ROCKIN' THE BOAT

Rockin' the Boat

Mass Music and Mass Movements

Edited by
Reebee Garofalo

South End Press

Copyright 1992 © Reebee Garofalo

Cover inset photo of Tiananman Square demonstrators
by Melanie Chapman
Cover background photo of Abidjan, Ivory Coast concert audience
by Neal Preston
Cover design by Jane Cook
Page design and production by the South End Press collective
Manufactured in the United States
Printed on acid-free, recycled paper

Library of Congress Cataloging-in-Publication Data

Rockin' the boat : mass music and mass movements / [edited by] Reebee
Garofalo.
  p. cm.
Includes bibliographical references (p.   ).
ISBN 0-89608-428-0 : $40.00. — ISBN 0-89608-427-2 ✓ $16.00
1. Rock music—History and criticism. 2. Protest music—History and criticism. 3. Music and society. I. Garofalo, Reebee.
ML3534.R6348   1992
781.5'92—dc20
                                                          92-8334
                                                            CIP
                                                            MN

99 98 97 96 95 94 93 92   1 2 3 4 5 6 7 8 9

South End Press, 116 Saint Botolph Street, Boston, MA 02115

This book is dedicated to the memory of
Rick Dutka
for whom the connection between
popular music and political struggle
was a fact of everyday life.

Permissions

An earlier version of "Understanding Mega-Events: If We Are The World, Then How Do We Change It?" by Reebee Garofalo, appeared in Constance Penley and Andrew Ross, Eds., *Technoculture*. Minneapolis: University of Minnesota Press, 1991. It is reprinted with the permission of the publisher.

An earlier version of "Nelson Mandela, the Concerts: Mass Culture as Contested Terrain," by Reebee Garofalo, which deals only with the first Mandela Tribute, appeared in Mark O'Brien and Craig Little, Eds., *ReImaging America: The Arts of Social Change*. Philadelphia: New Society Publishers, 1990. It is reprinted with the permission of the publisher.

"The Politics of Marginality: A Rock Musical Subculture in Socialist Hungary in the Early 1980s," by Anna Szemere is based on earlier research which was originally published as "'I Get Frightened of My Own Voice': On Avante-Garde Rock in Hungary," in Simon Frith, Ed., *World Music, Politics and Social Change,* Manchester: Manchester University Press, 1989. It is used with the permission of St. Martin's Press, the exclusive U.S. distributor.

"Don' Go Down Waikiki: Social Protest and Popular Music in Hawaii," by George H. Lewis, is based on earlier research which was originally published as "Storm Blowing From Paradise: Social Protest and Oppositional Ideology in Popular Hawaiian Music," in *Popular Music,* Vol. 10, No. 1, January 1991. It is used with the permission of Cambridge University Press.

"Music Beyond Apartheid?" by Denis-Constant Martin is a translated and revised version of "La Musique au-delà de l'Apartheid," originally published as the "Afterword" of the French edition of David Coplan's *In Township Tonight!: South Africa's Black City Music and Theatre,* Paris: Editions Karthala, 1992. It is reprinted with the permission of the publisher.

An earlier version of *Rock Nacional and Dictatorship in Argentina,* by Pablo Vila, appeared in *Popular Music,* Vol. 6, No. 2, May 1987. It is reprinted with the permission of Cambridge University Press.

An earlier version of "Popular Music and the Civil Rights Movement," by Reebee Garofalo, was published as "The Impact of the Civil Rights Movement on Popular Music," in *Radical America,* Vol. 21, No. 6, March, 1989. It is reprinted with the permission of *Radical America*.

"Chicano Rock: Cruising Around the Historic Bloc," by George Lipsitz, originally appeared as "Crusing Around the Historical Bloc: Postmodernism and Popular Music in East Los Angeles," in *Cultural Critique,* No. 5, 1986. It is reprinted with the permission of *Cultural Critique*.

Acknowledgements

It is with a profound sense of loss that I have dedicated this book to the late Rick Dutka. Ricky was one of my closest friends and a music-and-politics soulmate of the highest order. As one of the organizers of the Sun City project, an executive director of the New Music Seminar, and a vice president at Island Records, Ricky was, for me, an invaluable connection to the inner workings of the music business. But far more importantly, he was a force for change within the industry who embraced—indeed, set in motion—the kinds of cultural developments described in this book. I wish he could be here to see it.

Naturally, much of the credit for a volume like this goes to the contributing authors. They have contributed important new insights to a growing body of knowledge and have been consistently helpful and cooperative in the preparation of the manuscript. Together, we are part of a larger international network of musicians, academics, journalists, and other cultural workers who have taken on the task of analyzing the significance of popular music and mass culture and particularly their role in social change. This collection is a sampling—hopefully, a representative one—of this work.

I was first approached by Todd Jailer to edit this collection for South End Press. Given Todd's interest in music, I was looking forward to working with him. But before we finalized a contract, Todd left for El Salvador, where he continues to do valuable cultural work. He passed the baton to Tanya Mckinnon who unfortunately left the Press before completion of the manuscript. My main editorial help has come from Loie Hayes, who, in a very short time, has offered a number of valuable suggestions. I wish I could have availed myself of her assistance earlier in the project.

Because South End is a computerized operation, this project has also introduced me to the wonderful world of desktop publishing—a world in which I am largely illiterate—and to the joys of converting from IBM to Mac and back again across multilingual keyboards which apparently send different commands to the computer. The manuscript literally could not have been completed without the magic of the computer wizards at the University of Massachusetts at Boston. Paul Paquin from the UMass Computer Center earned my eternal gratitude for retrieving the entire chapter on East Germany from a disc which came up empty on the screen. I still marvel at how he did that. Troubleshooting kudos also go to Paul O'Keefe and Andreas Thanos from the College of Public and Community Service.

I would also like to extend my gratitude to Line Grenier for roping

Val Morrison into translating Denis-Constant Martin's chapter on South Africa from the French original. She/they did a great job.

Finally, I am indebted to Debby Pacini for her friendship and emotional support, her knowledge of world music and insightful comments on the manuscript, and her helpful hints and power-user shortcuts for using Microsoft Word.

Amnesty International tour, Abidjan, Ivory Coast. Singers from left: Peter Gabriel, Tracy Chapman, Youssou N'Dour, Johnny Clegg, Sting, and Bruce Springsteen. (Photo: © Neal Preston)

Table of Contents

Introduction

Reebee Garofalo

On the eve of Paul Simon's 1992 South African tour—the first such tour by a major U.S. artist since the lifting of cultural sanctions—the offices of the promoter and sound company were bombed by the Azanian National Liberation Army. While the tour was supported not only by the white minority government, but also two of South Africa's main black organizations—the African National Congress and the Inkatha Freedom Party—other anti-apartheid tendencies held that the lifting of sanctions was premature. Simon was undoubtedly considered an appropriate target because of the controversy that surrounded the release of his 1986 Grammy Award-winning album, *Graceland,* which was based largely on South African musical styles and was recorded mostly in South Africa under questionable circumstances, in violation of the UNESCO cultural boycott. Just as the bombing incident can be seen as one indicator of the degree to which culture—and popular music in particular—is taken seriously as a force in political struggle, the controversy surrounding *Graceland* raises a number of issues which must be confronted head-on in any analysis of the role of mass music in global political change.

Graceland was, in many ways, a pivotal album of the 1980s. It was released during the ascendancy of the so-called "charity-rock" phenomenon, and no doubt benefited from the unprecedented international focus on Africa created by "mega-events" such as Live Aid and Sun City. (Simon himself appeared as a soloist on "We Are the World," but interestingly refused to participate in the more radical Sun City project, which directly opposed violating the cultural boycott.) Historically, the album has taken its place as one of the defining contributions to the amorphous category of "world beat" or "world music," and as such has been at the heart of highly politicized discussions concerning musical appropriation and ownership on the one hand and "cultural imperialism" on the other. Because such issues invariably accompany discussion of the global political role of mass culture, they will surely surface among the readers of this collection.

Rockin' the Boat is about the relationship between mass-mediated popular musics—that is, musics which share an intimate relationship with mass communication technologies—and political struggles around the world. From West African highlife to political cantopop in Hong Kong, from Hungarian punk to the Aboriginal rock styles of Australia, the collection focuses primarily on musics which have combined mass cultural elements—primarily Anglo-American and African-American—with indige-

1

nous musical styles and/or those which have made conscious use of advanced technologies aimed at reaching a mass audience. The essays in this collection deal with the role of these musics in a myriad of political functions: survival/identity, resistance/opposition, consciousness raising/education, agitation/mobilization. While all of the contributors to this collection would probably agree that the political potential of mass-mediated popular musics has been largely overlooked, if not systematically devalued, the essays in *Rockin' the Boat* do not endeavor to present mass culture in an uncritical light. Rather, it would be more correct to say that mass culture is treated as "contested terrain." It is regarded as one arena where ideological struggle—the struggle over the power to define—takes place. While there is no question that in this arena the forces arrayed in support of the existing hegemony are formidable, there are also numerous instances where mass culture—and in particular popular music—issues serious challenges to hegemonic power. In analyzing and reflecting on a number of such instances from around the world, *Rockin' the Boat* attempts to explore the potentiality of mass culture, while being ever-mindful of its perils.

While there is nothing particularly new about establishing a link between music and politics, historically that link, at least in the United States, has usually involved a connection between progressive political movements such as labor or civil rights and folkloric musical forms generally associated with the black church, agricultural workers, and the urban proletariat. Mass culture has been seen by leftist intellectuals and conservative elitists alike (albeit for different reasons) as a debased culture, produced only for profit and manipulated from above, which invariably renders its audience passive and mindless in the corporate search for the lowest common denominator of acceptability. In this view, mass culture is disparagingly seen as the vacuous culture of an undifferentiated mass whose only function is consumption, as opposed to folk culture which expresses the values and ideals of an identifiable group of real people. As a result, mass culture has been regarded, certainly until the late 1960s, as being fundamentally incompatible with a progressive political agenda.

Musically, this view was challenged in the pop explosion of the 1960s. As popular music added the rhetorical appeal of folk music (Dylan, Country Joe and the Fish) and the self-conscious experimentation of the avant-garde (the Beatles, Frank Zappa) to the compelling rhythms of rock 'n' roll and rhythm and blues (MC 5, James Brown)—and, in the process, became associated with the political turbulence of the decade—it became increasingly difficult to dismiss mass music as aesthetically or politically bankrupt. Just as "politicized" popular music problematized the traditional view of mass mediation, the social movements of the 1960s challenged historical notions of radical politics—indeed, the very notion of what is political.

Movements based on issues of race, age, and gender confounded simplistic analyses of class antagonisms. Organizing based in the community rather than the workplace broadened a narrow focus on economic issues and working conditions to include issues of leisure, culture, and the quality of life. These changes were accompanied by reformulations of political theory which invariably assigned culture a more prominent and relatively autonomous role in political struggle. Such developments have, in turn, forced a rethinking of the role of mass culture in political work. In the current period, it is primarily the electric styles of mass-mediated popular music (Peter Gabriel, Living Colour) rather than the folkloric forms of an earlier time (Tracy Chapman being a notable exception) that have come to be associated with progressive politics. It is the intention of *Rockin' the Boat* to analyze this phenomenon critically and concretely.

Given its thrust, one of the central themes of *Rockin' the Boat* concerns the global appropriations and uses of rock, in all its Anglo-American and African-American variants. While accounts of politicized rock in the United States no longer come as a surprise to most readers, the political uses of rock-derived styles in Tiananmen Square, on the eastern side of what was the Berlin Wall, or in Argentina's Luna Park stadium may be less familiar. This is not to suggest that rock is the only music which is used oppositionally—many chapters speak of other musics as well. Nor is it to suggest that rock is invariably progressive in its effects—one needs to look no further than the well-known use of rock in the invasion of Panama and in the Gulf War to see its power in a reactionary context. There are any number of instances where rock has been perceived as threatening to overwhelm indigenous musics. A number of writers have written eloquently about the development of salsa as a Latin American working-class defense against the encroachments of rock.[1] While the seductively neat division of salsa as nationalist (as if this or that Latin American country "owns" salsa) and rock as imperialist (as if rock belongs only to the United States) has elements of truth, ultimately it denies the dynamic complexity of cultural development and change. The implication that rock serves imperialism, of course, cannot be conveniently dismissed, but neither can the music be reduced solely to this function. I will return briefly to the discussion of *Graceland* to illustrate this point.

As a multi-platinum album, *Graceland* added millions to the coffers of Warner Brothers Records and increased Paul Simon's personal fortune measurably. Simon is a talented musician with a fine ear for "exotic" sounds; he is respectful of South African music, if not anti-apartheid politics. He worked with notable, if not the most progressive, black South African musicians on the project, offering three times union scale for sessions and appropriate co-writer credits on collaborative songs. Far from being overwhelmed by the power of rock, *Graceland* is dominated—indeed, defined—by performance styles which are clearly South African. Contributing mainly lyrics, Simon himself is vulnerable to the charge of avoiding political content. But under considerable international pressure, he was forced to add explicitly anti-apartheid performers like Miriam Makeba and Hugh Masakela to the *Graceland* tour. Their renditions of selections like "Soweto Blues" added a decidedly progressive dimension to international broadcasts and public performances. As a result, *Graceland* has been variously celebrated, according to Steven Feld, as "a melding of mainstream 'world' pop and African 'folk' musics; the major anti-apartheid consciousness-raising and publicity event of 1987; and a major international market breakthrough for the South African musicians."[2]

This does not mean that *Graceland* should be above criticism. Simon should certainly be taken to task for reserving the producer's credit and all the copyrights for himself. If his purpose was to showcase black South African music, one has to wonder why he named the project after the estate of the white North American who captured the rock 'n' roll crown by employing—some would say imitating—African-American musical styles. He also added insult to his own injurious violation of the cultural boycott by using as a back-up vocalist on the album Linda Ronstadt, who made front page headlines for performing at Sun City and refusing to apologize. Still, the point to be made is that, for all its flaws, *Graceland* cannot be neatly contained within a formulation like cultural imperialism. On balance, its effect has been progressive.

The concept of cultural imperialism developed as an idea of the left describing the cultural analog of international political domination. According to Dave Laing: "It depends on an analogy between the historical colonizing role of Western nations in politically subjugating the third world and the current role of transnational media and electronics corporations."[3] Although the concept has proven to be attractive and widely invoked, it remains vague and limited as an analytical tool for a number of reasons. First, there is a tendency to privilege the role of external forces, while overlooking the internal dynamics of resistance and opposition that work against domination. In addition to underestimating the strength and resiliency of indigenous cultures, this tendency assumes audience passivity in the face of dominant cultural power and neglects the active, creative dimension of popular consumption. Closely related, there is also a tendency to conflate economic power and cultural effects. Here it is assumed that patterns of ownership determine cultural forms and preferences. Finally, the notion of cultural imperialism rests on the premise that the "organic" cultures of the third world are somehow being corrupted by the "unauthentic" and "manufactured" cultures of the West. Each of these assumptions needs to be examined critically in order to arrive at a more accurate view of the role of mass music in worldwide political struggle.

In one of the only book-length studies to date that deals with this concept in relation to popular music, Roger Wallis and Krister Malm postulate the existence of cultural imperialism "when a culture, usually that of a powerful society or group in a society, is imposed on another in a more or less formally organized fashion" and when "the cultural dominance is augmented by the transfer of money and/or resources from dominated to dominating culture group."[4] There is both a cultural and an economic dimension to the concept. With respect to popular music, then, the cultural imperialism thesis is inseparable from the pattern of internationalization which has characterized the operations of the music industry since its inception.

U.S.-based record companies have never been shy about exploiting their international connections. As early as 1878, the Edison phonograph was demonstrated for enthusiastic audiences all over Europe; there has been an international market for U.S. music ever since. When Paul Simon first heard South African popular music, he remarked that "it sounded like very early rock and roll to me, black, urban, mid-fifties rock and roll."[5] This is hardly surprising since South Africa, like many other countries, was the recipient of a steady stream of African-American musical styles in the 1950s and 1960s. At the time, such international sales provided a handsome source of additional revenue to an ever-expanding domestic industry. The systematic exploitation of the world market *as a condition of further growth,* however, did not become dominant until the 1980s.[6]

In 1979, the U.S. music industry suffered its first recession in 30 years, with sales dropping off some 10.8 percent. The rest of the world soon followed suit. Record companies responded in two ways: concentration of product (the number of new releases in the United States was cut nearly in half between 1978 and 1984); and expansion into new markets, aided significantly by the development of music video and the full deployment of satellite broadcast. By 1984, the U.S. industry was back on its feet, and by 1990, it could boast year-end sales of $7.5 billion in a world market estimated at well over $20 billion.[7] Given the sluggish state of the recessionary U.S. economy, however, this recovery did not come about without some profound structural changes in the ownership patterns of the transnational music industry.

A handful of transnational record companies have long occupied the power center of the international music business. At present, the five largest companies control roughly two-thirds of the world market.[8] Each of these companies is, in turn, owned by a larger transnational conglomerate. EMI Records is a division of the British electronics firm Thorn-EMI, which also controls Capitol, Chrysalis, IRS, and Rhino, among others. Polygram, which includes Polydor, Deutsch Grammaphon, Mercury, and Decca as well as the recently purchased A&M and Island, is owned by the Dutch-based

Phillips electronics corporation. The German publishing conglomerate, Bertelsmann, bought RCA Records and its affiliated labels when the record division was dumped in the General Electric takeover of RCA. In 1987, Japan's Sony corporation bought CBS Records (now Sony Music) for $2 billion. Only one of the top five transnational record companies—WEA (Warner Brothers/Elektra/Atlantic), a division of Time-Warner—remains in U.S. hands, and in 1991, Time-Warner entered a partnership agreement with Toshiba and C. Itoh to the tune of $1 billion. Further, with its $6.6 billion purchase of MCA in 1990, which included Geffen Records and Motown, Matsushita has also made a bid for a share of the international marketplace. To the extent that the United States is identified as the main imperialist culprit in the exportation of pop and rock, it must be noted that the United States is no longer the main beneficiary of the profits. The economic foundation of the cultural imperialism thesis is thus questionable.

The persistence of the cultural imperialism thesis in the face of economic restructuring can perhaps best be explained by the fact that it is still U.S. Top Forty which dominates the world market. In asserting the relative autonomy of culture, one could conceivably argue that Western culture, technology, and organizational forms exert an imperialist influence even in the absence of strict economic control. The very fact of industrializing—which is to say commodifying, commercializing, and technologically mediating—musics which have developed primarily in live performance certainly alters their character, at least to the extent of rendering them more amenable to the processes of exchange. That this change introduces a complicating economic element which can affect the use value and social functions of these musics is undeniable. Whether or not this places these musics totally in the service of imperialism is another matter. One would be hard pressed to argue, for example, that the primary function of reggae—itself a product of interaction with U.S. rhythm and blues, commercialization, and Western technology—is to serve the forces of imperialism.

Further, we must question the very nature of cultural "ownership," especially as it applies to U.S. popular music. Can it be that the 25 million or so people outside the United States who bought Michael Jackson's *Thriller* were all simply the unwitting dupes of imperialist power? Or, is it conceivable that Jackson produced an album which resonated with the cultural sensibilities of a broad international audience. Taking a closer look at the roots of our own popular music lends considerable weight to the latter proposition. The United States is a nation of immigrants, willing and unwilling. Its cultural forms have historically come from many other places. Scrutinizing rock 'n' roll—the formative influence of all currently popular styles—reveals this multiculturalism. Its defining characteristics are, of course, its Africanisms brought forward through African-American genres and performance styles. There are also familiar European elements as well as a host of other influences as diverse as Latin American, French creole, and Hawaiian.[9] "It is difficult to argue, therefore," as Andrew Goodwin and Joe Gore point out, "that rock music is 'Western' in quite the same way that Hollywood cinema or British television news are."[10]

There is one final cultural aspect of the cultural imperialism thesis which must be called into question—namely, the imagined "purity" of third world musical cultures. Just as *Graceland* benefited from an infusion of South African township jive, *mbaqanga, kwela,* and Zulu choral music, these South African popular styles were themselves heavily influenced by African-American rhythm and blues, soul, jazz, and gospel from the 1950s and '60s. Similarly the emergence of West African popular styles such as *juju* allis, highlife, and afrobeat can be traced to the influence of the African-American end of the U.S. popular music spectrum. There is a particularly interesting dialectic as regards this process in Africa, since most of the U.S. popular music influences in question had African roots to begin with. In Chapter 11 of this collection, "Some Anti-Hegemonic Aspects of African Popular Music," John Collins effectively argues that in many instances, this process is better described as the culture of the diaspora returning home rather than a clear-cut instance of cultural imperialism.

That the international entertainment business may be motivated by imperialist practices is not in question. The results as regards music, however, are usually closer to what Wallis and Malm call "transculturation"—a two-way process whereby elements of international pop/rock are incorporated into local and national musical cultures, and indigenous influences contribute to the development of new transnational styles.[11] The emergence of world beat, described by Goodwin and Gore "as Western pop stars appropriating non-Western sounds, as third world musicians using Western rock and pop, or as the Western consumption of non-Western folk music,"[12] is a testament to the complexity of this process. While it is true that U.S. Top Forty is still disproportionately represented in most of the world's markets, local and national musical cultures continue to appropriate these influences in ways that serve their own ends. *Rockin' the Boat* attempts to document this process.

Organization

The mega-events of the 1980s were the most dramatic examples of the use of mass-mediated popular musics in consciousness raising and mobilizing masses of people. Accordingly, the first section of *Rockin' the Boat*, "Mega-Events: The Global Stage," is devoted to a critical analysis of the best known of these events including Live Aid, Farm Aid, Sun City, the Amnesty International tours, the Nelson Mandela Tributes, and the Greenpeace project. These projects were pre-dated by local and national efforts through-out the world. The second section of the book, "Rock Around the World," focuses on a number of examples from Eastern and Western Europe, Africa, Latin America, and Asia and the Pacific in which mass music has been instrumental in subverting hegemonic control. In the final section, "Bringing It All Back Home," *Rockin' the Boat* concludes with examples of the empowering aspects of mass music in the United States.

Mega-Events: The Global Stage. As stated, the most dramatic example of the mass culture/mass politics connection in the 1980s has been the phenomenon of mega-events. In addition to creating shared international experiences of staggering proportions, mega-events have also made it clear that mass-mediated popular music has taken on a new and different role. In the sixties and before, music generally served as a cultural frame for what were more or less developed political movements. That role was consistent with a theoretical position which relegated culture to a position of second-ary importance in political struggle. Since the late 1970s, however, music has taken the lead in the relative absence of such movements. In all of the mega-events, music itself was the organizing vehicle. It was mass music—not particular issues or (with the possible exception of the second Mandela Tribute) political personalities—that mobilized masses of people.

Chapter 1, "Understanding Mega-Events," offers a broad analysis of the convergence of social forces which produced this unique social phe-nomenon. The cultural spaces opened up by these events hold out possi-bilities for new and interesting political work. In Chapter 2, Neal Ullestad deepens the analysis of these "Diverse Rock Rebellions" in distinguishing between the "internal hegemonic shifts" of what he refers to as "Media Aid"—the more charity-oriented mega-events—and the "disruptive effects" of the more radical events. Chapter 3, "Nelson Mandela, the Concerts," offers a detailed case history of the contestation which occurs on the terrain of mass culture. Needless to say, mega-events are not without their contra-dictions. While most observers agree, however reluctantly, that mega-events have had a generally progressive, or at least humanitarian, effect, it is also the case that they have provided transnational record companies with inexpensive access to new audiences numbering in the hundreds of millions. It is, thus, important to look critically at the impact of mass-medi-ated popular musics around the world.

Rock Around the World. It is, of course, difficult to ignore the destruc-tive role the U.S. government plays in the international arena—a role in which culture is often conceived as one more weapon in the arsenal of domination. Still, as I have argued, the cultural imperialism thesis is simply not adequate to capture the complexity of the social relations of popular music. Because popular music is seldom exported as a finished product—what gets exported most often are master tapes which must be manufactured and distributed locally—the interplay between the transnational music industry and the local music scene cannot be reduced to a relationship of simple domination. Rather, it is a relationship in which there is a relative autonomy in the interaction between local and foreign musics. Particularly in cultures with strong musical traditions of their own, the threat of cultural domination exists in tension with the ability of local cultures to incorporate "foreign sounds" in ways that are counter-hegemonic. In Chapter 11, John Collins identifies "nationalism" and the "cultural tenacity of traditional music" as two of the "Anti-Hegemonic Aspects of African Popular Music." Such strengths exist in other countries as well. This is the other side of cultural imperialism.

In this section, *Rockin' the Boat* addresses the political role of popular music in a diversity of contexts: (corrupt) socialist governments in China, East Germany, and Hungary; liberal reformist governments in Australia; dictatorship in Argentina; and conservative bourgeois democracies in Britain and Hawaii (deriving from its status of U.S. statehood). England, of course, has often taken the lead in the connection between popular music and political struggle. In Chapter 4, "Rock Against Racism and Red Wedge," Simon Frith and John Street analyze two of the most notable music-and-politics movements of the last 20 years. Their successes and failures are discussed in the historical context of different moments of British political history.

During the last 20 years, rock music—in both its Anglo-American and African variants—became a global phenomenon with profound political implications. In fact, Wallis and Malm have noted that the 1970s and 1980s were characterized by "the almost simultaneous emergence of what could be termed 'national pop and rock music'" in countries throughout the world.[13] In countries like Cuba where the government implemented conscious policies to build the indigenous cultural forms, rock was a minor influence. But, even in those instances where this music gained a foothold, it is simply too facile to tally the results as a victory for cultural imperialism. This point is clear in the case of *rock nacional* in Argentina. In Chapter 13, "*Rock Nacional* and Dictatorship in Argentina," Pablo Vila argues that in this instance, U.S.-based rock styles served as the basis for the most oppositional cultural voice during the dictatorship. Similarly, musicians throughout Eastern Europe, the Pacific region, and Africa have incorporated Anglo-American pop and rock into local cultural forms and music movements in ways that enhance the local culture.

In his compelling essay on "Rock Music and Political Change in East Germany," Peter Wicke analyzes the substantive role of rock musicians in the political upheaval that lead to the disappearance of the German Democratic Republic. Because of the particular conditions of the production and consumption of rock music in the GDR, musicians were in a position to raise a political voice that was in critical ways independent of state-controlled media. Initially intent on seizing the opportunities presented by *glasnost* and *perestroika* as a way of envisioning a new socialism in the GDR, the momentum which they played a significant role in generating was soon swept up in historical forces whose direction could not be determined by this dedicated cadre of cultural workers.

Wicke also details a common theme which runs through many of the chapters—particularly those describing totalitarian regimes—which is the suspicion on the part of the authorities that even the most innocuous songs contain subversive political content, which is received as such by a "knowledgeable" audience. This tendency has had the effect of politicizing music which is not intentionally political and enhancing the power of music which is; this was the case in localities as diverse as China, Argentina, and Hungary. While perceptions such as these can increase the oppositional power of the music, there is—as Anna Szemere points out in her essay on "A Rock Musical Subculture in Socialist Hungary in the Early 1980s"—the danger of creating the expectation that musicians should function as political leaders when the musicians themselves do not perceive this to be their role.

Rock 'n' roll also took up the voice of opposition in the People's Republic of China. In Chapter 7, "Rock and Roll on the New Long March," Tim Brace and Paul Friedlander detail the historical development of the Chinese variant of this music and its emergence as an oppositional form primarily in the music and unprecedented popularity of Cui Jian, one of the musicians who performed at Tiananmen Square. The events of June 4, 1989 also precipitated a highly democratic—if petit bourgeois—support movement in Hong Kong. Again, mass-mediated popular music, in this case a genre called political cantopop, was the primary organizing vehicle. The process of its rise and impact is detailed in Chapter 8, "All for Freedom," by Joanna Ching-Yun Lee.

Given the state of modern technology, Marcus Breen argues in his essay on "Australian Aboriginal Music" (Chapter 9) that the music of even the most isolated of Australia's aboriginal groups, can no longer be reduced to discrete, folkloric cultural forms. Rather, they interact in a highly complex fashion with the other cultural forms around them. It is interesting to note that the CAAMA (Central Australian Aboriginal Media Association) artists have actually embraced this process as a way to help preserve traditional values. In Chapter 10, "Social Protest and Popular Music in Hawaii," George Lewis argues that Hawaiian musicians made a similar use of the advanced technology which was put in place to meet the needs of the growing tourist trade.

The African musics described in John Collins' overview (Chapter 11) and in Denis-Constant Martin's essay on South Africa (Chapter 12) have also merged the traditional with international pop styles. Particularly in South Africa, as Martin points out in "Music Beyond Apartheid," black musicians have emerged as the progenitors of new musical genres based on truly multicultural influences which hold out the possibility of a culture "from all, to all, for all." These are musics which look forward to a nonracial future, free of oppression. In Argentina, the *"rock nacional"* artists, described by Pablo Vila in Chapter 13, made a strategic appropriation of U.S. folk-rock to confront the oppression of dictatorship.

There are also two other seemingly unrelated themes which run through many of the projects described in this book—namely, the importance of cassette technology and the notable absence of women performers. Cassettes provide the transnational culture industry with an efficient format for expansion into remote areas; however, the technology is also effective in the production, duplication, and dissemination of local musics. Thus, while cassettes generate huge sums of money for transnational corporations, they also decentralize control over the production and consumption of music. Indeed, given the ease with which cassettes can be edited and duplicated, the very distinction between producer and consumer begins to blur.

Decentralized control over production holds out the possibility that new voices will find new avenues for expression. Such developments augur well for the future participation of women in the popular music enterprise. While the exclusion of women from musical performance often has its roots in antiquated notions of women's roles, it is by no means limited to traditional cultures. The development of popular music in the United States is certainly no stranger to the issue.

Bringing It All Back Home. The popular music of the rock era was born a music of outsiders. It has often drawn its power from its outsider status and, as a result, has generally been associated with rebelliousness. As mass-mediated popular styles became further politicized by the social movements of the 1960s, the music became identified with a more explicit oppositional stance. Chapter 14, "Popular Music and the Civil Rights Movement," provides historical background for this development by chronicling the trajectory of the movement through trends in popular music. Since that time, mass music has been generally seen as having a progressive or humanitarian bias. In sharp contrast to this general tendency, the perennial problem of misogyny has always blunted popular music's progressive edge.

It is for this reason, as detailed in Chapter 15, "Women's Music: No Longer a Small Private Party," by Cynthia M. Lont, that women's music was forced to develop its own sensibilities and structures outside the established "malestream" channels. In Chapter 16, "Reconstructions of Nationalist Thought in Black Music and Culture," Kristal Brent Zook argues that the nationalist project in general, and rap in particular, has often suffered from the construction of "narcissistic mirror images of the dominant patriarchal and heterosexist culture." Zook, however, sees hope in the recent emergence of strong female voices within rap. The Chicano culture that George Lipsitz writes about in his essay on "Chicano Rock" (Chapter 17) is not immune from criticisms of the same sexism that characterizes other sectors of our society. But Lipsitz sees in the "bifocality" demanded of ethnic cultures "a complicated cultural strategy designed to preserve the resources of the past by adapting them to the needs of the present." It is in this way that popular music provides a link between that which is most highly valued and that which is yet untried.

Other Issues and Concerns

Rockin' the Boat documents a representative sample of instances of the role of mass music in political struggles. It is not an exhaustive study (nor is it intended to be). There are any number of other examples of "politicized pop"—reggae and calypso, among others—which are not included in this volume. In some cases, a considerable amount has already been written about these styles and it seemed more beneficial to present examples that were less well-known. In other instances, acceptable chapters could not be secured within the time constraints of the publication schedule. Finally, space was a consideration in the desire to produce an affordable book. The contributors to *Rockin' the Boat* have tried to bring fresh insights to the more well-known phenomena, while breaking new ground in reporting on more obscure or unexpected examples.

The selection of contributors for a volume like *Rockin' the Boat* presents certain problems in itself. Most of the writing on mass music is done by white men from Britain, Western Europe, and/or the United States. Given the legacy of domestic racism and sexism in these countries and an international pattern of colonialism and imperialism, not to mention the limitations of English-language publication, this reality is hardly surprising. In progressive circles, the need to include indigenous and alternative voices in the research enterprise has long been recognized. As a general rule, I believe there is value in soliciting work by authors—women and men— from the areas/cultures being investigated. I would also point out, however, that the desirability of insiders versus outsiders is not automatically open and shut. The companion pieces on Hong Kong and Bejing offer a case in point.

Joanna Ching-Yun Lee's chapter on political cantopop clearly benefits from an insider's knowledge of the cantopop phenomenon. (Her parents are actually in the leadership of the Hong Kong Alliance, the organization which is the main financial beneficiary of the musical movement.) It is not difficult to imagine, however, that such a position might make it difficult to maintain an openly critical position on the contradictions that would characterize any mass cultural phenomenon like the one she describes. She has done an admirable job. Perhaps more to the point, the Tim Brace/Paul Friedlander chapter on oppositional rock 'n' roll in the People's Republic of China probably could not have been written by an insider. Even some of their interviewees were given anonymity. Given the current political climate, their analysis might have entailed grave risk to a local researcher. What Brace and Friedlander lack in insider knowledge is more than balanced by their ability to offer a critical perspective.

Finally, I would note that, within certain broad areas of agreement, the methodologies, writing styles, voices, and at times political perspectives of the contributors to *Rockin' the Boat* differ widely. Some of these differences can be explained in terms of the class, race, ethnicity, gender, and sexual orientation of the authors. Others may be linked to cultural and linguistic conventions. Still others have to do with the nature of popular music studies itself. Popular music studies is still an emerging field. With inputs ranging from journalistic to highly theoretical, the field is not yet bound by any particular canon or tradition. Even within the academy, its practitioners are often found in the margins of sociology, anthropology, communications, history, political science, and economics, as well as ethnomusicology and musicology itself, each drawing on the expertise of other disciplines. The essays in *Rockin' the Boat* reflect individual and cultural differences as well as a multidisciplinary approach. While this may create a certain unevenness in the flow of the text, one can only hope that it contributes to the vitality of the enterprise as a whole.

Bruce Springsteen on tour for Amnesty International. (Photo © Neal Preston)

Understanding Mega-Events

If We Are the World,
Then How Do We Change It?

Reebee Garofalo

*Bob Geldof should be remembered in history for suggesting that a
lot can be done if we tap this power source.*
—Bill Graham

I would like it to be a movement, but it is not going to be so.
—Bob Geldof

In one of those moments that cried out for a grand social gesture, Joan
Baez opened the Live Aid concert with the words: "Good morning, you
children of the eighties. This is your Woodstock and it's long overdue."
While there was undoubtedly a historical connection between the two
events, close examination reveals as many differences as similarities.
Woodstock was experienced as participatory, communitarian, and non-
commercial (indeed, anti-commercial), with no great spiritual or physical
distance between artist and audience. Interestingly, these are all terms
which come from the vocabulary of folk culture. But it was Woodstock that
ushered in the big business/mass music culture of the contemporary era.
To deal with the seeming irreconcilability of "folk" values with the commercial imperatives of mass culture, counterculturalists often sought refuge
in the social relations of an idealized past. The hippie diaspora that was the
"Woodstock Nation" reflected a longing for the imagined simplicity of an
earlier rural life even as it embraced the electronic—not to mention the
sexual—revolution.

Live Aid, by contrast, was hardly an occasion for folksy nostalgia
(Baez's comments notwithstanding); it was an unabashed celebration of
technological possibilities. While Woodstock was hailed as countercultural,
there was precious little at Live Aid that could have been vaguely construed
as alternative or oppositional. If Woodstock represented an attempt to
humanize the social relations of mass culture, Live Aid demonstrated the

full-blown integration of popular music with the "star making machinery" of the international music industry. Paradoxically, Live Aid may have opened up spaces for cultural politics that would have been unthinkable at the time of Woodstock.

Part I: Background

Many observers have commented of late on the degree to which rock music, in its myriad forms, has become mainstream U.S. music. "Rock & roll is now the music of the land," opined Bill Graham. "Broadway. Movies. TV commercials. Miami Vice. It's the music of America. It's certainly not the music of the alternative society."[1] Pronouncements such as these often serve to confirm the inevitability of cooptation and incorporation. How, then, do we explain the fact that there is scarcely a social issue in the eighties and early nineties which has not been associated in a highly visible way with popular music and musicians? Hunger and starvation in Africa, apartheid, the farm crisis, peace, political prisoners, the environment, child abuse, racism, black-on-black violence, AIDS, Central America, industrial plant closings, and homelessness have all been themes for fundraising concerts, popular songs, or both. Even a cursory look at these projects reveals a liberal-to-left-leaning bias in both the choice and treatment of issues.

Chiefly responsible for this development has been the phenomenon of mega-events—that string of socially conscious mass concerts and all-star performances beginning with Band Aid, Live Aid, and "We Are the World" which has been dubbed, in true liberal fashion, "charity rock." While the designation itself indicates a conception that exists well within the bounds of mainstream political debate, the impact of this phenomenon represents a more serious challenge to the existing hegemony. Consider for a moment one outlandish possibility: that in the most conservative political period in decades (perhaps even because of it), there is one arena where, at least for the time being, progressive forces seem to have real power.

From Bruce Springsteen's "Born in the U.S.A." to Public Enemy's "Fight the Power," the link between popular music and political issues is more explicit than ever before. There is also a significant difference in the role of popular music in building political movements. Even in the music-and-politics sixties, music generally served as a cultural frame for what were more or less developed political movements. The civil rights and anti-war movements engaged millions of people in the politics of direct action primarily on the strength of the issues themselves. In the process, these movements exerted a profound influence on the themes and styles of popular music.[2] Since the 1980s, music—which is to say, culture—has taken the lead in the relative absence of such movements. With the decline of mass participation in grassroots political movements, popular music itself has come to serve as a catalyst for raising issues and organizing masses of people.

This situation not only turns the traditional Marxist analysis on its head, it renders inadequate even the more sympathetic "culturalist" treatment of mass culture. Historically, our attempts at understanding mass culture have been fraught with false starts, misconceptions, and faulty analyses. Culture currently occupies center-stage as a category for investigation—sometimes to a fault—but, as yet, we have no agreed-upon models or analytic tools for thinking about it. The phenomenon of mega-events represents a unique convergence of forces which challenges the very terminology of mass culture as well as our thinking about the nature of political work.

Culture Theory

In the classical interpretation of Marx, culture (which is part of the superstructure) is presumed to be "reflective" of ideas that are favorable to the ruling class. Because culture is "determined" in this way, it does not possess a social effectiveness of its own. Social transformation comes about as a result of radical political activity based on class contradictions in the economic realm (the base). The cultural arena, therefore, is not conceived of as a primary site for political struggle. Subsequent applications of this model to a systematic analysis of mass culture—most notably the work of the Frankfurt School—invariably yielded gloomy conclusions:

—Mass culture is produced only for profit. In commodifying human interaction, mass culture reduces culture to its exchange value and negates the possibility of any real use value.

—The production of mass culture is top-down and totally manipulated. The culture industry is in complete control and responses are determined in advance.

—The consumption of mass culture is necessarily passive and mindless. There is no possibility for resistance/opposition within mass culture.[3]

Is it any wonder that politically minded people avoided association with mass culture at all costs? High culture could be appreciated for its literacy, folk culture for its historical significance. But popular culture—that messy third tier which was itself a product of industrialization, commercialism, and the transition to capitalism—belonged to neither camp. Most often commodified and sold as mass culture, popular music could be, at best, tolerated as "entertainment" or, worse, dismissed as hopelessly reactionary. The music that has always played an important, if supportive, role in political movements—from labor to civil rights—has been what we think of as "folk" music. But, already there is a problem with terminology and, therefore, with the analysis.

There is a significant difference between the sociological use of terms like "folk," "popular," and "mass," and their meaning in everyday language. Woody Guthrie, for example, is remembered as a folk artist. But, "folk" in this sense is a marketing category that was created by the music industry, in part, to separate performers like Guthrie from commercial country music. In the sociological use of the term, Guthrie exhibited none of the characteristics of a folk performer. He was a known artist. He was a paid professional. He was not a member of the community he sang about. He appeared in formal settings which separated artist from audience. It would be more correct to say that Guthrie was a popular artist performing in a folkloric idiom. When his work was recorded and sold, he became a product of mass culture. Still, as late as the mid-sixties, the distinction between "authentic" folk and "commercial" pop was a significant dividing line politically. Remember that Bob Dylan was booed off the stage at the 1965 Newport Folk Festival simply for appearing with an electric guitar (his classic rock Fender Stratocaster).

When activists finally acknowledged a connection between politics and popular music in the late sixties, the music was valued precisely when it was thought to be something other than mass culture or when it was deemed to be progressive despite its being mass culture. *Sgt. Pepper* was art. Dylan's lyrics were poetry. Woodstock was community. And, Motown...well, Motown was black. At no point was this music celebrated as mass culture, even though this was clearly the basis for its widespread—mass, if you will—appeal. This failure to embrace mass culture as mass culture has contributed heavily to our inability to grasp its political potential.

Interestingly, it was, in many ways, the movements of the sixties which forced a reconsideration of the traditional Marxist model at the experiential level. Participation in the major movements of the decade— civil rights, anti-war, the counterculture, Black Power, student power, welfare rights, and women's liberation—often included contact across strict class lines. In all of these struggles, the locus of organizing as well as the major political victories were in the realm of the superstructure. Marxist orthodoxy offered little in the way of explaining these admittedly short-lived successes. Building on Raymond Williams, formulation of culture as a "constitutive process, creating specific and different ways of life," the "culturalist" critique proposed a conception of the superstructure as "productive." The narrow interpretation of simple "determination" was replaced with a more dialectical process of shaping and influencing. Culture was, thus, accorded a certain "relative autonomy."[4]

In the area of popular music, culturalists have tended to focus their investigations on the power of the audience to "reappropriate" culture, to determine meaning in the act of consumption. This perspective has had the positive effect of freeing the human subject from the prison of economic determinism and restoring people to their rightful place as the actors who make history. But, in concentrating to such a degree on the power of the superstructure, culturalists have also tended, often by omission, to accept the mode of production as a given. In the extreme, economic relations are overlooked as the abstract process of "resignification" magically eludes material market forces. The production of culture is no longer seen as a necessary component for thinking about political struggle.

Regarding the political potential of mega-events, this is not only a grave theoretical error, it's a missed opportunity. The progressive effects of mega-events have every bit as much to do with the intentions of their artists/organizers as they do with creative consumer usage. It is in the dialectic of production and consumption that the politics of these events is realized. While the culturalists are to be credited with elevating culture to a position of greater significance on the political agenda, they can also be criticized for privileging the act of consumption in such a way as to ignore not only the political intentions of artists and cultural workers, but also the political economy of production and, in particular, the influential role of the culture industry itself. In exploring the power of the consumer, the culturalists have identified certain possibilities for resistance and opposition within mass culture. It is equally important to understand (and influence) the relative power and political tendencies of artists, recording companies, and the mass media on the production side of the equation.

Artist Power

In the early fifties, the power center of the music industry shifted from an alliance of publishing houses and film studios to record companies. This shift corresponded to the ascent of records as the leading source of revenue in the industry. The market was dominated by a handful of major labels, with dozens of hungry independents, "indies," waiting in the wings. As per the conventional wisdom of the day, popular artists were kept on a relatively short artistic leash, as the majors controlled the production process from start to finish. Everything from song-writing, artist and repertoire, arranging, production, and engineering, to mastering, pressing, promotion, marketing, distribution, and, in some cases, retail sales, was organized as an in-house function. It was expected that audiences would respond favorably to gentle changes in popular styles, which would render the market that much more predictable.

The eruption of rock 'n' roll into this placid scenario demonstrated not only the relative autonomy of the cultural sphere but also the limits to which public taste could be determined from above. Far from being passively consumed, rock 'n' roll was a music which engaged its audiences—in the social ritual of dancing, in celebrating the sounds of urban life, in multicultural explorations. In resisting this new music, the majors not only acted against their economic self-interest, they contributed significantly to the oppositional posture of the form.

By the late sixties, the majors had learned from their rock 'n' roll mistakes. As it became clear that the key to profitability lay in manufacturing and distribution, record companies began contracting out most of the creative functions of music-making. Far from resisting artistic innovation or the creative impulses of independent producers, the majors simply bought up successful independent labels and artist-owned companies, entered into joint ventures with them, or contracted with them for distribution. Accordingly, among the top-selling records in the United States today, there is seldom a single entry which is not owned and/or distributed by a major label.

Like all capitalist enterprises, the music business tends towards expansion and concentration. In 1978, five transnational music corporations controlled—through ownership, licensing, and/or distribution—more than 70 percent of an international music market worth over $10 billion.[5] Following a period of recession which plagued the industry from 1979 to 1983, revenues from the international sale of recorded music grew to more than $20 billion in 1988.[6] Many U.S.-based major labels now report that more than 50 percent of their income comes from sales outside the United States. At the same time, the number of new recordings released in the United States—by far the world's largest producer—declined significantly during this period. Far from scouring the world for new, exciting, and diverse talent—fortunately, the indies do that—the major companies reaped greater rewards from fewer artists.

The commercial imperatives of the music industry limit, both quantitatively and qualitatively, the range of musics available to the public. Major record companies maintain separate divisions or subsidiaries for different genres of music such as rock, country, rhythm and blues, latin, jazz, and classical, which are, in turn, marketed to different publics with separate and unequal promotional budgets. In practice these different audiences are divided not only along the lines of musical taste, but often along lines of class, race, ethnicity, and age as well. Restrictive radio formats and selective reporting in the music press serve only to increase audience fragmentation. A handful of major corporations maintain a tight control over the music market by heavily promoting only those artists who are considered to be sure bets. It is therefore important to consider the economic and social relations of cultural production as a site of struggle.

It is also important, for our purposes, to note that acquiring the lion's share of the market is not entirely synonymous with controlling the form, content, and style of popular music. If anything, record companies have relinquished this control in their relentless pursuit of higher profits. As the industry has expanded, record companies have moved farther and farther away from the creative process. Particularly in the 1980s, music, to these corporate giants, has come to represent a "bundle of rights." Far from being limited to the manufacture and distribution of a fixed sound product, the exploitation of "secondary rights" for things like television, movies, and advertising has become an ever-increasing source of revenue. Content to focus its energy on the development of such new sources of income for music, the industry has shown little inclination to intervene in its content (except when forced to do so by organizations like the PMRC—Parents' Music Resource Center—but that is another discussion). Artistic autonomy is virtually assured for the big names in popular music.

As is the case with other culture industries, the music business is organized according to a star system. The difference is that only a handful of superstars from other cultural sectors can match the earning power of international rock stars. The top names in popular music, such as Prince, Michael Jackson, or Bruce Springsteen, take home tens of millions of dollars in a good year. In the United States, the revenue from the sale of recorded music alone rivals that of all organized sports and the entire film industry combined. Only television is bigger, and very few of its stars can compete with popular musicians for earnings. In addition to their considerable economic clout, top popular musicians enjoy an artistic autonomy which is unsurpassed anywhere in the cultural sphere. As Sun City organizer Little Steven states: "These guys are in complete control of their own destinies."[7] But, what is the impact of their music on other cultures?

Transculturation

The exportation of Anglo-American pop, catapulted to new heights in the phenomenon of mega-events, is often seen as a prime example of cultural imperialism. There is a sense in which transnationalization encourages a kind of cultural domination, but almost never by the direct suppression of local musics. Rather, it is in the establishment of a commercial music industry that the social relations of culture are irrevocably altered. The process can have particularly deleterious effects on traditional music cultures which are based on live performance and artist/audience interaction. Commodification thus begins to separate culture from everyday life. The establishment of a star system and the introduction of restrictive radio formats can further the process and limit the diversity of musics which are produced.

But to the extent that the concept of cultural imperialism is envisioned as the uni-directional imposition of one culture on another accompanied by a concomitant drain of financial resources from the host country, this concept is simply not adequate to capture the social relations of popular music. With the United States usually identified as the main imperialist power, the economic dimension of cultural imperialism is complicated by the fact that, at present, only one of the five largest transnational recording companies is U.S.-owned. Further, the concept underestimates the strength and vitality of indigenous musics and fails to acknowledge the extent to which domination breeds resistance. Indeed, it does not even describe accurately the normal operations of the international music industry in producing local musics.

Most mass cultural products, such as film or video, are generally produced and manufactured in one country and sold as finished products in the international market. This is to be contrasted sharply with international popular music. According to Larry Shore:

> The vast majority of the international flow of music is not in the form of finished products but rather a master tape which is then manufactured locally. What is particularly important to an understanding of the international music industry in addition to this predominance of local manufacture, is that in many countries the TMCs [transnational music corporations] are thoroughly involved in marketing local music. It is true to say that a large share of their revenues come from the sale of what are called international artists—usually American or British musicians—but in almost all countries in which they operate, especially the larger markets, the TMCs need to generate local hits for the commercial success of their subsidiaries.[8]

The exportation of international pop encourages the development of a whole production and distribution infrastructure within the host country which contributes positively to building both the local economy and the indigenous culture. The employees of the subsidiaries of multinational recording companies, for example, are most likely to be residents of the host country. The availability of production facilities also encourages the development of ancillary small businesses such as clubs and retail outlets, owned and operated by local residents. On a deeper, cultural level, and particularly in those countries with strong musical traditions of their own, the introduction of international pop seems to present as many opportunities as it closes off.

In their groundbreaking study of music industries in small countries around the world, Roger Wallis and Krister Malm found that "the world had been flooded with Anglo-American music in the fifties and sixties. This influenced, but did not prevent local musicians from developing their own styles, adapted to their own cultures."[9] The process of cross-cultural influence they report is more nearly described by the concept they call "transculturation" than by the more imposing notion of cultural imperialism. Acknowledging the dangers of reducing music to "the lowest common denominator for the biggest possible audience," they conclude that:

> What happens in practice is that individual music cultures pick up elements from transcultural music, but an increasing number of national and local music cultures also contribute to transcultural music. The resulting process is a two-way flow…[10]

There is, thus, an interaction between U.S. pop and local musics which isn't found in the exportation of other mass cultural forms. This interaction does not negate the destructive tendencies of cultural domination, but it does hold out the possibility that even Anglo-American influences can be appropriated to advantage by the host country. Far from simply being overwhelmed by outside influences, there have been many instances—for example, reggae, salsa, highlife, and *mbaqanga*—where local musics have incorporated outside elements in ways that have actually strengthened the indigenous culture. Additionally, the global stage of mega-events provided a moment of opportunity, albeit a limited one, where internationalization itself was a two-way process. While Anglo-American music was disproportionately broadcast to a worldwide audience, the international sounds of artists like Youssou N'Dour, Aswad, and Sly and Robbie also gained some access to the coveted U.S. market.

To a great extent, the process just described is the inevitable result of countries being exposed to international media. In the final analysis, the internationalization of the music industry and the transculturation of popular music cannot be separated from the technological advances which propel us ever closer to a global culture. As in the case of transculturation generally, a concrete analysis of the relationship between music and technology is key to understanding the politics of mega-events.

Technology

Popular music and musicians currently bear a different relationship to the tools of artistic production than was previously the case. Prior to the rock era, it was the function of recording to approximate the sound of a live performance. Now it's the other way around. It is the task of the live performance to reproduce what is possible in the studio. One of the reasons that the Beatles stopped touring after 1966 was that, given the state of portable technology at the time, virtually none of the material from *Sgt. Pepper* could be performed live. Touring groups today routinely use "sampled" sounds and pre-recorded tracks as an integral part of the music performed in concert. The question is no longer, "Is it live or is it Memorex?" but, rather, "What is 'live'?"

Rock 'n' roll differed from previous forms of music in that records were its initial medium. They were one of its defining characteristics. Since that time, it has become more and more difficult—in many cases, downright impossible—to separate "music" from the technology used in its creation. Recording equipment can no longer simply be viewed as the machinery which reproduces something called music, which already exists independently in some finished form. Ever since magnetic tape first mediated "direct-to-disk" recording, successive advances in studio technology—editing, overdubbing, multi-tracking, and digital effects—have been used—ironically, in the name of higher "fidelity"—to create products which bear little resemblance to anything that can be performed "live" in the traditional sense of the term. Particularly with the advent of digital electronics, technology exists as an element of the music itself. Music, musicians, and technology are inseparably fused in the process of creating popular music.

The cultural products which make use of this technology, therefore, cannot be dismissed as the commodities which reduce culture to an exchange value and put that much more distance between artist and audience. Recordings, worldwide broadcasts, and music videos must be seen as new forms of communication which create new modes of consumption, different, perhaps, from a "live" performance, but not automatically alienating because of that. From the time the voice was first accompanied, music-making has been intimately connected to increasingly complex technologies. As was the case with earlier technologies, the music being composed on the current generation of electronic devices represents simply the most recent development in the extension of our control over the production of sound. It isn't that this music is somehow less "authentic" than other musics, it's that our feelings about authenticity—like our copyright laws and our theories of culture—have not kept pace with technological advances.

While it is true that technological advances serve the capitalist goals of expansion and concentration, it is important to note that capital itself is not monolithic in these developments. The economic self-interest of Japanese hardware manufacturers who make digital audio tape (DAT) recorders, for example, is quite at odds with that of record companies whose primary task is to protect the "integrity" (i.e., financial viability) of the "artistic property" which is their economic lifeblood. There have been a number of "summit" meetings between these two segments of the industry to try to arrive at solutions to the problems posed by developments like DAT which would give consumers the capability of making studio-quality recordings in their livingrooms. This tension has sometimes been played out among different departments of the same firm (e.g. Sony, which owns CBS Records).

Perhaps more importantly, capital is not the only player in the game.

Technology is invariably a double-edged sword; in its development, artists and consumers also gain significant power. The same electronic advances that permit simultaneous worldwide broadcasts and the construction of international mega-audiences for capital have also encouraged decentralization in the creative process. Explains producer Niles Rogers:

> We're working out systems where if somebody who lives in England, say, has a system similar to what I have, and he's got a track and he wants me to play on it, well, he can send it to me over the satellite to New York. My system can then pick it up. It will go down on tape. I can listen to it, put my guitar overdub on it, send it back to him, and it'll all be digital information. It will sound exactly the same as when I played it. I can play on your record if you're anywhere.[11]

In this instance, technological advances have altered the social relations of industrial production with the result of greater and greater degrees of artistic freedom.

On the consumption side, the electronic items which have caught the public's fancy have been those which have delivered improved sound quality and provided for maximum flexibility and portability of use. In the words of Simon Frith:

> The major disruptive forces in music in this century have been new devices, technological breakthroughs developed by electronics manufacturers who have very little idea of their potential use. The only lesson to be learned from pop history (besides the fact that industry predictions are always wrong) is that the devices that succeed in the market are those that increase consumer control of their music.[12]

Particularly since the advent of digital recording technology, the very distinction between production and consumption has become less clear. Producers who make use of sampling devices and "found" sounds in the creative process are, in a very real sense, acting as consumers of sounds which have been provided for them. Conversely, home taping enthusiasts who make their own recordings by mixing and editing different LPs and radio broadcasts are producing their own cultural products. And, with the sophisticated consumer equipment just on the horizon, they will soon be able to do so with professional quality. Once again, we are forced to rethink the conventional wisdom of theoretical categories. The advent of mass culture can no longer be seen as that historical schism which marked the transition from active music-making to passive music consumption. Quite to the contrary, recent developments in the technology of mass culture have transformed consumption itself into a potentially creative act.

If the cultural sphere generally is relatively autonomous, then popular music may well be its most potent sector. By virtue of the economic power and artistic freedom of popular musicians, and the particular relationship between music, musicians, and the new technology, popular music enjoys an unparalleled access to the means of international communication. The political potential which accompanies this access has been played out most dramatically on the terrain of mega-events and performances.

Part II: Mega-Events

Typically, mega-events involve the creation of a variety of cultural products—live performances, worldwide broadcasts, ensemble recordings, compilation LPs, home videos, and/or "The Making of…" documentaries—each of which can be produced and consumed in a variety of ways. It is now literally possible for hundreds of millions of people to "attend" the same concert simultaneously, be it at the "live" event, at a public broadcast, or in the privacy of their own livingrooms. For those who tape a broadcast off the air or purchase a subsequent audio or video recording, the event can be relived any number of times, publicly or privately, in any number of new contexts. Audio and video recordings which illustrate a particular issue can also be used effectively as educational tools for classrooms, interest groups, and community meetings. A feedback loop is thus completed as the consumption of the original event is used in the service of producing another. How are we to weigh the impact of all these possibilities politically?

Tony Hollingsworth, producer of the Nelson Mandela Seventieth Birthday Tribute, outlined four functions of the Mandela concert which could apply equally well to other mega-events. These included: fundraising; consciousness raising ("to raise the profile of Nelson Mandela's name as the symbol of fighting against apartheid"); artist activism ("to demonstrate to the world and to South Africa the enormous popular and artistic support for all those who fight against apartheid"); and agitation ("to make the show act as a flagship…whereby the local anti-apartheid movements could pick up from the enormous coverage that we had and run a far more detailed political argument than you could have on a stage.")[13] While some of these functions proved more worthwhile than others at the Mandela Tribute, they, nevertheless, provide us with useful categories for assessing the impact of mega-events.

Fundraising

Perhaps the most obvious—if not always the most important—use of mega-events is that of fundraising. As Will Straw points out: "The most under-rated contribution rock musicians can make to politics is their money, or ways in which that money might be raised."[14] For all the reasons articulated above, popular recording artists are in a particularly good position to exploit the fundraising potential of mega-events. "Give me another element of our society that could have drawn as many people as Live Aid," remarked promoter Bill Graham. "A sporting event? An international soccer match? I don't know. I'm trying to show what a rare position these artists are in—that a group of people can say: You want to raise $10 million?"[15]

In this regard, it is interesting to note that almost all the estimates of Live Aid's fundraising potential were low. Not even the producers understood the power of what they were dealing with. Bob Geldof was originally shooting for $35 million. *Newsweek* predicted that the event could "make as much as $50 million." *Rolling Stone*'s computations put the net at "more than $56 million." The actual take was $67 million. By anyone's fundraising standards, that is a staggering amount of money to be generated from a single event.

To be sure, there are worse things that one could do with $67 million than try to feed starving people in Africa. On the other hand, $67 million is a drop in the bucket compared to the sums that are spent to create and perpetuate such problems in the first place. Given the numbers affected by starvation in Africa, $67 million averages out to nickels and dimes per capita. And even at the level of $67 million, there remains the question of the extent to which the event served the issue at hand vs. the extent to which it served capital. At the 1986 ceremony of the British music industry's BPI awards, Norman Tebbitt from the Thatcher administration "extolled Live Aid as a triumph of international marketing."[16] On this side of the Atlantic, Pepsi vice president John Costello said: "Live Aid demonstrates that you can quickly develop marketing events that are good for companies, artists, and the cause."[17] Mega-concerts may be uniquely capable of generating mega-sums of money, but they are equally capable of opening new markets, constructing new audiences, and delivering new consumers. Artists, record companies, and advertisers such as Pepsi, Eastman-Kodak, AT&T, and Chevrolet, for example, gained access to an international audience of 1.5 billion people very cheaply because of the "humanitarian" nature of the event. Still, there's $67 million which wouldn't otherwise be there.

As for the fundraising function of mega-events, there are even more questions on the expenditure side of the ledger. The most obvious of these is, of course: "Where does the money go?" Huge concerts may be unsurpassed in their fundraising potential, but they have not always had an exemplary track record in getting the money to its proper destination. That check for $243,418.15 that was pictured on the back of the *Concert for Bangledesh* LP, for example, languished in an IRS escrow account because of the organizer's failure to set up proper tax-exempt conduits. The quarter of a million dollars or so that the Rolling Stones raised for Nicaraguan earthquake victims in 1972 probably went straight into Somoza's pocket. By the 1980s, event organizers had gotten considerably more sophisticated about things financial. USA for Africa was set up as a tax-exempt foundation to receive and distribute the proceeds from "We Are the World." The Sun City project chose as its conduit the Africa Fund, a tax-exempt foundation with a demonstrated track record in getting the money to its proper destination.

The more pressing question about fundraising is: "What is the money used for?" In the aftermath of the concert, Live Aid was beset with reports of food rotting on the docks and trucks that didn't work—charges which Geldof refuted repeatedly as inaccurate. We are not just talking about the mechanical problems of implementing any large-scale project. There was considerable evidence which suggested that Geldof and the producers of Live Aid did not fully understand and were not equipped to deal with the political implications of the struggles going on in Ethiopia and Eriteria at the time. Further, we must raise questions in a broader philosophical context. In thinking about fundraising politically, it is important to distinguish between charity and change, dependence and self-determination, quick fixes and long-term development.

To their credit, many artists and organizers of mega-events have at least thought about these distinctions. While the character of Live Aid and certainly most of the reportage about the event were decidedly apolitical, the Band Aid Trust did entertain proposals for: "the purchase of water-drilling rigs to help with irrigation; various agricultural projects, including reforestation; medical aid; and the purchase of trucks and trailers for transportation of food and supplies."[18] The Africa Fund distributed the proceeds from Sun City in more or less equal shares to: "political prisoners and their families...in South Africa;...the educational centers and college set up by the ANC in Tanzania and Zambia;...grassroots educational outreach by the anti-apartheid movement in the US."[19] In the case of the Amnesty International tours, the proceeds went to fund the on-going political work of the organization.

It must be noted, however, that the operations of the mass media make it more difficult to get the public to think about the long haul. "Long-term aid is less exciting than the Seventh Cavalry arriving with food to bring people back to life," said Geldof. "And that's a problem."[20] Further, the crisis orientation of the media exacerbates a more general problem with fundraising as a strategy: namely, the idea that simply generating huge sums of money can solve problems which are fundamentally political. Which is why the consciousness raising function of mega-events is so important.

Consciousness Raising

If the power of popular music readily lends itself to fundraising, then its form is equally well-suited to consciousness raising. It is laudable that a tennis star like John MacEnroe has refused million-dollar deals to play in South Africa on more than one occasion. But there is no way that tennis as a cultural form can portray the horrors of apartheid. While any cultural event can be dedicated to a particular cause, popular music is further distinguished in its ability to reflect the issue at hand in its very content. Of course, other cultural forms such as film or theater have this capability, but they seldom combine the versatility, responsiveness, and impact of popular music.

It is always tempting—and more often than not, too facile—to write off projects like USA for Africa. Greil Marcus, for example, has argued that "We Are the World,"

> sounds like a Pepsi jingle—and the constant repetition of "There's a choice we're making" conflates with Pepsi's trademarked "The choice of a new generation" in a way that, on the part of Pepsi-contracted song writers Michael Jackson and Lionel Richie, is certainly not intentional, and even more certainly beyond the realm of serendipity. In the realm of contextualization, "We Are the World" says less about Ethiopia than it does about Pepsi—and the true result will likely be less that certain Ethiopian individuals will live, or anyway live a bit longer than they otherwise would have, than that Pepsi will get the catch phrase of its advertizing campaign sung for free by Ray Charles, Stevie Wonder, Bruce Springsteen, and all the rest.[21]

There was perhaps an even more distasteful element of self-indulgence in the follow-up line "We're saving our own lives," where the artists assembled proclaimed their own salvation for singing about an issue they will never experience on behalf of a people most of them will never encounter. With hype, glitter, and industry gossip often taking precedence over education, analysis, and action, Live Aid was also vulnerable to any number of criticisms.

At the same time, we must not underestimate the political importance of the momentum these projects generated. In the first place, they effected an international focus on Africa that was simply unprecedented. In the process, they created a climate in which musicians from countries all over the world felt compelled to follow suit. A partial list of African famine relief music projects is sufficient to illustrate the point:

—Great Britain – Band-Aid – "Do They Know its Christmas?" (37 artists)

—United States – USA for Africa – "We are the World" (37 artists)

—Canada – Northern Lights – "Tears are not Enough"

—West Germany – Band fur Ethiopia – "Nackt im Wind"

—France – Chanteurs Sans Frontieres – "Ethiopie" (36 artists)

—Belgium – "Leven Zonder Honger"

—The Netherlands – "Samen"

—Australia – "E.A.T." (East African Tragedy)

—Africa – "Tam Tam Pour L'Ethiopie" (50 African artists including Youssou N'Dour, Hugh Masakela, Manu Dibangu, and King Sunny Ade)[22]

Even the most cautious humanitarian efforts can create the cultural space for bolder undertakings. Just as Live Aid begat Farm Aid, the whole "charity rock" phenomenon has inspired other, more politicized ventures like Amnesty International's Conspiracy of Hope and Human Rights Now tours. The Mandela Tribute would have been unthinkable without Live Aid.

An artist's involvement with political issues and events can also be the occasion for the emergence of a more politicized popular music. In the words of Simon Frith and John Street: "The paradox of Live Aid was that while in the name of 'humanity' it seemed to depoliticize famine, in the same terms, in the name of "humanity" it politicized mass music."[23] The focus on Africa, which began with the relatively safe issue of hunger, quickly targeted the more compelling issue of apartheid. Using "We Are the World" as a model, Little Steven assembled more than fifty rock, rap, rhythm and blues, jazz, and salsa artists to create "Sun City," a politically-charged anthem in support of the cultural boycott of South Africa. The *Sun City* LP also includes "Silver and Gold," a contribution of U2's Bono, as well as "No More Apartheid" by Peter Gabriel and Gil Scott-Heron's "Let Me See Your I.D." Gabriel's "Biko" and Scott-Heron's "Johannesburg," of course, preceeded this more organized focus on apartheid, as did Peter Tosh's "Fight Against Apartheid" and Special AKA's "Free Nelson Mandela." Following the release of "Sun City," Stevie Wonder jumped into the fray with "It's Wrong (Apartheid) " and dedicated his 1986 Grammy to Nelson Mandela. Kashif took on the issue of apartheid with "Botha, Botha." The Mighty Sparrow called on the United States to "Invade South Africa." Jim Kerr of Simple Minds wrote "Mandela Day" especially for the Mandela Tribute. Stetsasonic delivered the searing rap and video "A.F.R.I.C.A."

Politicized popular music has extended to a broad range of other issues as well. There was a clear connection, for example, between John Cougar Mellencamp's involvement in Farm Aid and his "Rain on the Scarecrow," a song about the despair of modern rural life. Jackson Browne's interest in Central America led to "Lives in the Balance," a moving criticism of U.S. intervention in Central America. A number of rap groups including Public Enemy, Boogie Down Productions, and Stetsasonic participated in "Self-Destruction," the anthem of the Stop the Violence Movement, protesting black-on-black crime. In recording "Fight the Power" for Spike Lee's *Do the Right Thing,* Public Enemy contributed the soundtrack for the most powerful statement about racism in recent memory. As more and more songs born of political experience enter the popular market, the development of a more politicized culture gets validated.

Early in 1989, Geffen Records and cable music channel VH-1 teamed up to promote a mega-project to benefit Greenpeace. As their part of the project, VH-1 produced more than two dozen 60-second spots called "World Alerts," which feature celebrities discussing a range of environmental issues. Additionally, artists ranging from U2 and Talking Heads to John Cougar Mellencamp and Belinda Carlisle donated 27 hit songs to a compilation album entitled *Rainbow Warriors.* The same double LP was also released in the Soviet Union as *Breakthrough.* It soon became the top-selling record in the U.S.S.R., with all proceeds split between Greenpeace and the Soviet-based Foundation for Survival and Development of Humanity. A few months later, a number of Western heavy metal acts including Ozzie Osborne, Motley Crue, and Bon Jovi participated in the Moscow Peace Festival, the first Soviet mega-festival to be broadcast worldwide. Popular music forced a level of cross-cultural communication that governments had resisted for years.

Our Common Future was another environmental extravaganza that was staged at Lincoln Center in the spring of 1989. Participating were Bob Geldof, Richard Gere, Sting, Midnight Oil, and Herbie Hancock, among others. In addition to top-notch entertainment, the show provided a platform for a number of scientists and world leaders to voice concern over global environmental decline. It was a little unnerving, however, to see Margaret Thatcher delivering a pre-taped message about Britain's concern for the environment. It may be that the politics of the show were complicated by the sponsorship of multinational corporations, including Sony, Panasonic, and Honda, all of which had their corporate logos prominently displayed during the syndicated telecast.

Dave Marsh in particular has been critical of corporate involvement in mega-events for robbing "charity-rock of one of its most important selling points: the selflessness of its motivation."[24] Given the scale of mega-events, however, most would be impossible without some kind of corporate involvement. Amnesty International's Human Rights Now tour would have gone bankrupt had not Reebok bailed it out at the last minute. Further, there is a more optimistic reading of the situation: that the power of popular music—and, in particular, the phenomenon of mega-events—has obliged corporations and world leaders to accommodate to initiatives which are essentially left wing or progressive.

Artist Involvement

Celebrity endorsement has long been used to bolster campaigns, support charities, and sell products. Why not promote social causes? In this regard, it is important to note that mega-events and socially conscious mass music have been the beneficiaries of a left-leaning orientation which has characterized popular music since the rock era. As explained by *New York Times* critic John Rockwell:

> Rock's leftist bias arose from its origins as a music by outsiders—by blacks in a white society, by rural whites in a rapidly urbanizing economy, by regional performers in a pop-music industry dominated by New York, by youth lashing out against the settled assumptions of pre-rock pop-music professionals.

> That bias was solidified by the 1960's, with its plethora of causes and concerns.... Rock music was the anthem of that change—racial with the civil-rights movement, and also social, sexual, and political.[25]

For the most part, popular music still seems to draw from that sixties spirit, but as the music becomes more and more mainstream, there is no guarantee that this will remain the case. The late Lee Atwater, George Bush's campaign manager, managed to coopt blues and soul artists such as Joe Cocker, Albert Collins, Steve Cropper, Bo Didley, Willie Dixon, Dr. John, "Duck" Dunn, Sam Moore (of Sam and Dave), Billy Preston, Percy Sledge, Koko Taylor, Carla Thomas, Stevie Ray Vaughn, and Ron Wood, among others, for an inaugural performance for Bush. White supremacist organizations have discovered the power of punk in recruiting skinheads to their cause. Anti-abortion activists, locked arm-in-arm, sing "We Shall Overcome" as they sit-in at abortion clinics. In these politically conservative and economically uncertain times, there are any number of forces which eat away at the progressive edge of the music and complicate the nature of artistic involvement.

In producing mega-events, there is an inevitable tension between recruiting "name" artists who will ensure the financial success of the event versus local artists or artists who have a demonstrated commitment to the issue at hand. From another angle, one has to wonder what motivates an artist to become involved—political commitment, economic considerations, public relations, mock heroism, ego, etc. Different events require different levels of political commitment. "We Are the World" was recorded essentially in one session on the night of the 1985 Grammy Awards ceremony when all of the contributing artists were already in Los Angeles. Similarly, Live Aid demanded only one day of the artists' time and no particular political commitment to anything beyond some basic notion that starvation is a bad thing. Still, Bob Geldof did not hesitate to resort to what was referred to as "moral blackmail" in recruiting artists. With 21 dates in 18 countries, the Amnesty International Human Rights Now tour made far greater time demands on its artists. Still, headliners Bruce Springsteen, Peter Gabriel, Sting, Youssou N'Dour, and Tracy Chapman not only made all the dates, but also participated in press conference after press conference.

To the extent that exposure is the name of the media game, one must question an artist's motivation for performing at a live mega-event. Even though artists technically play for free for most of these concerts, when one considers the impact of having an audience of hundreds of millions in terms of, say, record sales over the next few days, then every artist who performs probably has one of the biggest paydays of his or her career. Questioned along these lines regarding his appearance at Farm Aid, Billy Joel retorted: "We don't need exposure."[26] To be fair, it must be noted that overexposure is just as big a concern for many of the artists who headline mega-events.

There are times when an artist's personal politics can be perceived as having a direct effect on the political character of an event. The Mandela Tribute was criticized for booking Whitney Houston. It was felt that Houston's widely rumored insistence on a non-political event could only lessen the impact of the show. Hollingsworth defended his choice on the grounds that it was the idea of a musical tribute that defined the politics of the Mandela concert and that Houston "agreed to pay tribute to Nelson Mandela as the symbol of fighting against apartheid."[27] Nevertheless, the degree of "fit" between artist and issue is one variable that can affect the public perception of a mega-event. The relative absence of black acts at Live Aid (and the poor coverage of some of those who were there), for example, was especially noticeable given the nature of the issue and the fact that black artists had provided all of the leadership for "We Are the World." A less obvious, but equally important, contradiction was the presence of performers such as the Beach Boys, Queen, Tina Turner, and Cher, all of whom had played South Africa in spite of the UN-sponsored cultural boycott.

On the positive side, many of the artists who headline mega-events have donated their time and talent to local communities and political organizations. Little Steven immersed himself in the issue of South Africa for the Sun City project. Following that, he turned his attention to organizing in the Native American community. Because of his involvement in Central America issues, Jackson Browne did a series of benefit dates for the Christic Institute. Bruce Springsteen rallied when 3M proposed closing its plant in Freehold, New Jersey. All of the profits (including artists, record company, producers, publishers, and participating unions) from Dionne Warwick's "That's What Friends Are For," which also featured Elton John, Gladys Knight, and Stevie Wonder, were donated to the American Foundation for AIDS Research (AMFAR). The rap artists who initiated the Stop the Violence Movement have played an on-going role in protesting the explosive conditions which exist in communities of color.

Agitation/Mobilization

The intentions of artists and producers clearly exert a profound influence in shaping the political character of our popular culture. At the same time, cultural products may have unintended consequences as well. Who, for example, would have predicted that striking black South African students would be chanting "We don't want no education. We don't want no thought control," a line from Pink Floyd's "Another Brick in the Wall," as they boycotted schools? In order to assess the impact of a cultural phenomenon, it is essential to look at its cultural usage.

Tony Hollingsworth envisioned the Mandela Tribute as a "flagship event" to be used by local anti-apartheid groups. In England, the site of the live event, the controversy generated by the concert was used to advantage by the local Anti-Apartheid Movement. According to Hollingsworth, the resulting momentum forced a change in the media coverage of Mandela and the ANC. Even in the United States where the concert itself was less effective, Little Steven's editorial in the *New York Times* criticizing the depoliticization of the event, capitalized on the shortcomings of the U.S. broadcast to deepen the analysis of apartheid and to raise issues of media censorship.

Sun City broke new political ground in its attempt to encourage an activist audience response. The *Sun City* album jacket, for example, was filled with facts and figures about apartheid. In addition, the Sun City project issued a "Teacher's Guide" which showed how to use the record and the video as educational tools in the classroom. As part of this educational effort, the "Teacher's Guide" reported on numerous anti-apartheid student projects from all over the country which had been inspired by the *Sun City* recording. Here the attempt was made to build on the familiarity of the mass cultural product to create exercises which could be tailored to local use.

Amnesty International also encouraged political activism in the way its tours were organized. The Conspiracy of Hope tour targeted six political prisoners as part of the event. One of the goals was to recruit new "freedom writers" who would participate in the letter-writing campaigns Amnesty uses to call attention to the plight of prisoners of conscience. As a result of their efforts, three of the prisoners were freed within two years. In addition, Amnesty/USA added some 200,000 new volunteers to the organization.

"Previous to 1986, we were an organization post forty," said Executive Director Jack Healy. "Music allowed us to change the very nature of our membership."[28] The mass cultural events were used to enlist people directly into the on-going political activity of the organization.

Conclusion

It is likely that mega-events will continue to happen, if for no other reason than our utter fascination with their technological possibilities. But, beneath the gleaming surfaces of the pop scene, mass culture exists as a site of contested terrain. It is in this fertile arena, with all of its contradictions, that progressive forces must either make their voices heard or risk being relegated to the margins of political struggle. Thus far, mega-events have been staged, for the most part, in support of reasonably progressive causes. Indeed, in most instances, they have shifted debate to the left. But, as Bob Geldof cautioned those who envisaged Live Aid as a sixties-style movement,

> [W]e've used the spurious glamour of pop music to draw attention to a situation, and we've overloaded the thing with symbolism to make it reach people. But people get bored easily. People may have been profoundly affected by the Live Aid day—some were shattered by it—but that does not translate into a massive change in consciousness.[29]

Geldof's case may be a bit overstated. It has been demonstrated that popular music is capable of far more than "spurious glamour." At the same time, we would do well to acknowledge its limitations. While one hesitates to borrow metaphors from Keynesian economics in this day and age, it would, perhaps, be fair to say that mega-events appear to be quite useful for priming the political pump. But, for those interested in lasting structural change, it has to be recognized that they are no substitute for a political movement.

From the making of the *Sun City* video. Front row from left: Little Steven, Darlene Love, Jimmy Cliff, David Ruffin, two members of Viva Afrika, and Bruce Springsteen. (Photo © Reuven Kopichinski)

Diverse Rock Rebellions Subvert Mass Media Hegemony

Neal Ullestad

An exciting tension surrounds popular music in the 1990s: invention facing tradition, creativity confronting stagnation, tolerance versus intolerance, rebellion against authority, commercialism versus authenticity. This tension is not a simple struggle of positive and negative, "good" or "bad." But the tension does tend to subvert the pervasive control exercised by corporate mass media over our experience of daily life. This subversion is first a struggle for democracy, justice, and everyone's equal right to pursue his or her own happiness. It is much more than a struggle to decide what music we hear, when we hear it, where, and how.

We *are* hearing more diversity and dynamism in popular music these days—across the radio dial, at county fairs, in small clubs and dance halls, at benefit concerts, and in all recorded formats—than at any time since the mythical 1960s. But that diversity isn't valued and nurtured everywhere. Most often the music industry and mass media in general barely tolerate diversity. Mass media and the "music business" tend to subvert multicultural pleasures that are difficult to commodify, subordinating such pleasures to the power of pop to absorb a little of everything, diverting diverse desires into compulsive consumerism.

The current articulation of popular culture and the entertainment industry with mobilizations of hundreds of thousands of individuals for social responsibility is one of the most intriguing moments in these times of cultural awareness and resistances to corporate hegemony in the mass media.

1991 opened with the release of the "Give Peace a Chance" single and video by the Peace Choir, organized by Sean Ono Lennon and Lenny Kravitz.[1] And, on Earth Day 1991, many major stars brought us an eclectic message against militarism and for peace. In December 1990, Lou Reed, the Roches, and Pete Seeger played a benefit concert in New York City—News

Aid—for the striking *Daily News* workers.[2] A strong intervention by women rappers, such as Queen Latifah, Monie Love, and Salt-N-Peppa (see Chapter 16), has drawn majority attention toward "positivity" rather than the randy "adolescent" male rants so popular in the early '80s. And the Stop the Violence (STV) Movement—including KRS-ONE, Ms. Melodie, and Just-Ice—earned a substantial amount of support for the National Urban League in the late 1980s, focusing attention on alternatives to inner-city despair and self-destruction.[3] Bonnie Raitt, Bruce Springsteen, and Jackson Browne went acoustic in Los Angeles for the Christic Foundation (whose research has consistently challenged many Reagan/Bush lies on Iran, Iraq, and Central America). The *Red Hot & Blue* Cole Porter revival offered up sizzling AIDS/HIV *edutainment* on the centennial birthdate of one of Broadway's most successful songwriters—featuring interpretations by Aaron Neville, Sinaed O'Connor, Neneh Cherry, and many more. Greenpeace built on its successful 1989 *Rainbow Warriors* release (Peter Gabriel, Chrissie Hynde, David Byrne, and even the Grateful Dead) by sponsoring a benefit concert in Phoenix in conjunction with Arizona Native American Indian Rights groups and anti-nuclear forces, which featured John Trudell, Bonnie Raitt, and Bruce Cockburn.

To understand how such political rock could assert itself so strongly in the face of media war hysteria and the general indifference to the deepening social crises, we must go back to rock's roots—before the many mass media events of recent years, before Amnesty International's Human Rights Now tour, before the Mandela Seventieth Birthday Tribute, before the Sun City project, Live Aid, Rock Against Racism, Rock Against Sexism, MUSE, and No Nukes!, and before the Lennon/Ono bed-ins, Bob Dylan, and Phil Ochs. The tension inherent in rock 'n' roll's emergence from the segregated and authoritarian culture of the 1950s is the source of its dynamism today.

"The '50s were a time of flux, of sound and fury." The sound was generated by young people "creating their own culture; and the fury, that of the older generation resisting, hating, and opposing something they could not and [often] did not want to understand."[4] There was also the fury of the Ku Klux Klan against civil rights activists, the fury of McCarthyism against "communism" in the labor and cultural communities, as well as the fury of the literary establishment against the Beat Poets. The fury of the Black Panthers and radical feminists was yet to come.

In the mid-1950s, authoritarianism—so entrenched throughout the 1940s and early 1950s—was tentatively but confidently challenged on significant cultural levels, especially in rock 'n' roll. Madison Avenue's cynical advertisers gloried in smug satisfaction as they worked to manipulate consumer interests with relative ease. And, many men actually believed, as Mick Jagger sang, that another guy couldn't "be a man, 'cause he doesn't smoke the same cigarettes as me."[5] But in rock 'n' roll music, youthful desires, feelings, and concerns were expressed as never before. Rock 'n' roll was the "soundtrack" for the emergence of a youth culture that has had significant effects on social discourse and intercourse over the past half century.

Can't Get No Satisfaction

Subversion of satisfaction is the name of the game in pop/rock. If we are unhappy—dissatisfied with our lives—it is our own inadequacies, and not the social system we inhabit, that make us so. In mass media the system of advertising makes a single proposal: transform yourselves—your lives— by *buying* something more. "This more," advertisers promise, "will make us in some way *richer*—even though we will be poorer by having spent our money."[6] It is the buying that counts, "which is one reason the buyer is insatiable."[7]

Hegemonic corporate forces encourage constant changes in artists, sounds, and products, perpetually fostering dissatisfaction, subverting conventional meanings of desire and pleasure until we "can't be satisfied."[8] Consumer mythologies of style and fashion condense fulfillment of our desires into the act of buying that which is "new," *now.* Clearly, such change seldom includes any significant disruption of the day-to-day, "natural" acceptance of the "given" order of things—of received "reality." Since meaningful change can be a serious threat to corporate control, superficial change—through the subversion of satisfaction—has been institutionalized. And every repackaged sound or product is pronounced new and "revolutionary."

But occasionally the relentless new, now of pop is genuinely shaken by something radically different. Pop/rock has succeeded in tapping and absorbing youthful rebellion as a rejuvenating force. But pop hasn't been as successful in strangling social awareness. Several mass media music projects in the last few years have significantly activated social consciousness within the realm of popular music. These include: Live Aid, Farm Aid, Sun City, the Mandela Tributes, Amnesty International's tours, Greenpeace's *Rainbow Warriors,* and the *Red Hot & Blue* Cole Porter review. These seven challenges to the status quo offer lessons of difference and similarity that have implications beyond their immediate impact on mass media entertainment.

Difference/Similarity/Politics

The differences and similarities of these mass media events are visible in their genealogy—their emergence, their sustaining efforts, history and consequences; in musicians, product, and "success" (popularity and profitability). Significant differences distinguish what is referred to here as "Media Aid"—primarily "charity" benefit events such as Live Aid and Farm Aid—from the more radical events such as Sun City and the Mandela and Amnesty concerts, and from *Red Hot & Blue* and *Rainbow Warriors,* which have quite different implications in the context and format being considered. Addressing these interventions in chronological order exposes an increasing self-awareness over the years as artists become more outspoken and audiences more actively supportive. This, in turn, indicates cumulative effects, especially for some artists and particular audiences. But outlining certain basic features of popular music first helps compare the differences and similarities we observe.

Artistic expression is best understood by analyzing and comparing four major aspects of its totality: artist, audience, the product or musical piece itself, and the music industry in all its complexity.[9]

We can assess each individual artist's expressed intent, conditions of existence, biographical information, and interaction with the audience, other musicians, and "management." The reception of the music by an audience can be even more complex than the artistic expression itself. The composition of each audience—young/old, black/brown/red/yellow/white, female/male, gay/straight, rich/poor—is only one level on which to compare different listeners and viewers. The relationship of a particular audience to broader national and international cultural and political realms, the uses to which people put musical products, group and individual interpretations of meaning, as well as perceptions of the artist, and the livelihood and life experiences of those involved, all require investigation.

Musical products in Media Aid mega-events range from songs and benefit concerts to paperback books, video and audio releases in various formats, T-shirts, buttons, posters, and related educational campaign materials. These forms, their specific content, and their existence separate from the producing artist all affect our understanding of the music and its message.

Finally, addressing the role of economic and political power structures in the music industry includes examining who controls access to performance venues, recording studios, mass media outlets, and distribution networks, as well as what that control means for artists, audiences, and artistic expression in general. Attempts to manipulate production and consumption relations in more "profitable" avenues dominate corporate policy—but what are the long-term effects of such actions? What alternatives might be appropriate?

This brief outline of artistic expression can help address the seven mass media musical events cited above in economic, ideological, and political terms.

All pop is political. Even the most avowedly non-political work of art has political implications in its conception, its expression (production), exhibition (distribution), and reception (enjoyment/consumption). And, self-conscious political activism isn't limited to speeches, meetings, or voting. Cultural and social activities of diverse origins and expressions produce distinct effects.

Live Aid

The recent flurry of rebellious and subversive influences in pop/rock—such as the Human Rights Now tour, the Mandela Seventieth Birthday Tribute, and Sun City—all emerged in the wake of Live Aid's initial disruptive effects.[10] Staged simultaneously in London, Philadelphia, and Sydney, Australia on July 13, 1985, and broadcast to an international audience of 1.5 billion people, Live Aid featured a core line-up of international superstars. It generated what some critics claim were significant challenges to dominant relations in the musical fabric of our lives, disrupting complaisant pleasures and apathy. Live Aid showed that rock—even in the post-1984 era—still carries certain compassionate ideals, a conscious break with the arrogantly self-satisfied rock 'n' roll of the "Me" and "Greed" decades.

Live Aid jump-started the current round of cultural political activism. Events which followed—Sport Aid, Comic Relief, Food Aid, EAT in Australia, reggae's "Land of Africa" from Jamaica,[11] Hear 'n Aid by metal rockers, and the many other mass media events[12]—have exposed millions of people to alternative information on the Ethiopian famine that was not readily available through established channels. Now, years later, we can see Live Aid's limitations. At the same time, we cannot ignore its long-term effects of validating cultural intervention in the global political arena.

One view of Media Aid holds that this trend was a renewal of the "true" spirit of rock 'n' roll, a revitalization of the audience, musicians, and industry in a socially relevant way. The other preponderant view has it that Live Aid was just another example of pop/rock's cooptation, a rip-off of the hard work that put together other musical/political expressions. This view holds that Media Aid was nothing more than a glamorous charity gambit, virtually the antithesis of Sun City and Amnesty's concerts, a ripe opportunity for cynical manipulative media hounds.[13] As well-intentioned charity and philanthropy without political significance, Media Aid serves the status quo by containing individual concern and sharing within corporate and governmental channels.

Some of these critics claim that the cooptation was so complete that Live Aid was a part of the problem and not a solution of any type, not even a "band-aid." But significant questions remain if such conclusions are reached too soon: Were the consciousnesses of particular audiences raised? What effects were there upon specific musicians? What are the implications of Media Aid cooperation and "profit-sharing" on the production, copyright, royalty, and distribution relations of the entertainment industry? What are the differences between Media Aid and the Jerry Lewis Telethons? Few critics fell between the two poles of opinion on Live Aid (etc.), though both camps had those who tempered their discourse by conceding specific points to the opposition.

This polarization of views was particularly unproductive because it blocked meaningful dialogue and critical cooperation. Further, it reflected a recurring problem that has limited effective discussion for many others, and not just rock critics. Such a polarization has been a part of the debates on popular culture for decades.

Historic Tension

In the 1930s, theories of Theodor Adorno and Bertolt Brecht regarding the social role of popular culture, and appropriate responses to it, were similarly polarized. Adorno held that popular culture primarily manipulates people to be happy consumers, pawns in the hands of authoritarian forces accountable only to the bottom line.[14] He emphasized the cooptation and control inherent in consumerism. Brecht, on the other hand, had a more optimistic view of modern society. For him the mass media offered opportunities as well as manipulation and restrictions. Brecht acted within cultural media to transform them into institutions and practices that better served the people. He anticipated the popularity and significance of the call-in talk shows of radio and TV, and advocated "functional transformation" and "subversion" of the hegemony of corporate powers in mass media. For Brecht the concept of *montage* addressed issues of perspective, context, and situation, where codes of behavior produced in one set of circumstances can be contrasted, or juxtaposed, to a radically different context.[15]

Building on Bertolt Brecht's *praxis*, Walter Benjamin held that the wide availability of popular culture serves to break down some of the mystery associated with art—fostering a democratization of artistic appreciation. Further, Benjamin held that the "shock effects" of day-to-day life expressed in art can serve to stimulate a need to overcome the crises that confront us.[16] Adorno, Brecht, and Benjamin provide useful insights for today, but their theories remained polarized, as have those who have come after them, except in certain isolated instances.[17]

With the emergence of rock 'n' roll, there were those who rejected it and those who embraced it, lining up with reasons remarkably similar to those of Adorno and Brecht. Punk rock also was greeted with conflicting reviews—denounced as decadent degeneracy and ultimately coopted, or encouraged as the true essence of the working class emerging from the fringes of the pop mainstream. More productive analysis grew from the exploration of theories of empowerment.

Within a framework that conceptualizes "the problematic of power as the organization of desire," Larry Grossberg set out in 1984 to describe the parameters and limits of rock 'n' roll's "empowering effects" in terms of the production of "affective alliances."[18] He argued that despite a general cooptation of much of rock music, alliances of rebellion can build on the emotional articulations that form the rock "community," and can disrupt the corporate power-brokers' hegemonic control over that community's desires and pleasures. Levels of cooptation—or "incorporation" for Grossberg—are not always so dominant that rebellion is totally invisible. Recurring open rebellions crack the mythical monolith of corporate rock and its "harmonious" facade.

To be coopted in any segment of society, and not simply in rock culture, means to be immersed in the mystification of reality at the level of social consciousness. It is to accept as inevitable—to be resigned to—current and future social conditions of existence and relations of power, unquestioning the overwhelming "truths" of the mass media. To survive in modern society is to be "coopted" to one degree or another. Yet, total sell-out isn't inevitable. Island Records' Rick Dutka describes particular "pressures of commercialism" that situate musicians in diverse "arenas of struggle" which "necessitate compromises that produce varying degrees of cooptation."[19]

Seldom complete, cooptation functions with various degrees of realization. Further, cooptation does not just offer the goal of becoming successful. It holds that there is no alternative but to succumb to the pressures of the current configuration of modern capitalism that work toward the atomization and control of almost all of everyday life—a considered life of consuming, working, pleasure-seeking, and suffering. To be fully coopted is to be "fooled quite easily," believing the "Fabrications on T.V. [that] distort the news"[20]—fabrications that sustain the powers that be in the exercise of their control.

Empowerment

Certain processes of rebellion can be understood to have "empowering effects"—a liberation from aspects of authoritarian control. Empowering effects tend to clarify reality and verify truths. No matter what the intent or attempts to control the outcome, such effects can reveal new layers of truth and address issues of perspective, as well as global versus local implications. Rock can remove signs, sounds, objects, and styles "from their apparently meaningful existence" within dominant cultural relations, and relocate them within the sensibility of the rock community, an "affective alliance of differentiation and resistance" centered around the rebellions of youth.[21] In that process of "excorporation," rock can and does speak truths. A constant ebb and flow exists between incorporation and excorporation, such that there is a simultaneous intertwining of effects. According to Grossberg, rock offers an alternative choice within, not an oppositional pole from without. So, while rock produces its own boundaries of existence in relation to hegemonic structures, its resistance remains generally "within the political and economic space of the dominant culture."[22]

But there are exceptions to most rules, and John Lennon's "Imagine" stands as one of the most eloquent poetic rebellions against dominant economic, political, and cultural institutions of the day. His sentiments have been repeated and elaborated in rock by many others in the past 20 years. The vast majority of those who participated in Media Aid have never dreamt of such open challenges to rock's pop hegemony. But while Grossberg's theory had rock 'n' rollers resisting, removing, and demarcating, we can see other things happening within the rock community's experience of Live Aid. Live Aid drew in and brought together, and at the same time confronted certain relations of domination.

Hegemonic relations exist as a complex set of mechanisms that structure actions and thoughts, practices and expectations, desires and feelings. Hegemonic structures work to control these relations in the interest of the ruling powers, controlling "reality" but also simultaneously leaving room for discontent, for interest in change, and even for certain rebellions. We are channeled and coaxed, as well as coerced and prohibited. But, hegemony is not a consolidated force. It is a fluid process, successful in containment because it is flexible and encourages our active consent.[23] Nonetheless, power is ultimately rigid in the limits it sets. Within the limits much seems possible. But, we are constrained from going beyond the boundaries—short of radical thought or action. And so resistance, rebellion, and other struggles for excorporation would seem inevitable. Or, as Malcolm X explained, "As long as explosive ingredients remain...You're going to have the potential for explosion...."[24]

The Place of Media Aid

Live Aid, Band Aid, and USA for Africa *did* exist quite solidly within the structural limits of the hegemonic framework. They functioned at a level that reproduces ideas of charity, even as they sold millions of records and other merchandise that profited—among others more deserving—the record industry. But, this is not all they have done. Media Aid has also tended to subvert conventional meanings of pleasure. Such charity events seem to have built on general feelings of compassion, latent in the United States, to encompass an outpouring of social concern across society. Live Aid affected the commonly experienced meanings and values of its viewers.

Live Aid was first and foremost a media event of the highest order. The aid, the music, and the musicians were quite secondary to the event itself. Its significance as a true extravaganza was such that even Ronald Reagan had a desire to participate. Any mass media event of such an order, with global cooperation by so many corporations and governments, is firmly situated within the limits of the dominant social structures; including hegemonic relations at the level of social consciousness. It is, in fact, a part of the "common sense" reality—the mirage—of the "natural" and "inevitable" order of things as they are.

The concrete material effects of such a mirage tend to obscure, distort, or hide the "true," complex, and multilayered "nature of things" in the mind's eye. There isn't necessarily an intent to deceive and manipulate; nor is there anything "wrong" with the reception of the perceiver. No "untruth" is expressed. Yet, there is the *material impact* of the observable distortion. The mirage of pop peace and harmony—quite real in its own strange ways—obscures the very real conflicts and suffering inflicted upon the world by corporate capital.

The recognition of hegemonic incorporation by various means does not negate the fact that power relations are constantly shifting and changing to various degrees. Live Aid served to disrupt the smooth flow of ideas and beliefs because it was a window onto another part of the world, a window through the haze of the mirage, a view behind the screen of consumer "reality." Such a view can have empowering effects. Hegemony is an historical process where one picture is *preferred* but not ensured. There are changing "frames" and "windows" that have different effects.[25] Not only was the obsessive "star" discourse shifted from its totally superficial and self-centered focus, but also the global political discourse was shifted to include cooperation with the Soviets, shining a shaft of light onto that section of humanity shrouded by rhetoric regarding the "evil empire." Since the Reagan/Bush/Thatcher frontal assaults on the Liberal/New Deal/Labor coalitions have narrowed the hegemonic discourse and shifted it far to the right, it is subversive to question that which they present as acceptable discourse and received, or "true" reality. The incorporation of Live Aid within the hegemonic rock discourse didn't eliminate its effective resistance against the global power structures on certain key levels. Rock is simultaneously co-opted and rebelling in Media Aid. In these cases charity had additional—unplanned—subversive effects.

Dave Marsh considers the main accomplishment of Live Aid to be "the reawakening of a section of the rock audience to its own social potential and a quantum leap in public awareness of the horrifying problems of poverty, hunger, homelessness and racism."[26] In this sense Live Aid resisted and challenged ideas that the world is best served by greedy self-interest and the side-stepping of social responsibilities, as put forward by Reagan, Bush, and Thatcher. In Grossberg's theoretical terms, this is a part of the process of excorporation.

Media Aid was a partial demystification of reality, a disruption of conventional meanings—a shock to the system of received ideology. Structures of the "conscious mind of collective youth" were shaken.[27] The immediate sensuous character of everyday life was confronted with another sensual experience, another part of *reality*. Such confrontation has very real "truth effects."[28] Truth can lead to empowerment in the appropriate context.

Live Aid was a media event that structurally emphasized charity and philanthropy (for others not so much like us), as well as global cooperation at a time when the narrow dominant views have atomized and deadened the majority of the pop audience and locked us in our lonely rooms. Live Aid opened windows from our rooms to the world and made it "legitimate" to *care*, and called on us to *act*. Significantly, Media Aid called on the people of the United States and Britain—societies well-known for overt acts of racial hatred—to act *for* black Africans.

The effects were not externally oppositional. The events spoke for internal alternatives, for action *within* the system. And there was no guarantee that the effects were substantial or long-lasting. But the call to action and interaction is crucial in these times of enforced apathy. Could this subversion of conventional meanings of pleasure indicate the regeneration of special forms of desire and pleasure, the desire to help and the pleasure of giving (rather than the charitable *guilt* of giving)? In hindsight, we can see the lasting effects of these events. But at the time, the immediate effects of the event were contained within existing hegemonic relations, effectively perpetuating the suffering that was being confronted.[29]

Shifts and Openings

Two resulting developments are significant: internal hegemonic shifts, and disruptive openings. Shifts *within* hegemonic structures alter them in ways that leave the possibility for the development of more favorable power relations. Politically there is a challenge to what is seen as the "natural image" of reality, the mythological distortions that give a sense of inevitability to that which *is* now. Legitimating "liberal concerns" is a rebellion against resignation.[30] In Live Aid, we witnessed a step in a direction that showed more concern for human rights than for property rights. This concern has had material effects in attendance at large concerts and the acquisition of recorded releases to assist those in such diverse situations as Kurdish refugees, Mexican and Central American earthquake survivors, and people with AIDS.

Musically, within the dominant relations, our mass media aid events were a pleasurable expansion of cooperation in singing, composition, and general performance. Such expression broke some of the structures of isolation and atomization that so control human interaction, especially among successful musicians. Media Aid has generated new possibilities in musical interaction, even innovation. Sociologically, these events gave the audience and performers a sense of belonging—to the human family, as well as the rock community. Media Aid shows that there *is* hope in the post-*1984* era; and hope is vital for empowerment.

The second development, that of disruptive openings, is a more radical one. The disruption of the usual order of the day caused by Live Aid provided openings for further, more radical challenges to existing relations, such as Central American Sanctuary Defense (confronting administration policies on Guatemala and El Salvador), the Mandela celebrations, and Human Rights Now!, as well as the *Sun City* recording sessions. The relations of a particular event, in disrupting the general processes of pop culture, can provide a radical space or "revolutionary opportunity" for *conscious* subversion of the reproduction of authoritarian social relations.[31]

Farm Aid

The first Farm Aid emerged directly out of Live Aid in September 1985. Farm Aid focused public attention on the plight of U.S. family farmers, and also openly exhibited some of the controversy and contradictions that the parent event was able to conceal.[32] Farm Aid grew from a comment by Bob Dylan to Willie Nelson at Live Aid, that in the process of helping Ethiopians, U.S. farmers, too, could be helped. "Keep America Growing" was the theme of Farm Aid II. Help "the men and women who feed us all" was a dominant sentiment. As Farm Aid went on to subsequent annual affairs, including Willie Nelson's co-sponsored 4th of July picnic in Austin, Texas, the farm crisis deepened. Nelson and John Cougar Mellencamp kept the fire going with the help of local and national activists.

But Farm Aid exhibited strong expressions of the ideology of isolationist populism deeply rooted in the agricultural heartland of the United States. "Help our own" rang out more than once from the stage; and the spirited nationalism (including advertising to buy U.S. beef and jeans) harked back to that mythical Disney past when family farming was an occupation for millions and agribusiness wasn't in control. Farm Aid also brought black and white artists together on stage. And, diverse '80s audiences were exposed to new or rediscovered musicians, such as Judy Collins, War, and Rita Coolidge.

But the most significant political statement in Farm Aid wasn't spoken from the stage and didn't emerge from any of the songs. Though important things were said and sung, the exposure of a different reality from that espoused by the Reagan administration served to confront viewers with questions; questions without easy answers. All the cheerful babble from the announcers in the control room couldn't hide the fact that this event wasn't just fun, and that family farmers *are* in trouble.

The unavoidable question was: What's being done about it? When questions are raised and previously concealed aspects of reality are exposed, people tend to look for answers. Such answers needn't come from within the hegemonic system, but someone must be available with radical answers when they are being sought, otherwise answers internal to the ruling system will be found.

Sun City

"I Ain't Gonna Play 'Sun City.'"[33]

Sun City, the hard-edged political pop/rock statement—a visual and aural montage—released in October 1985 by Artists United Against Apartheid (AUAA)—was another interruption of the orderly course of business-as-usual in the music world. But this event was more radical from the start. "Sun City" visually and verbally challenged entertainers to endorse the United Nations boycott of South Africa: don't "endorse" relations of apartheid by performing at the Sun City entertainment complex in the "black homeland" of Bophuthatswana. This is not just an issue of solidarity with a political mass movement, but also a recognition that those involved are fighters, not simply victims. By calling for a boycott of the mostly white elite of South Africa, co-producers Steve Van Zandt and Arthur Baker put a different sort of pressure on the hegemonic powers enforcing the official segregation of the Afrikaners.

First erupting as a single at the New Music Seminar in New York, "Sun City" grew into an album on Billboard's Top Forty that winter, a video that received "heavy rotation" on MTV, and a quality paperback book—all offering serious challenges to popular perceptions of the status quo on issues of South Africa, pop success, and cultural legitimacy. "Sun City" was much more than a political challenge to the Reagan administration's policies on South Africa. "Sun City" challenged musicians to consider the deepest implications of their work and success, taking thoughtfulness far beyond the tentative steps of Live Aid. Further, Artists United Against Apartheid—including Pat Benatar, George Clinton, Bruce Springsteen, Bonnie Raitt, Jimmy Cliff, Ruben Blades, Darlene Love, the late David Ruffin, Lou Reed,

Bob Dylan, Miles Davis, Stanley Jordan, Peter Gabriel, Gil Scott-Heron, Nona Hendryx, and dozens more—openly challenged the audience to consider the world situation in light of specific policies and their effects. As an avowed educational campaign, Sun City reached many people who otherwise would have remained ill-informed.

Musically, the radical fusion of rock, rap, pop, and jazz in this production could have far-reaching effects. The musics are genuinely *fused* on the album and in the songs. And the interaction of the musicians has other implications because of their diversity in age, style, ethnic and racial heritage, and "recognition" (stars versus unknowns). No previous rock event brought together such a wide range of rockers and rappers; Latin, African, reggae, and jazz musicians; women and men alike. The generation of the album was equally radical, with various individuals working together and alone, thousands of miles apart, to build on the original demo tape and to contribute tracks and eventually even entire new songs. Technologically, the production of the album and video explored new ground. And the fast-paced juxtaposition of shocking images of police brutality and masses of protesters, contrasted to the life of leisure lead by most white South Africans, was a montage of sights and sounds, educating and entertaining simultaneously.

The *Sun City* musicians were the first group of internationally recognized artists to take a stand against apartheid; and they stood with gusto. *Sun City* was a frontal cultural assault on the institution of apartheid in South Africa. It was a turning point in the genealogy of pop/rock.

The Mandela Tribute

The Seventieth Birthday tribute for Nelson Mandela in Wembley Stadium—even as he and other ANC leaders were locked in South African jails—is quintessential rock rebellion in a mass media event, as Reebee Garofalo describes in Chapter 3. As a hopeful—yes, fun and playful—cultural intervention in the hegemonic political discourse, it was one of many assaults against apartheid that eventually led to the release of Mandela. But it stands as a nodal point in pop/rock, similar to *Sun City* in its radical thrust and implications.

Though Whitney Houston signed early but refused to be involved if the event was "political," the very conception of a mass media birthday party for an imprisoned liberation leader is radical in and of itself! Because all pop is political, the politics of apathy and unquestioned acceptance of authority have every bit as significant effects as active and self-conscious participation in the voting franchise, and consumption relations can have every bit as much of an impact as coercive force, product boycotts, and strikes. Social effects result from diverse and divergent activities, some of which are none too obvious. Four years after the Mandela tribute Reagan and Thatcher are gone, Mandela is free, and Amnesty and AIDS Aid have yet to crest.

Conspiracy of Hope and Human Rights Now!

Amnesty International's Conspiracy of Hope/Human Rights Now! concert tours represent the coming of age of rock's self-conscious political intervention in the mass media and with mass movements. Again we are treated to genuinely exciting music. Stanley Jordan, Joan Baez, Little Steven, Third World, Miles Davis, and Carlos Santana were among those who graced the stage in New York's Giants Stadium in the summer of 1988. This conclusion of a six-city U.S. tour was a kick-off for the six week world tour that covered 20 cities: London; Paris; Budapest; Turin; Barcelona; San Jose, Costa Rica; Toronto; Montreal; Philadelphia; Los Angeles; Oakland; Tokyo; Delhi; Athens; Harare, Zimbabwe; Abidjon, Ivory Coast; Sao Paulo; and Buenos Aires. The musicians included Tracy Chapman, Youssou N'Dour, Peter Gabriel, Sting, and Bruce Springsteen, all dedicated to human rights politics.

Springsteen's comments were indicative of the artists' reasons for getting involved. "I think that Amnesty makes the world a less oppressive, less brutal place to live, and I want to help Amnesty do its job."[34] Or, as Tracy Chapman explained, "I have faith in people...because in believing otherwise, there is no hope."[35]

It's hard to be critical of Amnesty's Human Rights Now! events. These artists would seem to have put a great deal "on the line" since Amnesty International is not a politically "safe" organization. Membership in Amnesty jumped following these tours, signifying a positive audience response. Many of the artists were radicalized even more by their interaction with stalwart human rights activists. And Amnesty's concerns remain on the pop agenda even today.

Rainbow Warriors

Greenpeace organized the release of a double album in March 1989 in the Soviet Union, where it was called *Breakthrough (Melodiya),* and in the United States, under the title *Rainbow Warriors.*[36] The recording included tracks by U2, Aswad, Sting, Bryan Ferry, the Eurythmics, Talking Heads, Peter Gabriel, REM, Sade, John Cougar Mellencamp, The Pretenders, and many others. The press release boasted "the very best of Western rock music," and the tracks were chosen because "they are hits or because they convey a hopeful message to young people in the USSR."[37]

Several musicians explained their involvement with Greenpeace with similar reasoning: "First, it was an *apolitical* organization, and second, the issues with which Greenpeace was concerned were *universal* [emphasis added]."[38] But other artists gave the opposite reason for joining ranks with Greenpeace, even as nuclear warships were being confronted, with claims that "Greenpeace is not a safe organization like…UNICEF."[39] It isn't always clear what *Rainbow Warriors* is about. Straight, sappy love songs mingle with articulate blasts against military might. The context of hope and confrontation offers vague insights into the politics of Greenpeace, but little can be judged as to the effects on audiences and political relations as compared to the Mandela, Sun City, and Amnesty concerts.

Compared to punk's anarchy and despair or to the politics of the Human Rights Now tour and Sun City, Greenpeace is much less declaratively political. But the political implications of such an amalgam emerge strongly when the songs and artists are observed more closely. David Byrne's "City of Dreams" and Lou Reed's "Last Great American Whale" are only two of the challenges to pop's mystical harmony, drawing attention to the situation of Native Americans in the United States. In the context of Desert Storm's victory in Iraq, songs such as REM's "The End of the World as We Know It," "This Time" by INXS, "Middle of the Road" by the Pretenders, "Throwing Stones" by the Grateful Dead, and World Party's "Ship of Fools," all can take on strong anti-war sentiments. There's a great deal of passion on *Rainbow Warriors*—confident, powerful pop anthems and searching introspection.

Red Hot and Volatile

Red Hot & Blue, "a tribute to Cole Porter to benefit AIDS research and relief," hit *Billboard's* Top Fifty in the fall of 1990.[40] As one of the many stirrings of consciousness in popular music toward human and civil rights politics, it is truly a landmark. Other events have been more overtly political; still others have raised more money. But never has pop/rock produced such sophisticated *edutainment* as exists in the video, audio, and printed product of these dedicated—some would say courageous—artists. Here, in service to suffering and neglected people, we have music laced with wit, romance, intelligence, and complex emotions, originally written by a homosexual, society "gentleman" of the Broadway stage. Cole Porter was a true wordsmith, and the songs collected here—"Down in the Depths," "Who Wants to be a Millionaire? (I don't)," and "Night and Day," among others—are indicative of his wide-ranging work.

In the video version, old movies clips feature Nat King Cole crooning and Frank Sinatra mugging for the cameras, among many vintage and contemporary short video takes. Again, montage is used to similar effect as in *Sun City*. Shocking images and information flash onto the screen as these *popular* artists sing and play with abandon, passion, and unfortunately at times calculated simulations of sincerity. Sinaed O'Connor impersonates Marilyn Monroe, k.d. lang offers a compassionate portrait of caring love in the face of despair in "So In Love," David Byrne and Tom Waits career across the screen, and Kirsty MacColl's "Miss Otis Regrets" is stunning.

State-of-the-art video techniques and playful scripting at times bring laughter to this serious subject—there are certainly enough "odd balls and weirdos" in the video release to signify post-post-modern interpretations of these pop and jazz standards. Neneh Cherry's rap "Under My Skin" stands as a monument to pleasure/desire/compassion/education/activism. What the other performances lack in innovation, they often make up in passion. Aaron Neville, U2's Bono, and Annie Lennox check in with inspired contributions, and nearly two dozen artists are represented on this radically diverse collection of covers and "makeovers".

Cole Porter's work expresses feelings of gut-wrenching loss next to the discovery of new experiences. With Porter, the exploration of bottomless sadness can reside "next to near indescribable joy, fierce intelligence, and a wink with the double entendre." Not unlike Elvis Costello, Suzanne Vega, or Tracy Chapman, Cole Porter gives a "sense of the eternal outsider,…having the sharpest eye in the room, chronicling details that others miss or are simply oblivious to."[41]

But despite the very real political implications of pop/rock pushing solid information, as opposed to pablum and fear about AIDS/HIV—and doing so while embracing the intellectual bent of Cole Porter's lyricism, and acknowledging his homosexuality—the deepest politics of this event are expressed in the juxtaposition of its video clips. Most of the songs have little or no "political" content. But a clear bias emerges as Sinaed O'Connor segues into Bing Crosby and Frank Sinatra intoxicated with their own sense of importance in "Well, Did You Evah?" This is followed immediately by Debbie Harry and Iggy Pop and their campy remake romp through New York City's homeless communities. Such contrasts reveal truths about the real world quite vividly.

Because of its many ambiguities, *Red Hot & Blue* doesn't take the full leap into radical rock. But, in conscious contrast to the emphasis on sharing in Media Aid, *Red Hot & Blue,* like *Sun City,* emphasized communication of hard information and relatively shocking images: the communication of *truth* to educate.

Cooptation or Rebellion?

The Media Aid mega-events disrupted the general processes of rock, unconsciously subverting conventional meanings of pleasure and certain hegemonic relations, as well as providing the "radical space" for the emergence of Sun City, Mandela, Human Rights Now! and Greenpeace—all *conscious* subversions of hegemonic social discourse. These attempts to subvert conventional social consciousness were not sufficient to generate lasting change in South Africa, or to decrease repression around the world. But, clearly they have been useful additions to the arsenal mustered against the reprehensible relations of apartheid and global racism. And, Mandela *is* free today.

Previous artists have asked us to act on political issues. And others have challenged hegemonic structures in their music. The Sun City, Mandela, and Amnesty artists took those challenges onto new terrain in vehicles of innovation. Their conscious cooperation disrupted the hegemonic discourse that surrounds the relations of apartheid. In so doing, they went far beyond the acts of charity of Media Aid.

The most significant difference between Media Aid events and their radical counterparts is not the topics of protest that are picked and the more radical implications of those choices. Rather, the deepest difference is the self-conscious action of the artists to disrupt and subvert existing meanings and relations. Media Aid wanted to help, and unknowingly disrupted and challenged. Sun City, Mandela, and the other radical events were consciously open challenges to the dominant political authorities.

The crucial question remains: How will all these events affect the future of pop/rock? Will the activist current go underground again as it so often does? Or, will new and more challenging events emerge? A Martin Luther King, Jr. package would seem timely now that Bush has sabotaged civil rights legislation and so many artists have paid King homage. (Such an event could be useful in confronting such states as Arizona and New Hampshire that continue to avoid a King holiday.)

No theory can tell whether or not cooptation or rebellion will dominate in the future. But the ferment of the day seems to signal more subversion of the pop mainstream. This will mean more and more people looking for answers to questions that are not easily contained within the hegemonic discourse. To paraphrase Pat Benatar, rock 'n' roll "is a battlefield."[42] The terrain of struggle requires advanced concepts for organizing mass movements for radical social change. Artists who have made the mass media their weapon have technology every bit as sophisticated—if not as destructive—as that used to obliterate Iraq in Desert Storm. Millions of people wait to be mobilized to create a more just and equal world. Missing are the tacticians and strategists who can translate desires and hopes into meaningful action.

Nelson Mandela Seventieth Birthday Tribute, Wembley Stadium, London. (Photo © Chris Rodley, courtesy of the photographer, Tribute Executive Producer Tony Hollingsworth, and the Barbara Gladstone Gallery, New York)

Nelson Mandela, the Concerts

Mass Culture as Contested Terrain

Reebee Garofalo

"We Shall Overcome" evolved from a religious hymn to a labor song to the theme of the Civil Rights Movement. It has been exported to dozens of countries around the world and has become familiar to millions of people. This process has taken well over 100 years. One performance of "We Are the World" at Live Aid, on the other hand, reached 1.5 billion people in a single instant of historical time. Some will shudder at the very thought of comparing the two songs. "We Shall Overcome," after all, is a time-honored anthem of liberation, which has spread through grass roots political struggle. It evokes images of courage, righteousness, and ultimate victory. "We Are the World," according to many, is a self-serving pop ditty that sounds more like a Pepsi commercial than a political song. Its message is, at best, paternalistic, and it has been accused of trivializing apartheid, one of the most important issues of our time. But beneath a discomfort with such a sacrilegious comparison, do we not also find a reaction of distrust for anything that smacks of mass culture? The purpose of this essay is to challenge that distrust.

The task of building a better world necessarily entails organizing mass movements. This means, by definition, attempting to reach masses of people. In this regard, mass cultural forms and technologies hold out hitherto unimagined possibilities. For better or for worse, we inhabit the society of the spectacle. Mega-events such as Live Aid will continue to happen for a number of reasons. They extend the reach of capital, while cloaking it in philanthropic garb. At the same time, they open up new opportunities for cultural politics. Given this reality, it is important to critically evaluate the potential of these events for social change, rather than to reject such happenings out of hand. In this spirit, I have chosen to analyze two huge rock festivals, one produced on the occasion of Nelson Mandela's seventieth birthday, the other celebrating his release from prison. Neither The Nelson Mandela Seventieth Birthday Tribute nor An International

Tribute for a Free South Africa, as the two events were called, was an unqualified success. Rather, they are selected for analysis precisely because they embody all the contradictions that enable us to see the possibilities and the pitfalls of mass culture.

Mandela: The Birthday

On June 11, 1988, the first Mandela Tribute was staged at Wembley Stadium in London. The 11-hour extravaganza featured a remarkably diverse roster of first-rate talent.[1] It was broadcast whole or in part to an estimated 600 million people in more than 60 countries. Historically, the Mandela Tribute takes its place as one extension of the "charity rock" phenomenon which began in the early eighties with projects like USA for Africa, Band Aid, and Live Aid. But in its very choice of theme, the Mandela Tribute called for the release of the imprisoned leader of a revolutionary organization considered officially illegal by most of the countries that broadcast the concert. With the stage adorned by a 30-foot scrim of Nelson Mandela's image perched tastefully atop the slogans "Isolate apartheid" and "The struggle is my life," and massive speaker columns flanked by exact replicas of the late Keith Haring's "Free South Africa" poster, the Mandela concert threatened to up the political stakes for mega-events. Just as Sun City pushed against the limits of politicized pop, Mandela held out the possibility of transforming charity into change.

The first Mandela concert was originally the brainchild of Jerry Dammers of Special AKA, who wrote "Free Nelson Mandela." Dammers is one of the founders of Artists Against Apartheid in London. He is passionate about his politics, to a fault in the eyes of his critics. A few years before the Mandela Tribute, he had been involved in producing an anti-apartheid concert at Clapham Common which attracted an audience of 200,000 and featured Peter Gabriel, Sting, Sade, Boy George, Gil Scott-Heron, Style Council, and Billy Bragg, among others. "The concert was a strong political event," according to Peter Jenner, Billy Bragg's manager and long-time political activist, "but it lost money."[2]

For the Mandela Tribute, Dammers engaged Tony Hollingsworth, then of Elephant House Productions, a company which handles both television and live events. Understanding that the concert "had to make money," Hollingsworth insisted that Dammers come up with at least "one major act" before proceeding. Dammers convinced Simple Minds to come forward with a conditional offer and then, according to Hollingsworth, absented himself from the process. Hollingsworth ran with the ball alone for the next nine months and is credited as the producer of the live event. In Hollingsworth's vision, the concert "had two points. It had to raise the consciousness of the situation of apartheid in South Africa and the way to do that was to use Nelson Mandela as the symbol of fighting against apartheid....And, furthermore, it had to show the sort of people that were prepared to make that statement were the favored stars of the public."[3] There is no question that the concert benefited from Hollingsworth's organizational abilities. However, particularly in the United States, it came under serious criticism for failing to deliver a forceful political statement.

Perhaps the most incredible thing about the Nelson Mandela Seventieth Birthday Tribute was that it happened at all in a country where the government itself is one of South Africa's staunchest allies. British royalty, who were conspicuously present at the less controversial Live Aid concert in London in 1985, were nowhere to be found at the Mandela Tribute. "We didn't have people dying of starvation," explained Hollingsworth. "We had a ninety year old political problem where there was an enormous amount of entrenched interests."[4] In England, the concert was broadcast live by the BBC, which in and of itself caused no small controversy. Within hours of the announcement of the BBC's decision to carry the show, the Thatcher government was besieged by protests from the South African regime acting through certain industrialists and members of the British Parliament. Their objections, according to Hollingsworth, served as "a wonderful publicity machine" for the event, which served to politicize the issue even more.

In the United States, the negative tendencies of the mass media were more apparent. Here the celebration was carried in its entirety by a number of radio stations in different regions, and televised nationally by Rupert Murdoch's Fox Television Network as "Freedomfest," a five-hour edited broadcast. The telecast was saturated with advertizing, often by firms doing business in South Africa. The political raps that some of the more outspoken artists like Little Steven ("Sun City"), Jackson Browne ("Lives in the Balance"), and Peter Gabriel ("Biko") used to introduce their performances were simply edited out. Most of the African performers were excluded from the broadcast altogether. The Fox broadcast was widely criticized for having depoliticized the event. Little Steven went so far as to write an editorial in the *New York Times* charging that "the show was neutered, the issue downplayed, and the message muzzled....If people didn't know who Mr. Mandela was before tuning in, they weren't any better informed after five hours of programming."[5] Fox's president, Jamie Kellner, offered a feeble response in *Rolling Stone* by saying, "Certainly, musically, you had 'Biko,' you had 'Sun City,' you had 'Mandela Day,' you had all of the important songs, which were the message."[6] Little Steven's sentiments were echoed in most reviews of the U.S. broadcast.

Given the purpose of the concert, one might logically wonder what would possess the promoters to go with a broadcasting company owned by the ultra-conservative Rupert Murdoch. Hollingsworth pointed out that there were relatively few options. "The three main networks, ABC, CBS, and NBC were obviously only prepared to talk to us about a couple of hours of network time...so, the pitch became between the Fox network and MTV," he said. "They were both offering about the same money. We went with Fox because their demographic figures gave a much, much higher viewership."[7] He made some attempt to preserve the politics of the event by having legal language built into the contract which "specified in general terms that they would honor the spirit of the day and reflect that spirit."[8] Accordingly, and in contrast to Little Steven's comments, the Fox broadcast was introduced by actor/director Robert Townsend (*Hollywood Shuffle*) with the words:

> It's more than just a concert. Just as with Live Aid, Amnesty, and some other mega-events, pop and rock stars from all over the world have gathered again to call attention to something they believe in—in this case the Anti-Apartheid Movement and its most visual and spiritual leader, Mr. Nelson Mandela. Imprisoned for over twenty-five years in a South African prison, Mandela and others have come to represent the struggle for freedom and equality in South Africa, an issue of worldwide attention. Welcome to Freedomfest.[9]

Although what followed clearly emphasized the entertainment function of the concert to the detriment of its consciousness raising function, a few memorable passages managed to slip through. Jim Kerr of Simple Minds introduced "Mandela Day," a song he had written especially for the event, by calling for "an end to the murder and the torture and the terror that's going on in South Africa."[10] Stevie Wonder told a non-attendant Nelson Mandela, "We're here celebrating your birthday, but I and we are all very conscious of the fact that this day you are not free. We are all very conscious of the fact that until you are free, no man, woman, or child, whatever color or culture they may come from, are really free...oppression of anyone is oppression of everyone."[11] As to the rest of the U.S. broadcast, however, even Hollingsworth admitted that he was "very disappointed. But, you can't cut out a picture," he added optimistically. "You can't cut out the backdrop of Nelson Mandela."[12] Still, there was some sentiment among activists in the music industry that Hollingsworth could have negotiated a stronger wording in the Fox contract and that by failing to do so, the politics of the concert may have been needlessly compromised.

The second goal articulated by Hollingsworth, that of linking the issues with "the favored stars of the public," was evident even in the U.S. telecast. Aside from the impressive line-up itself, the stars allowed themselves to be queried as to their feelings about the event. While their statements often added up to little more than what Little Steven referred to as "inane chatter" and "celebrity gossip," they were clearly supportive of the event in general and Mandela in particular. "I think that apartheid is a moral issue," said Annie Lennox of the Eurythmics in her off-stage Fox interview. "I'm obviously very much against it."[13] Even the reportedly non-political Whitney Houston managed to tell her Fox viewers, "I think it's important that they know that we are aware and that we do care."[14] But, while this goal was realized, it is important to recognize that in this instance, the goal itself was controversial. The question naturally arises: Are big stars appropriate spokespeople for a movement that they are not a part of?

It was Whitney Houston who most often served as the lightning rod for criticism along these lines. "The real mistake was Whitney Houston," said Peter Jenner. "The story around was that she would not do the show unless it was nonpolitical. The moment they agreed to those terms, they lost the battle."[15] Jenner argued further that the move offended lesser-known artists with a track record of anti-apartheid performances, like Bragg, who were passed over for bigger stars. "They're now reluctant to do any anti-apartheid events," he added.[16] Such a criticism must be considered in terms of the degree to which the concert was already politicized simply by its choice of theme. "What we were doing in this event was very different from the Live Aid situation," argued Hollingsworth. "We had a political issue. We were saying [to the artists],…'Don't come on board if you think that it is not politics.'"[17] At the same time, he acknowledged that the Houston camp made a "sharp division" between "what is humanitarian grounds and what is politics." While Jenner's criticism may be a bit overstated, it is true that such distinctions often obscure the reality that issues such as apartheid are fundamentally political. For Hollingsworth, however, the bottom line was that "Whitney agreed to pay tribute to Nelson Mandela as a symbol of fighting against apartheid."[18]

Houston, for her part, delivered easily the most animated performance of the day. She appeared in front of a backdrop containing the slogans "Isolate apartheid" and "The struggle is my life," which could be seen, albeit with some difficulty, even in the Fox telecast. While she is vulnerable to the charge of playing it safe (both musically and politically), it is also the case that she was one of the first artists to commit to the festival. Her overwhelming popularity contributed significantly to making a controversial event that much more attractive to broadcasters all over the world. And, interestingly, she was the "favored star" of imprisoned ANC leaders in South Africa. Ahmed Kathrada, one of the ANC rebels who received a life sentence along with Mandela, sent a message which was distributed by the local Anti-Apartheid Movement and quoted in *Rolling Stone*. "You lucky guys," wrote Kathrada from his cell. "What I wouldn't give just to listen to Whitney Houston! I must have told you that she has long been mine and Walter's [Sisulu] top favorite…In our love and admiration for Whitney we are prepared to be second to none!"[19]

As with most large events, trade-offs were evident in the Mandela Tribute. While the concert sacrificed depth of analysis for breadth of viewership, some 600 million people around the world ended up with a greater awareness of the importance of Nelson Mandela and the issue of apartheid than they had had previously. In the final analysis, a critical evaluation of the impact of an event like the Mandela concert cannot be limited to the merits and shortcomings of the production itself. Because the worldwide simultaneity of the festival created a shared experience of such staggering proportions, this is usually the focus for analysis. But it must also be noted that the Mandela concert was a very different event depending on where you saw it. Its impact was determined in large part by how it got used. In areas where local political movements were able to use the Mandela Tribute to advantage, it served as an important buttress to local organizing and education.

At Wembley Stadium in England, the site of the live event, a capacity crowd of 72,000 fans thrilled to half-a-day's worth of live performances complete with political commentary on the part of some of their favorite artists. There the concert dovetailed nicely with the needs of the local Anti-Apartheid Movement, which used the interest it generated to mobilize the troops for their "Nelson Mandela: Freedom at Seventy" campaign. Commenting on the level of politicization of the concert, Chitra Karve, a spokeswoman for the Anti-Apartheid Movement, told *Rolling Stone,* that in the context of the AAM campaign, "Every second of it was political."[20] According to Hollingsworth, the momentum produced by the concert even forced a change in the nature of media coverage of Mandela and the ANC. "When we first started this, Nelson Mandela was referred to by the BBC News Service as the leader of a terrorist organization, the ANC," he said. "What this event did was both to mobilize the existing support and create a much greater bedrock of sympathy within the general public, so it can no longer be reported in such stark terms."[21]

Rome, Italy, offers another such example. There the festival was sponsored by *Il Manifesto,* an independent left wing newspaper, and it was broadcast on public television channel 3, the communist channel. In the Piazza Farnese, a historic outdoor plaza, the concert was projected on a ten-by-fifteen-foot television screen to an audience of thousands for free. A small stage served as a platform for anti-apartheid speeches by Italian and African political leaders. Here the mega-festival was consciously used to create a local political event. The character of this outdoor gathering was described by Italian journalist Paolo Prato as "somewhere between Woodstock and a political rally," complete with "people on the ground smoking dope."[22] Again, the entertainment function of the event was consciously used in the service of political education at the local level.

The Anti-Apartheid Movement in the United States did not make direct use of the Mandela Tribute. Nonetheless, a progressive side effect of mega-events like Live Aid and the Mandela Tribute, along with the all-star performances of "We Are the World" and *Sun City,* has been the breaking down of the apartheid of our own music industry. In the United States audiences and radio formats are quite fragmented, ostensibly along lines of music taste but, conveniently, these tastes correlate highly with divisions of class, age, race, and ethnicity. The artists who appeared on "We Are the World" and to an even greater extent on "Sun City" encompassed a broad range of audience demographics and radio formats. "Whoever buys [the *Sun City* LP]," remarked co-producer Arthur Baker, "is going to be turned onto a new form of music, just as whoever sees the video is going to be turned onto an artist they've never seen before."[23] Similarly, any radio station which carried the Mandela Tribute in its entirety played artists who had never appeared on that station before. In Boston, for example, progressive rocker WBCN broadcast artists such as Salt 'n Peppa, The Fat Boys, and Freddy Jackson, not to mention Youssou N'Dour, probably for the first time.

Mandela II: The Release

It is not entirely clear whether the Anti-Apartheid Movement in the United States simply wasn't sufficiently organized to make better use of the first Mandela concert or whether Fox's involvement made the prospect politically unappealing. A third factor which is clear is that British organizers could have done better outreach in the United States. "The anti-apartheid movement in the United States was excluded until the last minute," says Danny Schechter, one of the organizers for the Sun City project and the producer of the video news magazine *South Africa Now*.[24] Adds Themba Vilakasi, the New England representative for the ANC and the executive director of the Boston-based Fund for a Free South Africa: "None of the [local] anti-apartheid groups initiated talks as to how it could be used to advantage."[25]

In any case, the United States as it turned out, also proved to be the Achille's heel of the second Mandela festival, staged once again at Wembley Stadium on April 16, 1990. Following the degree of criticism and analysis which accompanied the 1988 Mandela concert, those involved in the production of An International Tribute for a Free South Africa were in a particularly good position to learn from the first concert's shortcomings.[26] And, learn they did—or so it appeared initially. Tony Hollingsworth was again retained to oversee production; his contacts and production experience from the first concert were, no doubt, considered indispensable to the second effort. But this time, help in determining the political character of the event was supplied by Mike Terry of Britain's Anti-Apartheid Movement and the International Reception Committee established by the ANC to maximize the political value of Mandela's release. Convened by exiled South African anti-apartheid activist Bishop Trevor Huddleston in Britain, the committee was enthusiastic at the prospect of another rock show honoring Mandela. Given the worldwide coverage of the 1988 event, the committee reasoned, quite correctly, that a second extravaganza would be the perfect platform for Mandela to address an international audience directly for the first time outside South Africa.

With only 54 days to produce the concert, there were, of course, problems in booking artists. In addition to scheduling conflicts, there were also political issues to be considered. The production team was clear that the bill should be multiracial, but the tension between "name" artists and those with a demonstrated commitment to the cause had to be weighed, as always. The ANC apparently determined that all of the South African artists should perform together in two 25 minute segments, a decision which was itself controversial. "All these artists came out of the woodwork," says Schechter. "Jazz artists. Artists whose main qualification was that they were South African."[27] In the collaborative concert segments that resulted, there was also some tension as to whether better-known artists like Hugh Masekela and Miriam Makeba would receive star billing. It was resolved in the noticeable absence of Masekela and Makeba from the event. Still, with stars like Peter Gabriel, Tracy Chapman, Bonnie Raitt, Anita Baker, Neil Young, Natalie Cole, and Lou Reed, among many others on board, Hollingsworth had clearly assembled an impressive line-up of artists on relatively short notice. The fans responded favorably. The 72,000 tickets for the live event sold out faster than for any other event in the history of Wembley Stadium.

Whatever the problems with booking talent, it was widely assumed that the real headliner of the event, Nelson Mandela, appearing live at Wembley, would make the concert irresistible to broadcasters the world over. Embodied in the recently released ANC leader, after all, was the ultimate solution to the shortcomings of the first concert: star quality, political credibility, first-hand testimony, and in-depth analysis, all person-ified in a single individual—at that moment, perhaps the most important individual in the world. That assessment turned out to be largely accurate; broadcasters in some 63 countries signed on to broadcast the four-hour concert. (Even South Africa proposed to carry the show, a decision which was eventually nixed by the ANC out of support for the cultural boycott.) It is therefore all the more cruel an irony—as well as an affront to human decency—that not a single U.S. broadcaster could be persuaded to air the event. The only North American broadcast of the show was carried by

MuchMusic, Canada's rough equivalent to MTV, which broadcast the concert in its entirety.

Radiovision International, a Los Angeles-based firm with experience in selling the worldwide rights to rock concerts, was retained to find television buyers for the International Tribute. There is some evidence which suggests that Radiovision didn't do its job very well in the United States. Some of the U.S. outlets that were approached complained that the event was overpriced. Also, in leaving the U.S. contract for last, Radiovision may have offered potential buyers too little time to promote the event correctly. According to *Cablevision,* a leading cable trade magazine, "A Black Entertainment Television spokesperson says that BET might have cleared time, but it was never approached."[28]

Radiovision's imperfections notwithstanding, it also appears that U.S. television was being politically cautious, as well. After the networks passed on the show, *Cablevision* chided the cable industry for failing "to go where broadcast won't." PBS claimed that its programming guidelines prevented them from carrying benefits. Schechter, who tried to help Radiovision sell the show, argued that a cultural bias against rock shows was probably closer to the mark. MTV declined because they had already committed to airing a Muscular Dystrophy benefit shortly after the Mandela date. "In their minds, the Muscular Dystrophy benefit was the equivalent of the Mandela concert," complained Schechter.[29] In the face of such seemingly systematic rejections, Hollingsworth and Radiovision charged that the second Mandela Tribute was being suppressed. The entertainment newsweekly *Variety* agreed. According to Schechter, who also covered the concert for South Africa Now, "*Variety*…pinpointed political factors as central in the decision by broadcasters not to carry the event. *Variety* blamed their skittishness and a lack of consciousness as well."[30]

The inability to secure a U.S. buyer was devastating for this event. Politically, the United States is, of course, one of the most important countries for Nelson Mandela's non-racialist, anti-apartheid message to be heard. In addition, the United States also happens to be the single largest music market in the world. For an event like this, it is the U.S. market which most often determines the size of the profit margin. In this case, it *was* the profit margin. Whereas the 1988 Mandela concert eventually distributed over $1 million to six charitable organizations chosen by Bishop Huddleston, it is likely that there will be no surplus from the 1990 event.

Despite the U.S. blackout, An International Tribute for a Free South Africa did succeed in beaming Nelson Mandela and the concert's anti-apartheid message to more than 60 countries throughout the world. In the words of Danny Schechter,

> Nelson Mandela was received as a conquering hero, and spoke only after a seven-minute screaming ovation. His remarks projected

great dignity and presence, calling for continued pressure on the deKlerk government. 'Reject any suggestion that the campaign to isolate the apartheid system should be wound down,' he urged. His speech was page-one news in every newspaper in Europe. In the United States, only *USA Today* gave it that visibility, perhaps because it caters more to mass interests than elite concerns.[31]

Contested Terrain

As awesome and inspiring as mega-events may be, they are also tough acts to follow. It is possible for them to have a negative impact on other efforts. The first Mandela concert was "so big," complained Peter Jenner, "that no one wanted to do any other benefits at that time. It was a catastrophe for other events."[32] Jenner claimed that an AIDS benefit which featured George Michael the previous year had had to be canceled, and that an Amnesty International concert at Milton-Keynes at around the same time lost about $200,000 because it was so overshadowed. To the extent that mega-events are designed as fundraisers—as was clearly the case with Live Aid and Farm Aid—they pose the further problem of suggesting that simply raising money can solve political problems.

The Mandela concerts were supposed to be different. "This is a political concert," Jim Kerr insisted to *Rolling Stone* in 1988. "It's not a little namby-pamby money raiser."[33] The fact remains, however, that the concert could have been more politically oriented in its conception. At 1988's Nelson Mandela Seventieth Birthday Tribute there was no first-hand testimony and no in-depth analysis to drive the message home. The politics of the concert itself are evident in a home video since released by Elephant House Productions, Hollingsworth's original company. The video restores some significant moments that were edited out of the Fox broadcast such as the speeches by Harry Belafonte and Whoopi Goldberg and the performances of "Set Them Free" by Aswad and Sly and Robbie, "Soweto Blues" by Miriam Makeba and Hugh Masekela, "Talkin' 'Bout a Revolution" by Tracy Chapman, and "Free Nelson Mandela" by Jerry Dammers and friends. As a concert video, it is a fine piece of work. Still, one wonders whether a video of a concert for someone like Nelson Mandela doesn't demand more of a documentary treatment. In an edited video, for example, field interviews, narration, and documentary footage can be spliced in to produce a package that is both entertaining and educational. As controversial as Paul Simon's *Graceland* LP was, the video of the concert in Zimbabwe—with appearances by Miriam Makeba and Hugh Masekela and documentary footage of black Africans portrayed as normal human beings—succeeded admirably in putting a human face on black South Africa.

The presence of Nelson Mandela himself at the 1990 concert, of course, solved most of these problems. With his dignified but forceful demeanor and steadfast refusal to compromise his principles, Mandela capitalized on the platform provided by the International Tribute to drive home the anti-apartheid message literally to hundreds of millions of people all over the world. Mandela clearly understood the power of what he was dealing with. Backstage, he visited the artists to express his appreciation for their efforts. Said Mandela:

> Over the years in prison I have tried to follow the developments in progressive music...Your contribution has given us tremendous inspiration...Your message can reach quarters not necessarily interested in politics, so that the message can go further than we politicians can push it...We admire you. We respect you, and above all, we love you.[34]

With those words, no less a person than Nelson Mandela anointed the marriage of mass music and mass movements.

Mass culture is not without its contradictions. But it must be recognized that mass culture is also a site of contested terrain. Turning our political backs on this fertile arena will simply render us anachronistic in a world of high technology. Like rock 'n' roll, mega-events are here to stay. We must determine how their production can be influenced in progressive ways and how the current state of the art can be used to advance the struggle.

The Clash plays at the Anti-Nazi League Carnival organized by Rock Against Racism.

Rock Against Racism and Red Wedge

From Music to Politics, from Politics to Music

Simon Frith and John Street

The two most systematic attempts in Britain to use "mass music" to inspire a "mass movement" were Rock Against Racism (founded in 1976) and Red Wedge (founded in 1986).[1] These movements had much in common (not least, some of the musicians most actively involved). They were both explicitly socialist organizations focused on mobilizing youth; they both made populist assumptions about the equation of class experience and cultural expression; and they both sought to make pleasure educational and education pleasurable. Music was taken as the means to all these ends. But Red Wedge and Rock Against Racism (RAR) differed sharply too: Red Wedge was formed by and for a political party, Labor, with electoral aims; RAR was, ideologically at any rate, a spontaneous movement of musicians and fans, concerned with the politics of the everyday. And perhaps even more importantly, the decade between the two groups' origins, 1976-1986, marked a decisive shift in people's understanding of the possibilities of music and movements: RAR was a product of punk, Red Wedge of Live Aid. These differences of origin are now held by cultural commentators to explain the success of RAR (the marginalization of racist politics), and the failure of Red Wedge (the Labor Party's dismal electoral performance in 1987). Neither portrait is wholly accurate. There is no simple distinction to be drawn between the sources of the two movements. Nor are there any simple conclusions to be drawn about each's intention or their effectiveness. Together, however, their stories tell us much about how causes and chords become entwined, and about what happens to the politics and the music in the process.

Rock Against Racism

RAR was provoked into life by Eric Clapton's infamous remarks at the Birmingham Odeon in August 1976. From the stage, Clapton said he wanted to "Keep Britain White"; he also expressed support for the British politician Enoch Powell, who had made political capital since the 1960s from playing on the "dangers" of immigration.[2] One consequence of Clapton's outburst was a letter to *Melody Maker, NME,* and *Sounds,* written by Red Saunders, Syd Shelton, David Widgery, and others. They wrote:

> We want to organize a rank and file movement against the racist poison in music. We urge support for Rock Against Racism. P.S. Who shot the Sheriff, Eric? It sure as hell wasn't you![3]

This letter prompted 140 replies in the first week.

RAR's relatively modest origins were in stark contrast to its founders' ambitions. They were all veterans of 1960s libertarian politics and agit-prop work (now ensconced in the Socialist Workers Party [SWP]) and they still wanted to harness the political power of the imagination. David Widgery, by profession an East End physician, by inclination the SWP's most combative and entertaining cultural theorist, wrote of his plans for the movement:

> We aimed to rescue the energy of Russian revolutionary art, surrealism and rock and roll from the galleries, the advertising agencies and the record companies and use them again to change reality, as always had been intended. And have a party in the process.[4]

In this respect, RAR was partly defining itself against Music for Socialism (MFS), a group of progressive rock musicians and writers who had come together the previous year in a kind of last throw of 1960s idealism.[5] MFS (which was particularly influenced by Italian examples) was more interested in the politics of music-making and the music industry than in youth as such, and its initial response to punk (as voiced by the Maoist composer, Cornelius Cardew, for example) was overtly hostile: punk was denounced as "fascist." From the RAR perspective this reflected MFS's elitism. RAR's political activism was to be provided by "cultural autodidacts," people for whom Tamla/Motown was as important as Bertolt Brecht, and punks' shock value use of the swastika (key evidence for the Cardew line) would be challenged directly, on the streets.[6] In short, if Eric Clapton's mean sentiments provided the grounds for Rock Against Racism, its real political and cultural ambition was to seize the opportunity of punk and articulate a new form of proletarian cultural rebellion.

RAR was, then, the child of punk. It drew on punk's style, its rhetoric, and its music. Most of the musicians who played RAR gigs had come to prominence with the emergence of punk. Punk had re-established pop (as opposed to progressive rock) as the medium for political statement; it had created a new culture of street protest, through the do-it-yourself magazines, the market stall clothes sellers, the front-room recording studios, the slogans, and the politics of gestures generally. Punk allowed cultural auto-didacts to live out their theories.

But whatever the range of theoretical references behind RAR (and its street spontaneity depended as heavily on art school situationism as on Trotskyist agit-prop), it remained, in concert practice, confined to a surprisingly narrow musical spectrum. British RAR, unlike its U.S. counterpart, was focused musically on punk and reggae (and, ideally, demonstrated their integration formally—the Clash and the Ruts were the perfect RAR performers). It did not extend into other proletarian forms (heavy metal, for example) nor into other black pop forms such as funk or disco (to which RAR was explicitly opposed). This was not a racist position, as in the United States (though RAR's musical values did have an offputting effect for Asian British youth), but reflected punk contempt for "commercial" pop, for mainstream teenage dance music. RAR thus drew on a particular strand within British punk ideology, on what might be called its folkist wing. Although Johnny Rotten gave a sympathetic interview to the *RAR* magazine, *Temporary Hoarding,* the Sex Pistols were noticeable by their absence from RAR platforms. Their anarchist, disruptive aesthetic found little common ground with the worthier craft musicians: Joe Strummer, Elvis Costello, Tom Robinson.

As punk extended RAR's artistic context beyond the drunken mumblings of an Eric Clapton, so an upsurge in overt racism created a wider political context for anti-racist activity. It went beyond the music business or even youth culture. The National Front (NF), then the leading racist party, was collecting significant support in local government elections. It was also acquiring a considerable public presence through street demonstrations, often staged in areas which contained substantial black and Asian populations. RAR was intended, therefore, as a way of challenging all public displays of racism directly, whether contained within the music industry or within the wider political sphere. The cries and slogans captured its spirit: "Black and White / Unite we fight! NF = No Fun!"

The first RAR event was staged at a London pub in November 1976. The following month the venue was the Royal College of Art. According to Widgery, the audience was a mixture of 15-year-old girls, art students, and sixties freaks. Political leaflets and bookstalls occupied the side walls. "Something was in the air, not just dope, but a serious music-politics-black-white mix-up."[7] The founding conference was held in January 1977.

RAR's most memorable events were the big London marches and concerts organized in London in 1977 and 1978 with the Anti-Nazi League. These were outdoor events with all-star punk/reggae line-ups (Aswad, the Clash, Elvis Costello and the Attractions, X-Ray Spex, Stiff Little Fingers, Tom Robinson, Steel Pulse, and others) and short sets—the number of groups declaring for anti-racism mattered more than the quality of the music (this was the model of the Big Event later to be used by Live Aid). Their most striking feature was the make-up of the audience, as the 1960s generation of political activists sat on their blankets with their children and their leaflets gawking at the decidedly menacing display of punk and Rastafarian fashion (to the untrained eye there was little semiotic difference between the racist and the anti-racist punk, especially given the familiar sight of youths with an RAR button on one lapel, an NF button on the other).

Although much energy went into organizing an RAR tour in the summer of 1978 (a changing line-up of two or three acts from the central roster playing concerts around the country), RAR's most important achievement was to provide a model (and a name) for local activities that were put on without any reference to the central organization at all. 1978-79 saw not only a plethora of small town RAR gigs as local political groups of various sorts used concerts (religiously following the black/white line-up) to reach youth and to publicize particular local struggles, but also, more importantly, a series of instant public responses to local racial incidents. In Coventry, for example, local musicians (led by the Specials) were able to mount an immediate, powerful, and effective outdoor concert response to a spate of "Paki-bashing" incidents (street attacks on Asian British by skinhead gangs) which had resulted in a fatal stabbing.

RAR was not just a touring rock show, then, nor just an oppositional spectacle; it also set an ideological and organizational example. Its magazine, *Temporary Hoarding,* was thus a crucial forum for articulating the movement's message and its strategy. It mixed punk cut-up style with "our dubbed version of Marxism" and was a constant source of names, contacts, and addresses.[8]

A key ingredient in this was the Socialist Workers Party. The SWP was (and is) a Trotskyist organization with a keen eye for current trends and fashions. Its tactics are to focus on emergent struggles and movements, and to use these to build support for the SWP itself. It does not aim to take over these struggles but to educate and direct those involved, to provide a theory and a practice. With RAR, the SWP played an important supporting role, loaning it premises, providing a page for support and publicity in *Socialist Worker;* or, at least, that is how the party would describe its contribution. David Widgery explained the relationship like this:

> The music came first and was more exciting. It provided the creative energy and the focus in what became a battle for the soul of young working-class England. But the direct confrontations and the hard-headed political organization which underpinned them were decisive.[9]

This is undoubtedly true, if one adds the perhaps paradoxical rider that in some cities and circumstances the "hard-headed political organization" wasn't the SWP itself, but either another Trotskyist group like

IMG (International Marxist Group) or, more commonly, an ad hoc committee of local activists.

As cultural politics, RAR was a considerable success. Its outdoor concerts were immensely popular and hugely publicized (particularly in the music press) and are still recalled affectionately by those who gathered in North and South London in the summers of 1977 and 1978. By 1979, *Temporary Hoarding* was selling 12,000 copies and RAR's educational effects were plain. Brinsley Forde of Aswad explained what he saw as the intention and achievement of RAR:

> Racism is caused by people not being educated, being ignorant of different cultures. Before RAR, a lot of white people would be terrified to go to a reggae show. And it was a platform for saying things that wouldn't have been said. It was the start of more bands being politically aware.[10]

RAR could be seen, then, as an important inspiration for the anti-racist message of Coventry's 2-Tone label—inspiring not so much the content of the message as its form—and for the punk-ska bands like the Specials and the Beat, who became immensely popular with white working-class youth in 1979-1981. Indeed, these musicians could be said to have brought the RAR message into mainstream pop—the Specials' "Ghost Town" topped the charts in the weeks in which British cities exploded in black youth anger in 1981. Groups like Madness and UB40, with major pop followings throughout the 1980s, ensured that a particular kind of "realistic," working-class, political pop survived the collapse of punk and the rise of the New Romantics.

RAR, however, had more than cultural ambitions; it saw itself as having a direct political effect, and here one's judgement of its achievements must be more mixed. If RAR's intention was to rid Britain of the National Front, it could claim some success in doing this. By 1979, the NF was a spent electoral force (although it was to rise in different incarnations in the 1980s), and the SWP strategy of street confrontation undoubtedly helped both to deglamorize the NF's appeal to bored white youth and to mobilize black and Asian youth (it was striking that in the various city "riots" of 1981, black and white youth usually fought together against the police rather than—as in 1958—among themselves).

If, on the other hand, RAR's intention was to rid Britain, British youth, or the British music business of racism, then, not surprisingly, it failed. Racism found a new political home in the Conservative Party of Margaret Thatcher (who, in the run-up to the 1979 General Election, let it be known that she understood those people who felt they were being "swamped" by immigrants); the music industry continues to discriminate against black entrepreneurs (if not black musicians); and the pop/rock audience continues to be divided along racial lines even in the era of club music and acid house.

But this is to judge RAR by its most utopian rhetoric—demand the impossible!—and therefore to devalue its two most important achievements: first, to ensure, in the fraught political times of the late 1970s, when recession brought about both mass youth unemployment and a sharp political swing to the right, that racism did not become white youths' "common sense"; second, to sustain, through a period of disillusion with rock ideology, the 1960s belief that socialists can use mass culture to their own ends. Both achievements were necessary for the thinking behind Red Wedge.

Red Wedge

Like RAR, Red Wedge was to be a party with a purpose. Jerry Dammers (leader of the Specials, founder of the 2-Tone label, and tireless activist for Artists Against Apartheid) announced at the organization's launch: "We hope Red Wedge is like a party atmosphere, we just want to be part of the massive anti-Thatcher popular movement."

But even in the optimism of its initiation, Red Wedge was a much more cautious enterprise than RAR—it was only to be "like" a "party atmosphere." There was none of RAR's flamboyant rhetoric, no tributes to the power of the imagination. The contrast between Red Wedge and RAR is illustrated most graphically by each organization's journal. Where *Temporary Hoarding* was a chaotic collage of images and words, recalling the design styles of both *Oz* and *Sniffing Glue,* Red Wedge's *Well Red* was a neat, formal glossy, a lively *Marxism Today.*

The formation of Red Wedge was announced in November 1986. Significantly, the launch party was held at the House of Commons. It brought together trade unionists, Labor politicians, comedians, and rock musicians. There was no doubting, therefore, the political interests behind its creation. At the same time, the performers included both those associated with political causes (by now, the miners' strike rather than Rock Against Racism—Tom Robinson, Billy Bragg, Paul Weller) and those with no such association (Sade, Johnny Marr, Ray Davies, Dave Stewart). In a sense, the two performer strands represented two attitudes toward Red Wedge—for the first type of performer, it was an activist organization devoted, in this instance, to supporting the Labor Party; for the latter musicians it was simply a way of indicating an electoral position (like signing a party political advert). Musicians' involvement in Red Wedge activities varied accordingly.

A concert tour formed the backbone of the Red Wedge campaign. The musicians organized a traveling roadshow, just like the Tamla shows of the 1960s. Each performer would play a short set, and then everyone would get together at the end to sing Curtis Mayfield's "Move On Up." The emphasis was on musical entertainment (even if, for a performer like Billy Bragg, the songs were explicitly political), but just outside the concert hall, meanwhile, there would be a select group of Labor representatives (including Members of Parliament), who would chat to the audience and distribute party literature. On the day before the evening performance, these politicians and musicians would visit the local town, seeking out youth training schemes and photo opportunities; local groups would play a local Red Wedge concert.

Red Wedge was not confined to these events and visits. In the run up to the 1987 election, it also organized tours of women performers and of comedians. Coordination of these was the responsibility of a small London-based organization, which also published *Well Red* and produced the usual paraphernalia of pop: T-Shirts, stickers, buttons, posters.

Red Wedge was built upon a partnership between the Labor Party and the musicians. The party wanted Red Wedge to act as a means of reaching a youth audience. The musicians wanted Red Wedge to put pressure on the party to recognize the political interests of the young, and to adopt an effective cultural policy. Together, they wanted, at the very least, to bring youth to politics; it was a British equivalent of the U.S. voter registration campaigns. As one leaflet put it: "Red Wedge aims to create, through the world of the arts, a fresh and direct approach to politics, which ultimately will affect and involve *you*."[11]

As the Labor Party reflected upon its electoral defeats in 1979 and 1983, it was acutely aware of the desertion of first-time voters. The Party was convinced, too, that its victories in the 1960s had been achieved through support from the young. Then, Labor had been able to present itself as a youthful, modern party—an impression made all the easier by the elderly, aristocratic leadership of the Conservative Party. In the mid-1980s, however, Labor could no longer pretend to such an image. From 1979 to 1983 it had been led by the aged Michael Foot. And young voters' memory of Labor in power was of a party that presided over decline and industrial disruption.

Red Wedge, then, was part of an attempt to improve Labor's image among the young: simply, to make it fashionable. For the party officials who were engaged in negotiating with the musicians and were responsible for the modest funding that the party provided, Red Wedge was seen not as part of the policy-making process, but of the image-making process.

The musicians had different ideas. They saw Red Wedge as an opportunity to educate the party in youth politics, to force changes in policies of relevance to the young. The agenda was not confined just to those areas of direct interest to musicians: cultural policy, the music industry, copyright, etc. The musicians were concerned about youth training and youth unemployment. At the same time, the musicians were keen to maintain their distance from the Labor Party; they did not want to be the poodles of the politicians. Red Wedge was, therefore, run independently of the party.

What did Red Wedge achieve? As with RAR, the answer depends on what purpose we attribute to it. If it was intended to win Labor the 1987 election, it clearly failed. If it was intended to win the youth vote for Labor, then the results were more ambiguous. Labor made some small gains from the Tories among first-time voters, but this was against the background of a particularly bad 1983 performance. Intriguingly, Labor made most progress among young women. Young men remained obstinately resistant to Labor's message.[12]

The measure of Red Wedge does not, however, lie just with its ability to serve Labor's electoral interests. The musicians anticipated something from the relationship. They wanted more on youth and youth issues in the manifesto. They could point to some small steps here (around the commitment of resources for youth training, for example), but these steps were marginal and incremental, buried in the small print of the party's program. And certainly in terms of a policy on music—whether through using a tax on blank tapes to help support the independent sector of the record industry, or through expanding the remit of arts subsidy policy to cover rock and pop—Red Wedge suggestions seemed to fall on deaf ears. (Although, at a local level, Labor councils in such cities as Sheffield and Norwich were adopting "rock" policies, investing in a municipal recording studio in Sheffield's case, and investing in a live venue in Norwich's case.)

And what of the audiences, what did they get out of Red Wedge? They got a good-natured night out for a bargain price. The events were convivial affairs. There was little air of tension or adventure. Everyone knew they were gathered to support a good cause, so there was a general reluctance to complain about indifferent performances. Red Wedge offered a platform for polemic, but as Stuart Cosgrove once observed, "It is not political music that matters but using music politically."[13] Red Wedge failed to do the latter.

Role Models

Between the heyday of RAR and that of Red Wedge much changed in the world of musical politics. The most obvious expressions of the changes were, first, the willingness of musicians to become directly involved in established political organizations; and, second, the willingness of politicians to associate themselves with musicians. With RAR, the relationship had been tentative. The political organization was more organic, less overtly bureaucratic; it was more of a musical creation. The same was not true of Red Wedge.

The change owes much to Live Aid. It was this event that demonstrated the political power of popular music; it was this that gave musicians
a new role, that of statesman or woman. In his appeal to our "humanity,"
Bob Geldof moralized a mass music, a music which could no longer pretend
to be countercultural or subversive, but which was still able to articulate a
sense of concern and to raise vast amounts of money. He recognized the
huge, transnational appeal of Western pop stars, and he used the mass
communication technologies and industries which market Phil Collins,
Queen, and others. What Live Aid made explicit was that pop musicians
were able to represent a popular conscience, however sentimentalized;
indeed, it made them *responsible* for speaking up, for bearing witness to
causes and concerns.

The most obvious effect of this was to redefine the political impact of
rock as its power of publicity. It is easy to be cynical about this—if
musicians' willingness to support causes became conditional on the presence of the television cameras, then their own PR needs became difficult
to disentangle from those of the oppressed, starving, or homeless; both Live
Aid and the Mandela concerts effectively revived old rock careers and
launched new stars (Tracy Chapman, for instance). But the opportunism of
the performers (or, rather, of their managers and record companies) is not
really the issue. The fact was that it was the TV cameras that gave the
performers their political power in the first place, and what changed,
therefore, was the coding of rock *sincerity.* Tom Robinson's "true" devotion
to the RAR cause had been measured by his willingness to *muck in:*

> Tom took the RAR star everywhere, on tour and on TV, helped with
> our office, fitted RAR into tour schedules and loaned us money.[14]

Now political commitment meant making the most of one's three minutes
in the spotlight. What happened behind the scenes was irrelevant.

The Changing Politics of "Youth"

Part of the shifting character of political pop was an effect of the
change in its audience, or, rather, in the way in which that audience was
perceived. The cause lay as much with new marketing strategies as with
altered sociological conditions. In the 1980s, as the actual number of young
people in Britain fell, "youth" became an advertizer's design concept, and
political affiliations were rethought accordingly. Politics was increasingly
conceived as a matter of imagery. When the Labor Party-sponsored magazine, *New Socialist,* revamped itself, it hired the designer of *The Face,* and
its lead article was written by a *Face* "style guru," Robert Elms, who berated
the left for its outmoded fashions and lack of style. The parliamentary wing
of the party, itself under the guidance of an ex-TV producer, was reorgan-

izing its image, making itself media-friendly, giving Kinnock the same sort of advice about voice and clothes and gestures that had already transformed Margaret Thatcher's "look." It was into this packaged world that Red Wedge bought.

RAR, by contrast, was inspired by an idea of youth that had been fashioned by the rhetoricians of punk. For its ideologues, "youth" was a political, rather than a marketing, category; punk was the resulting sound of disaffiliation. The ethos of "do-it-yourself," the aesthetics of the sneer, set punk aside from established political institutions. The only acceptable form of political expression was a mass street movement.

The Aesthetics of Protest

If Red Wedge and RAR were marked by quite different political arguments about how to make protest music, there was, nevertheless, an obvious continuity between the two in terms of political imagery. Red Wedge borrowed its name directly from El Lissitsky's "Beat the Whites with the Red Wedge," while RAR organizer Red Saunders recalled his 1960s cultural education in these terms:

> I was just a working photographer and then the art got to me, typography, Rodchenko's posters, Mayakovsky's poetry. I was educated by the theatre group CAST (the Cartoon Archetype Slogan Theatre), it was the rock on which everything was based—brilliant minds and high energy—who taught me everything I know, about culture, politics, organizing. So that we would be reading Pre-obazhensky this week, right, then we're off to see the Prague Theatre of the Black and then it's *The Crimes of M Lange* at the Kilburn Grange. It trained you for cultural fanaticism. It wasn't just entertainment and you'd go out for a meal afterwards. We'd go back to the flat, eat sardines on toast, get herbed up and analyze it all night.[15]

The aesthetics of protest are not, of course, confined to images and artwork. There are also judgements to be made about the music, for which the Russian Futurists are less helpful, and in the cases of both RAR and Red Wedge it is clear in retrospect that conventional political assumptions determined tastes. For RAR, the value of a musical form lay in the proletarian authority of its performers—soul and R&B expressed the Afro-American working class; reggae expressed the Afro-Caribbean working class; punk the white working class. Music without such roots was worthless. This dogma had some odd consequences—as we have seen, both heavy metal and disco bands were excluded from RAR line-ups, for example, presumably on the grounds that they were a form of false consciousness. From

RAR's perspective the only real problem arose when an authentic band (working-class punk) had "inauthentic" followers (skinheads, racists).

This was the issue addressed when Jimmy Pursey's Sham 69 offered to play for RAR. The organization had to decide whether such a band was appropriate, and the tactic adopted was to schedule Sham 69 only with reggae bands. In the 1978 tour Sham 69 thus shared the bill with Misty in Roots. The audience was riven with tension, but the event passed off without incident, and RAR's decision was vindicated. In 1981, though, RAR confronted the problem in a new form. There was a proposal from some oi bands to play an RAR benefit. Oi was an offshoot of punk, but one which celebrated a peculiarly violent version of male working-class culture, and which had, like Sham 69, attracted a racist following. This time RAR refused them permission, less out of a fear of violence at a gig than from a determination not to give legitimacy to "incorrect" music.

Red Wedge held similar beliefs about the correct relationship of musical style and political principle. Two genres were prominent in Red Wedge shows: folk and '60s/'70s soul. When Gary Kemp from Spandau Ballet performed, he opted for an acoustic guitar. Kemp was establishing a political credibility for himself through his musical choice. His ability to do this depended on his (and, to a lesser extent, the audience's) reading of the meaning of musical forms. Some musics were deemed to constitute a basis for political authenticity and legitimacy, a way of conveying concern.

These aesthetic judgements were essentially exercises in ideology, ways of symbolizing ideas such as "integrity" or "compassion." The interesting question is how these judgements got made and how they were organized by the political and musical activists. At one level, there was simply a question of whom to play to and whom to play for. At another, there was the issue of what the music meant, and how these meanings were conveyed. The first dilemma addresses old arguments about the ability to cause change and the difficulty of preaching to the unconverted. The second dilemma touches on a less politically familiar territory.

David Widgery exemplifies the kind of political thinking that informed the musical choices of RAR. Writing of Carol Grimes, the white soul/R&B singer who performed at the early RAR events, he explained:

> …she was not only a great singer but play[ed] RAR's kind of music.…She loathed racism, lived in Bethnal Green with her son, came from a black music tradition, and, although she was one of the best blues singers in Britain, never got anywhere with the record companies because she refused to be prettied up and sold like a shampoo that could sing.[16]

Elsewhere, he recalls the cultural education that had taught him his aesthetics:

...black music was our catechism....We went for black music because it was so strong rhythmically, there was a passion in it, it was about life and had some point to it.[17]

Hidden in such recollections are a number of assumptions about "authenticity" and how it was captured in the conditions and tones of "black" music. Also in there are notions of integrity, defined by not "selling-out." These judgements of music and its performers have direct equivalents in Widgery's political ideology.

A similar match, but with different politics and different musics, could be read into Red Wedge. The re-discovery of '60s/'70s soul was partly informed by a sense that black music was somehow more authentic, but this time it was not measured by its roughness so much as by its style, its cool. These virtues in the music were paralleled by the political project upon which the Red Wedgers were engaged: to give the Labor Party and politics generally a desirable elegance. (There was, of course, nothing intrinsically socialist about the music, as Levi's use of Marvin Gaye testified.) The point was that certain musicians and writers were able to invest the music with this type of meaning.

The Medium and the Message

One key difference between RAR and Red Wedge was the way message and medium coincided more for RAR than for Red Wedge. RAR's political claims about racial equality could be demonstrated on stage. Red Wedge's concerns could not be symbolized so simply or so sympathetically. Racial harmony is a lot easier to sell than the British Labor Party (though Red Wedge did make sure it had a "balance" of black/white, male/female performers to demonstrate the party's "broad" concerns).

The problem is not just one of image. Differences of subject matter are also significant. Some issues or ideas translate more easily into song. Racial oppression is, of course, an established concern of popular music. Songs about forging alliances with a traditional, political party do not fit so easily in the repertoire of the average rock performer.

It's My Party...

The tension between musical forms and political ideas was replicated at the level of political organization. With RAR, the political organization (whatever the intentions of the SWP) grew from the cultural organization of the movement (and the moment). Red Wedge, by contrast, had to fit itself within—or set itself apart from—the Labor Party. Its politics had, at some level, to relate to the established electoral purposes of the Party. RAR was not so constrained. Its political ambitions were much less clearly defined.

More importantly, RAR could work with issues and ideas which fell outside the formal political agenda.

Even so, RAR remained wedded to a particular political perspective and the institutions associated with it. As Dick Hebdige has argued:

> RAR was widely identified with the Socialist Workers Party, and retained a residual commitment to the old sense of political priorities and tactics (marching, changing minds to change the world, exposing and explaining the historical roots of racism in *Temporary Hoarding*, identifying the enemy, "raising consciousness."[18]

For Dave Laing, RAR remained rooted in a determinist politics:

> ...the RAR's leadership's Marxist politics...led them to the view that an honestly realistic description of the state of things would *necessarily* imply a leftist politics...This position...lacked an awareness of the creative and moulding power of ideology.[19]

Both Red Wedge and RAR were, by this analysis, tied to, or influenced by, their political patrons. And despite the vital attraction provided by the music and musicians, the political interests so affected the music as to reduce both its power and that of the movement which it accompanied. RAR, just as much as Red Wedge, worked to confine its musicians, declaring that *this* is what punk or soul or reggae mean; they can stand for nothing else.

Both Red Wedge and RAR sought to connect the obvious power of music and musicians (to move people, to inspire people, to shape people) with the political power necessary to achieve their own ends (whether that power was mobilized on the streets or in the ballot box). The question is whether the different forms of power involved here are compatible. The histories of RAR and Red Wedge suggest that attempts to use mass musics to forge mass movements will always face two problems.

First, there is the problem of time scale. The power of popular music is by its nature momentary. Shock effects can't be repeated; novelty wears off; the history of rock is a history of jolts and routinization—the declining "buzz" of the big RAR concerts, for example, was apparent event by event; nostalgia is built into the pop experience. At the same time, the taste alliances which propel stars into sudden positions of authority (now David Bowie, now Bob Marley, now the Specials, now Boy George, now Madonna) are inherently unstable. The history of pop is a history of endless audience fragmentation. No political organization, not even one as street-conscious as the SWP, can sustain itself on bursts of power; all political organizations (even the anarchist ones) are part of the routinizing (thus disempowering) process. Reading David Widgery's retrospection on RAR, it becomes clear that for him, as for the other RAR activists, the importance of the movement was as much that, for a moment, it restored fun to politics as that it developed a politics of fun. All we would add is that the "momentary" politics of pop were, in this instance, well adapted to the task at hand—ending the "moment" of the National Front.

Red Wedge, lumbered with a rather more bureaucratic backing group, never suggested that politics was fun (voting was presented as a moral duty), but their shows did make clear the second problem of musical power—the confused nature of its "collectivity." The power of mass music certainly comes from its mobilization of an audience; a series of individual choices (to buy this record, this concert ticket) becomes the means to a shared experience and identity. The question, though, is whether this identity has any political substance. The Labor Party looked to Red Wedge to deliver the youth vote (just as advertisers look to certain sounds or stars to deliver the youth market), but it was never clear that Red Wedge's performers had the necessary authority to do this (to put it simply: Were they popular *enough?*) or that "youth" made sense as a collective category anyway. At one level the Labor Party had an old-fashioned and inappropriate view that Paul Weller, Billy Bragg, and others somehow "represented" young people (and were preferable representatives than the party's Young Socialist branches, long an entry point for Trotskyists). But the real problem for Red Wedge was that it was meant to appeal to everyone (along the lines of Live Aid) by using music, the collective power of which depends on its sense of *exclusion*. When people feel most passionately about music together it is because of its power to mark boundaries (this is obvious in the case of punk and heavy metal, for example); inclusive, "mainstream" music never has such power. RAR, at least, offered an enemy. Red Wedge, for all the targeting of the Tories, called on its audiences to be reasonable. And whatever else mass music may represent, it is not the power of reason.

The Times They Are A-Changin'

Rock Music and Political Change in East Germany[1]

Peter Wicke

Since World War II, nothing has affected the world as deeply as the breakdown of the East-West conflict in Europe resulting from the collapse of the Stalinist system of communism in Eastern Europe. What will come of this change—a more peaceful world or one that is even more unstable—remains to be seen. Certainly, cultural movements will play an important role in this struggle. Rock music played an important role in the dramatic changes which occurred in the former German Democratic Republic, the eastern part of Germany, in 1989—a role which went largely unreported even though the events surrounding these changes were widely publicized in the West. In fact, rock mucisians were instrumental in setting in motion the actual course of events which led to the destruction of the Berlin Wall and the disappearance of the GDR.

Music is a medium which is able to convey meaning and values which—even (or, perhaps, particularly) if hidden within the indecipherable world of sound—can shape patterns of behavior imperceptibly over time until they become the visible background of real political activity. In this way, rock music contributed to the erosion of totalitarian regimes throughout Eastern Europe long before the cracks in the system became apparent and resulted in its unexpected demise. Czechoslovakian President Vaclav Havel, for example, himself an artist, continues to number rock musicians among his closest political consultants. Ironically, in the GDR, it was precisely because the music was initially repressed that it became a medium of resistance which was more or less impossible to control.

Historical Background

The relation between rock music and politics in the GDR had a long and fluctuating history which preceded the events of the autumn of 1989.[2] This history began as early as 1965, on the occasion of the eleventh meeting

81

of the Central Committee of the Communist Party in the GDR. At that meeting, the conclusion was drawn, in an unprecedented and unacceptable attack on the party's own youth organization and media, that rock music was not and could not be in accordance with the goals of a socialist society. The author of this attack, the spokesman for the politburo, in its report to the Central Committee, was none other than Eric Honecker, the member responsible for security matters in the politburo which was still at this time chaired by Walter Ulbricht. It was remarkable enough that a speech about artistic and ideological matters should be delivered by the chief of the security services. It was even more remarkable, however, that rock music, normally not taken seriously in political matters, should be singled out for such a prominent place in this speech, and be subject to such sharp criticisms.

The substance of the criticism was that the party's youth organization and media had hitherto failed to counter in a decisive and systematic enough manner the Western influence communicated by this music. To make such a sharp public reprimand in fact ran counter to all previous customs in these matters. The question has to be asked as to what it was about this music that led it to be accorded the dubious honor of inviting such a vehement reaction on the part of the most powerful institution in the state.

The answer lies in the inalienably democratic character of the grassroots cultural movement of young people, which results from the fact that even with the most primitive means (for example, the use of a domestic radio receiver as a guitar amplifier) it is possible to create "publicity" in such a way that it lies outside the means of control or influence exercised by the state. The creation and organization of publicity was always one of the core issues in the socialist system because one of the most decisive preconditions for democracy is that people can articulate themselves. But the state and party authorities had been totally fixed on a conception of exercising power by a tight control of any kind of information and publicity. This gave all forms of art which could be exercised without the means of complex social organizations, and therefore without the bureaucratic apparatus of the state, an extremely important political status, particularly if they attracted a mass audience, because this meant an almost uncontrollable creation of publicity.

Before the emergence of rock music, the Stalinist system was never confronted with a cultural movement that threatened the state and party monopoly over publicity. The so-called serious arts attracted only a small fraction of the population and were easy to control because they were bound to state institutions like orchestras, concert halls, galleries, or publishers. Popular arts like film, television, or even popular music needed the state mass media. The early rock bands of the sixties needed nothing other than guitars, a drum set, and an amplifier. With only these primitive means and completely without any media support, they attracted masses of young people. In such instances the state's reaction was entirely predictable.

Be that as it may, seven years later, when the all-powerful politburo was chaired by Honecker himself, there occurred a complete reversal in the cultural policy of the party. "Youth dance-music," a euphemism created by the official bureaucracy to hide the true nature of the reversal, became recognized as a legitimate cultural activity of young people. The clear reason behind this change lay in the recognition that local officials were losing the battle against the mushrooming spread of rock groups.

In addition, the alienation of young people in their relationship to the state was becoming increasingly obvious. This alienation was evidenced, by the fact, among other things, that a song movement organized by the FDJ (Freie Deutsche Jugend, the party's youth organization) as a substitute for rock music along the lines of the American folk song movement was reaching only a small segment of young people, predominantly students. As the state body most intimately aware of the failure of its song movement, the FDJ began in 1972 to encourage the growth of an indigenous rock music movement, taking the bands under its political wing, and fighting for institutional spaces within society for these rock bands to practice their music.

However, even this action by the FDJ did not amount to a recognition of the right of young people to cultural self-determination. This lack of recognition was consistent with the history of a previous time when rock music was accorded no recognition at all. The actions of the FDJ have to be understood as an attempt to legitimize this form of music in terms of its political value as an agent of social integration at a time when the state was faced with the prospect of many young people attempting to live their lives outside the state-sanctioned social system.

"Political engagement through music" became the slogan among rock musicians which made the unthinkable thinkable. For the longest time, rock musical activities had been subject to an almost inquisition-like scrutiny. A broken beer glass during or after a performance had been enough to bring the musicians before the courts on charges of inciting hooliganism. It was nonetheless possible for the authorities to live with this slogan because it made possible, if not actually encouraged, the development of a critical potential expressed through the kind of political engagement vital to the future growth of GDR society. This political engagement involved discussions of the kinds of phenomena, such as unnecessary bureaucracy, corruption, and double moral standards, which worked against this future growth. There ensued a new spirit of criticism which gave rise to remarkable levels of creativity among the musicians, as well as to a new sense of identity. Rock music was accepted by large segments of young people in the GDR.

The fact that the state authorities had a rather different concept of society and culture was revealed as early as 1975 in an unmistakable fashion. Before this time, there had been discussions of statements made by rock musicians in their lyrics which were regarded as too critical. Until 1975, these discussions had been held as a public forum on the desirability or lack thereof of issues and topics raised in the lyrics. However, there now started a process of purposefully staged confrontations, a process which reached its culmination in the expulsion of Wolf Biermann, a pivotal figure in the singer-songwriter movement, from the GDR.[3] The authorities began a purge of the cultural landscape according to the philosophy of "whoever is not for us is against us," a purge which resulted in an unprecedented exodus of artists from the GDR.

The first band to suffer performance prohibitions was the Klaus Renft Combo, the most popular band in the GDR at this time. Those who expressed solidarity with this group suffered the same fate. In the years immediately following, almost all of the musicians affected by this kind of suppression, including Renft himself, left the GDR, based on a private application for cancelling their citizenship. It was the first mass exodus of its kind, which resulted in the loss of almost all of the most popular musicians. The state was more than willing to allow these prominent "trouble makers" to leave the country.

After these events the state authorities launched a political and cultural offensive. A large and expensive system was set up to support the activities of the rock groups, and thereby to depoliticize them. The depoliticization was achieved through the blatant creation of a dependency system through which bands were forced to rely on the state for resources and services such as passports, financial aid, apartments, telephones, permits for the printing of promotional materials, cars, permits to import instruments and replacement parts, and record contracts, among other things. The basis of the groups' dependency therefore changed dramatically. Instead of being dependent on an audience for their success, they became dependent on the state for the availability of their most basic needs. This form of dependency constrained bands to be conservative in their political orientation.

These strategies demonstrated the state's high estimation of the political effectiveness of the groups' music, and the potential within this music for subversion. Even single words within lyrics were viewed as being subversive enough to warrant consideration for censorship. To understand the impact of this practice, one has to imagine the political and ideological context in which it took place. In the GDR, for example, it was possible to censor—at least officially—the public mention of the term "assembly line," since assembly lines, while unavoidable, were not in congruence with the socialist goal of humanizing work. A rock song which told a love story could easily create a sensation if it spoke even implicitly of the assembly-line work of one of the lovers. The tighter the social and political controls, the more powerful such subtleties in public discourse could be. Moreover, it was impossible for the state to effectively counter the sensual power of the music or the uninhibited individualism that was celebrated through it.

Over the years, the musicians managed even more successfully to establish a political discourse about society and social realities in the metaphorical lyrics of their songs, such as those about flying, which served as a code to highlight unnatural restrictions against travel. This development is hardly surprising since official political discourse worked in a similar fashion—typical party rhetoric always contained even the most fundamental changes in political strategy "between the lines" of fixed linguistic formulas. Everyone in the society was familiar with the subtleties of discursive negotiation. Both musicians and their audiences realized the power of negotiation and utilized it to the fullest.

At the organizational level, the annual Rock for Peace festivals which began in 1983, were a model of such negotiated settlements. Organized formally by the state and the communist youth organization, and held in the House of Parliament as a symbolic location for state-run rock 'n' roll, the musicians succeeded quickly in taking over the festival operationally. In practice, the logistics of a three-day festival with some 50 bands performing and about 25,000 fans attending were simply not matters for bureaucrats. The musicians and the crowd easily turned the event into "their" festival. The results, of course, were not without contradictions. At first glance, seeing high-ranking state and party officials sitting beside "street punks" in such a formal setting appeared to be more a political manifestation of the party than a rock festival. But once the music started, party slogans evaporated into air as "the politics of rock 'n' roll" transformed the festival. In these ways resistance survived within strategies of political integration, and remained effective.

Within Eastern European communist regimes, radical purposes were often better served through the politics of negotiation. This strategy of survival prepared the ground for the dramatic changes that occurred in the autumn of 1989 by undermining official state ideology. Audiences for popular music placed much more emphasis on perceived elements of resistance in the music than they did on the quality of sound, often to the detriment of the groups themselves. The most successful groups, such as Pankow, City, or Silly, to name just a few, had little alternative but to build on this momentum and force the state authorities, little by little, to yield ground. In the process, the bands realized that their popularity gave them a remarkable political power.

Performance prohibition by the state was no longer possible without losing its face because the popularity of these bands was at least partly a result of the state's own support. The state had invested in rock music and became engaged in it, and it was precisely this action which put the state authorities in a position in which they could be confronted. Pankow challenged the authorities first during a festival in 1987, organized by the party's youth organization, when during a performance, they attacked the hypocrisy of the state's "peace policy"—fighting against the Western arms build-up, while the same time, fighting against internal peace initiatives which tried to put the military policy of the government on the agenda. The event had a signal effect because it demonstrated the helplessness of the state as soon as it was seriously challenged. Although the band was publicly attacked in the party's newspaper, this attack made it even more popular.

The economics of rock in the GDR also put the musicians in a position of considerable independence. The state's chronic shortage of hard currency played an important role in this respect. The most successful bands in the GDR had contracts with record companies located in West Germany. This situation was heavily supported by the authorities because the state badly needed the hard currency (75 percent of all revenue from copyright, mechanicals, and royalties of those deals went to the state). Although these contracts had been tightly controlled by the state, it was impossible to dictate to Western record companies what kind of songs they could publish from East German bands. As soon as the musicians realized their own power, they started to include critical songs in the versions of their albums produced in West Germany. Since these versions always reached the market earlier than the ones produced in East Germany, the authorities were forced to include these songs uncensored. Otherwise they would have demonstrated in public that they censored the bands. To blame the musicians for misusing the West as a critical platform was impossible because the West German companies could have a record released before the state-owned East German labels could even make a production decision. For a number of reasons, visiting reprisals on these bands would have entailed more trouble than it was worth for the state authorities—losing the badly needed hard currency, risking political trouble in a more than difficult situation, or losing the loyalty of a majority of the rock musicians, which could easily lead to a very dangerous confrontation.

Silly's 1987 album, *Batallion d'Amour,* was a milestone in this respect because the band had managed to get an album out completely beyond the approval of the state authorities. While Silly may have been the first, other bands followed in this practice, which meant that the state lost more and more control over rock music. Within the space created by these more popular groups, a younger generation of musicians began to sing lyrics that were aggressively and straightforwardly oppositional. This development was fueled in the late 1980s when the state distanced itself from one of its founding principles—a close relationship with the Soviet Union. As the state openly refused to follow Gorbachev's policies of *glasnost* and *per-*

estroika, the younger generation of musicians refused more and more to act within the framework of negotiation. Opposition was now expressed explicitly in song lyrics such as "I want to get out of here, I want to get out of here, because I don't want to live on the principle of a lie " (Mixed Pickles, "I Want to Get Out," 1989). A range of social issues became the subject of song lyrics—the destruction of the environment, the inhuman architecture of newly constructed East Berlin neighborhoods, the dissolution of meaningful public discourse, etc.

Faced with such open opposition, Honecker personally devised a strategy to split the rock scene into two camps and to foster opposition between them. He attempted this by leaving the younger generation of musicians alone to do as they wished while tightening, by means of the media, the conceptual and political space within which the more popular musicians could operate. They came under a double pressure. Suddenly the state started, despite the chronic lack of hard currency, to flood the country with the music of Western rock stars (Bob Dylan, Joe Cocker, Depeche Mode, Bruce Springsteen, etc.). Without the same kind of professional marketing and media presence their Western competitors enjoyed, the big East German bands found themselves at risk of losing their audience and with it their political power. This meant that they now needed the East German media more urgently than did the Western imports, which forced them into political compromises. Nevertheless, this strategy proved to be Honecker's eventual undoing. Its logic was recognized for what it was by the groups and their audiences alike. Instead of fostering opposition between two distinct camps, it had precisely the opposite effect of engendering solidarity between all generations of musicians and their audiences. In this way, both the rise of an indigenous form of GDR rock music and the full course of its history came to be intimately associated with the rise to power and political career of Honecker. There is a sense in which GDR rock music was born, lived, and died with him.

The Role of Rock

In order to trace more precisely the catalytic role of popular musicians in the dramatic events of 1989, it is necessary to describe the key events that took place between September 18 and October 10, 1989. These events provide evidence in support of the political effectiveness of rock music in certain situations. The events of these days were not, however, without their preconditions.

The most decisive of these preconditions was the state's 1972 initiative to organize all the country's rock musicians under the auspices of the Committee for Entertainment Arts[3] in an attempt to render them susceptible to forms of state-imposed discipline. Ironically, it was the creation of the structure necessary for this state-imposed discipline which made it possible for the musicians to organize successfully. Without these structures, such organization would not have been possible.

The second precondition derived from the fact that, because the GDR media did not provide a forum for meaningful political discussion, such discussion was forced to take place on the stages provided for the performances of GDR musicians and artists.

The final precondition derived from the way in which the GDR authorities tended to read into even the most innocuous songs a potential for serious political statement. This in turn led GDR audiences to read into such songs a more serious political content than was ever intended by the musicians themselves.

On September 18, 1989, members of the rock music section of the Committee for Entertainment Arts, that is to say, all prominent popular musicians in the GDR, met to plan a routine workshop for young musicians to help them to develop their musicianship. However, in the context of the exodus from the GDR of significant numbers of young people to West Germany, the members of the rock music section themselves were much more interested, as were the younger musicians, in discussing the implications of the exodus for the life of culture and popular music in the GDR.

At this time, political power was still firmly in the hands of the Stalinist regime. Officially, in the GDR media, the exodus did not exist. The fact that the vast majority of people in the GDR could receive reports of this exodus directly from West German television demonstrates the dismissive and cynical view that the political leaders of the GDR had of the political and cultural intelligence of its people. The leaders clearly did not believe that the situation was significant or serious enough to warrant discussion and defense through the media they controlled. In sad contrast, the media were full of euphoric reports of people joyfully anticipating celebrations marking the fortieth anniversary of the founding of the GDR.

In this context, the musicians felt that they had no alternative but to make a political statement of their own to the public. The full text of the statement appeared as follows:

> We, the undersigned of this declaration, are concerned about the current situation of our country, about the mass exodus of many members of our peer group, about the crisis of confidence in the social alternatives provided by the GDR, about the intolerable state of ignorance on the part of the state and party leadership, which minimizes contradictions evidenced within the social system, and continues to maintain an inflexible political line.

> We do not have in mind reforms which eradicate socialism, but reforms which make the continued existence of socialism possible in this country. Attitudes towards the current situation endanger it.

We strongly welcome the emergence of democratically constituted groups of citizens which will take the solutions for existing problems into their own hands. This country is badly in need of the individual initiatives of its citizens. The old political structures are clearly no longer appropriate. We take notice of the foundation of the New Forum, and find in this intended organization goals worthy of discussion and communication. We think the time is overdue for the reduction and elimination of old hostilities and reservations. It is important that the political will of large sections of the population find a resonance in the political leadership. This means, in addition, that the democratically constituted groups of citizens which are in the process of being formed should be recognized, tolerated, and included in discussions relevant to the running of this society as required by the constitution of the GDR. This country must finally learn to take account of minorities which think differently, especially if they turn out not to be minorities at all.

An increase in conservative and national, extreme right-wing elements in our society, together with an increasing subscription to general, pan-German ideals, are the result of the lack of a suitable reaction to, and the failure to properly assimilate the fact of contradictions which have stood in such high relief in our society. Forces of the left are once again becoming the victim of a stubborn inflexibility in political matters. We would like to live in this country, and it sickens us to have to watch helplessly as attempts at social analyses and democratization are ignored or criminalized.

We here and now demand an immediate public dialogue with all relevant parties. We demand that the media be made available for an airing of these problems. We demand a change in this unbearable situation. We wish to confront the current contradictions, because it is only by their solution as opposed to their minimization that a way out of this crisis will be found. Weak inaction provides the conditions within which pan-German thinkers can make their arguments. The time is ripe. If we do not take action now, time will work against us.

On the evening of September 18, 1989, approximately 100 of the GDR's most popular rock musicians signed this declaration.

Although the statement was crucial in sparking the sequence of events that was to follow, the nature of these events was such as to render the subsequent publication of the statement of little consequence. Despite the fact that the public announcement of this statement involved a high level of risk on the part of the musicians, and significantly prefigured the actions and statements of prestigious artists and writers for which it provided the necessary context, it has been left out of the accounts that have been constructed around the dramatic events of 1989. On September 19, 1989, as expected, there was a public announcement declaring the intended organization of the New Forum. This organization constituted a crime against the state. All expressions of solidarity with the New Forum, including the above statement, were also declared a crime against the state. This put all the musicians who signed the declaration at risk of being imprisoned by the state security services. Nevertheless, the rock musicians gave the GDR media seven days to make their statement public. This period of time ran out on September 25. On that day, the musicians carried out their declared intention of making the statement available to the West German media.

They also decided to make the statement public themselves by reading it aloud at the beginning of their own scheduled performances. The next day the state authorities became nervous and decided to cancel all important public performances in an attempt to prevent the musicians from making their statement public. But because it was impossible to effectively eliminate an entire cultural scene with so little advance notice, the statement was read publicly at a number of performances.

By October 3, 1989, the statement had been signed by more than 1,500 entertainers, including jazz musicians, singer-songwriters, pop singers, and disc jockeys. The state authorities began to enter into negotiations to prevent the statement from being read at public performances planned to mark the fortieth anniversary of the founding of the GDR, performances which could not be cancelled. But these negotiations failed to accomplish their intended goal. On October 7, 1989, the 40th anniversary of the founding of the GDR, during performances by rock musicians, singer-songwriters, and other artists throughout the whole country, the statement was read publicly. It precipitated an unprecedented degree of solidarity between performers and audiences. The state authorities in small towns and rural areas reacted without hesitation, and the security forces arrested young performers on stage and transported them directly to prison. But even during these actions the state security services didn't touch any of the prominent musicians or entertainers. In all big cities, security forces refrained from such confrontations. However, a course of action had been set in motion which could not be stopped. Audiences reacted with uncontrolled hostility toward the action of the security services.

Over the next few days, news spread informally, outside of official media channels, about the confrontations between state security forces and audiences at concerts. This resulted in young people taking to the streets in order to protest the actions of the security services, and led to further hostile and violent confrontations between the security services and young people, especially in big cities. The violence was completely on the part of the security services. The young people behaved in an orderly and passive manner, even at the risk of suffering bodily injury. There were more than a thousand arrests in Berlin alone. Despite the hostility and violence, there was no damage to property. Nonetheless, the dramatic pictures of these confrontations, edited and put together by the West German media, gave the impression that the situation in the streets was far worse than it actually was, and resulted in some 300,000 people taking to the streets in Leipzig to protest the situation as they now understood it. This tradition of Monday demonstrations in Leipzig, organized by the church, had hitherto attracted only a hundred or so people. Afterwards, prominent intellectuals, capitalizing on the momentum that had been set in motion by the concert confrontations, took credit for their engagement in the movement in such a way that the actions of the musicians themselves were left out. It was just at this point, as the state was already under pressure from hundreds of thousands of demonstrators, that prominent intellectuals in the GDR began to make public statements in support of change. The rest is history, and a matter of public record.

There is a common conception that recent dramatic events in Eastern Europe have signaled the triumph of the Western system and the defeat of socialism. This, of course, constitutes the perceived political reality, a political reality whose advent was overdue. The Stalinist versions of socialism, which more or less dominated the countries of Eastern Europe from the end of the World War II, were economically inefficient and also totalitarian. Their demise was not only inevitable, but highly desirable. There was therefore a strong motivation on the part of the populations of these countries to see political and economic change. And although the obvious alternative for these populations was to move towards the political and economic systems of the West, the inevitability of such a move was not a necessary outcome of the desire for change. The propensity of the Western media to couch the changes of Eastern Europe in the rhetoric of winners and losers—capitalism is the winner and socialism the loser—has removed from common consciousness an awareness that other political and economic systems could have come into existence.

It is important to make this point in understanding the changes in the GDR, because the intentions of the musicians and their young audience in this country—to effect political and cultural changes within the existing structures of socialism—were quite different from the changes which, in fact, took place. Once history is put in motion, there is no guarantee as to what the consequences of that motion might be. Although there was a clear understanding of this aspect of historical processes on the part of the musicians, the risks involved were deemed justifiable given the gravity of the political and cultural situation within the GDR. The exodus, in alarmingly high numbers of young people to West Germany through Hungary during the late summer of 1989, reinforced for the population of the GDR in general and its popular musicians in particular an awareness of the vacuum that existed in the cultural life of the GDR, and especially in that of its young people.

It is important to stress that while the political consequences of previous Stalinist regimes were unacceptable, it was the almost total lack of an attractive and stimulating cultural life within the mainstream of everyday experience for the majority of the population that constituted the concrete impetus for radical and fundamental social change. The importation of Soviet culture in the form of films, books, and magazines emanating from the changing political realities of *perestroika* gave a precise indication of the extent to which the authorities were prepared to go in providing a viable cultural life for the population of the GDR. The distance between the cultural aspirations of the people of the GDR and what the authorities were prepared to provide demonstrates the fundamental importance of cultural processes in putting into effect political, economic, and social changes, the outcomes of which were unpredictable.

These changes resulted not simply in the reformation, liberalization, and improvement of political and cultural life as it affected the everyday existence of people in the GDR, but the creation of a political and economic vacuum into which the incursion of capitalist forms of political, economic, and cultural processes was inevitable. In addition, a focus on young people as the instigators and harbingers of changes shifted swiftly to a focus on middle-aged career politicians as they took advantage of the opportunities offered through the lack of political expertise on the part of those who had initiated the changes. For the musicians this meant that they lost within months the opportunity to perform or to make records. In the crude market economy, with unprecedented mass unemployment and brutal real estate speculation, the dissolution of all GDR media networks, and the elimination of club and concert venues, the infrastructure for any musical and cultural life broke down almost totally. The extension of West German networks or new ones under West German management has made it difficult for indigenous rock musicians to survive as a local music scene.

But as we know from the Western rock classic, "Rock 'n' Roll Is Here to Stay." Slowly, a new rock music movement has begun to emerge amidst the alienation visited upon the eastern part of the new Germany. Under the slogan "Power from the East Side," former East German rock bands are performing again, in an attempt to revive their shattered careers, and to shake young people out of their lethargy and motivate them to fight back. In short, rock musicians now understand that the changes signaled by popular musicians over the past few years have resulted in the disappearance of socialism (even that limited form that was possible to practice under a Stalinist regime), and the irrevocable advent of capitalism as the new social form within which notions of social progress now have to be negotiated.

The Politics of Marginality

A Rock Musical Subculture in Socialist Hungary in the Early 1980s

Anna Szemere

What we prepare to welcome is never without some resonance in ourselves; it is the mirror in which each of us recognizes himself.
—Gadamer

In his book on American popular culture, George Lipsitz argues that

> Culture can seem like a substitute for politics, a way of posing only imaginary solutions to real problems, but under other circum-stances, culture can become a rehearsal for politics, trying out values and beliefs permissible in art but forbidden in social life. Most often, however, culture exists as a form of politics, as a means of reshaping individual and collective practice for specified inter-ests…[1]

Lipsitz's conception of cultural form existing as a form of politics was much in evidence during the early 1980s in Hungary when a highly innovative and influential set of rock musical styles emerged. Variably referred to as punk, new wave, avant-garde rock, and independent music-making, these labels defined various aspects of this musical movement by approaching it either as a subcultural style, an artistic-musical attitude, or as a particular position in the whole youth music field. Despite the fact that some of the musicians whose names were associated with the subculture still produce and perform under the radically different circumstances of today's Hungary, the punk/new wave movement articulating and drawing on a strong sense of subcultural identity was relatively short-lived.

As an investigator of the subculture and a fan of the music, I was initially interested in why and how this remarkable combination of creative energy, political-civic courage, and subcultural cohesion emerged seem-ingly out of nowhere; from where did it draw its resources; and what was its significance regarding the diversity and the institutional autonomy of the youth's music-making. Now with the collapse of the Eastern European Communist Party-states in 1989, I'm curious about the ways in which this music contributed to undermining the past social order by creating, through the music, an alternative social and cultural space where the dramatization of a severe cultural and moral crisis prevalent in contemporary Hungarian society was possible.

Robert Wuthnow suggests a strong relationship between the rise of social movements as producers of ideologies and the instability of social environments. He claims that the simultaneous production of numerous ideologies in a particular social setting can be seen as a response to uncertainty or disruptions in the moral order.[2] In the 1980s, Hungary witnessed the emergence of an increasing number and variety of cultural, religious, and strictly political movements and associations, a process characterized by Hungarian sociologist Elemér Hankiss as the self-organization of the society after decades of repression.[3] Wuthnow also asserts, rightly, that "the presence of the uncertainty in the moral order cannot be assumed to lead automatically to the production of new ideologies." His references to an authoritarian state which "may prevent ideas from being discussed" or to economic conditions which "may force [people to act] on short-term survival rather than giving attention to longer-range problems" are pertinent to the conditions in which popular music and youth cultures existed in socialist Hungary.[4] In order for the punk/new wave movement to be able to carve out its own subcultural space, as well as for other movements to surface in the broader cultural and political life of Hungary, significant processes had to take place involving, among other things, the loosening of the centralized political control exercised over the production and consumption of rock music.[5] Also, a new generation of amateur musicians broke into the popular music field, one whose members were either too young, or artistically too ambitious and, in terms of their relationship to the existing socio-political system, too marginal to be pressed or corrupted by the need to make "big money" through pop music.

The marginal socio-cultural location of the punk/new wave movement, the musicians' experience, and representation of marginality were central to the politics of the subculture and to the messages and the particular pleasures produced and articulated by the music. Marginality, in fact, expressed a multiplicity of simultaneous meanings. Besides defining the social and professional location of this group of young people, it was experienced and conveyed by them as the broader cultural and historical context of their existence. "Margin," as a metaphor, marked for them a set of spatial and temporal cleavages: disjunctions and splits within society between professional and underground art worlds; between official and forbidden (sub)cultures; between societies in the politically defined East and West; and between past and present, present and future. Marginality as the politics of the punk/new wave movement meant to highlight, to explore, and to dramatize these cleavages. It also defined a lifestyle and, although far less explicitly, a political stance elaborated and re-worked in varied and imaginative texts, performance practices, and even in real-life confrontations with officialdom. The Hungarian punks re-worked the Western punk bohemian ideology of marginality by adding new dimensions to it. They added a particular view and experience of history to it, a perspective from which the surrounding contemporary social world as a whole could be represented as "marginal," that is, historically anachronistic and ephemeral. Further, synonyms for marginality, emblems such as "alternative," "underground," and "independent" music-making, became the markers of subcultural identity and difference. These emblems also indicated and reinforced a connection between the popular culture of a particular youth group with the more "serious" and less young subculture of the political opposition and the avant-garde art world, loosely referred to as the "marginal intelligentsia."

How can the politics of the punk/new wave rockers' marginality, with its "carved-out" subcultural spaces, be interpreted within the framework of larger social processes marking the deepening crisis of Hungarian society at the turn of the 1970s? In what sense was the movement "political"? In other words, how did the specific conjuncture of art rock, history, and locality account for the elusive relationship this subculture maintained with politics?

The Politics of Rock in a Socialist Society

Iain Chambers observes in the introduction to his book on English pop history:

> Pop music is a field of continual novelties. In some cases, these merely involve the latest twist in marketing strategy, the quick business eye for a possible trend. More frequently, fresh proposals represent a real intrusion upon an earlier organization of the music and its surrounding culture. Whenever a sound powerful enough to threaten existing arrangements emerges, previous interpretations, choices and tastes are put in question.[6]

In the pop music field of socialist societies, such an intricate relationship between fresh musical proposals and imaginative business strategies was unprecedented. Typically, the centralized record industry failed or refused to notice the emergent innovative trends, partly because of the lack of incentives on the part of its employees, and partly because of the political control it was supposed to exercise over its products. When the audience demand was perceived by the gate-keepers of the music business as too much of a social pressure, the routine response was either an alteration of the material to be published, or a substitution aiming to redirect audiences to ersatz products, to recording artists of the industry's own choice.[7] More often than not, the demanded music with the original performers eventually came out, but with such delay that the recordings served at best as archive pieces reminiscent of some great moments in Hungarian pop history. As one punk musician put it: "By the time six committees and nervous officials come to decide whether this or that music should exist or not [on record], the music will simply no longer be around."[8]

Given their need for political control, the music industry and the mass media were fearful of allowing the ongoing public struggle for meaning which characterizes the reception of popular music under Western liberal capitalism.[9] Typically for authoritarian systems, the indeterminacy of meaning inherent in any particular cultural artifact tended to be seen and treated by the officialdom as a potential threat to the existing social and political arrangements. Processes of cooptation and marginalization were constantly charged with heavy moral and political implications, a condition only rarely to be observed in Western popular music where counter-hegemonic moments tend to be more or less smoothly reintegrated into the mainstream. The bureaucratic system of control rendered musicians and musical styles extremely vulnerable and corruptible, politically as well as commercially, which imbued the predicament of some "rock personalities" with a curious heroism. Popular histories of Hungarian rock and monographic portrayals of performers abound with accounts of the out-of-joint careers of prominent talents, legendary heroes of a particular generation or subculture, who broke in with a sound "powerful enough to threaten the existing arrangements." And yet, rather than re-shaping the whole popular music scene, they either disappeared without ever being given the chance to record their music, or misused their talents for the sake of mere survival. Many of them sought escape in alcohol or defected to the West without regaining the recognition acquired in their home environment. But bitterness and frustration pervaded virtually all the discourses on popular music, not excepting the autobiographic accounts of the successful musicians in the mainstream who, due to a fortunate combination of circumstance and individual talent, managed to balance between genuine popularity and official renown. In unison with their less fortunate colleagues, they too claimed that their creative talents and career chances had been curtailed by what they viewed as an arbitrarily operated, overbearing, and incompetent system of cultural production, including the recording industry, the concert management, the mass media, the licensing system, etc.[10]

Many of the musicians' clashes with the music industry or other agents of power took place behind the scenes over the issue of whether a particular composition should be published at all, rather than, as in Western rock, over the meaning of a text already out in the open. According to a 1986 survey of popular musicians in Budapest, virtually no recording artist had escaped censorship during his or her career.[11] Paradoxically, this form of coercive rather than hegemonic control over the production and dissemination of popular music resulted in musical texts layered with meaning. Not only marginal but a great number of mainstream musicians resorted to double entendres in their songs as a poetic and political strategy to avoid confrontations with the gate-keepers of the radio, the television, or the record company, themselves subject to political control. Due to the ubiquity of censorship, especially during the 1960s and 1970s, musicians' use of allusions, a sign-and-countersign language, grew beyond a political or creative strategy to deal with censors. It became an indication of "seriousness" in Hungarian rock 'n' roll until the rise of punk and new wave where lyrics were politically more outspoken and anarchistic.

The long tradition of writing allegoric texts with multilayered meanings, however, had taught audiences a particular mode of reading, or, rather, a mode of hearing. The politicization of rock thus had a self-perpetuating logic of its own.[12] In other words, the musicians' intentional and self-conscious use of the music for articulating political positions or messages played a relatively limited role in this phenomenon. The rock community's politicization was to a very large extent a process perpetuated by the system of controlling and regulating the whole domain of cultural production. In his discussion of GDR rock (see Chapter 5), Peter Wicke also draws attention to the state's role in rock's political perception and effects in Eastern Europe. Wicke observes that "authorities tended to read into the most innocuous songs a potential for serious political statement," as a result of which audiences were led "to read into such songs a more serious political content than was ever intended by the musicians."[13]

The political meanings and effects of rock music in East European social contexts therefore cannot be read off its surface any more directly than in the case of its Western counterpart. This is an important point to stress since the authoritarian institutional framework in which rock music had to find its niche did in fact produce creative strategies expressing and appealing to people's heightened political sensibilities, which in turn was a function of the larger historical network of repression in these societies. However, these circumstances, as I would like to illuminate with the example of punk and new wave rock, do not render the relationship between politics and popular music any more straightforward than in capitalist society.

"Ragged" Rock and the Rise of Pop Avant-Gardism

At the end of the 1970s, Hungarian youth music started to carry manifold social tensions. It was a particular moment in the ongoing economic recession when a sense of insecurity spread over and across diverse sectors of society. Typically, it was the young who were affected most painfully by a loss of faith in future prospects, and who suffered most from the apparent lack of stable, credible, and consistent sets of values to adhere to. Therefore, they responded in most desperate forms.[14]

While a craze for rockabilly revival raised a few groups to the top of the charts with escapist but extremely luring sounds and images of a mythical version of the United States of the 1950s, another youth subculture, whose members were downtrodden by the harsher realities of their own existence, was coming together. The most militant core included homeless and jobless males, some of them freshly released from state orphanages as they had turned 18; others were runaways from dysfunctional, predominantly working-class families. They sought release in drug trips, alcohol, and heavy rock.[15] Music provided them with the most effective medium through which they could articulate their nihilist despair and frustration to the outer world as well as to themselves. And their musical tastes actually identified them as marginal subjects with whom the establishment attempted to restore communication through favoring some of their "sincere and hard-as-stone" bands while disfavoring others. Those musicians who seriously undertook to be a mouthpiece of these youth groups inevitably clashed with the gate-keepers of the pop business. In fact, one wing of the early punk movement gained nationwide fame not so much by the music they played as by their resistance to the attempts of the media to domesticate them.

The Beatrice voiced social dissent in a crude and straightforward fashion. They presented themselves as intuitive rather than self-conscious, socially responsible rather than nihilistic punks. A British journalist, Chris Bohn, perceptively called them "social(ist) realists" because of their graphic description of lower-class life, of the bleak world of smoky outskirts, dirty subways, and pubs.[16] They were identified as the band of the "ragged crowd." For them to publicly admit to being a punk would have meant to subscribe to an ideology which the Hungarian guards of "law and order" declared to be right wing and fascistic. Still, the Beatrice could not escape the label earned by a concert whose main attraction was, allegedly, the grinding of a live chicken. The Beatrice never acknowledged that this incident ever happened. They were professionals intent on making their living out of music. They, however, had no control over their public image once the label punk was attached to it, triggering a campaign which eventually led to their silencing.

In the meantime, there was a notable revival of the amateur musician movement which reached a broad age range (from age 12 to 30) and social strata (from teenage apprentices to intellectuals). Some of these bands did not survive the second rehearsal. A self-conscious subculture with all the sartorial and hair-style extravaganza of punk was nurtured in centers such as the Young Artists' Club, art galleries, and college venues. Members of this subculture seemed aware of and well-informed about their British and North American prototypes. Better educated and older than the "ragged" punk subculture, they had the intellectual and political resources to challenge the official representations of the Western punk movement as fascistic.

Out of the venues where the avant-garde punks gathered, the Young Artists' Club deserves to be touched on because it hosted a mixed constituency loosely referred to as the "marginal intelligentsia." It was one place for connections and exchanges between the political underground, the so-called "democratic opposition"[17]—writers, avant-garde artists, popular musicians, academics, fresh college graduates, and other "floating" intellectuals in and out of jobs, on and off various blacklists. Its patrons enacted versions of marginality, negotiated its meanings, politics, but most of all, its style. The Club attracted members of the "ragged" working-class subcultures too, mostly through its hard-core punk events. This was a place notorious for repeated political scandals resulting from officially disapproved events (lectures or discussions with some oppositional artist or intellectual). These scandals then led to implementing various punitive measures such as temporary shut-downs, restricting eligibility to membership, wholesale removals of the club's staff, and so forth. The Young Artists' Club, located just a few blocks from the Soviet embassy, had a truly bohemian, casual, at times somewhat dire atmosphere, the latter caused by excessive alcohol consumption. In order to enter this atmosphere, one often had to push oneself through the crowds controlled at the door by heavily built and unfriendly guards, who were there to deny entrance to non-members who, in turn, were desperate to contest this rule.

Although the Club nurtured contacts and solidarity between the various groups of middle-class and working-class "marginal elements," it did not succeed in overcoming the social fragmentation among its constituency. The intellectuals' attempts to forge meaningful alliances with the "ragged" youth groups tended to fail, primarily because the intellectuals themselves were factioned and vulnerable vis-a-vis the ruling elite's political maneuvers.[18]

The beginnings of the art punk subculture date back to 1978 when Gergely Molnár and his band (the Spions) held three extremely brutal and provocative punk concerts for a selected elite. The sophisticated multimedia action may well justify the term "art punk" or "avant-garde" rock.

Faithful to the tradition of Hungarian avant-gardists, The Spions' leader defected to the West. As Feró of the Beatrice became the hero of the "ragged" punk rockers, Gergely Molnár's myth was fed by underground publications, and he was celebrated as the initiator of the avant-garde punk/new wave. The two divergent wings of the movement corresponded to Simon Frith and Howard Horne's distinction in the British scene between punk as a youth subculture and punk as pop style.[19] I will return to this issue later.

The new wave music scene began to appeal to a broader public when numerous bands emerged with harshly provocative or outlandish names such as Petting or Riding Coroners; others produced a shock effect by choosing the name of existing contemporary Hungarian institutions like Europe Publishing House (a name which also translates as Europe to Rent); or the (Albert Einstein) Committee, which was read by the audience as an allusion to the Central Committee of the Hungarian Communist Party.[20] The name URH was regarded by the public as a reference to the police patrol bearing the same acronym. Again, the band members elusively refrained from direct self-interpretation by saying that the name URH stood for Ultra Rock Agency. This "redoubling" technique of naming may be seen as an anarchistic assertion of an alternative social space with mirror images challenging and mocking the "real," that is the dominant social world.

Dave Laing has argued that the stage names of British punks marked only a mildly radical variation on hippie/underground precedents.[21] In the Hungarian history of rock, however, there had been no "Grateful Deads" or "Electric Prunes," no underground/psychedelic tradition; therefore, names such as the above proved extremely effective both in terms of recruiting followers and bewildering or outraging the public at large. But, as Laing has convincingly argued, shock tactics alone tend to lose their value fast. Punk, with its obsession with shock, soon gave way to new wave, which allowed for more subtle and individuated forms of artistic expression. The avant-garde new wave as a subcultural style was constituted, first, by a shared set of experiences deriving from its members' similar social location, age, and background; second, a commonality of perspective and attitude arising from a particular moment of cultural and historical awareness (postmodernism); and third, the textual incorporation of other art forms.

Music Making: The Alternative Network

Most of the performers of the punk/new wave scene came from bohemia or the professions, but many of these young people were "floating," uncertain about their career and earning their livelihoods primarily by unskilled freelance jobs. Their age varied between 20 and 30. Their marginality was more self-conscious and allowed for a materially far more secure existence than was the case with the "ragged" punks. The art punks had a middle-class background involving reasonably stable housing and living conditions. They had ties to the artistic and academic elite's networks, which occasionally provided them with rewarding and/or well-paying work projects (composition of film music or acting, for example). The new wavers were amateurs in music, but quite a few had simultaneously or previously been engaged in related art forms such as visual arts, filming, or drama. A few others had a musical past in jazz-rock or folk. Punk rock was "discovered" and used by them as just another outlet for experimenting with new ideas and forms of expression.

Initially, the punk/new wave seemed to revive the early informality of the beat club scene of the 1960s. Again, musicians and audiences were of the same age group and shared a similar social background. In comparison with the beat audience, however, this was a more mature and self-conscious group of people who sought an alternative space to nurture and communicate a particular artistic and political sensibility. They were not fans in the sense of pledging their loyalty to one star band only. The most popular groups attracted the same crowd to a live venue. Accordingly, there was no rivalry between the bands. Line-ups were fluid and the players of one band were frequently invited as guests to contribute at another's concert. The practice of joint live shows also reflected an emphasis on cooperation and inter-group solidarity rarely known among professional musicians. The undividedness of the public was sustained even as its composition changed. As the originally predominant bohemian/intellectual elite came to be absorbed into a younger and more ordinary rock audience composed of college and high school students as well as a smaller group of working-class hard-core punks,[22] the concerts were increasingly refashioned along the lines of ordinary rock events. This process also involved the widening of the audience in geographic terms, a break-away from the capital Budapest as the exclusive site of concert life.

Avant-garde new wave rock was never integrated into the Hungarian pop music industry. Although pop music in Hungary was considerably more commodified than in other socialist countries, political cautiousness prevented the music industry from developing business strategies to exploit the profit potential of new bands located at the margins. No quick business eye wanted to recognize that the avant-garde punk bands' live shows were attracting crowds of about a thousand people to venues designed for just a few hundred. Instead, barely known bands, dependent on the Hungaroton's tips for their musical ideas, were promoted and marketed under the fashionable label "new wave." Out of the seven or eight most significant avant-garde new wave bands, only two were given the opportunity to issue albums, even though each had enough of a repertoire for at least two LPs. Altogether three albums and a couple of singles came out to represent a large and varied set of styles, which had an impact not only for the next generation of amateurs but on mainstream rock as well. Even these records were sadly belated. The Committee's first LP contained material that had been played for three years at concerts. Their second album came out at a time when the band was ready to break up. The group Europe Publishing House had also been long past its heyday when Hungaroton assessed their competence worthy of producing an album.

There appeared to be a great deal of ambivalence and uncertainty in the overall manner in which the establishment treated these bands. Negotiations for record contracts were often started and then abruptly terminated. Apparently, the younger and more sympathetic label managers were not able to win their superiors' consent for these projects.[23] Similarly, the state-run radio recorded a number of concerts for its sound archive while seldom broadcasting them. Again, evidence suggests that the employees responsible for making the recordings were constrained in their decisions as to what kind of music, what bands, and what particular songs were or were not to get airplay. Another example for this split inside of the pop music establishment can be seen in the pop journalists' near unanimous admiration for the underground bands. In the annual official appraisals of rock bands, the Europe and the Committee were repeatedly listed among the critics' favorites. These lists were widely published. Thus, a uniquely controversial situation came about in which the top critics of the nation rated a particular music as the best indigenous music available at the time, while the very same music was denied access to the national music business, to its sophisticated recording and marketing facilities, without which genuine publicity was not possible.

The musicians did not seem extremely keen on gaining this kind of publicity. Although never turning down the possibilities of wider public exposure, they, in fact, disdained the whole system as incompetent and narrow. Playing for fun, staying a "leisure band," serving an audience which they saw as desperately needing them were crucial themes of their rhetoric.[24] Marking their difference from the institutionalized pop world was more important to them than reaching a broader audience and establishing themselves.

The ethos of marginality was forged within the framework of a second publicity, a network of alternative communication channels.[25] This publicity rested on the hard and dedicated work of the "enthusiasts." The term "enthusiast" comes from Wallis and Malm's discussion of small countries' music scenes invaded by the transnational music industry. The enthusiasts have been defined as active small-scale business people operating at the peripheries of the marketplace in order to protect spaces for "endangered" local music vis-a-vis the expansion of internationalized pop sounds. Their motive being cultural rather than economic, they normally make little or no profit out of their activities.[26]

In the Hungarian popular music scene, the "enthusiast" as a type of cultural broker emerged only as part of the art punk subculture. They operated to promote and preserve punk and new wave music which were endangered not by the transnational music industry but by a monopolized and rigid national music business with its in-built institutional brakes in responding to new musical phenomena. In most cases, the "enthusiasts" were students dedicated to organizing the concert life of their college club as well as to documenting live events by taping them. Their activity made possible an extensive circulation of duplicated tapes among the fans. This was an entirely non-commercial practice: for example, a recording of a 1981 URH concert, which never made it onto vinyl, rather than being sold, could be exchanged for a home-taped Joy Division album or some other relatively inaccessible piece of music.[27] Despite difficulties of travel, finances, and management, quite a few local groups could therefore participate at avant-garde rock festivals and other events in Europe and thus become part of a broader cultural scene.

Some local film studios were also responsive to the punk/new wave subculture, partly due to their personal involvement in it. Not only did the studios precede and surpass other media in reproducing and distributing tapes but they also encouraged musical creativity through commissions for composing film music, acting, etc. (The Committee and the Riding Coroners appeared in the late Gábor Bódy's feature film *The Dog's Night Song;* János Xantus' *Eskimo Woman Is Cold* featured the group Trabant.)

Nonetheless, live shows continued to be the chief site of communication between the bands and their public. As amateurs, the musicians worked under very poor technological conditions with unresponsive technical crews hired by the venue. The concerts were often canceled at the last moment, either for political or technical reasons, but usually for a combination of both. The audience was typically oversized in terms of the clubs' capacities. This posed a threat to the safe operation of the venues, in a physical as well as a political sense. Many directors did not feel comfortable taking the risk of clashes between their guards and the frustrated crowds by the entrance, desperate to get in. Therefore, the atmosphere was always pregnant with violence. Police forces armed with nightsticks at the gates were not an unusual sight. Despite the risk and anxiety involved, the shows were fairly lucrative for the venues due to the predictable full house that such concerts ensured. An extremely exploitative remunerative practice prevailed in which bands, because of their status as amateurs, received extremely low or no fees at all, while the audience paid ticket prices in the same range as if they had attended the performance of licensed musicians. This practice epitomized the specific ways in which the cultural establishment's adherence to old restrictive bureaucratic regulations (licensing) on the one hand, and its unscrupulous exploitation of audience demand, on the other, combined to simultaneously stifle and capitalize on underground music.

Marginality as an Artistic Ideology

The Hungarian punk/new wave movement, as I argued above, replicated the British dichotomy between punk as a youth subculture and punk as pop style, but in a somewhat modified form. Punk as pop style, or the art punk wing of the movement, produced its own subcultural formation. This group of youth were ideologically more articulate, more self-conscious, and, therefore, less vulnerable to the repressive measures of the ruling elite. Due to their cultural background and connections with the more prestigious art world of film makers, sculptors, painters, performance artists, and academics, they could mobilize considerable intellectual and material resources for attaining a degree of tolerance for their activities. This tolerance was always partial and threatened, but it allowed for a relatively protected borderline existence within the contemporary cultural field.

The politics of marginality marked not only disruptions and cleavages such as within the pop music scene between amateurs and professional musicians; it also created alliances. For the creative ideology and practice of the art punk/new wave, the most consequential alliance was forged between visual artists, amateur dramatic actors, and musicians.

In British rock, as Frith and Horne have observed, a connection between the arts and rock music had existed from the very beginning. In their book devoted to the exploration of this connection, they provocatively suggest that the art school graduates' involvement with music as a commercially viable practice created British pop as an international superpower in that the art students added style, image, and self-consciousness to the Afro-American sounds. In the Hungarian history of pop and rock, the tie-up between the two cultural fields was only stimulated by the emergence of punk as a musical fashion, but it also turned out to be extremely significant in terms of self-reflection, innovation, and style. Most remarkable was the adoption of the term "rockandroll" with a new meaning. Whereas in mainstream discourses on popular music in Hungary it signified the 1950s dance music style (rock 'n' roll), the punk/new wave musicians took over the broader, affectively charged understanding of rockandroll with its elitist connotation of authenticity and relevance.[28]

Also, the reshaped definition and practice of rockandroll highlighted the music's "traditional" preoccupation with sex and drugs, a feature which, in general, had been suppressed in Eastern Europe: in music, lyrics, and performance styles alike. The use of the term rockandroll thus indicated a new appropriation of the Anglo-American rock tradition. The art punks were anxious to remind their fans that rock music was more than just sounds; visual images and stage choreography were treated as no less important in conveying and encouraging "forbidden" ideas, feelings, and pleasures. A group named Kex had had an entirely marginal and ephemeral existence in the '60s music scene but, thanks to its surrealistic, cabaret-style pop eclecticism, it attracted a remarkably devoted following, mostly among middle-class high school students in Budapest. To most members of the 1980s audience or even to the musicians themselves, the Kex evoked no personal memories since they had been too young to go to concerts at the time. Nonetheless, in digging out some extremely poor-quality amateur tape-recordings, older fans resuscitated the music and, along with it, the cult in popular memory.

In many other respects Hungarian punk and new wave echoed the artistic ideology of their Western counterpart. As an effect of the different cultural and political milieu, however, it emphasized different themes and dramatized different splits within the cultural terrain as a whole. For example, the alliance created between visual arts, drama, and rock implied the problematization of the conventional boundaries between diverse artistic forms and practices such as performance, video, painting, slides, film, and, of course, music. The avant-garde/punk tie-up also led, once again, to questioning the separation between art and everyday life, the gap between artist and audience—concerns which had recurrently been on the agenda of 20th-century "isms."

The use of avant-garde discourse within the realm of popular music implied also the subversion of the distinction between high ("autonomous") and popular ("commercial") arts. In the British prototypical punk subversion this conventional antagonism intersected with notions of political credibility (authenticity) and "sell-out," resistance, and hegemony. In discussing the Sex Pistols' manager Malcolm McLaren's play on these tensions, Frith and Horne observe that

> Previous pop art musicians had been recuperated either as "stars" (like Pete Townshend) or as "artists" (Brian Eno) or as both (Bowie and Ferry); either way, they lost control of themselves. McLaren's aim was to stay sharp by burrowing into the money-making core of the pop machine, to be both blatantly commercial (and thus resist the traditional labels of art and Bohemia) and deliberately troublesome (so that the usually smooth, hidden, gears of commerce were always on noisy display)...[29]

It was impossible to play such a game with the music industry in Hungary because of the radically different, far less smooth, and very visible gears of commerce. Pop music, as I have tried to show above, could not, typically, be viewed as a site of subtle hegemonic absorption. The antagonism between high and popular arts was explored and reassessed by Hungarian punks in the context of the prevalent cultural caste system where "high" art was often treated as synonymous with the politically compromised forms of artistic respectability. This caste system marginalized not only various forms of popular culture but also certain types of avant-garde expression, most of which in Western capitalism had long been commercialized and coopted. Therefore, the collapse of a distinction between "high" and "popular" at the conjuncture of punk and the avant-garde in Hungary marked the dramatization of a conflict between "legitimate," official, and respectable art on the one hand, and rejected, forbidden, outcast forms of expression on the other. These specifically Eastern European cultural conditions provided the following programmatic ideas introducing the underground publication Jó Világ *(Good World)* with a sharp political edge:

> We cannot assume that this narrow terrain [of marginal culture] is at the façade of nationwide interest. Nonetheless, it seems remarkable that at the rock concerts of the bands covered by our journal thousands of people gather; that in the fine art world nothing evokes as much debate as the emerging processes herein represented; and that there always appears an established film director who arouses public interest through the portrayal of the "types" we have picked out to contribute or to be appreciated… *At the present moment we are more intrigued by a high school student's ideas as to why she/he is bored of the Kossuth-prize winner poet than by the ideas of the Kossuth-prize winner poet himself* (emphasis added).[30]

Music: A Textual Approach

The most common underlying theme of punk and new wave lyrics was a pervasive anxiety and frustration arising from a particular form of social and historical awareness. This awareness can most easily be captured in negative terms, in a lost or blurred sense of the spatial and temporal framework of existence. The particular existential despair encoded in the songs curiously reverberated a pre-modern Hamletian sense of time being "out of joint," but certainly was more directly rooted in what Lawrence Grossberg has described as the postmodern condition:

> We have been thrown into the maelstrom of constant change, apparently under no one's control and without direction. Both the past and the future have collapsed into the present, and our lives are organized without any appeal to the place of the present within an historical continuum. We have neither a sense of indebtedness to the past nor of our obligation to the future.[31]

The song lyrics frequently employed metaphors of travel to express a similar idea. But such travels seemed curiously directionless, de-centered, and lacking what travels are normally valued for, the excitement of the novel and the unfamiliar: "You arrive as a traveler who lost his way/ History is a rusty city." If the metaphor of travel is used to capture an aimless and bleak economy of boredom in everyday life, one cannot but feel a stranger, a tourist at home too: "I raise my head and look around/What can a tourist do? He's just happy to be here." The meaningless duality of "here" and "elsewhere" is relocated in the individual self in the form of an internal split: "I'm somewhere else/ Yet I'll be here" (Europe); "Existence is a background" (Trabant). The apparent randomness of the outer world sometimes appears as provoking the most desperate modes of regaining control over one's life: "No one called you and you will live here...But you'll disappear from here too since you're fed up" (Control Group); "No time!/ No space!/ A triple salto high up!" (Riding Coroners).

According to Dénes Csengey, postwar Hungarian generations grew into adulthood with the increasing awareness of their insignificance as social actors.[32] Following World War II, the youth of the 1940s were virtually drunken with optimism and self-confidence when they sang about "shaking up the world by tomorrow." Even the 1960s beat generation nourished at one time the illusion of being able to contribute to a then-renewing society: "I don't wanna stand when the minutes run fast, I don't want to stand when the earth moves," proclaimed the group Illés. The children of the 1970s and 1980s were deprived of even a disillusionment with the system since they had been outsiders from the start: "We are no one's children/ Just happened to be born here/ And are still alive"; "The messenger is coming and waving/ There have been no news for long" (Europe). The site of self-assertion is displaced: "Oversized souls hide in cellars" (Europe); an anarchistic separation from the straight world points to the possibility of in-group solidarity: "I am you and you are me/ We are in the same army" (sung in English, apparently to emphasize difference through the use of another language). And a sense of alienation and displacement may seek release in parodying the mainstream rhetoric of crisis: "Value, value, without value, without value-free value/ One can hardly react/ One cannot raise their voice/ One can hardly resist" (Committee).

The Committee was founded by visual artists, which explains their debt to contemporary multimedia performance styles. The stage-setting, the costumes, the movements and gestures were harsh and caricature-like. Speeches, jokes, and all sorts of "disruptive" comments ("word salads containing obscenities of every imaginable waste product of language," as Walter Benjamin would have it[33]) were vital elements of the performance. Therefore, the Committee's music had no studio version; it depended on the live stage show for its distinctive spontaneity and tongue-in-cheek humor. The Committee joked even with their self-imposed labels, one of which was "catastrophe music": this was an improbable collage of reggae, free jazz improvs, and out-moded *schlager* music.[34]

In contrast to the Committee's penchant for improvisation, the Control Group preferred to use carefully prearranged scenarios with sophisticated multimedia effects and, occasionally, audience involvement. Also, whereas the Committee celebrated the perceived disorder and chaos with a cacophony of harsh colors, the Control Group's dominant color was black. (The female singer, posturing as a chanteuse, was clad in black "fetishistic" clothing.[35]) This was a "rock macabre,"[36] replete with visions of suicide, death, and destruction. These visions oscillating between the experiential and the allegorical planes of representation were themselves embedded in a multilayered historical context: Orwellian images of totalitarianism translated into the "everyday" were blended with post-apocalyptic fantasies of a destroyed civilization.

The Control did not refrain from making direct political statements, even though they felt uncomfortable at discussing these statements divorced from their musical/performance context. At their gigs in 1982-83 they regularly played songs which barely concealed their sympathy for the Polish Solidarity. This was at a time when public demonstrations of loyalty (even in the form of wearing a badge) for the recently defeated movement provoked incidents of brutal harassment by the Hungarian police. Occasionally, the authorities abhorred members of the group for verses picked out from their lyrics, but these occurrences never led as far as to banning their acts.

The Europe Publishing House, with its all-male line-up and exclusive concern with the musical aspect of their performance, fell closest to mainstream rockandroll. Still, their proclivity for experimentation with musical forms and sounds positioned them right in the core of the alternative music scene.

The group was centered around a "front man," whose identity seemed inextricably bound up with the lyrical subject of his songs.[37] One aspect of the popularity of the Europe might have been precisely the powerful and intense ways in which a "personal history" unfolded in the sequence of the songs as well as the singer's affective investment in overt subjectivity. Paradoxically, his almost masochistic sense of self-inquiry and his desperate attempts to mark a purely individual difference resulted in songs that were appropriated by the audience as a kind of collective property, their sing-along hymns. One of the songs assuming a hymn-like character was "Deliver Me from the Evil," with a refrain replicating, as the title suggests, a line from the Christian prayer. The audience almost always demanded that this piece conclude the event. The verses, set to a simple, declining, open-ended melody, spoke poignantly to a generation's alienation, psychic wounds, and self-hatred. The gloom and anger of the song had an unmistakably Central European, Kafkaesque "feel" to it: "A bald censor is sitting in my brain/ With a thousand ears to hear each of my words/ Someone is thinking instead of me/ Someone is leaving instead of me./ I can't win and I can't lose/ Who cares if I'll be no more?"

Most remarkable was the fashion in which the Europe re-worked the punk ideology of "no future." In deconstructing "history" as a meaningful continuum of past, present, and future, punk musicians popularized the ideas spelled out in postmodern philosophies ("Ghosts in the depth of times/ Missing links"). Therefore, the future, on one level, appeared as unreal, a non-entity; not unlike the subjects for whom this absence translated into a loss of identity ("I raise my head and look around/ What can a tourist do? He's just happy to be here"). The future signified a lack by merging into the present ("The future is here and will never end"; "The future has become the present"). It became dated and, literally, anachronistic before it had actually arrived. Such a problematization of temporality on a global scale intersected with a special Eastern European sense of crisis: a depressing sense of backwardness of a society which appeared to have taken a dead-end route in history ("We will disappear like the last metro/ Everything's on sale but we've run out of everything"; "What is today has for long been past"; "My watch says it's been tomorrow for long").

However, on another level, which became increasingly dominant in the Europe's later songs, the future started to appear as challenging and fascinating. This idea largely came from science fiction representations of the awesome, even if bizarre, potentialities opened up by the late 20th century technological progress ("The machines wander away beyond the boundaries of imagination"). However, not even this meaning rendered the future to be the site of genuine escape. Rather, it was the excruciating tension between the fantasies constructed around it and the depressingly anachronistic everyday realities that provided the keynote of later texts.

The Trabant and the Balaton originally formed two separate groups, but they worked in symbiosis. They rarely made efforts to organize gigs for themselves but, rather, seemed contented with producing homemade, rather rudimentary recordings and circulating them through their friends. Their musical/artistic conception was modeled after that of the Velvet Underground, pop artist Andy Warhol's famous underground band of the 1960s. At the concerts the two bands employed mixed media techniques in a way which blurred the boundaries between art and performance, on the one hand, and real life, on the other. The song lyrics, similarly to the photo slides projected on the wall, seemed to chronicle and mirror their own everyday life, whereas their everyday life seemed to have been self-consciously fashioned and stylized along preexisting ideas and images.[38]

No clear boundaries were drawn between the individual musical items of their repertoire, either. The songs formed a sequence, a flow of loosely related, poetic narratives and mini-dramas. They spoke about the minutiae of private everyday life—suggesting thus that it only had minutiae rather than genuine events—refracted through psychedelia. The songs highlighted and celebrated the precariousness of the boundary between the "real" and the "unreal," between the "artificial" and the "authentic." The obfuscation of such demarcation lines produced a special ambience, a sensation of timeless and lonely "floating" in a completely self-enclosed, isolated space. The musicians' politics of withdrawal from public appearance thus corresponded to the extremely introverted world created and sustained by the music and the visuals.

The prominence of the Riding Coroners has been associated with their leader Attila Grandpierre's explorations of the relationship between shamanistic folk music and punk rock.[39] The musical explorations were complemented by some interesting theoretical work defining and legitimizing punk as the revival of shamanistic practices. Grandpierre has claimed that

> Punk returned to such forgotten underground layers of ancient culture which with their cultural impact and consistent radicalism are worthy of the attention of people in different fields of art…Totem music, the music of shamanistic ceremonies, was truly a working, effective magic force for its creators, which led to ecstasy, and, through its force, elevated the participant's relation to himself and the world into a symbolic order, and thereby the first step toward practical action was made.[40]

The author gives no clue as to the kind of practical action for which this modern version of shamanistic punk music may prepare its listeners. His establishment of the connection between shamanism and punk—the premodern and the postmodern—rests upon a not too original but very articulate instinctualist critique of modernity and the fragmentation of modern culture. However, the discursive and the musical elaboration of the interplay between shamanism and punk may be appreciated as an unconscious re-articulation of an ongoing theme in punk rock—an obsession with charismatic figures—with superstars, heroes, and leaders. Grandpierre reinscribes naturalness and authenticity onto punk radicalism: "All is artificial but we won't be artificial."

The Riding Coroners' live shows have been cultic rituals rarely failing to provoke the audience's active physical response through agitated body movements, shouts, and screams. Their skinhead "hard core" fans, in particular, display a willingness to act in total synchrony with the dynamics of the musical process and completely immerse themselves in it. Occasionally, there is also a visual emphasis on the musicians' part of "reconstructing" tribal rituals with make-up, hairdo, and bizarre costumes.

The music creates a completely self-contained and closed acoustic space. An apparently chaotic but carefully constructed soundscape is produced by the howling and screaming vocals, guitars, and an array of drums, timpani, and a host of other, non-conventional percussion. Excessive amplification, fuzz, and echo are heavily relied on to produce a thick noise which renders the lyrics almost completely incomprehensible. The typical concert is made up of just a few lengthy musical units bearing no title and following one another without a pause, without verbal introduction, comments, or talk of any kind. The whole process of the performance stimulates as well as acts out ecstacy, reminding one critic of "an ego trip with an entrance and an exit."

Epilogue

The year 1983 marked the onset of a decline in the punk and new wave avant-gardism in Hungary. Most of the groups were shattered by internal controversies and had difficulties in producing new work. The innovations in outlook, sound, and style introduced by these bands started to infiltrate mainstream rock but served more directly as a set of models for the younger generation of musicians at the fringes. More importantly, they created institutional spaces for alternative music-making even prior to the capitalist pluralization of the music industry in 1987. The avant-garde rock scene, nevertheless, lost its subcultural cohesion, identity, and much of its popularity. New trends emerged such as the industrial and instinct music, the latter influenced by the Riding Coroners' shamanistic ideology. These sounds rarely empowered their audience, or, as might be assumed, the audience no longer empowered the music nearly as much as was true for their forerunners.

An important theme in the punk/new wave ideology was a desperate search for new identities, which came to be reflected in a special sensibility toward any emergent or archaic cultural forms promising, however vaguely and ambiguously, the possibility of a spiritual renewal in the broadest sense of the word. This was epitomized by the powerful impact of "shamanist" punk as a "premodernist" critique of the present, or the Europe's preoccupation with the "posthistorical" representation of the future. As the expression of pessimism and frustration became virtually ubiquitous in mainstream discourses surrounding social, cultural, and political issues; as the rhetoric of crisis gradually found its way even into the traditionally optimistic editorials of the (then still hegemonic) Communist Party's daily paper, *Népszabadság,* the more pronounced and visible became the endeavor on the part of these artists and musicians to abandon the discourse of despair.

Already in 1984 the contributors to the underground publication *Jó Világ*—punk musicians, artists, and art critics—discussed the rise of a "new mentality" opposing what they saw as the depressed and decadent official culture. As editor László Beke argued, artists working in the spirit of a new optimism "are producing a 'good world' day by day, at times with hard efforts...constantly reiterating values such as beauty, goodness, friendship, love, dynamic yet intimate human community..."[41] Statements like these had an esoteric air of political elusiveness and thus effected little resonance among the wider public.

To pursue oppositional politics in society, even if on the terrain of culture, is a kind of vocation—a lifestyle—and is crucial in terms of providing identity. The position and politics of marginality as articulated by the avant-garde rockers became seriously threatened when emerging political forces per se started to undermine the existing power structure and the boundaries of the (political) hegemony started to get blurred. The meaning as well as the "established" forms of subversion, or the modes of merely sustaining *difference* in and through music activities, became undermined and needed to be redefined.

Avant-Garde Rock as a Form of Politics

To return to Lipsitz's ideas on the relationship between cultural forms and politics, it is arguable that the Hungarian avant-garde rock scene both rehearsed for politics—in trying out values and beliefs encoded in a particular art ideology and practice—and, more importantly, existed as a form of politics by virtue of its marginal professional, social, and political location. The "rehearsal" neither constituted a consistent political program, a preparation for social change, nor existed as a tool in the service of any organized political movement. Even though the artists and the musicians of the subculture formed part of the wider network of the marginal intelligentsia, which included an active core of political opposition, the politics of marginality itself signified a shared condition of "living on the edge" rather than any kind of organized activity. Apparently, politicians of the underground displayed more interest in this musical/artistic form than the musicians did in direct political activities. But then, this music did not exist solely as a form of politics; it was also a form of entertainment and leisure. Obviously, the jokes, the allusions, and the whole discourse of punk/new wave would not have worked for the members and supporters of the political underground had there not been a shared set of assumptions about the nature of the existing power structure, about the meanings and possibilities of subversion, and about the political, social, and cultural crisis of

Hungary as a colonized Eastern European country. This commonality of values and beliefs did not make up for a common ideology but rather, to borrow Raymond Williams' phrase, it constituted a "structure of feeling" resting upon collective experiences and interpretations of what it meant to grow up in postwar Hungary.

Whereas the political underground operated with a conceptual-analytic framework in investigating the respective historical alternatives of socialism and capitalism, the artistic underground never adopted a perspective in which concrete possibilities of social change were explored. Their mode of expressing political ideas indicated and reinforced, often just through brief verbal comments, suggestive metaphors, and jokes, a common awareness of the historical moment and of the past. These musicians gave highly individuated voices to collective traumas, anxieties, and fantasies of their generation. In doing so, they became ghettoized, a condition which they turned into cultural politics and practices.

Being "political" carried ambiguous connotations for many popular musicians and other artists in socialist Hungary. This has been a society where, for historical reasons, the arts, both "high" and "low," have traditionally been colonized by the realm of the "political." In other words, there was a tendency on the part of the ruling elite to treat the arts as either a potential tool of promoting the dominant ideology or, contrarily, as its adversary undermining the hegemony. The social organization of culture, as I pointed out in my discussion of rock music, rendered the arts to be the site of political meanings, whether or not such meanings were encoded in the texts by their creators. The centralized monolithic control exercised over the various art worlds—to which popular culture was considerably more exposed than the "high" arts—added a systemic component to the political perception and interpretation of cultural texts. The colonization and instrumentalization of culture by the political establishment thus led to another, more subtle form of constraint, one imposed on the artists by their audience, who were eager to read and hear texts in what may be called the "political mode." This was an audience possessing heightened sensibilities and sophisticated skills in deciphering multilayered texts—anything from pop song lyrics, filmic or literary narratives, to political speeches.

Certainly, the political framing of cultural texts by diverse social actors involved the producers themselves in using artistic forms for communicating political ideas in subtle ways. Most of the time, such communication strategies and skills between artist and audience formed the basis of (sub)cultural cohesion and identities and helped mark their difference from the official culture. However, the artists, while thoroughly immersed in politics, sometimes sensed any political framing and interpretation of their work as imposed-upon and therefore jeopardizing their control over the creative process. The more a musician or artist was affected by "high" art ideologies—and the art punk rockers, as Frith and Horne have convincingly demonstrated, brought "high" art assumptions into their practices—the more apt they seemed to define their work in terms of individual expression. And a concern for individual creativity entailed a great deal of ambivalence in their attitude toward politics or the politicization of their work.[42]

In a personal interview, the Europe's singer/composer Jenö Menyhárt asserted this distance from politics through making a distinction between "cultural matters" (their musical practices) and "Realpolitik." With a postmodernist bent for paradox, he said,

> Everybody is more oppositional than me...including the functionary at the record company. To be oppositional, you have to be a "Realpolitiker."...The level of Realpolitik means that you go out to the street to demonstrate, saying "Down with censorship!" or write a song against censorship. Cultural matters such as this [i.e. punk/new wave] are of no strategic importance in that they merely embrace and register an all-encompassing mood. These matters, I guess, speak to the ways we feel ourselves and the way we live in this place.[43]

Indeed, the punk/new wave movement was not political in this conventional sense of the word. One might even say that both the power elite and the audience read or heard the music in a more conventionally political mode, while the musicians sought to sustain control by pursuing the "politics of elusiveness." In a broader sense, the music existed as a form of politics through its ability to survive and thrive at the margins of the pop music scene and at the boundary between tolerated and forbidden subcultures. The marginality of the musicians also enabled them to create new hybrids between popular and "high" cultural forms, and between popular music and other art forms, thus subverting traditional frontiers. Carving out a space for this artistic practice in the cultural arena allowed them to register and dramatize the splits and disjunctions of a society undergoing a momentous political and moral crisis. In locating the existential anxiety of a generation in a wider historical context of schisms, the punk/new wave rock not only highlighted a hurting condition but, in doing so, it also helped people make sense of their experiences, of the insecurities that such historical processes incurred. Finally, the ethos of marginality, while dramatizing "otherness" and alienation, brought along moments of identity and solidarity as well.

Rock and Roll on the New Long March

Popular Music, Cultural Identity, and Political Opposition in the People's Republic of China[1]

Tim Brace and Paul Friedlander

To the youth of post-Cultural Revolution China, revolutionary songs and traditionally dominant expressive forms such as Peking Opera have lost much of their resonance. Instead, these youths have turned to Western-influenced rock- and pop-rooted forms as their music of choice. This music represents a serious and critical challenge, both to traditional musical forms (and to those who make their living with them) and to the hegemony of the government as the legitimate arbiter of Chinese culture.

Popular music has been, in the 1980s, increasingly and affectively embraced by the youth population. For them, it has symbolized, given occasion for, and contributed to the expression of feelings for a new, optimistic time—a time marked (until the late 1980s) by the opening of economic policies, new international relationships, and a sense of hope concerning the political future. It has become part of the everyday reality of millions of Chinese youth, many of whom do not remember a time without it. It has, in fact, become an integral part of their view of what Chinese culture *is*.

Popular music is an integral and strongly affect-laden component of the ongoing verbal and nonverbal dialogues which constitute the life-world of contemporary Beijing. The rise, development, and reactions to this music can show us much about where the lines are being drawn in the continuing—even escalating—battles over the future of Chinese culture. There is now in China a form of music which defines, binds together, and gives strength to an oppositional community of youth—a community which is volatile, impatient, and contemptuous of the present regime.

Historical Context

Cultural production in China is organized by the state. That is to say, there is an attempt made at centralized control of production in the service of the hegemonic needs of the Communist Party. The history of China since the Communist revolutionary victory in 1949 has seen vacillation between periods of more active and direct control and periods where the control is less obvious, less active, and less effective.

The period of the Cultural Revolution, which the Chinese consider to have lasted from 1966 to 1976, was the period of the most active and direct control since the founding of New China in 1949. The death of Mao Zedong and the defeat of the most radical movers of the Cultural Revolution (the so-called Gang of Four) led to a massive repudiation of the Cultural Revolution—a repudiation which was nothing less than a national obsession during 1977 and 1978, and which still informs personal and public dialogue.

With the ascension to power of Deng Xiaoping in 1978, instigating economic reform rather than social class-based revolution became the primary task of the Party and therefore of the Chinese government. The Open Door Policy of 1978 codified this new direction, and called for a new openness in China's relations with foreign countries (especially the West) in order to facilitate economic reform and the ultimate goal, "socialist modernization." The Party was—and is—still firmly in command. But its credibility was tarnished by the Cultural Revolution, and it is in constant danger of being further tarnished as a result of the Chinese people becoming more aware of conditions and ways of life outside Chinese borders. However, this is a danger the Party (or at least those who currently lead it) feels it must face. Modernization and reform are the only ways for China to survive. The goal, for the Party, is to be open, modern, economically viable, internationally respected—and to retain power.

Gangtaiyue: The Dominant Style

As a result of the Open Door Policy, mainland Chinese were able, for the first time in over ten years, to listen to "foreign" popular music. The first popular music to be widely disseminated on the mainland was from Hong Kong and Taiwan. This *gangtaiyue*[2] was initially promulgated, as the Chinese say, "half openly." This is a term used among mainland Chinese to describe an action or process whose political acceptability is not yet known; in this case, it means that the government had not taken a stand, pro or con, on the active dissemination of this new popular music style. Its importation and spread, therefore, at first advanced slowly and cautiously. Its method of dissemination was usually hand-to-hand, involving the borrowing and copying of cassettes brought into the mainland by foreigners, Chinese travelers returning home, and visiting overseas Chinese. It is significant to note that its early dissemination was not via state-controlled radio or television. In the words of one informant:

> *Gangtai* popular music was the first to enter the mainland. At first, it was spread "half-openly." It did not appear on radio programs, but people borrowed cassettes from friends or visitors, and copied them. I would go to my friend's house, and if I heard some music I liked, I would borrow the tape and copy it...I never listened to the radio. It only had folksongs. I only used the cassette part.[3]

The embracing, by the mainland audience, of this music from Hong Kong and Taiwan was explained, fairly consistently, as tied to the audiences' relief from the stifling artistic atmosphere of the years immediately prior to 1978.[4]

After the repressive cultural policies of the Cultural Revolution and the Gang of Four, this music seemed a wondrous breath of fresh air. The people were tired of hearing the same things over and over. They wanted something new and different, and this was new and different.[5]

Gangtai style has remained, since the late 1970s, the favorite and dominant style of youth-oriented popular music in mainland China. It circumscribes in a particular way the Chinese conception of what popular music "is"—and more importantly, what it "ought" to sound like.[6] This *gangtaiyue* typically has the following characteristics: smooth, flowing melodies, which usually have no direct or obvious relationship with traditional Chinese melodic and rhythmic pattern construction; a type of vocal production which was described as the "middle way" (a term carrying a positive connotation) between Western full, ringing vocal style and Chinese folksong style; lyrics emphasizing feelings of love between young men and young women; a relatively high level of technical sophistication, from the standpoint of studio production; and an easy, dance beat background (provided by the instruments most commonly used in Western popular musics), which North Americans might commonly associate with "light" disco-inspired dance music, or with the popular music style commonly known as "easy listening." *Gangtai* style performers are either from Hong Kong or Taiwan, or are mainland singers imitating the style of those from Hong Kong or Taiwan. *Gangtai* singers normally do not write their own music or lyrics: the pieces are professionally written.

As the dominant style of popular music, the *gangtai* style has become the standard by which popular music itself is defined. Stylistic parameters (vocal delivery, melodic construction, formal patterning, harmonic accompaniment, instrumentation) have become, not one possible style among many, but constitutive of the notion of popular music itself. This notion carries with it strong internationalistic elements. It is certainly felt that the *gangtai* style owes much to international styles of popular music, especially those of the West. This feeling is reproduced and reinforced by the small amount of Western popular music which is heard daily over the government-run Radio Beijing, music which most Americans would call "easy listening." Smooth-flowing, melodic, professionally produced in technologically advanced studios, this Western music conspires with the *gangtai* style, with which it shares these stylistic features, to reproduce a conception of what popular music "ought" to sound like. This music, especially as performed by entertainers from Taiwan and Hong Kong, expresses and enacts a particular relationship between Chinese and Western cultures—a relationship that more and more mainland Chinese, especially youth, want for themselves and for their country. Since the Open Door, the most important influence is from Hong Kong: it is close, it is Chinese, and its relation to the West is long and deep.

Xibeifeng: The First Challenge

In the mid-1980s, a new style emerged: a style which was interpreted by many Chinese as an indigenous alternative to imported forms.[7] This music, simply put, adapted folksong melodies, or imitations of folksong melodies, to the dominant accompanimental style as defined by the music from Hong Kong and Taiwan (and updated through stylistic adaptation from the newest imported musical fad of the mid-'80s, North American disco music). Several of these styles, each based on the folksong style of a different region of the country, sprang up almost simultaneously. The one that achieved the most widespread popularity is known as *xibeifeng,* or Northwest Wind.

Stylistically, *xibeifeng,* despite certain differences from the popular musics of Hong Kong and Taiwan, still refers strongly to these musics in its instrumental accompaniment, quality of studio production, and professional quality of the voice. However, there is within this style a reemergence of a residual musical element which had been selected out as inappropriate—in other words, rejected—by the forces guiding the development of popular music[8] in mainland China: namely, a rough vocal delivery received as imitative of the folksong style of the Xibei (Northwest) area of China (the provinces of Shanxi, Shaanxi, and Gansu). This vocal production, when combined with melodic and rhythmic construction imitative of Xibei folksongs, presents an obvious and dramatic break with the dominant *Gangtai* style.

For many Chinese youth, *xibeifeng* calls forth national pride in the emergence of an indigenous popular form which is taken to speak more directly, in its use of (modified) northern folksong melodic and singing styles, to mainland Chinese realities and lives. This is a strongly affective response, stated in terms evoking feelings of national identity and a deserved international membership.

Yaogun Yinyue: The Second Challenge

Recently, a new form has arisen, a form which is seen as a much more direct challenge to the dominant musical parameters of the Hong Kong/Taiwan style. The Chinese call this style *yaogun yinyue,* which is a translation into Chinese of the term "rock 'n' roll." As a result of the Open Door Policy, international commerce and cultural exchange reached levels previously unknown to Communist China. Chinese students and business people left for the West, flooding their friends and families back home with packages containing Western commercial items, including Western popular music. This music gained cult-like popularity with some urban students as the English language and Western cultural artifacts achieved a degree of political acceptability. For example, in 1978, at the Shanghai International Studies University, a tape from the United States called *The Best of Twenty Years After* (including such pop hits as Bobby Vinton's "Blue on Blue") made its appearance on campus. Soon, Shanghai students were listening to music from Bob Dylan, John Denver, Karen Carpenter, Simon and Garfunkel, and, later, the Beatles. In major urban coastal centers, young people with radios heard rock music broadcast from Hong Kong, Taiwan, South Korea, the Voice of America, and other short-wave services. However, they generally preferred music that emphasized melody and lyrics rather than heavy distortion and a strong beat. In this sense, it fit into (and reproduced) the emerging *gangtaiyue*-determined popular music aesthetic.

In the mid-1980s, in a move seen at the time as progressive, some artists recorded Chinese language versions of American and English pop songs. In 1985, Cui Jian, then an aspiring rocker and trumpet player with the Beijing Symphony, recorded a cover of the Paul McCartney/Michael Jackson hit "Say Say Say." Also at this time, accessibility to recorded music rapidly improved as state factories produced portable cassette players and radios, and record labels manufactured and released cassettes of local, regional, and national artists. By 1988, the more than 240 record companies in China were producing and distributing over 100 million cassettes per year. Most of these were of popular music, predominantly *gangtaiyue* style.[9]

But a few musicians, reacting to a more open economic and political situation, began creating a louder, more rhythmic kind of music based more on Western rock music than on the easy, smooth sounds of *gangtaiyue* or on the by-now disco-dominated style of *xibeifeng.* This style, called *yaogun yinyue,* is practiced by a growing number of urban youth. However, at this time, due to the widespread fame of his performances and recordings, Cui Jian's'is the name which comes to the lips of most Chinese when they are speaking of *yaogun yinyue.*

Stylistically, Cui Jian's music presents the following characteristics: pinched, rough vocal style; a foregrounding of rhythmic elements, both in the accompaniment (which borrows heavily from Western rock music) and in the melody; a melodic construction which is often taken to be closely related to that of northern folksong; lyrics often interpreted as politically oppositional in content; and occasional use of traditional Chinese instruments, such as the *suona* (a reed instrument), the *dizi* (a transverse flute made of bamboo), and the *guzheng* (a zither).

Cui Jian's *yaogun yinyue* shares an important stylistic characteristic with *xibeifeng:* both feature a rather rough vocal delivery, decidedly contrasting with the smooth, open vocals typical of Hong Kong/Taiwan style. And, in fact, many Chinese associate Cui Jian's music with *xibeifeng.* Cui Jian himself, however, strongly denies this association, stating that any similarity between his music and *xibeifeng* is simply "coincidence." He describes his music as *"yaogun yinyue,"* or rock 'n' roll.

Yaogun Yinyue as Political Opposition

Cui Jian's audience comprises chiefly intellectuals and young male workers. Intellectuals, responding to the lyrical content, see this music as a form of thinly veiled political criticism—criticism of life in modern China in general, and of the current government and its policies in particular. For the workers, the attraction stems not only from its oppositional lyric content, but also, and perhaps mainly, from its aggressive sound. For many of them, the figure of Cui Jian has taken on heroic proportions: he is a young male, he speaks out boldly, he appears unafraid of governmental suppression, and his style is forthright, not overly sophisticated, and uncompromising.

The most widely known Cui Jian piece is *"Yi wu suo you"* ("I Have Nothing"). Here is a translation of its lyrics:

I used to endlessly ask
When will you go with me?
But you always laughed at me.
I have nothing.

I want to give you my dreams
And there is still my freedom
But you always laugh at me.
I have nothing.

Oh...when will you go with me?
Oh...when will you go with me?

The ground still passes under my feet;
The deep water still flows.
But you always laugh at me.
I have nothing.

Why haven't you laughed enough?
Why do I always have dreams?
It is hard to face you;
I forever have nothing.

Oh...when will you go with me?
Oh...when will you go with me?

The ground still passes under my feet;
The deep water still flows.
But you always laugh at me.
I have nothing.

I tell you, I have waited a long time.
I'll tell you my last request:
I want to grab your two hands;
So that you will go with me now.

Your hands are trembling
Your tears are flowing
Can it be that you are now telling me
That you love me? I have nothing.[10]

This piece is taken as deeply political, a form of protest music by many Chinese. Of course, it is within a particular interpretive framework that this reception of Cui Jian's music takes place: a framework of poetics, historically conditioned, which has as one of its characteristics a tendency to look for indirect, yet powerfully oppositional, political statements in ostensibly innocuous lyrics.

As an example, let us look at the title to this piece. The Chinese phrase *"Yi wu suo you"* does not present us with a subject: a literal English translation would be "To Have Nothing." However, subject omission is common in colloquial Chinese, and so English translations of this phrase usually (and appropriately) insert the subject "I." The title then translates as "I Have Nothing." This translation fits with the rest of the piece's lyrics, as they appear to be directed from one subject ("I") to another. However, many Chinese, when translating this title into English, translate it not as "I Have Nothing," but as "We Have Nothing." The political ramifications of this interpretive move—of the extension of "I" to "We"—are obvious and powerful.

Due to this practice of interpretation, at which members of the government are also no doubt gifted, one might think that Cui Jian would quickly find himself silenced, in jail, or worse. However, this has not happened yet. Cui Jian's relationship with the government is an interesting example of the particular intersection of politics with economics which contributes heavily to the unstable character of life in China today.

Cui Jian is very famous right now in China. His music is liked very much by a large number of people. The government, for its part, is certainly concerned over the dissemination and popularity of this music. However, silencing one so well-known is not easy, especially at a time when the government is trying to regain a semblance of trust in the wake of the events culminating in the catastrophe of June 4, 1989. Also, the government, which is presently in bad financial shape, benefits financially from Cui Jian's fame and popularity (for example, he raised over a million Chinese dollars in February 1990, in a benefit concert given in the name of the Asian Games). Therefore, although Cui Jian must be careful with regard to direct challenges to the current regime, he in a sense has a certain control over the government due to his financial worth and his popularity. This mutual give and take—this mutual control—is dynamic, fluid, tense, and unstable.

In March 1989, Cui Jian gave three concert performances at Beijing's 2,000-seat Council Hall, a massive "Soviet" building converted into a theater. There he performed "I Have Nothing" and "Rock and Roll on the New Long March." Students and others in attendance jumped to their feet and began to sing, a practice previously uncommon among Chinese audiences, but which is becoming more frequent at rock 'n' roll concerts. The authorities, who had already banned Cui Jian from performing live during parts of 1987 and 1988, felt severely threatened by the boisterousness and intensity of the audience's physical response. Shortly thereafter, Cui Jian released the cassette *Rock and Roll on the New Long March:* a musically broad, lyrically incisive, nine-song effort. The title cut reflected an interesting nostalgia about Mao, referring to the historic march as authentic and meritorious, while casting aspersions on Deng's "materialistic" new Long March to modernization. To Cui Jian, rock 'n' roll was potentially an authentic manifestation of the people's best aspirations, just like the real Long March, while the current autocratic and materialist trends were corruptions of that ideal.

Other selections on the cassette included the rap-style number "It's Not That I Don't Understand," a work that cited the fast pace of societal change and the awakening of the singer (or perhaps the Chinese people) to find a future unlike the one imagined 20 years before; and "Start Over From the Beginning," a piece about the anxiety and alienation of contemporary Chinese youth, with the title suggesting a possible political solution.

In this recording, Cui Jian not only expanded the lyrical and political boundaries of Chinese pop/rock, he also experimented stylistically with a variety of musical influences. The title cut contains some rhythmic references to reggae; there are several places where an interest in North American country music is both rhythmically and melodically apparent; and rhythm and blues-style saxophone solos permeate the work. All in all, this recording stands as the most important work yet released within the realm of Chinese popular music. It is consistently sold out in stores from Beijing to Hong Kong, and there is a healthy black market in the sale of dubbed copies.

Anti-Hegemonic Aspects of Chinese Popular Music

In the field of popular music, the masses' conception of popular music results, to some extent, from that selected part of the world's popular music culture which the government allows over the mass media. In this respect, the mass media can be effective partners with the dominant forces in the hegemonic process. To the extent that the Chinese populace conceives of popular music as that which they hear over these media, and to the extent that the government can and does actually control what is heard through these media, this music becomes affectively defined in such a way as not to oppose the government's hegemonic objectives—objectives which, simply stated, involve the control of meaning. In practice, control over what is and is not heard over the mass media is problematic, as is control over the meaning of a musical event once it takes place. There are many areas or foci of the struggle for meaning which involve mass-mediated culture; we would like to emphasize three which seem particularly relevant.

First, the dominant power cannot completely control what is presented via the mass media. The dominant technology in China for the dissemination of popular music is the cassette tape. These are sold on the streets in Chinese cities, and foreign music tapes are constantly being brought in from outside by returning Chinese and by visitors from other countries. The reproducibility and ease of transport of cassette technology has profound effects on the producer-consumer relationship: it, in fact, restructures this relationship by frustrating any attempt, by the government, at total control of distribution and content.[11]

Second, the ways people experience music through the mass media are varied and also uncontrollable. The exceptional flexibility of the mass media regarding the possible situations in which media can deliver cultural products is a two-edged sword. On the one hand, this flexibility extends the "reach" of government-controlled messages deep into the lives of the populace. On the other hand, this reach, in a sense, exceeds the government's grasp, for there is less control over the specific and concrete reception and use of a given broadcast. Modern electronic mass media, therefore, do not lend themselves easily to totalized manipulation.

And finally, people's responses are not so easily controllable. Seemingly innocuous love songs are capable of becoming burning torches of political commitment; songs meant to influence affective and conceptual development one way can be immediately, or at a later time, subverted into the service of oppositional positions. One good example of this second type occurred when university students in Beijing, fed up with being forced to attend "meeting after boring meeting" where they were to be "re-educated" into Marxist thought, spontaneously broke out into revolutionary songs, confounding, confusing, and frustrating the meeting's Party cadre organizers, who were there, after all, to try to re-instill (after the events of June 4, 1989) a revolutionary spirit into the "counter-revolutionary" students. The various possible uses for music, and the situational pressures of the music-listening event preclude any dominant power from totally controlling responses and interpretations.

In sum, it is in the very nature of mass musics to simultaneously provide increased resources for the hegemonic programs of the dominant power (in this case, the Communist Party) and for the anti-hegemonic programs of either special groups within the populace (as in the case of Yaogunyue performers and fans) or the populace as a whole. The endemic indeterminacy of musical meaning couples with the mass media's tendency—through the objectification of performance into a commodity (the cassette)—to provide great freedom vis-a-vis the potential contexts of musical experience to severely compromise governmental attempts at the control of this experience—and therefore of musical meaning and social response.

There are, of course, moments when anti-hegemonic statements on the part of some performers are there for all to see. In the spring of 1989, Cui Jian performed one of his pieces, called "A Piece of Red Cloth"—a song that attacks governmental abuse of power—with the students in Tiananmen Square. An Agence France-Press photo from a January 28, 1990 concert pictures Cui Jian performing this song while blindfolded by a piece of red cloth. The statements within this song and by these performance gestures are undoubtedly anti-government, and serve as powerful foci—as enactments of and invitations to community—for a youth alienated from and angered by government corruption, inefficiency, and insensitivity.

But it is the intention of this chapter to point out that, in addition to such moments as described above, it is in the very nature of popular music, as a mass-mediated and mass-distributed commodity "consumed" through performance on privately owned (and therefore privately controlled) playback machines, to evade the control of experience/meaning/response by any power whatsoever. And in China, where the majority of popular music is heard via cassette decks (the dual cassette deck—with dubbing capability—is the most popular), governmental control is further compromised by the empowerment of the individual listener to record and/or dub as he or she pleases.[12]

We believe that this argument adds a subtlety heretofore lacking in most discussions of the meaning—too often reduced to the effect—of popular music for an audience. The forces working against hegemony within China are not limited to the fact that "cassette technology…offers the potential for diversified, democratic control of the means of musical production"[13] through the empowerment of unofficial channels of distribution—though they certainly include this development. Rather, these forces are endemic to the nature of the construction of meaning as a creative act—a relational act in which an individual invests (and simultaneously creates) him or herself. As Peter Manuel correctly points out, popular music can be viewed as an "arena of negotiation," an "active participant in mediation and expression of broader conflicts and tendencies."[14] In China, this negotiation—always power-based—frequently breaks out into open struggle. But the struggle is not simply over what music will be heard, what it will sound like, and who will control its production; it is also over what it means. And the latter cannot be reduced to the former.

Since June 4, 1989

The government, since the events culminating in the violence of June 1989, has begun a process of tightening its control, both economically and politically, over the Chinese population. It seems that this incident shook awake those arms of the Party which had, in the 1980s, remained largely dormant: included were arms whose function it is to oversee the implementation of the Party's typically didactic artistic policies. For example, appeals are being made to install a program of music education at the primary grade levels, a program whose goal would be instilling in children a love for and appreciation of traditional Chinese folksong. This would be part of a general program of recommitment to the political education of the young—an education which would, of course, emphasize Marxist-Leninist-Maoist tenets, and presumably would have little sympathy for any type of popular culture not useful toward this end.

The government is beginning to move against those involved with popular music. The popular Taiwanese singer Hou Dejian, who participated in the demonstrations in Tiananmen Square, was forced to leave the country, and his music is banned from sale. Several concerts of Cui Jian's have been canceled, and his pieces have been directly criticized by music officials.[15] Those few scholars attempting to work in the field of popular music constantly run a great risk of criticism and censure by the Party.

In addition, striking changes have taken place since the Tiananmen incident in the music that appears over the mass media, especially television. Before June 1989, it was common to see popular music broadcasts on television any night of the week. After June 1989, these shows gradually disappeared from the screen, to be replaced by showings of films (mostly made during the 1950s) exalting the events and heroes of the Communist Revolution.

These moves on the part of a government which has lost the confidence of its people intensify the struggle over the control of musical meaning. By eliminating certain voices from the social dialogue, the Party hopes to tip the scales in its direction vis-a-vis the construction of this meaning. But the social practices of production and consumption—the creative aspects of popular music as process—are constantly breaking through the governmental nets which try to control them (and through them, the people). Instead, people are using these empowering moments to give impetus to a new revolution: a kind of affective restructuring,[16] the creation of which does not bode well for the totalitarian goals of the current regime. Struggles over the meaning of popular music are struggles between different visions of what China is and (more importantly) what it should be, and reveal what has been called a "schizophrenic conflict between [the government's] vision...and a quite different reality."[17]

Having adopted the Party's mandate for modernization, the people now reject the Party for its lack of progress toward this goal. Having been asked to be (and taught to be) angry about life's conditions (so that they would get involved in the Socialist Revolution), the people now direct this anger at the Party itself—at its corruption, its inefficiency, and its insensitivity to the people. For many young people and many intellectuals as well, *yaogun yinyue,* and especially that of Cui Jian, both expresses and gives objective presence to this anger; and the anger, in its turn, empowers the music in its opposition. Governmental attempts to control popular music practices may be effective with some, but they fuel the anger of many. And this anger is outside the control of the Party. As one university student said:

> Cui Jian says things that we all feel, but cannot say. We all hate the government. Cui Jian speaks for us. He says my feelings. This is one tape that I will keep forever.

Postscript

In the summer of 1991 a second Cui Jian recording was released, entitled *Jiejue* (China Beiguang Audiovisual Art Corporation, BSL 029). This title is difficult to translate directly into English: its use, usually as a verb, tends toward meaning an activity of solving or resolving a difficulty; but it can also carry the connotation of "getting rid of."

The music on this recording continues the stylistic traits of *yaogun yinyue* discussed in this chapter. In addition, several features should be noted. There is a move toward a rougher and faster sound, using a more distorted guitar timbre and quicker tempos; the vocal delivery is rougher, less melodic, and more rhythmic; the album as a whole sounds less studio-produced and more spontaneous (it contains one live performance); and the lyrics continue to express the anger and frustration of the Chinese youth. One song ("The Last Shot") obviously refers the audience to the events of June 4, 1989 (the lyrics of this piece are omitted from the cassette notes).

This cassette album was originally banned from sale within the boundaries of the People's Republic of China. It has since been released. This again shows the ambivalence of the regime toward Cui Jian, and is indicative of intra-party debates over the removal of this voice—and the anger it embodies—from the arena of public discourse. But given what we know about the anti-hegemonic activities of Chinese youth and intellectuals, it should come as no surprise to discover that the sounds of this new cassette were well-known within these communities prior to its official release. As the dubbing of cassette tapes has become a political act, opposition to the governing regime has become simultaneously suppressed and empowered. And since its release, the wide availability of this music of anger and frustration has continued to empower opposition to the regime. *Yaogun yinyue's* role as an objectification of anti-government feeling—as a resource for use in political opposition—has intensified.

Concert for Democracy in China, Hong Kong. (Photos courtesy of the Hong Kong Alliance in Support of Patriotic Democratic Movements of China)

All for Freedom

The Rise of Patriotic/Pro-Democratic Popular Music in Hong Kong in Response to the Chinese Student Movement

Joanna Ching-Yun Lee

> I, in the past, was too lazy to think.
> I have never been concerned about my old home.
> I only look for the easy life and peace of mind.
> You, knowing that you will be fatally wounded,
> Still bare your chest to the guns,
> Determined, though it means death
> For democracy to reign.[1]

The Chinese student democracy movement produced a tremendous impact on indigenous Cantonese popular music (cantopop) in Hong Kong from May 1989 to December 1990.[2] Cantopop assumed a transformed identity as a political tool during this period. Its lyrics mobilized the masses in political rallies that supported Chinese students in the heyday of May-June 1989, and more varieties of political cantopop lyrics continued to appear in Hong Kong long after the crush of the movement. Political cantopop originates from and is fully integrated into mainstream cantopop. It is commercial in nature.

The types of political cantopop lyrics have changed during the process. Patriotic, community-mobilizing lyrics (produced prior to June 4, 1989) are immediately succeeded by satirical lyrics that ridicule claims of the government of the People's Republic of China, lamentations that mourn the dead students, and pledges to continue the democracy movement. Much cantopop produced in 1990 contained indirect social references or political analogies, and this repertoire is still growing.

Political cantopop evolved into commentaries that extended beyond the issue of democracy in China by early 1990. Although such cantopop began as a response in support of the democracy movement in China, it assumed a different identity soon afterward in its place of origin. It evolved into direct commentaries on the political changes in the home front. Directed not only at the "mother country," such cantopop involved the listener in social and political issues of Hong Kong.

A preliminary catalogue of 65 such cantopop songs appeared in a Hong Kong cultural weekly, *Contemporary,* in February 1990.[3] More political cantopop was produced and released after February 1990, either relating to the situation in China, or blatantly commenting on the bleak political future of Hong Kong. Since March 1990, more productions of quasi-patriotic popular music for Hong Kong have appeared in Hong Kong. One of these projects was even promoted by the government radio station and subsidized by the Hong Kong-based International Bank of Asia.

The Political Context of Hong Kong

Hong Kong, a British colony since 1842 which blossomed into the principal financial center of Southeast Asia in the 1980s, is a city hypersensitive to the smallest changes in the People's Republic of China's political climate.[4] A city of more than 5.7 million inhabitants,[5] 99 percent ethnically Chinese, with a certain but rather pessimistic political future, Hong Kong will be returned to the People's Republic of China's sovereignty starting on July 1, 1997, under the prescribed political arrangement of "one country, two systems."[6]

Political uncertainty and hence financial pessimism have plagued the colony ever since the early 1980s.[7] An emigration wave started from the late 1970s and has grown three-fold since 1987.[8] As of 1990, the British colonial system had not instituted democracy at any political or legislative policy-making level for the average Hong Kong citizen.[9] However, Hong Kong citizens were also known for their political apathy.

Hong Kong, according to many who live there, is a transitional stopover where money is easily made, and from which to depart to a "permanent" country.[10] According to them, Hong Kong is not a permanent home, and no roots are to be left. Since no roots are to be left, and all that is to be gained is financial, few Hong Kong citizens were ever active in politics in their own city, let alone in the People's Republic of China. However, the events in China in the spring of 1989 became the catalyst for many in Hong Kong in their search for an identity.[11] This phenomenon was new, and was also widely reported in the international press.[12] The Chinese pro-democracy movement became a storm that moved tens of thousands in Hong Kong to demonstrate their love for their "mother country." The birth of Chinese patriotism, therefore, provided the impetus for subsequent political concern and involvement within Hong Kong itself.

The Chinese democracy movement started on April 15, 1989 to mourn the death of Hu Yaobang, who was revered by youths as one of the most "uncorrupted" of the Chinese leaders. Hu was disgraced and forced from power by the authorities in January 1987.[13] The student protest in April 1989 was in no way politically threatening, nor did the students expect their movement to develop and to be empowered by the international media. By early May, the Beijing students organized more rallies to commemorate the seventieth anniversary of the May 4 Movement.[14] Participants used banners that expressed their love of their country, wish for a less corrupted government, and their hope for the well-being of the political system. They did not know that their small beginning would become the spearhead for a new order in Chinese politics.

The main event that triggered worldwide attention during those months was the declaration of martial law on May 20 and the subsequent news blackout. This single decision by Deng Xiaoping, Li Peng, and Yang Shangkun became the turning point of the whole movement and directly changed the nature of the protest. The outcry against this brutal decision shook every Chinese, especially overseas Chinese, who prided themselves as upholders of their "mother country" and supporters of their "brothers and sisters" living in the homeland.[15] From May 20, 1989 onward, an unprecedented number of Hong Kong citizens participated in numerous rallies. One of these, held on May 28, 1989, was attended by one-fifth of the population.[16]

It is difficult to ascertain the numerous reasons why the democracy movement of 1989 created such a concerted response from the people of Hong Kong while earlier democracy demonstrations in Beijing in 1986 created no effect. One of these reasons, however, is clear. As the date of July 1, 1997 drew near, Hong Kong citizens became more sensitive in their political consciousness and more daring in their political acts. When Hong Kong citizens were not consulted in 1983 about their own political future, a sizeable portion of the society suddenly realized its own powerlessness. This portion is mainly the educated middle class. Many learned an important lesson from this experience: they began to understand the importance of active participation in political and social movements. The 1986 democracy movement was short-lived, and there was too little time for the masses to be mobilized. When the opportunity for supporting the Chinese democracy movement came again in 1989, Hong Kong citizens did not hesitate to show their power. However, the power of Hong Kong citizens is very limited: they could only support the Beijing students from afar. This frustration at being unable to contribute more to China dampened the morale of Hong Kong citizens. This same frustration intensified as soon as the democracy movement faced difficulties after June 4, 1989. Large-scale popular support in Hong Kong almost vanished without a trace by 1990.[17]

The Chinese democracy movement of 1989 is also full of contradictions. First of all, the student leaders themselves did not have a concrete plan for an alternative government or social system if they were to succeed in toppling the government. The student group itself was not cohesive. Second, the democracy movement in China was limited to the big cities, and only students, intellectuals, and urban workers participated. The ideals and motives for joining the movement were mixed, especially when patriotic fervor and various opportunisms came into play by late May 1989. When demonstrations became a daily affair, participation became more voluntary, less a function of social pressure. Third, the international media made the movement much larger than life, as it became more and more euphoric.

The Musical Context of Hong Kong

Before the 1970s, Hong Kong's popular music scene was clearly divided between the mainstay of Hong Kong-Taiwanese popular music sung in Mandarin, rather than Cantonese (the indigenous dialect in Hong Kong), and Anglo-American popular music.[18] Almost none of these songs contained local references, since they were neither solely produced nor exclusively marketed for the population of Hong Kong. Mandarin songs were popular in the colony, since melodies tended to be "Chinese" in character, and the dialect was still accessible. Anglo-American popular music, however, was closely associated with better-educated urban youth. This Anglo-American pop is imported and consumed without either dubbing into the local dialect or mediation of any sort.[19] The local folk music tradition is very weak, since Hong Kong does not truly possess its own cultural traditions, but only inherits forms of art and entertainment from China and the West. The People's Republic of China, from the 1950s to the early 1970s, was not successful in exporting much of its own "popular music" to Hong Kong. Although revolutionary songs and revolutionary operas were the staple "music for the people" in mainland China in those decades of the Cultural Revolution, they were simply not readily available in Hong Kong, nor was their dissemination encouraged by the British government.[20]

Cantopop became the dominant entertainment music in Hong Kong only from the mid-1970s, with the development of Hong Kong as a thriving financial city, and the growth of the popular music and entertainment industries that were to dominate all of Southeast Asia.[21] The style of cantopop is derivative of the production, marketing, and promotion of contemporary Japanese popular music. Cantopop attracts mostly urban youth, who can surely afford to support the market. The whole entertainment business is most lucrative, since the media specifically cultivate such popular culture.[22] Pop singers often become film stars with the same level of popularity, since fans and followers are often devoted and supportive. By the 1980s, the local production of cantopop evolved and stabilized into a style of contemporary soft rock.[23] Lyrics are almost exclusively of an amorous nature. Heavier rock music is rarely used for the setting of Cantonese lyrics.[24]

The reasons for the rise of political cantopop in 1989 are multifarious: patriotic fervor, political idealism, and commercial entertainment-business incentives all played their parts in this phenomenon. Without the commercial apparatus of cantopop, the various cantopop projects in support of the Chinese students could not have been organized and mobilized. Without the patriotic fervor and political idealism of many of the cantopop stars, fundraising concerts could not have taken place. By no means did all of Hong Kong's prominent cantopop stars participate in these activities. However, there is a core of around ten popular musicians and entertainers who have participated throughout this cause. They have devoted time, energy, and have also given themselves freely to the service of fundraising for the pro-democracy political organization, the Hong Kong Alliance in Support of Patriotic Democratic Movement in China.[25] According to the Hong Kong Alliance's financial report, by February 1990 a total of US $3.2 million had been raised since the establishment of the organization. Out of that total, $1.9 million was raised from the 12-hour Concert for Democracy in China.[26]

All for Freedom

On May 23, 1989, 150 leading singers and entertainers of Hong Kong showed their solidarity with the Chinese students by recording a newly composed song entitled "All for Freedom." The song was hand delivered by one of the Hong Kong singers to the Beijing students and broadcast in Tiananmen Square on May 24, 1989. On the same day, it was also broadcast in a "Down with Li Peng" mass rally in Hong Kong. The song lyrics, as well as the simplified score, were also printed in local newspapers on May 24. "All for Freedom" was released in Hong Kong as a cassette in late June 1989, and all the proceeds were donated to the Hong Kong Alliance.[27] The delay in the release of the "All for Freedom" cassette was due to negotiations regarding royalties and rights among record companies, since the 150 singers belonged to different record labels. The copyright of the recording now belongs to the Hong Kong Alliance in Support of Patriotic Democratic Movement in China.

When the cassette was released, the liner notes contained a list of all the participants, and a statement that supported the Beijing students: "We fervently respond to the Beijing students' democracy-seeking, freedom-seeking, patriotic activities. Together we recorded 'All for Freedom' on May 23, 1989 to express our support in the spirit of democracy."

"All for Freedom" is a unique dual-dialect song: the verse is sung in Cantonese; but the key phrases are sung in Mandarin (italicized below), the official dialect of the People's Republic of China.[28]

> Surging high, the great ambition in our chests.
> Righteousness fills our hearts,
> Bravely creating a new territory.
> Risking our lives, we march forward—
> Unending road—we rely on our passion.
> You and I will hold hands forever,
> To face the road full of brambles and thorns.
> Our hot sweat flows, but we will not tire.
> Our hot blood flows, but we have no fear.
> *We love freedom,*
> *All for Freedom.*
> You and I, bravely advance
> Hand in hand.
> *Nothing can disperse,*
> *Nothing can ward off*
> Our determination, which swells to fill the earth
> And wraps around a thousand mountains.

The first of its kind in which two Chinese dialects are interpolated, this is a cantopop song in which Hong Kong popular singers are seemingly establishing a dialogue with Beijing students. The ideas of connection and support are clearly evident in phrases such as "You and I will hold hands forever" and "You and I, bravely advance hand in hand." The concept of a "united front" is also evident—the identity of Hong Kong singers is tied in with the Beijing hunger-strikers and their supporters. Every phrase in this song is a slogan, referring to support and encouragement in a struggle that seems hopeful and uplifting.

The musical style of "All for Freedom" belongs to heavier rock, which is rather unusual in the milieu of cantopop songs. The composer, Lowell Lo, is known for his deviation from conventional cantopop.[29] The nature of the lyrics and the timing of the political events, however, conditioned the reception of the song. "All for Freedom" entered the pop chart in the last week of May 1989, and went immediately to the top for three weeks (June 4-24, 1989).[30] There was already media-hype while the singers were recording in the studio—young teenage fans mobbed the small EMI studio while the recording was in progress, and measures were taken to prevent the crowds from disturbing the singers.[31]

There are, in fact, two versions of "All for Freedom." The initial choral version was recorded on May 23 in the EMI studio in Hong Kong, within

24 hours of the completion of the song.[32] The media gave this recording a very high profile, and quoted many of these singers and their thoughts about the suffering students in Beijing. The second version, finished a day later, involves the "We Are the World" format: every singer is allotted a solo phrase, and the extended version lasts twelve and a half minutes. It is understandable that managers and record companies were reluctant to have their stars included only in a chorus of 150. The wish to isolate the voices and create the same "big star" effect of "We Are the World" is realized in the extended version.

The production and reception of "All for Freedom" already attest to the inherent problems of the support activities in Hong Kong. "All for Freedom" marked the first time in Hong Kong's history that cantopop became a politically rallying force. While patriotic and pro-democratic fervor is predominant in the singers' minds, commercial instincts of the record companies hampered the immediate release of the extended version of "All for Freedom." The core of cantopop singers, who were themselves heavily involved in the democracy movement, became the organizers and the motivating force guiding other cantopop stars. As a movement, "All for Freedom" is idealistic on the one hand, and promotional on the other. It is impossible to separate these two elements. While it is important to preach democracy, it is as crucial that the activity is given a high public profile. The high public profile, however, would naturally bring in commercial interests, since every cantopop star is also a commercial artist. Hong Kong's record industry, however, was also very sensitive to the political issue at that time, and the proceeds of the sales were eventually agreed upon and the money donated to the Hong Kong Alliance.

Under the auspices of the Hong Kong Alliance, the first Concert for Democracy in China was organized and televised live on May 27, 1989 as a 12-hour music marathon. Most of the singers who recorded "All for Freedom" participated in the Concert for Democracy in China, which lasted from 10 am to 10 pm on that day.[33] While this was a benefit concert in which singers participated out of their free will, it is impossible to rule out publicity motives in their participation. However, most of the singers who were involved also spoke openly about their opinions and feelings about the Chinese democracy movement. Many of these conversations and interviews were subsequently published in the local newspapers. This musical celebratory marathon was attended by more than 200,000 people, all of whom waved yellow ribbons throughout the concert.[34]

Another political pop song was first performed in the Concert for Democracy in China by local cantopop singer Danny Summer. "Question" is, in fact, a Cantonese setting of Giorgio Moroder's "Circles of the Human Chain."[35]

Why is there mud on their hands? Why is the crowd trembling?
Why are they fervently praying to heaven but do not know to
   question?
Why do we doubt what's right or wrong? Why do we hesitate to go
   ahead?
Why do we mutter our curse but dare not question?
Layers of encircling walls on all sides. Though the road is long, we
   have to go on.
Why did the crowd cry on that day? The message of their hearts is
   clear.

Although the lyrics might appear vague and general at first glance,
the timing of this song, as well as the context of its first performance, can
be construed as providing questions for the people, asking them "questions" about their own destiny. One could interpret the lyrics further: they
describe the political situation in China before the democracy movement,
the doubts of the people, and a pledge to carry on the fight. These lyrics
challenge the listener to get involved in the movement and to question the
authorities—exactly what the Beijing students intended to achieve. The
musical style of "Question" is similar to that of "All for Freedom." "Question"
is another marked departure from the usual cantopop, because it has a
much heavier beat and more angular melodies.

Danny Summer also premiered "Mama, I've Done Nothing Wrong" at
the May 27 concert. The title of the song is inspired by a hunger-striker's
banner which was shown in the television news.[36] The reference to
"mother" extends beyond the human relationship, and includes the relation
between the motherland and its diaspora.

I don't need others to decide for me whether this is right.
I don't want anyone to determine my crime.
I don't want the sun to rise again, rise again once more just to
   imprison the truth.
I don't want to helplessly whisper my grievances.
I don't want to numbly sigh about the storm.
I cannot let my sorrow go—that sorrow—and coldly ignore it again.

Mama, let me hear the words from your heart.
How many nightmares you'd rather not think about,
You do not dare scold me for.

Mama, I'm going far away, please forget about me.
The wind is blowing, rain beating.
I don't want to, don't want to be weak again.
Mama, I've done nothing wrong.
Mama, I've done nothing wrong.
Together, you and I, let's continue on,
We have undying courage.

The heavy footprints of the people,
As they step on the road of eternal struggle.
The angry breathing of the people,
Overwhelming the voices of repression.

A coldness still infiltrates the air in the wind,
Tears of the spring rain still flow across the earth.
How I hope that one day, one day,
The world will become beautiful forever.

Danny Summer's album, *You Awaken My Soul,* which contains the two songs discussed above, is the first commercially released cantopop album in which more than half of its songs are devoted to the Chinese democracy movement. The album was also clearly marketed as such: the cover of the album portrays Danny Summer standing in front of a blood-red background.[37] It was released in mid-July 1989, but did not enjoy very good sales: only 60 percent of the singer's earlier albums.[38] However, "Mama, I've Done Nothing Wrong," which was already released to the radio stations by early June 1989, was among the Top Thirty on the pop charts for almost two months.[39]

The Concert for Democracy in China became a symbol of Hong Kong's solidarity with the Chinese students, and it was blatantly organized against the wishes of the Chinese government. The artists were not afraid of being "blacklisted" by the People's Republic of China, and their participation in the concert was seen as a challenge to the Chinese leaders. The possibility of retaliation from China was already in every journalist's mind even when the first recording of "All for Freedom" was in session.[40]

The political message of the above examples is clear—there was widespread support for the Chinese students among the Hong Kong populace, and the cantopop singers' involvement in this political cause elevated the profile of public fervor and support. Hong Kong citizens were constantly encouraged to actively participate in the cause, which, at that time, included monetary donations and participation in demonstrations. The above song lyrics were all produced by the end of May 1989. Although the lyrics were wary of the struggle, they were still hopeful of the future.

Cantopop after June 4, 1989

After the massacre of June 4, 1989, the lyrics of pro-democracy cantopop took up different themes, and were set with much darker tones. The most blatant reference to the crush of the democracy movement is Lowell Lo's album *1989,* with title songs "1989 Prelude" and "1989."[41] Both songs were composed and set to lyrics by Lo and Susan Tang, who are the creators of "All for Freedom."[42] The title "1989" already provides an immediate temporal frame of reference for the singer and his audience. Since the album is an undisguised critique of the Chinese government, it was received with caution by the media when it was first released. By late 1989, the Hong Kong media was wary of criticisms from China.[43] "1989 Prelude" and "1989" were tacitly banned at the Hong Kong radio stations, where they received no airplay.[44]

"1989 Prelude"

Why is the sky so dark?
The stars are not shining, maybe it'll soon be dawn.
Thousands of people awaiting the rise of the brilliant sun,
Its beams to enlighten China.
The whole sky is gloomy, from the bottom of my chilly heart rosy
    clouds arise;
The furious, fearful cries of the democracy movement rise from four
    corners in chorus,
The will of the people becomes a new commandment, unity brings
    new strength
To usher my country, my homeland into a new era.

"1989"

How heavy, my heart.
Bitterness covers the great earth.
Hope is overshadowed.
People's expectation has become naught.
How bitter, this China.
Our hope for democracy has neither been abandoned nor for-
    gotten.
Our movement hasn't seen its end. Where there's a will, there's a
    way.
The human will has not eclipsed. The people's determination will
    become strong.
Our hearts forever united. Our hands forever joined.

The lyrics contain clear references to the undying pledge of the people to the cause of democracy. The musical style of these two songs is much mellower and ballad-like. "1989 Prelude" and "1989" also contain introductions played on Chinese instruments, and melodies that are quasi-Chinese, pentatonic, and highly folklike.

"Blood-red Dawn," another song from *1989*, contains similar politically intense lyrics.[45]

Who gave the order?
Who opened fire?
Who fell on the ground—this night?
Who can redeem this sin?
Who can stop it?
Who can disperse this omen?

Wounds dripping with blood.
The time of struggle passes slowly.

The eternal scars—
The result of this suffering is a road overflowing with blood.

The gradual dawn—
The sword that slaughtered the city—
Who can wash the blood-red road?
Wounds dripping with blood—
Let great anger breed more anger.

The dawn to which the lyrics refer is obviously that of June 4, 1989. The events that happened in Tiananmen Square are vividly depicted in the above lyrics, and the last phrase shows the determination of people who are still willing to continue the fight for democracy.

Another wave of anti-People's Republic of China propagandistic cantopop was produced during Christmas 1989. One of Hong Kong's foremost lyricists, James Wong, set ironical and farcical democracy lyrics to well-known Christmas tunes.[46] Phrases such as "Deng Xiaoping is coming to town" and "Li Peng asked me what I want for Christmas, and I said I want a passport" epitomize the frustrations of average Hong Kong citizens about their future.

Many political rallies were organized by the Hong Kong Alliance in late 1989 and 1990, and cantopop was always an essential part of these gatherings. The issue of the performance or the broadcasting of popular music in political rallies led to an incident on September 12, 1989, during "the Hundredth Day Mourning of the June 4th Massacre" rally, and created much dissent among the Hong Kong Alliance's supporters.[47] The controversy resulted in some supporters leaving the rally to protest what seemed to them more like a cantopop concert than a political memorial.

Concerts for Democracy in China: U.S.-Canada Tour in May 1990

A considerable number of singers and entertainers have participated in almost all of the rallies organized by the Hong Kong Alliance since May 27, 1989, and in concerts that are fundraising as well as spirit-raising for the democratic cause.[48] In May 1990, a U.S.-Canada, six-city Concerts for Democracy in China tour, with a core of eight popular singers, raised a net amount of U.S. $380,000.[49] These funds were then contributed to North American-Chinese democracy associations in the United States and Canada. These Concerts for Democracy in China were blatantly political: Mr. Wah Szeto, the chairman of the Hong Kong Alliance, traveled with the performers, and spoke and sang at every concert.[50] The atmosphere of the North

American Concerts for Democracy in China was charged with patriotic fervor. Rallying political cries were heard loudly and clearly even in these concert halls in North America, 11 months after the crush of the democracy movement in China.

Political, entertainment, and fundraising motives were mixed in the Concerts for Democracy in China tour. In many ways, these concerts were organized along the same lines as the original one on May 27, 1989, but on a much smaller scale. The concerts began with "All for Freedom," after which each singer took a turn to sing one or two solos, and these songs included not only cantopop, but also Mandarin-pop, Chinese folk songs, patriotic songs, protest songs used in May-June 1989 in Beijing,[51] and even "Blowing in the Wind." The mixture of cantopop, a few Mandarin songs, and a few English-language songs reflects the organizers' wish to engage the entire audience—overseas Chinese and non-Chinese who identify with any of the dialects or languages. In order to broaden the popular appeal of these concerts, and not restrict them to the Chinese who emigrated from Hong Kong, the organizers also invited Taiwanese pop singer Lo Dayou to participate. During the concert, all the performers walked into the midst of the audience, holding donation boxes in their hands.

Cantopop 1990:
Issues of Chinese and Hong Kong Politics

Other cantopop lyrics may not be as direct as "1989 Prelude," but they may contain subtexts that are inherently political in nature. For example, love lyrics can provide an analogy of the relationship between government and its people. Some songs employ titles such as "Dialogue," inferring the dialogue between the authorities and students in late May 1989; and "Lying," alluding to the lies the Chinese government told the world about the massacre.

Another cantopop song, "Ten Firefighter Boys," is a parable about the democratic spirit.[52] It uses the analogy of ten youths to chronicle the sequence of events in the democracy movement, and to warn people not to be afraid, and not to be overcome by solitude in the struggle to free China. However, the musical style of this song is markedly different from earlier examples given in this article. The light, Latin dancing rhythm accentuates the playful quality of this parable. "Ten Firefighter Boys" is one of 11 songs from a recording entitled *Madness* performed by the Tat Ming Pair, released in January 1990.[53]

On a certain midnight, fire alarms resound all over,
The volunteer firefighters in town
All gathered by the bridge.
Of the ten determined firefighter boys,

One felt he lacked training.
Since it looked rather dangerous, he just registered and left

…

Of the ten determined firefighter boys,
At this juncture only seven remained.
They gathered by the bridge,
Only to argue about the way to fight the fire.
Three of them were cross and left,
Swearing never to see the others again.
There still remained four reliable ones,
But one is all talk with not much action.
Earnest in his theories, but he won't tackle the real smoke and fire.
The three who were left behind
Could not stop the blazing fire.
In an instant they were buried under this great catastrophe

…

10 minus 1 is 9,
9 minus 1 is 8,
8 minus 1 is 7,
7 minus 1 is 6,
6 minus 1 is 5… [fades]

The Tat Ming Pair specifically created "Madness" to focus on the Chinese democracy movement and the impending political future of Hong Kong. Another song in this album is in fact a "catalogue," in which the names of famous personalities of Britain, Hong Kong, and China are listed one after another. The song title reads: "This list contains left, right, good, evil, big, and small: arranged not in order of importance."[54] This cantopop song is a blatant political pun, and is certainly received as such. The melody is in fact traditional: it is a "rock" version of a famous Cantonese operatic tune.

Another song from the same album of which the lyrics are exceptionally brilliant is "Questioning Heaven." Lyricist Zhou Yaohui researched old traditional Chinese legends in order to evoke the story of the Mid-Autumn Festival. The subject matter of this song deals with a traditional Chinese character trait—people blame heaven, but do not take the initiative to change circumstances around them. "Questioning Heaven" ("Tian Wen") is originally a section taken from the Chinese classic "Chuci," a shamanistic song.[55] The images are very vibrant, colorful, and mythical.

Miserable, beneath the flame in the sky,
The earth is wordless and silent.
The wind stirs up purple mist and clouds.
The people huddle in terror.

Who was he who raised his bow and arrow,
Aiming at the flame in the sky?
Who was she who stole the magic pill and rose to the sky,
Watching over the dark sky in her moon palace?

...

Raving beneath the dark flame,
The coarse cries are from the crows.
A sky of red snowflakes swirl.
When will the curse of a thousand autumns end?
Who dares raise his bow and arrow,
To aim at the arrogant flame?
Who won't try to steal the magic pill and rise to the sky,
Even to watch over the dark sky in the lonesome moon palace?
Although there are complaints about Heaven, Heaven can't be
    questioned.
All the sentient lives sigh; life can't be questioned

...

"Questioning Heaven" was at the top of the pop chart from December 3-16, 1989, and it was among the Top Thirty up to February 3, 1990. Although this song contains no direct reference to the democracy movement, the focus on "questioning heaven" as the ultimate authority evokes much food for thought in the Chinese mind.

In 1990, Hong Kong cantopop witnessed an increased output that referred specifically to the situation of its own people, especially regarding politics and emigration—Hong Kong citizens are not British by nationality, nor are they totally Chinese in identity. The people face the dilemma of staying or leaving as the cloud of 1997 hangs above the city.

The Tat Ming Pair also commented on British-Hong Kong relations in "We Are Both Watching" by the use of another analogy: the bridal pair. The phrase "national status" in the chorus refers pointedly to the political issue at hand in late 1989, when the Hong Kong People Save Hong Kong Campaign lobbied for Hong Kong citizens' right of abode in the United Kingdom.[56]

Changes in this world are too great. I only hope
That we welcome the future and walk towards it together.
Changes in this world are too great. I only hope
We quickly walk together and enter a beautiful country.

Behind the bridal veil, pearls of tears fall.
Gladness within the heart; secretly rejoicing.
The priest said, in joy or sadness,
Our hearts join in harmony in our love song

...

I want to be with you day and night
I want to follow you in your adventures.
Our hearts join in harmony in our love song.
I want to be enthusiastic with you.
I want to be lonely with you.
Whether or not you give me a national status,
Our hearts join in harmony in our national anthem.

It is clear that "national status" is the issue presented in the subtext. The ending of the song is in fact the first three phrases of the British national anthem, "God Save the Queen," played on a synthesizer. Although there are no accompanying words to the anthem, the melody itself is already symbolic.[57]

Other references to 1997 include "Farewell to England," a song which was produced prior to but released after the democracy movement.[58] This song paints the picture of Hong Kong, the sentiments of its people, and the lowering of the British flag on June 30, 1997, the last day that Hong Kong will belong to Britain. The ending also evokes a plea to Prince Charles, by that time, perhaps, the ruler of Britain.

The flag is quietly lowered.
At that moment, the whole world watches—
A hundred year dynasty has ended.
Comrades are once again standing up to say:
From this day, people should remember to unite for 50 years.

Once I laboured from morning till night,
I've remained to the present.
You still seem not able to give up your old passport,
And haven't changed for the one with a new stamp.
This year is an important time.
Of course, with one mind, we'll face the dawning future.
You said you've been to England ten times,
But you didn't even go to see Big Ben once

...

England, farewell, farewell on this day.
My King, farewell tomorrow.
My King Charles, it's now your turn.
Heros can still speak up now.

Other cantopop might not have as clear a political agenda in its lyrical content, but it might contain commentary on the emigration wave. The idea of departure is taken up in other cantopop songs. "Farewell Song" is not directly related to politics or to the democracy movement, yet it reflects the concerns of Hong Kong citizens of the 1990s.[59] The lyrics comment on the brain-drain situation, and lament the situation of a rapidly disintegrating city. Although the lyrics are rather introspective, they provide a very candid commentary of contemporary Hong Kong society. The musical style is most typical of cantopop, and this song is recorded by the most popular male singer of the present generation, Alan Tam.

> Let me close my eyes and count carefully
> The few good friends around me
> Are now carefully checking into other countries.
> But every night, every morning, I only like
> To work diligently and not to look elsewhere.
> Right here, I said, I'll grow old.
>
> Into this city, I've woven my own history.
> To charge ahead in its prosperity, I still love the city;
> To lean on its brilliance, I can't forget its sincerity.
>
> But you said, close your eyes and count backwards.
> Hurry, it is not too soon now.
> You also said you have to start cramming English
> And add up your accountbook,
> Determined to take away every piece of root, every blade of grass.
> Smiling, you ask me to heed your advice.
>
> Though difficult, give it a try anyway. No need to depend on others.
> Toughen your heart and mind, you've got to give it a try.
> There are old friends in other lands to charge ahead with you.
>
> The sorrows of parting entwine my heart.
> The good friends around me who can leave, have gone.
> Like an ant trying to find its way,
> Is it true that one day, I shall be the only lonely one left?

Promoting an Identity for Hong Kong Citizens in 1990: "Dreams of Hong Kong"

Hong Kong is a third world city with the communication networks and financial institutions of the first world. The power of the media is immediate and explosive, and popular artists are often very influential in promoting social causes. The success of pro-democracy cantopop in the market, in raising funds for the Hong Kong Alliance, and in nurturing the political and social consciousness of the average Hong Kong citizen, has empowered cantopop as a genre. "All for Freedom" became a formula for other causes, social or political.

Dreams of Hong Kong is an album released by the government-run Radio Television Hong Kong and financed by the International Bank of Asia.[60] It is only one among many cantopop albums that focus on the future of Hong Kong.[61] The objective of the *Dreams of Hong Kong* project is "to focus Hong Kong people's collective strength on consolidating the local community to build a strong and healthy future."[62] The album is an undisguised morale booster. Only three of its four songs are genuine cantopops: "Our Roots" is written by Angus Tung, a Taiwanese pop musician, and it is recorded in Mandarin by Hong Kong, Taiwanese, and mainland Chinese singers. Tung wanted to "reflect the common heritage bonding all Chinese regardless of their nationalities."[63] Apart from "This Is Our Home," all the songs are "shared" phrase by phrase among the cantopop stars.[64]

Since the early 1980s, Hong Kong has been going through many political changes in preparation for the Chinese takeover. The immanence of the political reality of 1997 never became so heartfelt until the Chinese student movement of 1989, when the population was mobilized for the first time in a common cause. The true identity of Hong Kong citizens, as British dependents without the right of abode in the United Kingdom and with no roots in England save for colonial history, became a pressing political issue in June 1989. Hong Kong citizens have begun to actively identify themselves as Chinese, and some also consider themselves patriotic Chinese, furthering the democratic cause.

Cantopop became an effective genre in sustaining the message of the democracy movement beyond 1989. It has since embraced other issues closer to home, and such lyrics have served to enlighten, to boost courage, and to uphold the image of a city that will hopefully be vibrant forever. It is certainly becoming a progressive force within Hong Kong culture, although it is also commercial in nature. Progressivism and commercialism are not mutually exclusive here. *Dreams of Hong Kong* is commercial and community-conscious at that same time. While "All for Freedom" is a dual-dialect cantopop song which motivated hundreds of thousands to rally for democracy in China, "The Lights of the City" uses Cantonese in the verse but English in the chorus (italicized below).[65]

> Passionate about Hong Kong, all our hearts unite
> To build up Hong Kong, our new hope.
> People of Hong Kong are fearless in self-renewal, and willing to
>   work hard.
> Even more prosperous
> Is this land;
> Even more prosperous
> Is the new Hong Kong:
> Together we build a brilliant tomorrow.
> *This is our home,*
> *This is our dream,*
> *This is our place,*
> *We love Hong Kong.*

Between May 1989 and December 1990, cantopop provided invaluable documentation about a major transition in the politics and society of

Hong Kong. It has charted new areas that were not addressed before: as a cultural form, cantopop is becoming a major force in highlighting political problems, social conditions, and the changing moods of the people in Hong Kong. It is difficult to predict how this political musical trend will develop in the 1990s and beyond 1997. However, as the main expression of popular culture in Hong Kong, cantopop has captured the aspirations, worries, joys, and sadnesses of the people and broadcast them far and wide in the short span of one and a half years.

Appendix 1: Selected List of Cantopop Albums

Album	Release	Artist(s)	Label & Catalog No.
—1989—			
*All for Freedom**	6/22	All Stars	Hong Kong**1989521
You Awaken My Soul	7/11	Danny Summer	BMG 4.280028
Chapter Two	8/9	Fundamental	BMG 4.280022
89	11/17	Lowell Lo	EMI FH-10130
Hong Kong X'mas	12/8	James Wong	Musicad MHS-1089
—1990—			
Madness	1/12	Tat Ming Pair	Polygram 125-4
Dreams on Stage	1/23	Alan Tam	Polygram 842 218-4
Love of Hong Kong	3/19	Sam Hui	Polygram 841 949-4
Dreams of Hong Kong	7/15	All Stars	Radio Television
Wish	11/16	Lowell Lo	EMI FH-10175

* The album contains only one song. Although the fundraising cassette was not available for sale until June 1989, this song was "unofficially" released from its first broadcast and short score publication in newspapers on May 24, 1989.

** Hong Kong Alliance in Support of Patriotic Democratic Movement in China

Appendix 2: A Selected List of the Major Rallies Organized by the Hong Kong Alliance in Support of Patriotic Democratic Movement in China (May 1989-December 1990)*

Date	Rally	Attendance
—1989—		
5/20	Mass Rally in Victoria Park	50,000
5/21	Mass Parade in support of Beijing students	1,000,000
5/24	"Down with Li Peng" mass rally	100,000
5/27	"Concert for Democracy in China"	200,000
5/28	"Worldwide Chinese Mass Parade"	1,500,000
6/4	"Mass Sit-in in Black"	1,500,000
6/24	Mass Rally against Retaliation	10,000
7/4	"Worldwide Chinese Mass Parade"	15,000
9/12	"The Hundredth Day Mourning of June 4th Massacre"	80,000
10/1	"The Road to Democracy in China in Blood—Reflections on October 1"**	15,000
12/24	"Christmas Carols for Democracy"	2,000
12/31	"Democratic New Year's Eve"	10,000
—1990—		
1/1	"New Year Mass Parade for Democracy"	20,000
4/5	"Chinese Democracy Mass Parade"	30,000
5/4	"May 4th, June 4th, and The Road to Democracy"	5,000
5/20	"Bicycle Parade for Democracy in China"	3,000
5/27	"Patriotic Democratic Movement Variety Show"	7,000
6/3	"Worldwide Chinese Democracy Mass Parade"	250,000
6/4	"Candlelight Mourning of the Souls Massacred on June 4th, 1989"	150,000
9/22	"The Sacred Torch Ceremony for Democracy"	1,000
12/9	"Mass Rally—Release Democracy Fighters in China"	2,000

* Figures and information supplied by the Hong Kong Alliance in Support of Patriotic Democratic Movement in China.

** October 1 is the national day of the People's Republic of China.

Archie Roach. (Photo courtesy Aurora/Festival Records)

Desert Dreams, Media, and Interventions in Reality

Australian Aboriginal Music

Marcus Breen

*"Black boy black boy
the color of your skin is your pride and joy"*
—Coloured Stone

Somewhere in the vast desert regions of Central Australia a small group of Aborigines sit around a cassette player, listening to the gentle country and western tones of a song by the Areyonga Desert Tigers. There's a concentration and sincerity here, as the sun beats down on people whose ancestors may have roamed this island continent 60,000 years ago. Incredibly, in the 1990s, they sit under a eucalyptus tree listening to "AIDS It's a Killer," a song with a special message about the virus that has caused serious concern among Australia's natives. The image is a potent symbol of how an ancient culture coexists in an uneasy alliance with the late 20th century, where a modern disease is challenged through the use of equally modern hi-fidelity technology. AIDS itself is a further symbol within this narrative, and in keeping with the history of Australia's Aborigines, it is more cruel than white media readings of AIDS would suggest. The disease, it seems, could be passed on to Aborigines through their sacred initiation ceremonies, where stone tools are used to make incisions and male circumcision is practiced at the onset of adolescence. Just as cruelly, the disease could circulate through the population through heterosexual relations. Everyday life for the subaltern of the Australian continent becomes a risk in itself. AIDS could wipe out Australia's Aborigines, thereby annihilating an entire civilization that just managed to survive the ravages of European settlement that began in 1788.

While stopping the spread of the AIDS virus is important for the survival of Aborigines, getting information to them about the disease is essential. "AIDS It's a Killer" is one practical means of communication, a fitting example of how Aboriginal music has a cultural and social value that goes to the heart of explaining contemporary Aboriginal society and its place in Australia.

Equally instructive and perhaps more relevant to North Americans, is the song "Munjana." The song grew out of the publicity surrounding the James Savage court case in Florida. Aboriginal James Savage was sentenced to death on January 24, 1990 for murder. He was born in Australia, but, under a perverse and racist program instituted by federal law in the 1930s, he was one of thousands of Aboriginal children who were sent away from their families to white homes and schools to be educated and socialized in an appropriately white manner. His trial and the circumstances of his life opened up to scrutiny the history of white oppression against black Australia. Aboriginal singer Archie Roach described this case in "Munjana," his most stirring song yet. It sounded the pain in a hollow echo of despair—a lonely man grasping for life in the face of an alien death sentence.

> Hello Russell this is your mother calling
> Please forgive me I can't stop the tears from falling
> You come from this land and sun above
> And always remember the strength of your mother's love.

Lyrically, the song mixed the intensity of maternal love with the deep-seated love of the open land, which is a permanent and challenging subtext of the Aboriginal experience that appears in much of their music.

Roach reinforced the agony of enforced isolation from the black family with "Took the Children Away," which unequivocally articulated black Australia's pain, while challenging white assumptions about black rights and progress toward equality. "Took the Children Away" almost reached the Top Forty charts in Australia late in 1990, opening up a new era of Aboriginal involvement within the mainstream music establishment. That Roach himself had experienced this appalling government policy, surviving it to sing about it, made the song more poignant still:

> You took the children away
> The children away
> Breaking their mother's heart
> Tearing us all apart
> Took them away.

Aboriginal music is making rapid headway into the Australian musical mainstream as well as serving Aboriginal people themselves. It is an exciting and challenging development involving remarkable determination and experimentation from Aboriginal musicians, activists, and bureaucrats. The history of Aboriginal music and its political economy show its funda- mental role within Aboriginal life. Now, representations of that life are being transported into the life of white Australia, upsetting the balance of white prejudice and apathy in a country whose attitude towards its natives has been likened to attitudes frequently associated with South Africa. A uniquely Australian form of black power has created the conditions to advance the Aboriginal cause for justice through contemporary music.

That Aboriginal music is becoming a popular medium in Australia is remarkable. Hardly ten years ago, descriptions of Aboriginal music were restricted to the exotic droning sound of the *didgeridu* (a hollowed-out stick, about the thickness of an upper arm, through which air is blown in a deep vibrating, rhythmic manner), clapping sticks, and chants of desert Aborigines. Their lives, it seemed, were dependent on white missionaries and government handouts. Alternatively, there were a few male country music singers and some remarkable women's church-style choirs. And yet it was always the exotic traditional Aboriginal music that captured the imagination of Australia and the world. In many ways the 1880 perspective of the Norwegian explorer Carl Lumholtz became the prominent white view of Aborigines, with its implied Victorian moralism: "The Australian natives are gay and happy, but their song is rather melancholy and in excellent harmony with the sombre nature of Australia. It awakened feelings of sadness in me when I heard it from the solemn gum-tree forest, accompanied by the monotonous clatter of the two wooden weapons."[1] This view married the high-minded European patronage of the "happy native" to the nostalgic, yet uncertain feelings about the vast Australian eucalyptus forests of the coastal regions and unexplored deserts of the center of the continent. It was an unequivocally generous view compared to that expressed by Baldwin Spencer in 1899, who described Aboriginal ritual, with its inextricably linked song and dance, as "eminently crude and savage... performed by naked howling savages."[2]

If the male explorers had views that reproduced their predetermined middle class European priorities, their anthropology was accurate for its day, in describing the antipodean experience of native song and dance. Their reports, and dozens like them, expressed consternation at the disorientation a meeting with Aborigines brought. These views predominated, seeping through school textbooks, media reports and representations of Aborigines, so that entire generations of white Australians thought of Aborigines as savages, or in some way inferior and useful only as entertainment—either as shooting targets, sexual objects (Aboriginal women were known as "black velvet," which became a nationally specific, derogatory racist term), or providing exotic song and dance.

While sympathetic academics, like G.H. Strehlow and Jeremy Beckett, introduced a liberal anthropology into a sympathetic sector of Australian academic life from the late 1950s, the vast bulk of Australians treated Aborigines as exceptions to daily life until the 1970s, when a new generation of academics and an activist Aboriginal black rights movement surfaced. The most important feature of the liberal academics' work was a commitment to comprehend Aboriginal life on its own terms and explain it sympathetically. While this may seem as patronizing as some of the earlier descriptions of Aboriginal life, it was an important milestone, simply because it recognized the culture of the Aboriginal people as worthy. More importantly, when examined, it was clear that Aboriginal civilization was mediated by song and dance. This was a major anthropological breakthrough which demanded attention.

A.M. Ellis identified some of the main features of traditional song from two tribes of the central and southern parts of Australia, the Pitjantjatara and the Aranda. He identified the relationship song has to the Aboriginal view of personal and social relations to the land, where ancestral beings traveled across the land, giving it physical and moral shape as they went. This is known as the Dreaming.

> Song is held by these people to be of great power in influencing non-musical events and that if performed correctly in all essential details it will enable performers to draw on supernatural powers left within the soil by the powers during the dreaming. This power may be used for evil as well as good, for which reason the teaching of songs is very strictly controlled. Only the eldest and wisest men know the most potent songs. Song thus is used as a means of social control, in that miscreants are sung about as well as talented hunters and the like, for legal and moral codes are perpetuated in the songs and they also serve to educate children morally and socially.[3]

Comments like this have clarified the intensity of song within everyday Aboriginal culture, while forming the basis for some questionable interest in the exotica of Aboriginal life, often from people with the best intentions. A recent example came from the pen of English writer Bruce Chatwin, who created a lyrically rich, but substantially misleading interpretation of traditional Aboriginal song-culture in his book *The Songlines*. For example, he used Eurocentric reference points to explain his experience of Aboriginal music, serving to deny the music its remarkable place in a unique system of belief: "What makes Aboriginal song so hard to appreciate is the endless accumulations of detail. Yet even a superficial reader can get a glimpse of a moral universe—as moral as the New Testament—in which the structures of kinship reach out to all living men, to all his fellow creatures, and to the rivers, the rocks and the trees."[4] Contextualizing Aborignal song by referring to New Testament morality reproduced 200 years of colonial values and represented the failure of most contemporary intellectuals to grasp the fact that a new or different conceptual and social apparatus is necessary to describe Australian Aborigines and their music.

The really important work that championed Aboriginal music came from Catherine Ellis, who brought none of the male aggression of either the explorer or the careerist academic and writer to her work. Together with her husband she studied Aboriginal culture and the role of Aboriginal song. Her conviction that Aboriginal music provided a new way of seeing Aborigines was the subject of an important book that opened up new avenues for music educators.[5]

 Through song, the unwritten history of the people and the laws of the community are taught and maintained; the entire physical and spiritual development of the individual is nurtured; the well being of the group is protected; supplies of food and water are ensured through musical communication with the spiritual powers; love of homeland is poured out for all to share; illnesses are cured; news is passed from one group to another.[6]

Modern Musical Development

Song stands as the director of cultural traffic within traditional Aboriginal culture. In the prematerialist world of Aboriginal society, song had a uniquely affirming role, objectifying existence and individuality to create an "essential power," namely the "human sense."[7] In this society, "universal communalism" meant that 500 different groups of Aborigines shared their territories and special meanings with one another.[8] But what about Aboriginal culture since the arrival of European civilization and in the present? What of the political economy of making music and of singing songs in the context of capitalist relations as opposed to preindustrial relations? The transformation from traditional "essentialist" readings to the dynamic contemporary is important at a number of levels. Aboriginal music no longer exists in one society, whether at a regional or national level. In the late 1980s and into the 1990s it is part of the flux of musical and cultural life of an entire country and planet. The cultural baggage of modern life—radio, television, film clips, and the cross fertilization of the media—no longer allow discrete cultural formations to comfortably exist isolated from those around them.

But it would be equally inadequate to reject the history of traditional Aboriginal life, in the face of the present. If there is any context in which history forms a particularly strong linkage between one generation and another, it is in societies where ancient values still resonate. Urban Aborigines in towns and cities of Australia as well as isolated rural Aborigines still share the ancient values of the Dreamtime and its values. At one level this may be axiomatic. But in advanced, postindustrial societies like Australia and North America, where the frontier ethic has overwhelmed the old with endlessly reproducible mythologies of newness, it is easy to forget that the values of the old still have a place. The history of degradation and abuse is absolutely necessary for an understanding of contemporary Aboriginal life and music. This history includes details like the successful 1967 national referendum to get white Australia to agree to change the Federal Constitution to allow Aborigines to be treated as Australians for census taking! It is necessary to explain the basic statistical facts of Aboriginal existence in the 1990s, to avoid a gross and unintended misrepresentation of Aboriginal numerical and cultural significance within Australia. According to the 1986 Australian Census there are 206,104 people who consider themselves Aborigines, while 21,514 consider themselves Torres Strait Islanders, making a total of 227,645, or 1.43 percent of the total Australian population of nearly 17 million, in 1986. (Aborigines and Torres Strait Islanders are lumped together in a rough ethnic mix, with far-northern Aborigines bearing some cultural resemblance to the Islanders, although Islanders are really Melanesian).

While these statistics may surprise some people who have believed that the substantial publicity Aboriginal people have generated reflected their vast numbers (as opposed to, say, North American Indians), clearly this is not the case. Indeed, the low numerical strength of Aborigines, combined with their isolation from the major coastal cities of Melbourne, Sydney, and Brisbane, means that their living conditions have often been like those of people in the underdeveloped world. For example, in 1984, the Task Force on Aboriginal and Islander Broadcasting and Communications, working from within the federal government's Department of Aboriginal Affairs, noted: "Aborigines are the most disadvantaged major segment of Australian society with respect to access to communications and the social and economic benefits which they provide."[9] Numerous other studies have noted that Aborigines are equally disadvantaged at every other social level—health, education, child care, and employment—while in 1991, the World Council of Churches noted the following:

> The impact of racism by Australians on Aboriginal people in this nation is not just horrific but genocidal, and must be addressed...
> We saw that the social conditions among Aboriginal communities are deplorable. We saw that the Government has not responded meaningfully to those conditions. We heard from the people their sense of frustration and alienation about a lack of meaningful control over their lives.[10]

This reality hits home when the vastness of the Australian continent and Aboriginal life upon it is understood as taking place largely outside the central population centers. About 70 percent of the Australian continent is considered "remote" and the population density is less than one person per ten square kilometers. Aboriginal representation in remote Australia accounts for about 14 percent of the region's population.[11] Equally, though, it would be wrong to characterize Aboriginal life in that mistaken colonial and idealized manner, as being restricted to one form (tribal or nomadic) or location (urban or rural). The same principle applies to the music. The range and scope of contemporary Aboriginal culture and musical expression stretches back to ancient times and forward through the 1990s. The diversity of the music is remarkable, with traditional music thriving among some desert communities, while newer forms of electric music also find a place, merging in a friendly relationship of support that unites rock with folk, pop with tribal, the joyous with the absolutely desolate.

Traditional music, as we have seen in the statements from E.M. and Catherine Ellis, encapsulated the entire Aboriginal value system. In various regions of Australia the musics differ, but there are some general attributes. Aboriginal tribal music is primarily vocal, with some purely instrumental forms: *didgeridu* solos in the north and songless sacred (non-Christian) performances in Central Australia, where dramatic acts are accorded reverent silence, broken only by the beating together of boomerangs or a stone shield on the hard earth. Most tribal instruments are percussive and continue this beating method. The instruments vary from hand clapping, body slapping, hitting paired boomerangs, thumping the ground with a stick, stamping while dancing, and striking long sticks together. Remarkable and unique instruments like the bullroarer are also used. This is a piece of wood attached to a long piece of twine that is spun in a circular motion above the head, with the air pressure on the wood creating a deep resonant roaring sound.[12] Singing has an important place in all this.

But to early settlers this was heathen mumbo-jumbo. These people and their music needed civilizing and as in many parts of the world in the early 19th century, Christian missionaries saw themselves as the purveyors of civilizing, Christian values. Settler-missionaries in Central Australia spent a considerable amount of time belittling Aboriginal culture while introducing Christian and European values. One of the major features of their proselytizing was the teaching of Biblical beliefs through hymns which were most frequently performed by choirs. "Christian mission music" directly challenged Aboriginal music and values.[13] The two systems—Aboriginal tribal nomad and European settler—especially where Aborigines were "settled" on mission stations, did not collide; European ways simply consumed the Aboriginal. The ammunition used at the forefront of their conversion from "heathenism" to Christianity and modernity was the song. There is no doubt that song, especially the hymn, in the religious and church context is the primary signifier for conversion to Christian belief.[14]

While Christian mission music may have been the main force of traditional cultural annihilation, white settlers were not only missionaries, but large cattle and sheep station or ranch owners, who made (and still make) claims to Aboriginal land. This is the same land which, according to

Dreamtime mythology, is sacred and the subject of the songlines. Nine-teenth century settlers introduced other forms of music which had a further impact on Aborigines, including: formal music training, bush folk culture, and the commercial music of touring shows. In the latter category, black minstrel shows were popular in country towns and cities, with Aboriginal performers singing "plantation songs" and Stephen Foster tunes like "The Old Folks at Home" and "Swanee River," which in their turn became part of the bush ballad tradition.[15] The bush ballad style is derived from American hillbilly, together with English, Irish, and Scottish folk songs, and the Australian colonial storytelling of progressive polemicist poets, such as Henry Lawson and Banjo Patterson, who reflected an earnest populism, often reflecting class antagonism with a distinctive narrative progression. As a musical style it comfortably fit into preexisting Aboriginal song and dance styles of Dreamtime story-telling. This mix of styles and influences is present in most conventional rock and roll songs, and is a style that has made its presence felt in contemporary Aboriginal music.

Gum leaf players also performed for black and white audiences, playing versions of the grand old North American popular songs and a few Australian tunes—some of them home grown. (The gum or eucalyptus leaf is played by holding it between the hands and up to the mouth and blowing air across it to make it vibrate. After the *didgeridu* and the bull roarer, it is probably Australia's greatest musical invention.) The introduction of radio in the 1930s brought its own style of cultural transformation, with the gradual development of solo Aboriginal singers in the Jimmy Rogers tradition, mixing hillbilly, folk, country and western, country blues, and yodeling.[16] Jimmy Little was the best-known exponent of this style from the 1960s on, singing "Telephone to Glory," a song straight out of the fundamentalist Baptist repertoire. This was followed by considerable inter-est in Elvis Presley and a strong passion for Kris Kristofferson (especially "Me and Bobby McGee") and Charley Pride songs. The relevance of this country-folk-rock combination is spelled out by Doug Petherick: "This ability of country and western to celebrate brawls, booze, and the low life on one hand and revival style religion on the other, sometimes in the same writer and even in the same song, has been a strong attraction for Aboriginal listeners."[17] This style of music, building on the bush ballad, is the prominent genre used today. Importantly, too, as with the world music movement in general, with which Aboriginal music has sometimes been associated, "the grain of the voice" has been an important factor in challenging recording, artistic, and commercial conventions.[18] It achieves this "challenging" mode because Aboriginal English sounds harsher, less refined, more nasal, even flatter, than European English. This difference in sound (a linguistic, dis-tinction, in fact) adds to the impact of the subject matter of many Aboriginal songs, which cannot avoid dealing with the daily hardship and history of abuse suffered by Australia's natives, illustrated by Archie Roach's "Took the Children Away," as noted earlier.

In recent Australian history, the musics described above permeated the Aboriginal community. Traditional Aboriginal music survived but had to give way to the transforming power of modern form and content. What the missionaries and settlers began, technology and the march of modernizing society took over. It needs to be said, however, that despite these considerable changes, Aboriginal music often managed to retain the spiritual sense of place and history, of dignity and purpose. It is significant that despite the transformations of Aboriginal music, community values and an intense connection with the land and the Dreaming distinguishes Aboriginal music from all other music in Australia. Aboriginal behavior based on unique notions of time, space, and non-materiality have never sat comfortably with Europeans, but it can be argued that those values and attitudes have become a part of the easy-going, relaxed Australian lifestyle. These elements have been reinforced since the 1970s, as Aboriginal pride and black consciousness have grown. Popular music changed Aboriginal music and culture, but Aborigines and their music undoubtedly challenged prevailing capitalist relations in European Australia as well. Their music reflected values that were not determined by Judeo-Christian beliefs and the work ethic.

Real and dramatic changes to Aboriginal music, combined with modest victories for Aboriginal people in general, had to wait until the 1970s and an Australian "black power" that saw how improvements could be gained by making use of the opportunities progressive governments made available. Black power in Australia had a major role to play in advancing the cause of popular musical development. In the first instance, traditional Aboriginal values were necessary for Aboriginal identity and survival. Secondly, traditional values which were conveyed most forcefully in music and dance could be conveyed using contemporary musical forms that had broad appeal. The 1970s ushered in this dramatic cultural and political development that is finding its feet in the 1990s.

Changing with Reformist Government

In the early 1970s a wave of optimism rode an unprecedented surge of enthusiasm for political change in Australia. The result was the election of the first federal Australian Labor Party (ALP) government in 23 years. A generation of reactionary government ended and, with it, the excesses that Australia's isolation from the rest of the world could bring. The cultural, economic, and political elite was horrified by its loss of power. Its disregard for the underprivileged (which included the Vietnamese) was effectively screened from most Australians who believed in the petty bourgeois suburban home-owning dream of existence that is so effectively marketed by capitalist establishments. In this scheme, Aborigines were not on the agenda. The election of Gough Whitlam as prime minister in 1972 turned Australia on its head. Youth culture, minorities, and Aborigines became part of the new Australia. "It's Time" was the slogan of the ALP for the 1972 election, and indeed it was. Empowerment was the key, and so a series of gradual reforms were introduced into Australia, one of which was to give Aborigines a greater say in their own lives and future, in particular by introducing legislation that would usher in a new era of land rights. The very act of trusting Aborigines with self-management (loosely defined) and control over their own land (land rights) and money was little short of revolutionary. Aboriginal life and Australia itself would never be the same again.

In 1971 Adelaide University opened the Center for Aboriginal Studies in Music (CASM), with Cath Ellis appearing there as a main player in the preservation and promotion of Aboriginal music. While arguably too much emphasis was placed on conventional musical skills at CASM, such as learning musical notation and classical instruments, tribal elders were also used to pass on musical traditions in the relevant (sacred) context. A new generation of musicians developed skills that made them a professional musician class within the Aboriginal community. This was a further major change. Formal education replaced traditional tribal ways, while the traditional and spiritual values were maintained.

Toward the end of the Whitlam ALP government in 1975—it was sacked under questionable circumstances by Queen Elizabeth's representative, the governor-general, with unproven assistance by the CIA—public radio was introduced as one of its final acts of defiance against the establishment. This single act opened up communication "from within" communities, rather than "from above," and ushered in "a significant cultural, economic and political break with the media status quo."[19] It provided all sorts of possibilities, including the promotion of Australian independent music and, as part of that scene, Aboriginal music. Other media then expanded and flourished, including an ethnic television station within the Special Broadcasting Service (SBS—which began as a foreign language radio station). Minorities had a voice of sorts. Although the voices were not mainstream, they could be heard simply by tuning in a radio or a television set. Culturally, it meant that for consumers, music could be more than Top Forty, because a different radio format was available. In the 1970s the political implications these changes brought were untried, but they provided a significant stepping stone for the advancement of Aboriginal music and the further advancement of Australian society as a whole.

In 1980, after a period of consolidation, Aborigines had made considerable social and cultural progress, with unlikely assistance from the conservative government of Malcolm Fraser, who allowed the bureaucracy to continue its support of Aboriginal programs established under Whitlam. Of course, much of the developmental work undertaken in these years could only flourish under a reformist government, and so it was that what had been Aboriginal activism in relation to the single issue of land rights during the 1970s became a vast series of activities with the election of the Hawke Labor government in 1983. The floodgates were opened and music was the bearer of the news and the means of articulating ideas and issues that needed to find a concentrated form.

While there is skepticism with governments around the globe, there is no doubt that reformist governments can and do have a major role to play in creating liberal democracies where institutions of state, even bureaucracies, act as "educators" in a Gramscian sense, to facilitate governance.[20] This is an important sub-theme to the discussion of contemporary Aboriginal music because the history of Australia's natives has brought federal and state governments face to face with the most difficult social and political question consistently facing the nation: What about the Aborigines? Developments in Aboriginal music have moved in tandem with the election of reformist governments and the modernization and liberalization of Australian society. These early changes, which led to the establishment of unfriendly bureaucracies for Aborigines, occurred through the activism of older Aborigines like Pastor Doug Nicholls, poet Cath Walker, administrator Charles Perkins, and, in the 1980s, Gary Foley. These people, along with activist Europeans like H.C. "Nugget" Coombes and Professor Fred Hollows, created a uniquely Australian Black Power Movement that could only succeed in its early days with a groundswell of white support for Australia's natives, that made Aboriginal rights and dignity a major platform of the ALP. But it was always black Australians who began marching in city streets in the early 1970s to bring attention to their struggles for rights.

Aborigines, with the help of sympathetic Europeans, created a black power that reflected the easy-going style of Australia. This was not the black power of African Americans like Angela Davis or the Black Panthers, but a brand that used collective support networks to conduct peaceful demonstrations that often generated enormous amounts of unintended publicity, due to the aggressive attempts of the police to break up the demonstrations. As Aborigines became more experienced at political campaigns, they began to more effectively target certain events, such as the Commonwealth Games in Brisbane in 1982, when Aborigines attracted attention from (British) Commonwealth countries to the plight of Aboriginal people. As the issues came into increasingly stark relief through these demonstrations, governments could not fail to take heed. White guilt affected conservative and liberal middle classes alike, so the relatively quiet Black Power Movement in Australia could make demands of state and federal governments. It was remarkable that from the early 1980s, all Australian governments at least paid lip service to the needs of Aborigines.

Real experience, of course, was another thing altogether. As late as December 17, 1990, Robert Tickner, then Federal Minister for Aboriginal Affairs in the Hawke Labor Government, had to admit that Aboriginal health was still at a third world level, particularly in isolated communities. At the end of 1990, infant mortality among Aborigines was three times higher than among European Australians, the death rate four times higher, and hospitalization five times higher. The "solution" to these problems in the 1990s was a decision to disburse federal funds of $230 million for water, sanitation, housing, and roads to Aboriginal communities. Nevertheless, the abysmal treatment of Aborigines continues. Reform is never fast enough. History is always there, insistently pressing against the present, reminding people that life has extreme demands. Music conveys this reality more effectively for Aborigines than any formal "political" campaign. For this reason, it is impossible to separate recent developments in Aboriginal music from progressive federal labor government support for Aboriginal people.

Aboriginal Popular Music in the 1980s

In the 1980s, the vast and mostly unhappy history of Aboriginal people began to appear in music. Until this time, Christian mission music, the bush ballad styles, the music hall, and male singer-guitarists had been an entertainment sideshow for Europeans to add to the list of other available exotic and traditional musics. Indeed, for most white Australians their only experience of Aboriginal music was in the late 1960s, when Lional Rose, former world bantamweight boxing champion and Aboriginal sportsman, had a hit with "I Thank You." Written by white former pop star and entrepreneur, Johnny Young, the song was a sentimental blast of indulgence that avoided politics of either a personal or social nature. Despite the radical changes sweeping the world to the accompaniment of popular music in the late 1960s, Lionel Rose was to remain an alien black man—a boxer, a solo guitar-playing Aborigine—playing entertainer in the bush ballad tradition perhaps, but never a polemicist or politician.

The 1970s were an important period of consolidation. The 1980s saw a substantial change. Young Aborigines, buoyed by the 1979 visit to Australia of Bob Marley, began to see music as a form of black celebration and resistance. Popular music, especially in Adelaide, the capital city with the largest per capita Aboriginal population, took on a new meaning. Music became an overt vehicle for political use. "Music as a utilitarian vehicle" could summarize the Aboriginal vision of the early 1980s. The Aboriginal use of popular music no longer allowed the cultural and anthropological indulgences of the exotic desert people and their tribal musics to be filed somewhere in the background of the European experience of Australia. There was no strange language or instrumentation to isolate the black person's experience from that of the European. Popular music brought the contemporary and historical experience of Aboriginal people into the open. "Rock and roll," as it was experienced through Bob Marley, created a groundswell of interest in the use of the electric band format. The everyday—for Aboriginal people, the pressing political and social issues that most affected them—could be displayed using the rock band medium.

For many European Australians locked into the middle-class urban lifestyle of the cities, the first suggestion that something fundamental had changed in Aborignal music was the film *Wrong Side of the Road*. Released in 1982, it showed Us Mob and No Fixed Address, two Aboriginal bands on tour. Their music was bursting with politically charged lyrics, while the sound—from the grain of the voices to the slightly awkward reggae-rock—was unlike anything else; unfamiliar, disorienting, and inspiring. It promised a new form of musical expression while opening political issues to public debate that were previously relegated to the serious and frequently disempowered realm of state politics. Of special note and something of a theme for musical progressives in the 1980s was the No Fixed Address song "We Have Survived":

We have survived the white man's world
And the horror and torment of it all
We have survived the white man's world
And you know you can't change that.

Soon after No Fixed Address and Us Mob began making waves, it became clear that a subculture of well-established Aboriginal musicians existed. Kuckles, with Jimmi Chi, came from Broome in far northwest Western Australia, singing protest music, arguing against uranium mining and for land rights. Chi's best known song, "Brand New Day," was written in 1975 "on the back of a truck during a demonstration against the Court Government (in Western Australia) for allowing mining on (Aboriginal) sacred sites."[21] A rough reggae, the original recording of the song uses a harsh, parodying voice that nervously expresses the Aboriginal plight. Somewhat similar in sound to West Indian singers like The Jolly Boys or Joseph Spence, its appeal comes from its lack of insistence compared to pop's demands. The song maintains its potency 15 years later, forming the basis for the first Aboriginal rock musical, *Bran Nu Dae*. The musical was performed at the Perth Festival in 1990 and is continuing to move around the country, attracting attention with its unflattering and disturbing view of Aboriginal life, as the title song shows:

Here I live in this tin shack
Nothing here worth coming back

> To drunken fights and awful sights
> People drunk 'most every night.

The history of "Brand New Day," as a song and as the basis for the musical, provides a model for other recent developments in Aboriginal popular music. Those musicians who saw potential in popular musical forms in the 1970s and made music in that decade created the foundation for those looking to advance the Aboriginal cause through music in the 1980s. In a similar sense, it took 15 years for the urgency of a song written with bold conviction in the back of a pick-up truck to gestate into a fully fledged musical, performed at a festival of the arts. (The question of whether this is a means of actually denying the popular its power, by incorporating it into the bourgeois buildings and cultural domains of middle-class consumers, is a matter that cannot be dismissed. The gulf between popular music's insistent demands and the red carpets of concert halls is vast, difficult to measure, and full of contradictions.) But survival, staying alive, and being part of the struggle for the long run, cliche-ridden as that may sound, is part of the process that Aboriginal performers have had to undertake.

Aboriginal songwriters and bands with intentions of instituting political change could achieve nothing without media support. While SBS, the Australian Broadcasting Corporation, and public radio could do something to publicize the music and issues through music, the mainstream was obsessed with classic hits radio and the Top Forty format that slavishly pursued *Billboard* prescriptions. In the total scheme of things, Aboriginal music has almost never seriously reached into this domain. It has, however, followed the historical process that was established by people like Jimmy Chi and members of No Fixed Address. Putting the media in place was the next step.

Media Conjunctions

Various projects have assisted the promotion of the music and its propagation through broadcasting. Undoubtedly the single most important Aborignal media institution in the country is the Central Australian Aboriginal Media Association (CAAMA). CAAMA in the 1990s is the fulfillment of the political ideals for change that manifested themselves during the Whitlam government from 1972 to 1975. It is an Aboriginal organization, controlled and run by Aborigines under the Aboriginal Councils and Associations Act of 1976. All members of CAAMA must be Aboriginal. A governing committee of at least 12 people is elected from the membership. Established in 1980, with assistance from various federal government departments, CAAMA blossomed through public radio, with a license to provide musiç to Aboriginal people. This was achieved by applying to the

Australian Broadcasting Tribunal for a license to broadcast a particular style of music and programing. Under the Australian system, a frequency allocation is made by the Tribunal after a successful application, with reviews every three or five years by the Tribunal to assess whether the station is in fact meeting its license obligations. The problem for CAAMA was not so much the incredible boldness of applying for and receiving a license to broadcast, as it was filling the air time with appropriate music.

Aboriginal music existed; it was just a matter of finding it and putting it on the air. This was a lot more difficult than it first appeared. To start with, CAAMA was based in Alice Springs, the major city in Central Australia. Intensely isolated, Alice Springs was and is a focus for Aborigines from Central and South Australia. CAAMA's original voluntary workers in the 1980s saw the opportunities public radio access provided for minorities, especially Aborigines, who, in isolated communities in Central Australia, deserved news and information as well as culturally relevant material that would promote their survival and a sense of purpose and empowerment. That ideal has grown and flourished. CAAMA Music, the most recent extension of CAAMA as a media center, is part of the Australian independent music scene and "the Aboriginal recording label of Australia."[22] CAAMA was and probably remains not so much an overt expression of black power as another necessary and practical part of the Aboriginal survival process.

In order to achieve their goals of broadcasting contemporary Aboriginal music, the CAAMA workers had to find musicians from obscure towns and settlements whose only experience of music was performing to other Aborigines. With AM radio station 8CCC at their disposal, CAAMA had an obligation to broadcast Aboriginal music for Aboriginal people six hours each day in three Aboriginal languages and in English. But the recordings were almost nonexistent, except for ethnomusicological recordings of traditional musics and the solo male bush balladeers with a predominantly sentimental style. According to Rodney Gooch, "There was very little Aboriginal music to use on the Aboriginal radio station, so we brought in a lot of people who could sing."[23] The process of recording these people began in a dilapidated two-track studio, and the first CAAMA cassettes were released late in 1980. They featured the bands Colored Stone and Warumpi Band, and solo male performers—Bob Randal, Isaac Yama, and Herbiee Lawton—who brought varying levels of community intensity to their work. "The framework for the label was simply Aboriginal music for Aboriginal people."[24] It was music about the Aboriginal experience using country music and early rock, while somewhere in the background the vastness of a virtually uninhabited desert beat like a heart.

After the first releases, a cassette featuring Kuckles appeared, bringing the music of *Bran Nu Dae* into circulation. The cassette, not vinyl, is important to the CAAMA story. In the first instance, the music was recorded

to be broadcast on the radio station to fulfill Aboriginal programing obligations. The circulation of the music for private and other consumption
became increasingly significant. In the extensive desert sands of Central
Australia, the only way to sensibly circulate the music was on cassette. Vinyl
albums and record players were impractical and had none of the portability
of battery-powered cassette players. At the end of 1990, thirty-one cassettes
were listed in the CAAMA Music Catalogue, with just one recording released
on an alternative format, the compact disc.

The move to CD is the next important step in this CAAMA story,
reflecting substantial leaps by Aboriginal music into the political and social
life of white Australia. A 1990 agreement between Polygram Records
Australia and CAAMA to distribute selected CAAMA recordings represents
a significant move to make this music accessible to the average Australian,
where before its distribution was restricted to mail order and a handful of
selected, sympathetic retail outlets. Among the material being distributed
is the CD sampler titled *From the Bush*. There is also a collection of tracks
about AIDS sung by Aboriginal bands, *How could I Know* (referred to at
the start of this article); a selection about alcohol abuse, *Wama Wanti:
Drink Little Bit;* a compilation about living conditions in a Central Australian
region *Uwankara Palyanku Kanyinijaku* (UPK); together with five other
cassettes by newly recorded Aboriginal bands. This move by Polygram
brings Aboriginal music and the political cause further into the foreground
of Australian and international life.

CAAMA has undoubtedly played a significant role in advancing the
cause of Aboriginal music, first among Aboriginal Australians and more
recently among European Australians, using music as a political weapon in
the long-term struggle of Aboriginal people for dignity, respect, and land
rights claims. Alternatively, for Aboriginal people themselves, taking the
music to them in desert settlements brought information and political
education where before, there was none, or very little. The CAAMA Catalogue puts it best:

> The past decade has witnessed stunning growth in the develop-
> ment of this music, a fact appreciated more with an understanding
> of the circumstances under which the music is produced. It is less
> likely that songs are written in an idyllic outstation setting and more
> likely that rough fringe camps, ravaged communities and town life
> is the wellspring of this music. It is no accident that the rise of
> contemporary Aborignal Music coincides with the growth of the
> Central Australian Aboriginal Media Association. Beginning in
> 1980, the fundamental objectives contained in the CAAMA charter
> were to provide full media services to its peoples. Arresting cultural
> disintegration through the broadcast of educational material in
> language and song demands a basic prerequisite in the form of
> recording facilities. The CAAMA Studios have recorded a massive

amount of material by the Aborignal composers and musicians of this country. The point of expression for these works is through 8KIN-FM Radio, the regional broadcast service operated through CAAMA.

Arguments that suggest that the media is a "legitimizing agent" that denies the true social and political value of a cultural or social activity by native peoples have been used against media creations like CAAMA.[25] In the case of Aboriginal Australians, the primary focus of CAAMA—namely, to provide music and information for Aborigines—has served to legitimize Aborigines, rather than denigrate their culture. Certainly, the existence of the media among them challenges and changes Aboriginal life and values, but it is more significant in advancing their basic living conditions. Aboriginal media also helps Aborigines to organize themselves. The Australian government's current inquiry into black deaths in custody, launched in the late 1980s and still running early into 1991, happened as a result of well-organized media campaigns in the mid-1980s.

CAAMA began with three volunteer staff, a radio license, and a commitment to the cause of Aborignal music. Now it is known as the CAAMA Group, an Aboriginal Arts and Crafts business which includes a television production company, and is a major shareholder in Imparja Television which was established along commercial lines in 1988. Imparja Television operates from the CAAMA base in Alice Springs, providing programs via satellite to the Northern Territory and South Australia under the Remote Commercial Television Service (RCTS) agreement. Its formation and subsequent successful license application was controversial, but served to reinforce the need for a voice for Aboriginal people. It was also timely, albeit late. In 1954, a Commonwealth Royal Commission on Television in Australia concluded that the provision of television to rural and remote Australia was necessary, but an economic problem. This is still the case, although the extension of access to television for people in remote Australia had to come through use of the AUSSAT satellite.[26] Buying time on the satellite has nearly bankrupted Imparja. Nevertheless, the satellite, which serves about 300,000 people, most of whom are Aborigines, has played an important role in promoting Aborignal music to Aboriginals. Moreover, developing skills, like film clip making (as well as radio programing), forms a further developmental stage in advancing Aboriginal interests in the media through a cultural seepage, whereby the sheer existence of Aboriginal "product" cannot go unnoticed by mainstream media programers indefinitely. "Serious" political campaigns and cultural agendas by reformist governments and activists find their place in advancing the voices of Aborigines by funding and supporting indigenous media organizations.

It is also important to note that satellite technology has a function and power that cannot be easily compared with a single radio station. For example, the transglobal nature of satellite technology "fundamentally challenges functions of the nation state and its agents in administering and negotiating communications, information, economic and social orders."[27] It also reinvests power. Satellites give governments, especially those of developing countries, and minority and indigenous groups a chance "to redress the immense power and strategic know-how of transnational corporations. Access to good quality information is critical to these processes."[28]

Public access models of communication, not to mention various forms of democracy, are based on some implementation of these processes. The empowerment of minorities has been a facet of advanced contemporary countries, which has unintentionally been aided and abetted by communication transnationals whose quest for ever larger markets has seen their tentacles reach into otherwise remote corners of civilizations—from the slums to the jungles to the deserts. While they reach into these places, bringing sounds, pictures, ideas, and information from their preferred massed suburban audiences of relatively willing consumers, a reversal also takes place. The pictures and sounds of poverty, notions of the non-consumer lifestyles of native peoples, and unconventional behavior challenge the modes of life of the idealized target consumer audience. As Freda Murphy, chairperson of CAAMA's board, said in 1987: "We cannot remain on the fringes of communication, as well as the fringes of town, forever."[29]

Postmodern discourse has indicated some of these articulations, yet often overlooked the multilayered, mutually inclusive, and dependant relationship between idealized target audiences and sources of information. One changes the other, in a dynamic osmosis. In doing so, it is possible for the minority to receive power and influence through the media over and above its numerical strength relative to the majority population or audience. There is, of course, no guarantee of this happening and an equal chance that a complete loss of the intended message will occur through its submersion into mainstream media activity. The osmosis theory demands, however, that at least a mutual, increasing interdependency between the mainstream and the periphery will occur. In the context of electronic media, music, and video in the 1990s, emotional and intellectual cues can be generated to act almost automatically for the idealized target consumer audience, building on the political black power campaigns that are inextricably linked to Aboriginal music. European audiences can respond sympathetically to the information and intellectual and emotional challenges put to them by Aboriginal music.

For CAAMA and Imparja, music provided the original vehicle for the development of both the radio and television outlets. Assisted by federal government funding, CAAMA organized itself to fulfill the needs of remote area Aborigines, first through a radio station, then cassette tapes, and finally a television station. The work of North American anthropologist Eric Michaels cannot go unmentioned here. Michaels identified the imperatives of community functions in the use of television by Aborigines in his book *The Aboriginal Invention of Television in Central Australia.*[30] Michaels championed the reconstruction of the medium, especially the video camera and recorder as used by Aborigines, as an act of monumental transformation and empowerment, suggesting that "Aboriginal cultural rights" would lead to "local, low power community television," which could, when implemented, "avert the cultural catastrophes of language loss and social disorganization in a region where economics and ecology have limited European colonialism."[31]

In a similar way, Imparja Television "made important allowances for local community control of incoming satellite television signals as well as fostering the development of production capacity at the same level."[32] This theme reappeared when the Federal Court upheld the decision of the Australian Broadcasting Tribunal to grant the RCTS license for the Northern Territory and South Australia to Imparja, after the decision was contested by Television Capricornia, the competitor for the license. The Tribunal thought that Imparja was preferable (to Television Capricornia) because of the nature and quality of its services, its responsiveness to the community and its ability to satisfy the needs of that community.[33]

This community function of Aboriginal media is recognized at an Australian federal government level as well. A statement by the former Minister for Transport and Communication, Kim C. Beazley on September 28, 1990 detailed the extension of public broadcasting licenses, with the aim of seeing 200 public radio licenses spread across the country, with Aborigines receiving special mention. The minister's statement said that "the Government continued to give a high priority to establishment of Aboriginal radio services. Special interest public radio license applications will be invited for Perth, Townsville, Kununurra, Broome and Fitzroy Crossing and community licenses to be made available at Katherine and Nhulunbuy will serve to increase Aboriginal radio programming in those areas."[34]

While Alice Springs has seen a proliferation of activity centered around CAAMA, other regional developments have also taken place. Once again, Jimmy Chi has a place here. In 1985-86, he was involved in the formation of the Broome Musicians' Aboriginal Corporation. (He was also involved in establishing the Aboriginal Rehabilitation Center, for people with alcohol problems.) Of the musicians' corporation Chi said: "We started that up to get something happening up here, to make musicians more aware of what they can do...music keeps people together in the community framework."[35]

The ultimate manifestation of media in the context of the community nature of Aboriginal society was the introduction, in 1987, of the Broadcasting for Remote Aboriginal Communities Scheme (BRACS). Once again, it is a program developed by sympathetic bureaucrats in Canberra and further indicates the significant conjunctions between government, policy, activism, and cultural production in creating Aborignal music. BRACS has several important characteristics. It is small scale and designed to be operated on a community basis by all community members and to transmit over short distances. BRACS communities will be able to produce their own video and radio programs or make use of AUSSAT programs.[36] Together with CAAMA there are now four other Aboriginal regional media organizations producing programs for radio and in some cases video programs for broadcast in remote areas. They are: the Western Australian Aboriginal Media Association (WAAMA), the Top End Aboriginal Bush Broadcasting Association (TEABBA), the Townsville and Aboriginal Islander Media Association (TAIMA), and the Torres Strait Islander and Aboriginal Media Association (TSIAMA).[37]

Gains in advancing the Aboriginal cause outside the Aboriginal community have been made by well-organized campaigns constructed by Aboriginal and European activists to bring the sounds and concerns of the people into the mainstream. Perhaps the best known of these efforts was Midnight Oil's *Diesel and Dust* album of 1988. That album and a subsequent tour attracted attention to the subject of Aboriginal land rights on a worldwide scale. The tour of the U.S. by Midnight Oil, accompanied by Aboriginal band, Yothu Yindi provided a useful propaganda tool for Aboriginal Australians overseas, just as Scrap Metal, an Aboriginal band from Broome was able to propagandize Australian audiences when they toured with Midnight Oil in Australia in 1988. Yothu Yindi has maintained its commitment to the Aboriginal cause, with the release on February 11, 1991 of a single titled "Treaty." Recorded with the assistance of two important European Australian singer/songwriters, Paul Kelly and (Midnight Oil's) Peter Garrett, it was written with the intention of gaining commercial radio airplay in Australia, and to draw attention to the need for a treaty between black and white Australia. The involvement of Kelly and Garrett suggests that committed activists are very much still a part of the process of advancing the Aboriginal cause through music. (It must be emphasized that these are particular examples from an increasingly diverse and active Aboriginal music sector within Australian rock music.)

Australia's independent record sector has always taken up the challenge of breaking new music before the major record companies take the music to a grand, possibly international scale. That is the case with Aboriginal music. Sydney-based Larrikin Records released Kev Carmody's groundbreaking Dylanesque *Pillars of Society* in 1990. Carmody, from Brisbane, spent a large part of the 1980s studying at Queensland University, and finished the decade preparing a doctorate on colonial history and the treatment of his people. His songs reflect the earnest intellect and radical vigor his academic training has given him, while his hard-headed poetic style maintains the tradition of narrative bush ballad morality. For its part, Australia's largest independent label and the second-largest independent in the world, Mushroom Records, launched a new specialist label called Aurora for Archie Roach's debut *Charcoal Lane*. Mushroom, the rock label, also has Yothu Yindi in its catalogue.

Building Bridges was a special development linked to major record companies. As a project it involved concerts featuring Aboriginal and non-Aboriginal musicians performing together in Sydney. The result was a double LP released through CBS, late in 1988. In some ways it was a gratuitous effort, with many of the white performers on the release having no ongoing record of involvement with Aborigines or progressive causes, unlike Peter Garrett or Paul Kelly, although members of Crowded House are well known for their support of Aborigines. For many of the artists appearing on *Building Bridges,* it was a "free kick" release with an opportunity to win publicity points and community good will. Building Bridges was, however, usefully exploited when the Australian Broadcasting Corporation Television broadcast a half-hour extract of the concert in January 1991, with a simulcast on the ABC youth radio network Triple Jay. Other majors have signed Aboriginal acts, including BMG signing Colored Stone—one of the first CAAMA cassette bands. BMG plans to release the Colored Stone back catalogue on CD in 1991. The move to the majors fosters a sense of confidence among Aborigines and a challenge to the potential isolation they often experience in their outback communities. It also promises to bring the music into the main arena of distribution and radio airplay.

Play Loud Play Long, the annual Aboriginal rock music festival in Darwin, Australia's northern capital city, ran for two consecutive years in 1988-89. It provided a further focus for the music and the people to get together to celebrate their identity in music. In 1990, the Aboriginal rock music festival was organized at a more local level in smaller outback towns. Other events, like the Barunga Sports and Cultural Festival near Katherine in the Northern Territory, bring an array of Aboriginal bands and performers together for cultural enrichment and an opportunity to exchange and develop ideas. Solo male performers like Archie Roach, Kev Carmody, Jimmy Chi, and Bob Randal make increasingly profound personal statements about the treatment of their people and their own experiences as black Australians. Press and media reporting, as part of the publicity drive to sell the recordings, occasionally reaches the front pages of newspapers and achieves high profiles in other media.

The appearance of recordings "in the language" makes the issue more challenging for white Australians. The rejection of English as the first language of communication incorporates an implicit rejection of European civilization. This challenge to the mainstream of contemporary Australian life is further on the fringes of popular music culture than Aboriginal music being sung in English. Songs and music "in the language" are becoming more prevalent, as people in remote areas grow confident, recording the songs they have created in ancient languages. Aboriginal rock bands singing "in the language" are also filtering through, and CAAMA has several tapes available, but Australian media, being rabidly Anglophone, will probably never play Aboriginal recordings in tribal languages. Public radio, ABC, and SBS will be and are the exception.

Observant readers will have noticed the absence of any reference to women. The Mills Sisters, from Thursday Island, are the exception. They sing melodious trios in a Hawaiian style. Nevertheless, there are very few Aboriginal women working in bands or as solo artists. Aboriginal culture appears to have a lot to do with this, although it can only be assumed that Aboriginal women will become more active. At the end of the 1980s, women could be most readily heard in small choirs, singing Christian hymns and country music favorites. The influence of the Christian missionaries lingers on in remarkable and ironic ways, reinforcing the collective female solidarity that was an important part of tribal life. CAAMA has released a collection of choirs, which features church hymns and secular tunes like "Bobby McGee."

Aboriginal music is part of the ongoing struggle by Aboriginal people for recognition and dignity. Its development has been a gradual process, steeped, as it must be, in the history of Aboriginal civilization and their decimation at the hands of European settlers. As Archie Roach put it when talking about his music: "In Victoria they almost succeeded in destroying the Aboriginal people. The languages have been lost and a lot of the traditions and rituals have gone. A lot of the old fellas (men) know it but won't talk about it because years ago they were punished by the authorities for talking about it. But the spiritual values are still there. That's what I'd rather get across to people. If the spirit dies nothing else is going to be much use."[38] This may be a long way from a eucalyptus tree in the middle of Australia's central desert, and yet Aboriginal music is helping Aborigines survive the evils that could kill them, while giving them a purpose and a strength to carry on, drawing on ties with the land and spirits that could benefit everybody. Aboriginal music is also giving an increasing number of non-Aboriginal Australians a chance to hear the Aboriginal voice and history first hand. As their polemic becomes part of the world's increasingly competent progressive political movements, they will find their rightful place in the corpus of the world's popular music.

Don' Go Down Waikiki

Social Protest and Popular Music in Hawaii

George H. Lewis

"Hey brah," Israel Kamakawiwaole waves his arm in the hot dusky air. His huge brown fist, clenched with the thumb and little finger sticking out at right angles, looks like a smoked ham with horns as he wags it up and down in the Hawaiian-pidgin symbol of greeting.

A bearded man in a red T-shirt and jeans smiles and waves from the back of the club.

Israel settles his 350 pounds back in his chair on stage, picks up an electric ukelele in a fist that nearly swallows the instrument, and announces: "Dis song tell how them stu-u-pid *baoles* fight ovah land, when it not theirs to fight ovah. It ours, yeah!" Strumming quickly, and amazingly lightly on the instrument he holds captive in his huge hands, Israel leads his group, the Makaha Sons of Ni'i'hau, in his own pidgin-clever version of "Waimanalo Blues." The four voices blend sweet as a choir in the dark smoky air of the rough-cut Honolulu club.

The cultural counterattack, spearheaded by popular music and dance, is in earnest in Hawaii. Local people are teasing out and uncovering their cultural roots while, at the same time, they are emphatically rejecting the artificial "tourist culture" that has been developed, packaged, and sold on the Islands by outside (mainland American and, increasingly, Japanese) concerns, and has all but swallowed up Hawaiians in its implications.

Haunai-Kay Trask, a local Hawaiian rights activist, has explained: "Hawaiians look to the land as something to feed them. Westerners look at land as a commodity, to be exchanged for something else, for money, for profit-making. When you take the land away from Hawaiians, you've cut them off from who they are. What's the alternative? You want us to go dance in the hotels and keep prostituting our culture? Is that being Hawaiian? Don't talk to me about the aloha spirit. That was an invention of Arthur Godfrey."[1]

The last two decades have seen, in Hawaii, the cultural and political rebirth of native Hawaiians. No longer content to dance in the hotels of the tourist industry or to act like mainland-created caricatures of themselves, Hawaiians have rekindled a pride in their heritage and have sought out their own cultural traditions, from a revival of their ancient forms of dance—*hula kahiko*—to the renewed popularity of slack key guitar and traditional chanting styles in Hawaiian songs.

Reacting against the commercial gloss of the tourist industry and the expectations it has created in the Waikiki audience for artificial Hawaiian songs and dances, Island musicians in the past two decades have forged a musical movement in search of their own traditional roots and culture, reaching back to encourage and embrace the few ethnic artists still alive and performing—merging this material with their own pressing social and cultural concerns to create a new type of music—part contemporary, part traditional, and all layered with social protest critical of non-natives who Hawaiians see as having nearly destroyed their culture, their self-identity, and their sacred land.

The lyrics of one of these newly constructed popular songs, "Hawaiian Awakening," reveals the tone and thrust of this concern:

> Deep in this tortured land all alone
> Hear the winds cry, the mountains moan…
> We followed their rules much too long
> Our protests are heard in our music and song…[2]

Kaona: Social Protest and Hidden Meanings

Social protest has always been a part of Hawaiian music, but—as with many oppressed peoples—this social protest has been hidden from the ears of outsiders. In January 1893, *"Mele Ai Pohaku"* was written in protest of the contrived annexation of Hawaii to the United States. The song, considered sacred when it was written, affirms the Hawaiian intent not to sign the papers of annexation—"We will not sign the *haole's* [whites'] paper, but will be satisfied with all that is left to us, the stones, the mystic food of our native land."[3]

The song's title, translated from the Hawaiian, means "Stone Eating Song," and the lyrics speak of the "children (flowers) of Hawaii, ever loyal to the land," who will back Lili'u-lani as queen monarch—"she will be crowned again"—lyrics quite bitter and subversive in nature, if one considers the context of their creation. And yet the song—because it was written and sung in Hawaiian—could be understood by almost no English-speaking American in Hawaii. In addition, its message was disguised with a bright and gay melody. It could, therefore, be sung in most public places without much fear of *haoles* deciphering its content.

As the song became a popular staple of Hawaiian singers at the turn of the century, its name was changed to *"Kaulana Na Pua"* (Famous Are the Flowers).[4] This change meant the song's title could be translated for non-Hawaiians, and the whole thing could be passed off as a gay musical tribute to tropical flowers, produced, sung, and enjoyed by "happy-go-lucky" Hawaiians—even as its deep political meaning continued to be understood by native people.

This disguising of meaning is called *kaona* in Hawaiian, and is a traditional element of the culture, found to as great an extent in the new, pop-oriented music of today as it was in these turn-of-the-century songs. The *kaona* style is also evident in *"Ku'u Pua I Paokalani,"* a song written by Queen Lili'u-o-Ka-lani herself during her imprisonment by the Americans in the 'Io lani Palace, and which has been revived by the new singers of today. The song title translates as "My Flower At Paokalani," which was the name of the Queen's home and garden. In Hawaiian, *paokalani* means "fragrance of the royal chief——the first layer of hidden meaning to the song. Also, this is a name song *(mel inoa),* a traditional form in Hawaiian culture, that is said to have been dedicated to the son of Evelyn Townsend Wilson (though this was never admitted to), an intimate of the Queen who voluntarily went into imprisonment with her. Her son, John Wilson, smuggled to the Queen newspapers, which were banned, by wrapping flowers picked from her gardens in them and delivering them to the palace. And yet the lyrics to this quietly beautiful song literally refer only to "the gentle breeze" that "blows to me the fragrance of my gentle flower."[5]

Finally, today, the site of Paokalani is occupied by the concrete parking lot and high-rise form of a Holiday Inn—a fact not lost on local audiences, nor on the artists, such as George Helm, who have revived the song.

Such songs of social protest have been kept alive among the people and sung in community gatherings throughout this century. They have become the touchstone upon which a fragile thread of musical dissent has stretched—connecting people and generations—from that earlier time of oppression until the current musical explosion in Hawaii that has brought these themes out, vividly, into the open.

Tourism and the Invention of Commercial Hawaiian Music

As the United States took over formal power in the Islands via annexation, interest on the mainland in things Hawaiian began to catch fire. In 1912, the Broadway production of "Bird of Paradise," with its Hawaiian theme and pseudo-Hawaiian music, was the talk of the nation. And when a group of Hawaiian musicians, singers, and dancers—featuring George E.K. Awai's Royal Hawaiian Quartet—were headline acts at the Panama-

Pacific International Exposition in San Francisco in 1913, a musical craze was born that was to sweep the United States and, later, Western Europe as well.[6]

The early Hawaiian musicians—Awai, Frank Ferara, and Sol Hoopii (who played background music for many Paramount movies)—inspired mainland music composers, the Tin Pan Alley people, to begin writing this sort of material for mass consumption. The result was a series of "phony" Hawaiian songs, many with nonsense lyrics that were supposed to "sound" like the Hawaiian language, such as "Oh, How She Could Yacki Hacki Wicki Wacki Woo (That's Love in Honolulu)," a big hit across mainland America in 1919.

The sexual suggestiveness of "Wicki Wacki Woo" was amplified in songs that were pointedly degrading to the Hawaiian, such as Harry Owens' "Princess Poo-Poo-Ly Has Plenty Papaya," which is not only racist and demeaning to Hawaiian women, but also mocks the recently overthrown Hawaiian monarchy in lyrics such as:

> The Princess Poo-Poo-Ly has plenty papaya
> She loves to give them away
> For all the neighbors, they say...
> Oh me, oh my, you really should try
> A little piece of the Princess Poo-Poo-Ly's papaya
> Ssa, sasa, sasa, sasa, say.
> She may give you the fruit
> But she holds on to the root
> Sasa, sasa, sasa, sasa say.[7]

At the time he wrote this song, Owens was band leader at the ballroom of the newly opened Royal Hawaiian Hotel (the "Pink Palace") in Waikiki.[8] Phony songs such as these, many of them written a continent and an ocean away from Hawaii in New York City, only added fuel to the emerging stereotype of native Hawaiians as lazy, happy-go-lucky, music-loving, sexually promiscuous primitives who were only too happy to perform for the civilized white mainlanders. Now, with Owens and others, these songs were coming "home" to Hawaii, to entertain the growing number of around-the-world cruise line tourists, and others, who were stopping off—and staying—in the newly constructed Island hotels.

The first of these hotels, the Moana, was built in 1901 in the Waikiki area, then primarily a marshy farmland where rice was grown and where a few people had beach homes.[9] The Moana, a grand, five-story structure, could be seen from all over Honolulu—the first of what was to become, by mid-century, an urban nightmare of high rises catering to the mainland tourist industry.

In its time, the Moana was a grand dame—tourists arriving by ship on the Matson Line could stroll on the beach or be entertained in the hotel's outdoor courtyard, shaded by an immense banyan tree. The tourists expected Hawaiian song and dance in the hotel, and they gòt it. Local entertainers, such as Frank Ferara and Pali Lua and his Bird of Paradise Trio would sing and strum gentle versions of Hawaiian tunes—as likely as not following arrangements made popular on mainland America, rather than in Hawaii.

In the early 1920s, an immense dredging and land-fill project in Waikiki displaced local rice growers and obscured several native religious sites, as it announced the conscious development of tourism as a major industry in Hawaii. Farms and rice paddies were replaced with white coral chip acreage. Later, sand would be hauled in and dumped, to create the famous beaches of Waikiki. In 1927, the Royal Hawaiian Hotel opened its doors—the first "resort concept" hotel of its kind—and tourists, traveling on world-cruise steamers, voted it "The World's Most Beautiful Hotel."[10]

As more hotels opened in Waikiki, commercial "Hawaiian" music seemed the natural sound for the stage shows and dance bands that sprang up with the tourist industry. Ragtime, jazz, blues, foxtrot—all were used in creating songs with Hawaiian themes, but with English lyrics and sensibilities. These *hapa haole* songs, played live in Waikiki and across the United States by touring bands, were broadcast throughout the world on radio programs such as the famous Webley Edwards-hosted "Hawaii Calls," as well as being featured in films such as Bing Crosby's 1937 *Waikiki Wedding,* (filmed entirely in southern California), from which the Harry Owens song "Sweet Leilani" won the Oscar for best song.[11]

This music, much of it commercially produced by non-Hawaiians, came to be defined as authentic Hawaiian music and was mistakenly assumed to represent and reflect the cultural identity of the people. Although the fragile tradition of authentic Hawaiian music was kept alive by some—mainly in the rural areas of the Islands—it was true, sadly, that even among Hawaiians themselves, many took on this "false culture" and the impact of its negative images of Hawaiians as part of their heritage. From 1930 and on into the 1950s, this "Hawaiian Sound" flourished commercially both on the American mainland (especially in the 1930s and 1940s) and in the lounges and supper clubs of Waikiki.

In 1959, the incorporation of Hawaii into the United States as a state and the increased ease of reaching the Islands via mass air travel intensified mainland interest in Hawaii. Middle-class tourist trade to the Islands heated up and was reflected throughout U.S. popular culture, in television programs such as *Hawaiian Eye,* books such as James Michner's *Hawaii,* and the infamous hula hoop craze. This new mainland interest was also reflected in the commercial music of the time, which added the "exotic" Island sounds of Martin Denny and Arthur Lyman (and Elvis Presley's "Blue Hawaii") to the commercial *hapa haole* standards of the 1930s and 1940s.

Completing the musical mix by incorporating into it the mainstream easy listening pop and country sound of the early 1960s, Don Ho and the Aliis, performing nightly at Duke Kahanamoku's, rapidly became the most popular act in Waikiki, playing such songs as "I'll Remember You," and the ever requested "Tiny Bubbles." With a mainland recording contract and hit songs that swept the easy listening American music market, Don Ho *was,* in the 1960s, Hawaiian music to most Americans. As the Don Ho Show became increasingly bloated with hoax and hype—middle-aged tourist women stepping on stage to be kissed by the entertainer and staying there to be taught, and dance, the "traditional" hula—many Hawaiians began to distance themselves from this spectacle that commercial Hawaiian music and culture had become. As Charles K.L. Davis, a noted traditional performer, said: "Hawaiian music is going right down the drain as far as Waikiki goes...it's a shame. Have you seen [Don Ho's] show lately? Awwwe! It's the most frightening thing I've ever seen...It was just dismal. God, it was awful! It's absolute amateur hour."[12]

Don Ho, in his turn, defended the show and its content and intentions: "I do it because people pay me a lot of money to do it...So what if the show's for tourists? What's wrong with tourists? I mean, why are local people so prejudiced against tourists?"[13]

The Creation of Popular Protest Music in Hawaii

That there was something new beginning to happen culturally and musically in Hawaii was evidenced by the decision, in November 1966, of a local radio station—KCCN—to broadcast Hawaiian music exclusively, 24 hours a day. Although a good deal of the available music was of the commercial, tourist variety, some of it was authentic, traditional, and "grassroots." This music was being made by a few artists, people like Genoa Keawe, Maki Beamer, Gabby Pahinui and the Sons of Hawaii, who were performing in the old styles and keeping alive a tenuous and fragile musical tradition—one that was supported mostly in rural and working-class, blue-collar Hawaiian areas and venues. This music, much of it programmed at first in order to fill the demands of 24 hours a day of programming, became, upon its exposure, increasingly popular with the more urban-oriented, socially conscious, and dissatisfied young Hawaiians who listened to this local station. As the station received feedback from this highly vocal audience, traditional Hawaiian music began to make up more and more of the playlist.

Due to pressure from the owners, in 1969 the station briefly entertained the idea of dropping the all-Hawaiian format, but abandoned its plans when it received 4,200 letters of opposition in one week's time.[14] In April 1971, KCCN sponsored a four-hour concert at the Waikiki Shell that featured over 50 local musicians, many of whom played traditional music in the old styles. The concert was a sell-out and a symbolic watershed in the resurgence of interest in authentic Hawaiian music.

Much of this interest from young Hawaiians who were searching for some sort of cultural roots resulted not only in their increasingly strong support of the few traditionalists who were still performing, but also in their own desire to play this music, to be a part of this tradition, and, soon following from this, to create new music within the old traditional forms. As Krash Kealoha, then station manager of KCCN, explained it in 1973:

> Up until that point [1970], we were playing old Hawaiian music and hapa haole tunes. Then several kids started talking to me, and it turned out they were disappointed because they were writing their own music and coming up with their own style, and some were even going into the studios and spending their own money—$5,000 or whatever it cost to produce a record. But when the record came out, it wouldn't get on any radio stations...At first there was a lot of resistance from our steady listeners [to us playing this new music], some of the older people who felt anything that wasn't sung in Hawaiian was rock and roll.[15]

KCCN, with its exclusive focus, became a key in dissemination and popularization of the new Hawaiian music, as well as a source of information about the music and the people who were creating it.

A second key to the launching of the new music was the interaction between an aging traditional singer from the poor town of Waimanalo, Phillip Pahinui (who died of a heart attack in 1980), and two young musicians, Peter Moon and Palani Vaughn. Pahinui, better known as "Gabby" or "Pops," had been active musically in the 1930s, '40s, and early '50s, playing mostly traditional music, though he was, at times, heavily influenced by mainland jazz and did play in the lounges of the tourist hotels early in his career. But his music had not been popular enough to base a career around, and he made his living working on street crews for the city of Honolulu. By the 1960s, he remembered: "I had just about given up, was working with the City and County then. The only time we'd play music was when we'd finish work on the road and sit down under a tree and strum."[16]

Peter Moon and others, attracted by Gabby's knowledge of the old songs and the techniques of slack key guitar playing, haunted him for lessons. As Moon said:

> Gabby is the truth master, the real thing. The old man down in Waimanalo with the chickens...He's just uncanny, he baffles us four or five times a year. He'll play slack key in these real old tunings, then smile at Cyril [his son] and me as if to say, "See, you didn't think I had it, did you."[17]

At the same time that Peter Moon was learning slack key guitar from Gabby Pahinui, Palani Vaughn was seriously researching Hawaii's musical past, looking for material upon which to build a career. Vaughn met Peter Moon in a course on Hawaiian art history at the University of Hawaii, and soon the two of them formed a band.

The Sunday Manoa, first recorded in 1969 and the most influential of the new Hawaiian groups, originally consisted of Moon, Vaughn, Baby Kalima, and two of Gabby Pahinui's sons, Cyril and Bla. Not only did all these young musicians have a strong interest and grounding in traditional Hawaiian music, they also had been extensively exposed to the popular traditions of 1960s youth music and politics, from Bob Dylan to the Beatles. Prior to his involvement with Pahinui, Peter Moon himself had gone to school in the early- and mid-1960s on the American mainland, where he soaked up the sounds of social change that were being created in American and British music of the time.[18]

Adding some amplification and increasing the number of instruments used, while experimenting harmonically, the Sunday Manoa developed a style of playing that pleased most of the purists, but still attracted the interests of the younger, pop-oriented listeners. Within a month of organizing in a garage in Waimanalo, the band landed a local recording contract and was playing regularly in the Kahala area, in many of the same clubs that were keeping Gabby Pahinui and other traditionally oriented singers afloat. In addition, their recordings began to be aired on KCCN, and the band began to attract a following. Their album *Cracked Seed,* recorded in the early 1970s, sold nearly 30,000 copies in one year in Hawaii—a huge number for a local band on a local label—showing that a band could remain faithful to traditional music and also be an economic success in the Islands.

But, having said that, it is important to note that the music of the Sunday Manoa was *not* traditional, acoustic Hawaiian folk music. It was electric, with a jazz/rock thrust that put the group in the mainstream of pop. As Peter Moon told an interviewer in 1972, who asked him why, when so much traditional Hawaiian music was written to be played as ballads or at hula tempo, did the Sunday Manoa play so many fast, up-tempo numbers. Moon replied: "It was because we were in a club 75 to 80 percent of the time. You've gotta sell drinks, you've gotta get the people going. We're pop music, no matter what people say."[19]

With the success of the Sunday Manoa, there quickly came other bands, intent on creating a new music of pop/rock through the late 1970s and 1980s that touched both the dissatisfied urban youth of Hawaii and, hopefully, their rural elders, who had kept alive the tradition of social protest against the *haole* outsider that they were drawing upon for inspiration.

The new musical groups of this movement refused to continue the tradition of "cute" group names of the hotel performers of the past, like the

Royal Hawaiian Serenaders or the Waikiki Beachboys—names that conjured up images of happy-go-lucky brown lackies of the Hawaiian films and nightclubs. Instead, they named themselves after Hawaii, the land: the Sunday Manoa, Ma Kapu'u Sand Band, Hui Ohana, Hokule'a, the Makaha Sons of Ni'i'hau.

This last group's name cleverly makes all the cultural connections of the new music. Makaha is an area near Honolulu that is poor, blue collar, and overwhelmingly native Hawaiian. Ni'i'hau is a small island that has resisted the cultural onslaught of the 20th century. The few native Hawaiian families who live there work the land in the old ways. There is no electricity, no running water. No one, not even the governor of the state, is allowed on Ni'i'hau without an invitation. Being "sons of" this island (which two of the group actually are) links them with the past and, at the same time, the land that means so much to Hawaiians.

The Sound of Social Change

This new music has had much in common with the music of many emergent social and cultural movements, performing ideological, motivational, and integrative functions for those who perform and listen to it. It is nationalistic and, above all, celebrates the traditions of native Hawaiians, in opposition and reaction to the cultural domination of the mainland United States and the entertainment needs of the booming tourist industry of the 1970s and 1980s.

An ongoing concern with the land is a theme strongly reflected in the lyrics of the new songs (such as *"E Kuu* Morning Dew," and *"Nanakuli* Blues") which celebrate the beauty of various Island places and lament their destruction by contemporary off-Island concerns, or the fact that the land—once Hawaiian—is now owned by foreigners who refuse to treat it with the care and reverence it demands. George Helm, a singer and activist who was lost at sea in 1977 while protesting against the U.S. military use of Kahoolawe Island as a practice bombing range, said in description of these new songs:

> Hawaiian views on nature are the subject of many songs and contain a true respect for nature. Many of the songs now openly express, if one understands the words, the language—pain, revolution; it's expressing the emotional reaction the Hawaiians are feeling to the subversion of their lifestyle—without the *aine* [land] and without the *aloha aina* [love of the land], we have nothing.[20]

The second major topic addressed in the lyrics of the new music is hostility toward the tourists and the U.S. military, and criticism of their impact on Hawaii in terms of land use, real estate development, and bastardization and cooptation of traditional Hawaiian culture. Walter Ritte articulated this feeling in a 1982 interview:

> We have no control over the tourist industry. It's like a giant malignant cancer and it's eating up all our beaches, all the places that are profound for our culture. It's grabbing them. They take the best. You know, at least Captain Cook gave us a nail—one nail for three pigs and caskets of water. They're not even giving us the nail back.[21]

Songs dealing with tourism and its impact include Chip Hatlelid's "Fujumina Store," which chronicles the tearing down of an old landmark business to build a shopping complex, and Olomana's songs about the re-zoning of Kawela Bay and Turtle Bay in order that new resort hotels could be built. As Olomana's Jerry Santos said: "Nobody even knew about it…but if you sing a song…all kinds of people will know."[22]

A third strong theme in this new music is that of an urgent concern for preserving the traditional ways of Hawaii, and even the Hawaiian race itself. Songs such as "All Hawaii Stands Together" and *"E Na Hawai'i"* are eloquent in addressing this theme. As Palani Vaughn, who has written a number of these sorts of songs, has said of his work: "By the third album, the content got rather political, saying things like 'the race is dying, but we must survive.' In fact I've been called a racist, but my answer is the Hawaiian race is a dying one and I don't find it a crime to foster its survival."[23]

Finally, these songs—in their messages and in the traditional instruments that are many times used in playing them—consciously attempt to connect themselves to that thin and fragile line of social protest in Hawaiian music that, since the time of annexation, had been kept alive mainly in the rural areas by a handful of respected artists. George Helm would always begin his concerts with the Hawaiian phrase *He punahele no 'e na Ka makua,* which translates to "You are the favorite of the generation before." In his choice of material, Helm (who, after his death, was elevated to the status of martyr by the movement) relied heavily on songs written in the first half of this century by native Hawaiians—songs that, in their fragile, rural voices, spoke out against the destruction of Hawaiian culture. He called these songs Hawaiian soul. As his close friend 'Ilimia Pi'ianai'a observed:

> George came to understand the political activism, the crying hurt and the unspoken dignity of the Hawaiians of the 1920s, the 1930s and the 1940s through these songs, which were very dear to him…a connection that flowered in his generation, in the movement he was a big part of.[24]

The Music, the Movement, and the Tourist Industry

From the mid-1970s on, this new, politically aware Hawaiian popular music was heard—not only on radio stations such as KCCN, but also at meetings and gatherings of the people. When the Hawaii Coalition for Native Claims held fundraising concerts on the 'Iolani Palace lawn, Hawaiian musicians, singers, and dancers performed from nine in the morning, non-stop, until dusk. When there were skirmishes with land developers, when demands were made for long-promised Hawaiian homestead lands, when the H-3 freeway drew fire from environmentalists, when protesters occupied the small island of Kahoolawe to protest its use as a bombing target by the U.S. military, the music was there, articulating an ideology of protest and opposition to the dominant, mainland controlled political and economic culture of the state.

By 1978, the movement—and its music—had brought enough pressure to bear that the Office of Hawaiian Affairs was created and official attention was paid to issues of education and land tenure at the State Constitutional Convention. The leader of that convention, John Waihee, called the new music of the movement the "glue that held this package together." In addition, Hawaiian was officially recognized, along with English, as a language of the state.

And yet, even as it proved effective in mobilizing cultural and social protest in Hawaii, this new music was popular far beyond the boundaries of these social movements. Peter Moon and the Sunday Manoa could sell 30,000 to 40,000 copies of their albums in this relatively tiny consumer market, sandwiched as it is between the world's two largest music markets—those of the United States and Japan. Songs such as Moon's reggae-tinged "Guava Jelly" and the wildly exciting "Cane Fire" (which documents with indelible Vietnam-tinged images the irresponsible burning of the cane fields—dark smoke obscuring the sun, poor native kids running to escape the flames, the helicopters of the establishment roaring above the inferno) shot to the top of the pop charts in Hawaii, and were clearly heard—and purchased—by some of the tourist trade, as well as by many local people who were not at all directly involved in the activist part of the movement. In fact, as contradictory as it may sound, there are those who speculate that without the tourist industry and the market it created in Hawaii, there could likely have arisen no strong musical and cultural movement to oppose it.

KCCN, the radio station that first aired the new music, did so in order to fill air space—space that was sold commercially primarily because of the tourist population of Honolulu and Waikiki. In addition, the studios and recording technology necessary to record the new music was already available and in place because of the on-going and lucrative business of recording tourist-oriented music for souvenir-type albums and cassette tapes.

As far as exposure of new acts goes, Peter Moon and the Sunday Manoa first broke into the urban Honolulu scene (from the more rural club dates they had been playing) at Chuck's Cellar, located underneath Don Ho's Polynesian Palace in the glittering heart of the tourist district. And Millie Fujinaga, a Japanese hotel manager who ran a Waikiki nightclub called The Noodle Shop, is generally credited by the new music community as having done as much, or more, than anyone in first bringing local Hawaiian musicians together. Moe Keale, a musician of the movement, said of Fujinaga: "Besides bringing Hawaiians together, she also keep us Hawaiians working."[25]

George Kanahele of the Hawaiian Music Foundation has claimed:

> Tourism has been good to Hawaiian music. It has created a vast new market; it has helped to discover and encourage new talent; it has inspired new songs and new styles of playing; and, above all, it has provided jobs to Hawaiian musicians. In a sense, the tourist industry is the grand patron, albeit a very impersonal one, of Hawaiian music.[26]

And, although they do not like a lot of what they have to do, a good number of the musicians of the movement do play some gigs in the tourist centers, in order to keep food on the table and also to stay in the music business.[27] Gabby Pahinui spoke of the feeling when "you have the right atmosphere with some old folks dancing. But when you go into a place with chandeliers and candles, you…have to play songs like 'Blue Lei,' and 'Sweet Leilani.'"[28] And Peter Moon has pointed out that "Hawaiian musicians adopt these other styles because they have to, in order to make a living. But you can only compromise so much."[29]

As Hawaiian music and culture moves into the 1990s, the compromises have taken on still another twist. As could have been predicted, by becoming as popular and as visible as it did in the 1980s, the new Hawaiian music has also become marketable in the tourist industry, especially to the younger professional mainland crowd who remember the 1960s and musical protest, and are in the market for consuming "authentic" culture. As Peter Moon has said, "People are interested now more in the real, the grass roots. And the recording industry is a very powerful media…A lot of people are looking at us…at slack key…like people are looking at reggae. The industry's always looking for something new, every hour of the day."[30] The Brothers Cazimero, originally a part of the Sunday Manoa, have been lured to the Monarch Room of the Royal Hawaiian Hotel, where they perform their "authentic" Hawaiian music for those tourists who want to experience the *real* Hawaii. Tickets for the annual concert of traditional Hawaiian music, *kanikapila,* are obtainable in the tourist agencies of Waikiki and in the major hotels. Hui Ohana, a popular movement band that had broken up, reunited in 1987 for a Waikiki Shell concert and reunion album that won them a *Ma Hoku Hanohano* Award—an honor created in 1977 by

KCCN radio and awarded annually by the Hawaii Academy of Recording Arts. Traditional slack key guitar styles, resurrected by movement musicians were fused with U.S. mainstream pop by Keola and Kapono Beamer to create the hit, "Honolulu City Lights," a bouncy tune that became the most popular Island song of the 1980s.

As the 1990s dawn, reggae-inspired Island music has become the latest "new" sound—likely inspired by Peter Moon's 1982 hit "Guava Jelly," which mixed Jamaican rhythms and Hawaiian images. Moon himself recently has reached back to Tin Pan Alley to record "Stardust," although he has not given up his commitment to songs of social protest. "Chinatown," on the same album as "Stardust" looks at what has happened to that area of Honolulu. "You can smell hell burnin' in times like these," he sings, as he paints pictures of gang wars, run-down tenements, and old men "living from a tin can."[31]

Conclusion

And yet, no matter how hard the culture industry tries to co-opt Hawaii's new music, the fact remains that change—political, social, and cultural—occurred in Hawaii in the 1980s in no small part due to the efforts of these artists and the effects of their music. The motivating force of any cultural renewal is stronger identity, greater self-esteem, pride, and dignity. Ultimately, these qualities become goals that can only be fully realized in the market place and in the arena of political power. Some of this is difficult to measure, but, in Hawaii, it does exist.

As George Kanehele saw beginning to happen in the late 1970s, Hawaiians are coming together far more now than they ever did before the advent of the movement—at hula competitions, musical concerns, political gatherings, and church meetings. The specific political gains made—such as the declaration of Hawaiian as an official language of the state, and changes in the allocation and tenure of Hawaiian land for native Hawaiians—are tangible and hard-won. But, in addition, this coming together has led to a spirit of awareness, of self-identity and pride—which, in turn, is reflected in the new music. This feeling of social solidarity and ethnic and cultural pride, awakened by the movement and nurtured by the music, is a force that now has to be taken seriously in the politics and culture of Hawaii.

Israel Kamakawiwaole finishes the smoky blues, sung in Hawaiian, with a flourish. "Someone tell me some *haoles* in dis place," he says with a grin, rolling his eyes. There's a laugh from the audience. "Poor *haoles,* don' unnerstan' dose Hawaiian words," Israel shakes his head sadly, "Hey, I got it," he says brightly. "You guys, you go down Waikiki. You unnerstan' *all* the words down there, yeah!" As the audience claps and whistles its appreciation, Israel says softly, "You unnerstan' us soon enough."

Youssou N'Dour (Photo © Karen N'Dour)

Some Anti-Hegemonic Aspects of African Popular Music

John Collins

There are many differing views held by social and developmental scientists on the role of popular culture, art, and music in relation to the expression and consolidation of social power. Some see it as a medium through which a central social group controls society; indeed, the structural-functionalists (pre-war British social anthropologists, Talcott Parsons, and others) saw all art and music, not just the popular variety, as part of a tension-managing mechanism regulating the values and "needs" of society. Opposed to these "consensus" models are the "conflict" ones; but these too treat popular culture as an ideological tool used by the ruling class or group to hold power or hegemony. For instance, the Marxist-influenced "Frankfurt School" of pre-war Germany was hostile to popular culture, seeing it as a form of instant gratification that helps create "false consciousness" and what Herbert Marcuse called the "repressive tolerance" of the ruling class.

However, the Italian Marxist Antonio Gramsci, who coined the word "hegemony,"[1] opposed his contemporaries of the Frankfurt School in treating popular culture as an anti-hegemonic or "people's art" that could potentially threaten the ruling class, whose hegemony was never permanent. Gramsci's ideas have never been very influential, and today many writers consider popular culture to have a dual aspect, for besides being hegemonic and associated with social and bureaucratic control, it can also be anti-hegemonic, decentralizing, and individualistic—what Hans Magnus Ensenburger calls "repressive" and "emancipatory,"[2] C.W.E. Bigsby "epithanic" and "apocalyptic,"[3] and James Carey "centripetal" and "centrifugal."[4] Raymond Williams also notes this double aspect when he distinguishes between popular culture which is "developed by the people or by the majority of the people to express their own meanings and values"[5] and mass culture (which incorporates areas of popular culture) which is "developed for people by an internal or external group, imbedded in them by a range imbedded in them by a range of processes from repressive imposition to commercial saturation."[6]

The recent history of African popular music throws light on the anti-hegemonic side of popular culture, for Africa has been faced with the hegemony of the colonial and neo-colonial powers, and some local popular musicians have attempted to overcome the resulting "cultural imperialism" in various ways, three of which will be discussed here in some detail. First, African popular musicians have "indigenized" their music; second, they have utilized the black music of the New World; and third, they have continued the African tradition of using music to voice protest and social conflict.

The Indigenization of Acculturated African Popular Music

It should first be noted that modernization in Africa does not necessarily imply "cultural imperialization," as an indigenous culture may actually employ external influences for its own purposes, by first imitating and then assimilating them into its own cultural experience. This process has been noted by the writers James Lull,[7] D. Marks,[8] and Paul Rutten[9] to apply even to the popular music of European countries undergoing Anglo-Americanization. And this is also one of the conclusions in Wallis and Malm's book[10] on the popular music industry of 12 small countries (including East African ones) being affected by Western multinationals; for this process of "transculturation," as they call it, besides leading to the formation of a standardized music reflecting Anglo-American culture, also includes the catalytic influence this imported culture has in generating a thriving indigenous music scene. Likewise, David Coplan's work on the black South African popular music scene[11] also demonstrates this double hegemonic/anti-hegemonic aspect of acculturation, which he connects with Western domination on the one hand and the struggle for African cultural autonomy, retrenchment, and indigenization on the other.

The indigenization itself of modern African popular music can be linked to three factors: the geographical diffusion of Western ideas, the cultural tenacity of traditional music, and the emergence of nationalism. And turning first to the indigenization resulting from geographical spread, which may occur when an acculturated music develops in cities, or in the coastal ports where there was the first contact with Europeans, and then spreads into the rural hinterland becoming de-acculturated as it does so. An example of this is the progressive Africanization of coastal brass-band music, such as the late 19th-century West African *adaha* music, which in the 1930s influenced the local Akan recreational music called *konkomba* or *konkoma*.[12] Another example is the East African *beni* music of the local African "askari" troops of World War I, which turned into the Kalela "tribal" dance of the 1930s and 1940s.[13] The geographical factor also applies when an acculturated popular music develops in one African country and then spreads into other African countries where it creates secondary local varieties. For instance, Zairean rumba-influenced "Congo Jazz" spread into Tanzania during the 1960s where it became the "Swahili Jazz" of the mid-seventies.

Indigenization also can take place when an African popular music "re-models"[14] a tenacious traditional genre. It can happen in traditional rural villages, which was the case when the brass band-influenced *konkomba* music, mentioned above, affected the traditional recreational music of the Ewe people of Ghana and Togo during the 1950s—becoming a neo-traditional drum and dance style known as *Borborbor*. Remodeling may also occur in towns where there are large numbers of new rural migrants or where there is a strong "residual" performance style[15] that has "[survived] from the past and [is] available to be re-worked to form new styles."[16] Another example from Ghana is the neo-traditional dance style known as *kpanlogo* which grew up in the mid-1960s through the impact of acculturated highlife music on the traditional recreational music of the Ga people.[17]

The indigenization of popular music is also related to the growth of African nationalism—both of the pre- and post-independence variety. The early nationalist movement began partly as a result of a change in European colonial policy in the late 19th century. Up to the middle of that century it had been policy to foster the growth of a Europeanized African class, but later, with the "scramble for Africa," the Berlin Conference of 1885, and the discovery of quinine (enabling white traders to settle in malarial areas), the Westernized African elite and merchant princes became a threat to late imperial expansion. At the same time, "scientific racism" was concocted and Africa was depicted as a "Dark Continent" with no history. Consequently, African nations were ideologically demoted to "tribes," and there grew up an intense imperial hatred of the African elite whom racists believed disguised their natural "inferior" condition under a thin veneer of European dress, customs, and art forms. For instance, in Nigeria, up to the 1880s the black elite replicated European dramatic, literary, and musical forms through such organizations as Friends of the Academy,[18] the Lagos Philharmonic Society,[19] and the Handel Festival.[20] However, the increasing colonial institutional racism and progressive exclusion of the African elite from administrative jobs and the economic sections they had previously dominated led to an African "united opposition from 1897 to 1915,"[21] and the "nationalist generation."[22] Similarly, in late 19th-century South Africa, when the African imitation of Western culture "failed to achieve major gains in autonomy, contrary tendencies towards cultural retrenchment emerged...leading to a heightened sense of cultural nationalism."[23] The musical consequences of this were the Africanization of hymns by separatist Christian churches, such as the United Native African Church of Nigeria (established in 1891) and the Nazarite Faith of South Africa (established in 1911), and the use of traditional music by the African elite. For instance, Yoruba music "played an important role in the labyrinthian maneuvers of the nationalists of the 1920s and 1930s."[24]

Since independence in Africa, this indigenization and national cultural revival has become even more important—and even government policy. Some examples are Tanzania, where President Nyere banned foreign pop music on national radio in 1973, and the following year set up the Ministry of National Culture and Youth "which encouraged dance-bands to compose music that supported the policies of the party and the government."[25] And when Guinea gained independence in 1958, President Sekou Toure expelled French musicians and supported local groups like Bembeya Jazz and Les Ballets Africain.[26] In a similar vein, during Zaire's "Authenticite" campaign of the early 1970s, President Mobutu ordered all local musicians to use their African rather than their European names;[27] for instance, the famous *soukous* or "Congo Jazz" artists Franco and Rochereau became known as Luamba Makiadi and Tabu Ley respectively. Likewise, Ghana's Dr. Nkrumah attempted in the late 1950s to change the name "highlife" to an indigenous one, *osibisaaba*,[28] although in this he was unsuccessful due to resistance from local musicians. Indeed, this search for African identity has spilled beyond national borders in the form of Pan African festivals such as those held in Dakar in 1966, Algeria in 1969, and Nigeria in 1977.

The Musical Influence on Africa of the Black Diaspora

The black music of the New World has and is playing a part in the African pursuit of autonomy and identity, and this influence can be traced as far back as to the introduction of Jamaican *gumbey* or *gombe* music to West Africa in the 1830s[29] and the syncopated brass-band music of West Indian regimental bands stationed there from the mid-19th century,[30] followed first in South Africa[31] and then West Africa[32] by a craze for black minstrelsy and ragtime music. This influence from the black Americas, however, occurred later in Central Africa, where the rumba became popular from the inter-war period, and last of all in East Africa where local popular dance music arose after World War II "primarily from influences not of 'European' but of Afro-American origin."[33]

In fact the black American influence on Africa, both musically and non-musically, has both enhanced and hindered colonial and Anglo-American domination. On the hegemonic side, West Indian troops were used by the colonialists, as were West Indian and African American missionaries. And some of the first African elites who introduced Western ways were the descendants of freed slaves. These include the Krios (Creoles) of Freetown, Sierra Leone, who were returned from North America from the 1790s onward, and the Americo-Liberian elite who were returned from the 1820s by the American Colonisation Society; and the West African Brazilian elite who came from South America from the 1840s, bringing with them Afro-Brazilian Calunga and Carata masquerades[34] and the samba drum.[35]

The anti-hegemonic effect of this influence from the black diaspora is noted by David Coplan, who relates it to "African urban cultural adaption and identity";[36] he also adds that some of the black American Christian missionaries, such as Bishop Turner,[37] actually helped the black South African nationalist cause. Similarly, some of the first African nationalist ideas were introduced to Africa by African American and black Caribbean writers such as Edmund Blyden, Aimé Cesaire, Marcus Garvey, George Padmore, W.E.B. DuBois, and others. Music has also been involved as African musicians have partially been able to by-pass or short-circuit white "cultural imperialism" through the selective borrowing and incorporation of ideas from the black part of the spectrum of imported Western popular performing arts. Some early examples are the catalytic effect of West Indian regimental brass band musicians who played calypsos as well as martial music and made an impact on the *adaha* variety of highlife[38]; the Brazilian influence on early *juju* music, for instance the small square *samba* drum[39]; the impact of the *rumba* on "Congo jazz"; and of ragtime and jazz on the growth of South African popular music.[40]

Since the 1950s and 1960s many black American musicians who play jazz, samba, soul, reggae, rastafarian, and other "roots" music have been inspired by the message of black power, black pride, and the African heritage; indeed many have visited Africa, including James Brown, Jimmy Cliff, Bob Marley, Max Roach, Tina Turner, Randy Weston, and Gilberto Gil, to name a few. This in turn has contributed to black African cultural autonomy, for paradoxically, in copying these black American artists, Africans are being turned toward their own resources, which in recent years has led to the creative explosion of numerous African "pop" styles, such as Afro-rock (e.g., Ghana's Osibisa), Afrobeat (e.g., Nigeria's Fela Anikulapo-Kuti), and Afro-reggae (e.g., Côte D'Ivoire's Alpha Blondy). This imported black American influence has also encouraged the exploration of local roots by contemporary African musicians which has resulted in such music styles as the Ga "cultural" music since the 1970s and the *mbalax* music of Youssou N'Dour of Senegal in the 1980s.

The major reason for this long-term selective African preference for the black rather than the white music of the New World is due to their similarities in socio-historical experience and music. For, as noted by various writers on social and musical change, similarities between interacting cultures provide "cultural analogues" that enhance acculturation[41] and create a familiarity or shared environment that fosters "co-orientation"[42]—or what Luke Uche, in his study of the Nigerian popular music industry, calls "cultural triangulation."[43]

Coplan notes the first type of socio-historical similarity, or shared environment, when he states that "the appeal of black American performance styles in South Africa derives from a comparable experience of two peoples under white domination"[44]—that is, "colonialism" in Africa and the old "Jim Crow" laws in the United States. Since the 1950s, the similarities remain, but are different; for there has been the success of black civil rights in the United States and independence in the Caribbean and Africa.

The musical similarities or analogues between Africa and the black Americas stem largely from the fact that millions of African slaves were taken to the New World during the black diaspora, taking their culture and music with them. And this has remained, either in transmuted form or— particularly in South America and the Caribbean—more or less intact. However, even in Protestant North America, where the suppression of African culture was more thorough, there is much musicological evidence of African retentions in the blues, jazz, and many other types of music. (See writers such as Melville Herskovitz,[45] Rudi Blesh,[46] Richard Waterman,[47] LeRoi Jones,[48] and Paul Oliver.[49])

The other half of the story, the return of black New World performing arts to Africa, has not been so well documented as has the study of African retentions in the Americas. Nevertheless, most writers on African popular music have noted this imported black influence, and, according to John Storm Roberts, "there is no mystery about why the different Afro-American styles were influential in different parts of Africa. In West Africa and the Congo, Cuban music was returning with interest something that had largely come from there anyway, so there was a most natural affinity."[50] Indeed, because the Cuban rumba and other black New World dance music coming into Africa are partially of African origin, this trans-Atlantic cycle of music leaving Africa during the diaspora and then returning can be treated as a form of cultural "feedback." In short, what was taken from Africa to the Americas in the days of slavery has, in various transmuted forms, been reclaimed by Africa in the 20th century.

Popular Music and the African Tradition of Protest and Social Conflict

African popular music is also anti-hegemonic, by carrying on the tradition of using music to express group conflict within the context of social change. The old European image of traditional Africa and its music as only geared to social cohesion and static equilibrium is in fact an ideological concept—like "primitive" and "tribes"—created by colonialists who wanted passive subjects without their own history.

But far from static, modern historians are now stressing the dynamic aspects of pre-colonial Africa; and as the Ghanaian musicologist J.H.K. Nketia states in connection with traditional Akan dance-music styles, "the creation of new musical types is encouraged in African societies."[51] And these traditional styles have often been associated with social tension. Male and female age-sets and secret societies would sometimes demonstrate conflict with the older generation through musical ridicule, for instance by the masked dancer of the Poro secret society of the Mende people of Sierra Leone;[52] and the Akan warrior of Asafo Companies could literally drum a despotic chief or elder out of town. Indeed, the talking drums were actually employed in warfare, which is one of the reasons why the traditional drums of the African slaves were banned in the New World. Then there were songs and rhymes of mutual insult, such as the *tshikona* dance and musical duel of the Venda people of the Transvaal,[53] a tradition carried through to the New World as African American "dozens"[54] and the *picongs* of the Trinidadian calypso "tent wars."[55]

One specific way in which the dynamic musical tradition has been used in modern Africa is in the struggle against colonialism; and just as the vernacular hymns of the African elite played a part in the nationalist movement, so too did the popular music of the masses. In East Africa, the inter-war clash between the Beni supporters and the missionaries was because Beni tried to "capture and use European symbols,"[56] and the hostility of the colonialists to *beni,* with its drill-like dances and uniformed ranks of performers, was because they thought it was subversive—and, in fact, *beni* did play a role in the 1935 copperbelt strike. Just after World War II, the *gombe* bands of the multi-ethnic youth associations of Côte D'Ivoire were absorbed in the nationalist movement.[57] In Ghana, "John Brown's Body" (a black American Civil War song) was adapted by the nationalists to criticize the British imprisonment of Kwame Nkrumah,[58] and on his release the Akan highlife musician E.K. Nyame welcomed him with the song *"Onim Deefo Kukudurufu Kwame Nkrumah"* (Honorable Man and Hero Kwame Nkrumah).[59] In addition, nationalist sentiments were voiced by some local comic opera songs and plays, such as Ghana's Axim Trio's plays "Nkrumah Will Never Die,"[60] and the Nigerian Hubert Ogunde's play "Strike and Hunger," about the 1945 Nigerian general strike.[61] More recent are the revolutionary *chimurenga* songs of the mid-1970s guerrilla war against the Smith regime in Zimbabwe[62] and the anti-apartheid songs of exiled popular South African musicians such as Miriam Makeba, Hugh Masakela, Dudu Pukwana, and Dollar Brand (Abdullah Ibrahim).

Popular music also has a bearing on social stratification and is particularly identified with the poorer layers of society, as popular musicians in Africa usually come from "intermediate"[63] levels of society such as newly urbanized rural migrants, semi-skilled workers, "laborers, messengers, drivers, railroad men, sailors and clerks."[64] Popular music styles also symbolically help create, amongst both players and audience, shared perceptions of group boundaries and social distance. One of the earliest studies of this phenomenon was of the *kalela* dance of young men in the southern African copperbelt region, carried out in the 1950s by Clyde Mitchell, who considered it to be "an analogue or metaphor for the essential patterns of urban social relations"[65] and connected to modern class distinctions; as the *kalela* was only played and danced by lower class "miners, domestic servants and 'lorry boys.'"[66]

Some popular musicians also make a protest on behalf of the poor and downtrodden, one of the most well-known being Nigeria's Fela Anikulapo-Kuti, whose open political defiance of his government has often gotten him into trouble—for instance, his controversial 1976 album *Zombie* that mocked the military mentality, and later releases such as *V.I.P.* or *Vagabonds In Power* and *Coffin for Head of State*. However, usually in African music, political protest against those in power is not direct but oblique—for instance, in the form of animal parables such as the Ghanaian African Brothers Band's highlife song of the late 1960s, "Ebi Te Yie, Ebi Nte Yie" or "Some Sit Well, Whilst Others Do Not."[67] This song is about a group of animals sitting around a fire (i.e. the national cake), with the smaller animals protesting that the larger ones are hogging all the warmth (i.e. wealth). The title of the song has entered into common Akan parlance, a language in which previously there had been no indigenous word or concept for social strata based on wealth and class. However, according to N.K. Asante-Darko and Sjaak van der Geest, there are two ways in which a highlife song can become political; it "may be intended by the composer, or the public may give it a secret political meaning"[68];—that is, the songs are semiotically given a new "signification"[69] or "handled" in a different way.[70] A Ghanaian example is the 1964 song "Agyima Mansa" by Dr. Gyasi and his Noble Kings highlife guitar band, about the ghost of a mother lamenting the plight of her children. The song was banned from the radio as President Nkrumah believed (although Dr. Gyasi denied it) that the song was secretly being used to criticize his regime—"Mother Ghana" lamenting the plight of her population.[71]

Another protest tradition carried through into popular music in Africa is the expression of new ideas of youth and the conflicts they may have with each other and with the older generation. For instance, the Ambas Deda ethnic union of modernizing Temme immigrant youths in Freetown, Sierra Leone often clashed with the Temme elders.[72] Then the Ghanaian *kpanlogo* music of the mid-1960s, mentioned previously, was created by Ga youths and initially frowned upon by the elders as indecent, and indeed, there was an attempt to ban the *kpanlogo* dance by the Ghana Arts Council, until President Nkrumah himself intervened in the matter in 1965 and patronized a display of *kpanlogo* groups at the stadium at Black Star Square in Accra.[73] In Central Africa the Zaiko Langa Langa guitar band, which was formed in 1970 and, first associated with juvenile delinquents, became a focus of the Zairean youth culture. Since then many bands have modeled themselves on it and there is fierce competition amongst them as to who is the leader of youth fashion.

In recent years women musicians, who have been largely excluded from popular music development in Africa, have been struggling for prominence, one of the first being South Africa's Miriam Makeba, who became a professional dance-band singer in 1954. The feminization of popular music began later in West and Central Africa, partly inspired by Makeba and partly by foreign (including black) artists. According to Dr. Omibiyi-Obidike, "by the middle of the 1970s a generation of Nigerian female pop artists had emerged and had started making their mark on the Nigerian music scene,"[74] although there was male opposition to this development, as expressed, for example, in the 1973 Nigerian highlife song by Godwin Omogbewa called "Man on Top."[75] Likewise, since the 1970s women have entered the Ghanaian concert party (local comic opera) business which previously only employed female impersonators; this process began in the early 1960s, when President Nkrumah set up the Workers Brigade Band and Concert Party that employed both actors and actresses. Although Ghanaian highlife has been a "mainly male affair,"[76] through the separatist church choirs that since the late 1970s have begun playing "gospel highlife," women are finally playing guitar-band music. Previously the guitar was always associated in West Africa with palm-wine bars and drunkeness, and so was put out of bounds to women performers by their parents and families.

Finally, it should be added that African musicians today are able to fight for their rights through organizing themselves into trade unions, the first of these being the Nigerian Union of Musicians formed in 1958, the Ghana National Entertainments Association set up in 1960, and the Musicians Union founded in 1961.[77] Both these Ghanaian unions were dissolved after the 1966 anti-Kwame Nkrumah coup due to the unions' link with Nkrumah's Convention People's Party. However, in 1974 a single unified Musicians Union of Ghana (MUSIGA) was formed to replace them. In short, the tradition of African performers expressing political, social, generational, gender, and organizational conflict and protest has been carried through into the modern context.

To summarize, 20th century African popular performers have found three ways of circumnavigating the problem of "cultural imperialism" and producing a viable contemporary art form in touch with the common person. These are through the progressive Africanization or de-acculturation of genres that were initially modeled on foreign ones, by the creative use of the black dance-music "feedback" from the New World, and by continuing the old African tradition of protest music. Moreover, all these three ways of regaining autonomy have become more important and more self-conscious in postwar times, with the climate of indigenization and cultural awareness in the new independent African nations, and the search for the African "roots" by black performers in the New World.

Miriam Makeba

Music Beyond Apartheid?[1]

Denis-Constant Martin
translated by Val Morrison

South Africa was, and remains, although undoubtedly not for long, the only state in the world legally founded on racial discrimination. It has taken nearly 40 years for world powers to acknowledge this peculiarity and apply pressure to the Pretoria government to move towards democracy. Prior to this long-overdue "awakening," political parties and social movements struggled to attract international attention to the heinous theories and practices which were occurring in the country. The success of these actions has resulted in the international condemnation of South Africa's institutionalized racism and the elevation of Nelson Mandela from political prisoner to internationally applauded negotiator. This evolution of international relations coincided with a resurgence of exotic musical vogues in Europe and North America. As South Africa has been thrust into the international limelight, the country has offered rhythms capable of arousing developing societies and supporting a cause worthy of being defended. South African musics, despite the UNESCO cultural boycott, have thus been "discovered" by the outside world while simultaneously undergoing profound changes from within.

On the musical front, an extremely complex picture emerges in which musical genres reminiscent of earlier eras of South African history interact with those of more recent times. Adding to the complexity are the fruits of labors undertaken outside of South Africa through interaction between European and U.S. artists and South African musicians living in exile since the 1950s or early 1960s (Miriam Makeba, Hugh Masekela, Abdullah Ibrahim,[2] and Chris McGregor, to name the most important). A rich diversity, if not a certain confusion, is one of the distinctive features of South African musics as they appear on the international scene.

Among the first to be discovered, Johnny Clegg practices a rock style which mixes in varying proportions, depending on the period, Anglo-Celtic and Zulu influences. Vocal group Ladysmith black Mambazo, whose poly-phonic a cappella is reminiscent of *Isicatamiya,* became famous following their association with U.S. singer Paul Simon. Ray Phiri, the man behind the scenes of the whole *Graceland* operation staged by Simon, was also able to promote his band, Stimela. Simon "Mahlathini" Nakbinde, the kingpin of the ghettos and uncontested master of *mbaqanga,* or more precisely of *mqashiyo,* began, with the Mahotella Queens, a second career outside of his country. More recently, the group Mango Groove mixed rock and the sounds of 1950s South Africa—*kwela* and *marabi.* Finally, some stars from the contemporary South African scene, such as Sello Chicco Twala or Lucky Dube, the local incarnation of reggae and rastafarianism, have achieved success outside the country.

While this diversity accurately reflects the effervescent quality of South African music, such musical proliferation is not invariably seen as positive. South African music, argues pianist Rashid Lanie, head of the South African Musicians' Alliance (SAMA), "lacks orientation; is going in no precise direction," but he adds, "art always reflects the atmosphere of the society."[3] The musical situation, then, corresponds to the political one, where amidst confusion, uncertainty, and violence, a new South Africa is being born. Artists and producers are spurred not only by a desire to participate fully in making history, but also by a will to take advantage of the reorganization of entertainment markets provided by social advances and the erosion of segregationist barriers. This tension, with all its contra-dictions, has arisen after a period of systematic suffocation of all artistic creation. The current wave of creativity is, thus, an integral part of the radical and rapid transformations in the country today, expressed in indigenous languages. Because music touches people, most notably the young, it shapes and influences their perception of what is important politically, as well as their aspirations and the ways in which they are expressed.

Historical Background

What is striking about contemporary South African musics is that they (almost) all make reference to the genres of the 1950s. Whether it be in rock, disco, or jazz, to name only the principal categories, the fragrance of *marabi, kwela,* and *mbaqanga* often color the interpretations of various groups. These styles, dating back some 30 years, are themselves insepara-ble from the social and cultural life prevalent at the time and of which only the most brilliant representations have been preserved. Re-editions of recordings from this era are multiplying, and books and films are bringing the period to the fore.[4] It is as if the rebirth of hope—hope for freedom, hope for social mobility, and finally, hope for peaceful cohabitation—is based on an idealized vision of the past. In the 1950s:

There was that air of "something is going to happen"…it was the best of times, it was the worst of times…But the saving grace was that there was much less polarization between the different race groups…if the child is father to the man, the 1950s begat the present—and perhaps the future.[5]

Creativity was inextricably linked to the social and political battles and the immense coming together of energies which lead in 1955 to the adoption of the Freedom Charter and to support for those of all races accused during the "treason trials," which dragged on from 1956 to 1961 only to be declared groundless. This creativity was expressed, above all, in music. *Marabi,* South African jazz, and even *kwela* were the offspring of mixture: musics from the city, in which supposedly tribal origins disappeared to make way for the input of all; interracial musics carrying a European stamp, reworked by all the "non-whites" who found themselves in South Africa. These musics were intimately associated with places: Sophiatown (near Johannesburg) and District Six (near Cape Town), where people of all colors came to work together. Sophiatown was "the most cosmopolitan of…black social igloos and perhaps the most perfect experiment in non-racial living."[6] District Six, the reputed "colored" district, accommodated people from diverse communities, including recently arrived European immigrants. The sector was poor, but had "soul":

the jazz session really brought all kinds of people together…Marked as it is by its bitter past, and standing as a daily reminder to the world of apartheid's most heinous face, few places have better credentials as a healing symbol for a new and reconciled South Africa.[7]

It is not possible here to retrace the recent political evolution of South Africa. It is nonetheless indispensable to recall a few key moments. The banning of the African National Congress (ANC) and the Pan-African Congress (PAC) in 1960 after the Sharpeville massacre, the arrest of Nelson Mandela in 1962, and the whole trial of Rivonia, which ended with the imprisonment of principal black nationalist leaders in 1963, marked a discernible hardening in the implementation of apartheid by the government of the National Party. This translated specifically into massive transfers of population destined, on the one hand, to erase what were considered "black spots" (sections where the segregation of groups was not "perfect"), and, on the other hand, to give fictitious existence to homelands *(bantustans)* which promised "independence" to all black citizens, thus making them foreigners in their own country, South Africa.

Both Sophiatown and District Six were "black spots." As meeting places and centers of creativity, it was imperative for the apartheid regime to wipe them off of the map. This took time, however, as resistance was ardent. Between 1955 and 1962 Sophiatown was progressively emptied of its residents, who were transported to Meadowlands, which developed into Soweto. The area was renamed Triomf. Evacuated and partially razed between 1966 and 1984, District Six remained, for the most part, a wasteland where a few remaining churches and mosques bore witness to a lively past. As for musicians in Sophiatown, District Six, and elsewhere, their possibilities for work were substantially diminished. The clubs which welcomed bands and mixed audiences in Johannesburg, Durban, Cape Town, and other cities were increasingly subjected to police or Special Branch raids. It became more and more difficult for the most creative groups—especially when they were racially mixed—to meet and work together.

Under these circumstances, many of the most talented South African musicians chose exile.[8] Political repression and a will to systematically separate South Africans had tragic consequences for the development of music. As a result, it has taken approximately 20 years (from the mid-1960s to the mid-1980s) for South African music as a whole to come back into its own. In the meantime, individuals (notably, Abdullah Ibrahim, when he returned to South Africa, and Philip Thabane and Malombo) continued to affirm the originality of what was considered to be black South African culture.

For those who remained, the extension of apartheid to radio and the recording industry, combined with the banning of non-segregated concert halls, made artistic life nightmarish. Discrimination and racial separation effectively meant discrimination and musical separation. The attempts at "retribalization" of black populations under the homeland policy carried with it a determination to promote traditional or neo-traditional musics given indigenous labels (zulu, xhosa, sotho, tswana, venda, etc.) and, concommitantly, to stifle all "modern" creativity born of cooperation between different groups.[9] South African radio (SABC) was divided into virtually airtight departments whose role was to furnish each group with music which was supposedly "theirs." Radio Springbok was directed at Afrikaaners and broadcast not a single note of "black" music. On the other hand, "black" radio was programmed according to the "homeland" target and was rigidly controlled by white officials. In different regions of the country, local stations broadcast "ethnic" programs. Whenever the censors picked up the slightest political allusions suggested by the lyrics (for example, "peace" or "power" surfacing in a love song) the song was immediately condemned by a cohort of linguistic experts and declared unsuitable to the project of apartheid.[10]

With the same organization imposed on record companies, there was no communication between "white" and "black" music departments. Outside of genres said to be "traditional" and religious hymns broadcast according to the language in which they were sung, "black" production was channeled into a sort of standardized and impoverished *mbaqanga*. This policy was not totally successful. Independent producers continued to support creativity, but their records didn't stand a chance of getting widespread airplay, even when radio permitted experimentation, such as broadcasting the big band of Victor Ntoni at the end of the 1970s, only to bury it when the audience became too large.

On the whole, this policy encouraged a decline both in the quality of commercial products and in public taste. Generalized mediocrity pushed those who were searching for something more to look to sounds from elsewhere. The U.S. influence had always been a strong one in South Africa, whether country and western for the Afrikaaners or African-American genres for blacks. Jazz, gospel, and musicals had long been used as a point of departure for the development of South African arts. One yardstick of musical quality revolves around the capacity to imitate what comes from overseas, just as ambition for success often centers on the possibility of penetrating these outside markets. In the 1960s and 1970s, however, the relationship to these "foreign" expressions of creativity was reduced to one of mimicry. Radio 5, the "in" station, played the Beatles and white U.S. rock groups; imported soul music from the United States swept black South African townships. Beginning in the late-1960s, rock groups blossomed, and Soweto "soul music" was born. For whites as well as for the black "elite," African music itself was dismissed as "country bumpkin music."[11]

But even as the realization of "grand apartheid" projects appeared to have advanced irrevocably (homelands were declared independent by Pretoria but would never be recognized internationally), even when South African culture seemed to have retracted to a point where it no longer dared think of originality, the cry for creativity resurfaced as paramount.

In the political realm, black students had, in 1968, quit the multiracial National Union of South African Students (NUSAS) and formed the South African Students Organization (SASO); Steven Biko was the principal harbinger of this organization which preached the affirmation of a "black consciousness." This ideology was then recaptured by the Black People's Convention (BPC), created in 1971. The ideology had a strong influence on students who rose in 1976 in Soweto to protest against the extension of the Afrikaans language to the teaching of blacks. The repression which hit the young activists of the movement and the outlawing of the BPC forced numerous militants into exile, where they reestablished contact with the outside organization of the ANC. The latter was thus able to reconstruct their clandestine network within South Africa, enabling their military branch, *Umkhonto we Sizwe,* to intensify the armed struggle. At the same time, union pressure was becoming stronger and stronger. In 1983, several political organizations joined together to form the United Democratic Front (UDF), which benefited from the involvement of prestigious clergymen such as Desmund Tutu and Allan Boesak.

The balance of tendencies within the National Party was modified by a number of circumstances, including the struggle of anti-apartheid militants, who associated more closely as "charterists" (partisans of the Freedom Charter included in the ANC program) and inheritors of the Black Consciousness movement; the recomposition of white communities (particularly the appearance of a group of Afrikaaner intellectuals ready to envisage non-racial projects); the changes brought to bear on the region (the independence of Angola and Mozambique in 1975, and Zimbabwe in 1980); and outside pressure. The presidential and "multiracial" (separate chambers for whites, Indians, and "coloreds," no representation for blacks) Constitution adopted in 1983 on the initiative of P.W. Botha appears, in retrospect, to have been the last gasp of institutional apartheid. In 1989, P.W.Botha was obliged to abandon his position as president of the party, and then the state, to the moderate reformer, F.W. De Klerk. From that moment on, the march to change has been accelerated. At the beginning of 1990, groups opposed to apartheid (ANC, PAC, the Communist Party, and a practically paralyzed UDF) were again authorized. On February 11, 1990, Nelson Mandela was freed and, in the name of the ANC, became the primary negotiator with the leader of the white state. In 1991, the primary pieces of legislation which defined apartheid (the Population Registration Act, the Group Areas Act, the Natives Land Act) were abolished.

The Reinvention of South African Music

Throughout this period, guitarist Philip Thabane, with his band Malombo, persisted in his unprecedented search for the heart of South African culture. He provided the inspiration for Jabula, who chose exile in London, and also for the Malopoets who, in 1978, furnished prophetic signs of the renewal of music in South Africa. But Philip Thabane is a musician's musician, immensely respected, regarded as living proof that it was possible to resist calmly and wordlessly the enterprise of musical destruction. An artist solidly implanted in his township and internationally appreciated, Thabane is, nevertheless, not really known to the larger South African public.

With greater fame, Abdullah Ibrahim is the person more identified with awakening South African music. While pursuing a brilliant career between Europe and the United States, close to the avant-garde of jazz, he remained in contact with his country and in 1974, returned to record a theme entitled, "Mannenberg Is Where It's Happening." "Mannenberg" refers to the area where the residents of District Six were forced to install themselves. Musically, it is an interpretation which comes alive with the intense richness of *marabi,* staggered rhythms, and cyclic progessions, and gives an opportunity to saxophonist Basil Coetzee to create a memorable solo (indeed, he kept the nickname "Mannenberg"). The recording, produced by Rashid Vally, was offered for distribution to major South African record companies and was refused across the board as it didn't fit the narrow compartment of musical apartheid. Vally had to see to its commercialization himself.[12] The record[13] enjoyed immense success.

On the rock front, young black musicians, among them Sipho "Hotstix" Mabuse, who formed a group called the Beaters (an obvious reference to the Beatles), began to show an interest in Black Consciousness. In the mid-1970s, the Beaters played in Salisbury and discovered the existence of authentic modern African musics, notably Zairian rumba. They "Africanized" their style by mixing the rock and soul music they played with elements of popular musics from South Africa and the rest of the continent. They rebaptized themselves and chose to sport the name of a black suburb in the Rhodesian capital: Harari. With the release of their album *Rufaro, Happiness*,[14] popular success was, once again, immediate.

In 1976, in Natal, brothers David Masondo and Moses Ngwenya formed the Soul Brothers, adding the colors of *mbaqanga* to those of U.S. soul music. They went to Johannesburg to record *Mshoza Wam*, which sold more than 300,000 copies.

Earlier, a young man of British origins named Johnny Clegg had become passionate about Zulu music. He began to associate with urban street musicians, learned their repertoire, and danced with them. From this "field," he even wrote a master's thesis in anthropology.[15] But above all, by combining Johannesburg's street music with a British-inspired rock accompaniment, he invented a new genre which he went on to perfect on stage with his mentor Sipho Mchunu. In 1976, "Johnny and Sipho" released their first recording of songs interpreted solely in Zulu. Their first album, *Universal Man*, released in 1979, included lyrics in English. Despite the hostility of record producers and radio, Clegg and Mchunu conquered South African youth. The racial mixture of their band, Juluka, and the cultural mix of their music enabled them to reach all audiences.[16]

It was thus from the inside, during an intellectual current of African rejuvenation, that South African music took off again by reclaiming its own roots. The watchful eye of outsiders also contributed to the consolidation of this movement. Beginning in 1976, U.S. jazz musician Darius Brubeck, son of pianist Dave Brubeck, visited South Africa regularly to play exclusively with black musicians. He managed to break the iron-clad rules of Bantu education (which did not allow for artistic education for blacks) by creating a jazz course at the University of Natal, a limited initiative which nonetheless had an important symbolic reach.[17]

In the mid-1980s, Paul Simon came to South Africa under controversial circumstances in search of original formulas which might furnish material for a new album and bolster a flagging career. In 1986, he released

Graceland,[18] a series of songs arranged for the most part by Ray Phiri, which feature, besides Phiri, musicians like saxophonist Barney Rachabane and vocal group Ladysmith Black Mambazo. A video and world tour completed this operation, making South African music known everywhere major music markets existed.

Paradoxically, this outside recognition, this appreciation of South African talents in the international show business arena, provoked a renewed interest in local musics in South Africa itself. The sought-after world penetration was attained, not by those who had attempted it by imitating outside models, but rather by those who represented either the most popular genres (Ladysmith Black Mambazo or, outside of *Graceland,* Simon Mahlatini) or the most original music (Ray Phiri) within South Africa. As a result, local musicians have been encouraged to re-Africanize (or South Africanize) their music.

On the margins of this process, the importation of reggae also played an important role. In the 1970s, Jamaican song, carried by an international vogue,[19] penetrated South Africa. The mystique surrounding it, the tone of contestation of certain lyrics met the frustration of a young audience from whom censorship had amputated rebellious music. Although considered "revolutionary" by South African authorities, reggae was widely circulated. Following Bob Marley's visit to Harare for Zimbabwe's independence ceremonies, Carlos Djedje attempted to transplant Jamaican music to South Africa without much success. It took Lucky Dube, coming from an African-ized soul music, to adapt reggae to the South African situation successfully. In the 1980s, a dozen or so bands made South Africa one of the countries, outside of Jamaica, where reggae was most alive.[20] In this case, the frank black origins of the musical genre (perceived as less Westernized than African-American musics) counterbalanced its coming from outside. Even without direct musical references to South Africa, reggae was able to offer an incontestable pertinence to the ears of township youth.[21]

South African Music Today

Today, South African music must sound like South African music. This is not simply a self-evident truth but rather the result of a tormented evolution which involved political consciousness raising as well as the maturation of musical taste. Behind what appears to be a statement of the obvious, the particular history of this country is profiled through a double affirmation manifested most clearly in music: the proclamation of the "Africanness" of South Africa and the acceptance of the multiracial character of South African culture. Music, in effect, is one of the domains where the most effective reconciliation between these two seemingly contradictory propositions can be realized. Efforts to accomplish this reconciliation and the difficulties encountered result in the diversity—and "lack of orientation"—which characterize South African music today.

Foreign musical forms, imported and well received in the 1960s and 1970s, have not been abandoned. They have been remodeled into a more African shape by incorporating elements borrowed from historically South African musics. These elements are themselves composite. Their harmonic structure rests on the same European model as that of rock and African-American genres. What is strictly South African is the treatment of rhythm described by musicologist Andrew Tracey as "kaleidophonic."[22] It is thus this harmonico-rhythmic combination which now colors genres occasionally difficult to distinguish: disco, rap, rock, fusion, jazz.

Interpreters of what we might call South Africanized disco have the highest record sales. They maintain the primary tendencies of disco affirmed in the early 1980s, but bend it in two directions: the Africanization of the music and the relative politicization of the lyrics in a way that evokes that of reggae.[23] Chicco (Sello Chicco Twala) is undoubtedly the most popular artist in this domain. While he advocates reconciliation and reconstruction in his own recordings,[24] the album he produced for Brenda Fassie, is even more openly political. Notably, we hear a song with a religious feel which praises the "black president" who remains nameless, although we can't help but recognize Nelson Mandela.[25] "Be proud to be an African," exhorts Yvonne Chaka Chaka, another artist in this genre, who then particularizes the message by asking for "peace for you and for me."[26] In all three of these examples, traits typical of U.S. disco are illuminated by imprints of *mbaqanga,* or South African jazz, and the occasional splash of reggae. We find the same atmosphere with the vocal group Pure Magic[27] or again, with Umoja and Peto. Prophets of the City, for their part, have adapted rap, but as an ingredient in a very richly South African mix which includes *mbaqanga* as well as the music of Cape Town's Malayans and that of the Boers. Their message includes denunciations of drugs, alcohol, and violence.

Jazz, jazz-rock, and fusion are also well-represented in South Africa. Jazz musicians like Barney Rachabane or Jonas Gwangwa continue to produce very high-quality recordings.[28] Sakhile, extremely popular with black audiences, offers a formula of soft "fusion" where the South African sound serves as a backdrop for lyric saxophone solos,[29] a recipe also found in the music of Ratau Mike Makhalamele.[30] Sankomota foregrounds a clearly religiously inspired voice.[31] More well-known on the outside, Tananas draws on the specifically Cape Town culture for a style close to jazz where the Latino-Mozambiquian influences combine with an old Boer-Malay background.[32]

This proliferation of musics, characterized by renewed interbreeding, does not negate the presence of much older genres which do not have the benefit of the same commercial promotion. *Mbaganga,* jive, all of those musics previously referred to pejoratively as "township music," today find themselves revalued as sources for creativity. *Isicatamiya,* popularized by Ladysmith Black Mambazo, still inspires the popular practice of competitions between groups formed by the inhabitants of hostels for migrant workers.[33] Religious music, sometimes similar to *isicatamiya,* sometimes copied from North American gospel songs, resounds each Sunday in all kinds of churches. Finally, there is not a march, not a protest, not a burial during which *toi-toi* is not heard. This chant, which accompanies bodies in movement and gives rhythm to their motion, draws its inspiration from old-time war songs as well as from modern hymns.

Crossing the Line in Music

The political negotiations prefiguring the advent of a non-racial South Africa, the dismantling of apartheid already underway, the changes surfacing in television programs, the toleration of "grey zones" (non-segregated residential areas), the timid beginnings of multiracial publicity,[34] testify to the social transformations occurring and to come in South Africa. The realization that apartheid is finished carries with it changes in individual behavior and, as a consequence, adjustments in commerical strategies. Music escapes neither of these.

Contemporary South African music is fundamentally mixed. It realizes, in practice, the fusion of cultures which met in South Africa. Because the mixture gave birth to genres whose elements came from diverse cultures and were present in varying proportions, the innovations which emerged could be typed by community and social class. We can thus speak of "white" or "black" music, music consumed by either the petty bourgeoisie or by the proletariat, knowing full well that they have all been cross-fertilized. If a fear of the Other is inextricably linked to desire for the Other, a passage may be more readily initiated by music, in that music ignores the language censor, to let the body speak, all the more easily in this case because the musics are so closely related.[35] The acceptance of the community of the Other may well be discretely announced by a widening of musical tastes. Since music is also a commercial product, this opening toward "different" musics signifies the widening of a profitable market as well. Here, the economic is inseparable from the social, the political, even the realm of pleasure. This analysis begins to explain a major turn recently taken in South African music, namely that of "cross-over"—"crossing over" racial boundaries, "crossing the line" of sound.

Because Johnny Clegg and Sipho Mchunu were somewhat independent of the powers of the music industry from the beginning, they were able to build their mixed popularity from the audience, even without the support of the SABC. This direct contact (through concert or record) with the audiences, reinforced by international celebrity status, permitted Clegg's bands Juluka and Savuka, insistent on performing only in venues open to all, to impose an image of black/white twining, indivisible in dance as in song.

Sipho "Hotstix" Mabuse, who participated, with Harari, in the "re-Africanization" of South African music, was also one of the first to touch white as well as black buyers with "Burn Out,"[36] a song, released in 1984, whose unique arrangement for the time combines a Western structure and the insistence of the piano with riffs borrowed directly from *marabi*. He has since continued on this thrust and his music represents the most advanced synthesis of South African rock (rock, *mbaqanga,* jive, *kwela,* and even *toi-toi)* supporting politically toned lyrics.[37]

Ray Phiri is perhaps the most imaginative and most complete musician in South Africa as the 1990s begin. Guitarist, arranger, composer, he is capable of drawing from all genres, of using all forms (Western, African-American, African, South African) to conceive of a music whose richness is equaled only by the balance of the construction and the logic of the melodic and harmonic development.[38]

In the mid 1980s, another mixed band, Zia, blending rock, *mbaqanga,* vocal polyphonics, and Zulu dances also began to perform. Initially supported by the black public, they succeeded in "crossing over" five years later. At the same moment, Mango Groove, another black and white ensemble playing rock to the background of *marabi* and *kwela,* exploded. With the success of Mango Groove, "the darlings of South African music,"[39] the commercial possibilities of going beyond race—the marketing of cross-over, if you will—became patently manifest. The strategy of cross-over, once considered politically subversive in South Africa, is becoming a commercial imperative.

So much so that the brother duo of Marc and Alex Rantseli (known as Marcalex and launched in 1989 with immediate results) projected "a marketing concept as much as a band."[40] Posing for the cover of *Talk* ("the magazine for trendy adults"), sandwiching Mary Slater, beautiful blond winner of the "model of the year" title, they wear the mildly exotic latest in clothes fashion. Clones of African-American disco singers, this time without much of the "South African" in their style, they represent the young black bourgeoisie acceptable to those white South Africans who are ready to evolve, up to a point.[41]

Cross-over, by definition, seeks to find common elements in the tastes of disctinct groups. For record companies and artists with a certain ambition, the objective is to find a way to please everyone. Cross-over therefore runs the risk of leveling aesthetic quality and standardizing products on a market basis rather than a creative one. Marcalex is a flagrant example of this tendency. At the same time, we must recognize the talent and progressive effects of a Johnny Clegg or a Mango Groove.

Neither is the cross-over strategy unidirectional. While it is generally true that crossing the line is executed in the direction of black artist to white market, there is at least one recent example that the reverse is also possible. Well-directed by Mike Fuller, the white singer P.J. Powers crossed over to the black public with a disco-soul formula in which South African and reggae references are innumerable. Her energy and her voice unequivocably give soul to the English and African language texts. For Powers, music, lyrics, and politics are closely connected. "We have to be like a big family...we are all the same," she states, "our leaders are finally free...from now on, we can no longer be arrested for these opinions."[42]

Finally, without actually conquering the township audiences, white rock groups have also attempted to "Africanize" their music, thereby crossing the musical line in another way. Cape Town's Bright Blue didn't hesitate to incorporate the melody of the nationalist hymn "Nkosi Sikeleli Afrika" and let the political critique point from behind the poetic metaphor.[43] Elsewhere, a certain tradition of contestation in white rock[44] is being perpetuated by bands such as the Gereformeerde Blues Band, who offer a provocative image of Afrikaaner "counterculture," wherein the "noble" traditions are mocked.

A Song of Reconciliation

Over 30 or so years, from 1960 to 1990, South Africa has changed considerably. For years, repression stifled all hope for change when most other countries of black Africa were becoming independent. With the erasing of "black spots," with the forced displacement of the black population, with the blood of those who, persisting to fight, fell under the blow of "pale power," and with the silencing of those banished to Robben Island, the creativity born of meeting and mixture was denied the opportunity for expression. The hope offered by the tragedy of South African history resides in the failure of oppression and the refusal to share. Undoubtedly, as it stands, reconciliation is yet but a wish, but one expressed more and more clearly, and more and more forcefully, despite the violence, the hesitation, and the fear.

As affirmed in different ways by the advocates of the Freedom Charter and the theologians of black liberation, it is because oppression was visited upon blacks that they have the possibility of, and have assumed the responsibility for, rendering liberty to all, including the oppressors. Music is one of the areas where the manifestation of this not-so-new dream is crucial, in that contemporary South African music, in its origins and its lively reality, is in a very real sense from all, to all, for all.[45] In many ways, the musical situation parallels the political situation. Because these musics of mixture and cross-fertilization were innovated by blacks and refused by a large part of the white population, black artists occupy a position of cultural leadership, just as black political leaders are determining the course of structural change. Because of these aberations of history, it is "black" music which reveals the real South African culture.[46] It is black artists who are the carriers, the regenerators of the culture of all. They are the ones who can bring it to everyone. With them, white artists in growing numbers are participating in the work of building a common South Africa. And the public, a soon-to-be reunited public, is finally poised to accept this vision.

Luis Alberto Spinetta. (Photo courtesy Claudio Martínez)

Rock Nacional and Dictatorship in Argentina

Pablo Vila

The innocent are the guilty
says his highness, the King of Spades.
—Charly García

Years of the Dictatorship

Between 1976 and 1983, Argentina witnessed the full development of a phenomenon which has come to be known as *rock nacional* ("national rock"). At first sight it might appear no more than a matter of musical consumption, fashioning its participants simply as "artists" on one side and "public" on the other. But it has proved an original form within which the young created and inhabited a space of their own, symbolically protected from the assaults of the military dictatorship (which had made them its principal victims), and has come to constitute, with the passing of the years, a counterculture and a social movement.

The mass nature of attendance at concerts is only one of the indicators of the social relevance of the movement. Dozens of magazines published over 16 years (with print runs of up to 25,000 copies) and some 4,000 "underground" magazines served to give voice to the thought of youth, silenced by a violent and authoritarian society. From within those spaces (the concerts and magazines) a "we" was constructed, an identity within which the musicians became leaders who, through the lyrics of their songs, gave form to an alternative, countercultural proposal which challenged the ideology of the dictatorship.

This genuine phenomenon of cultural resistance was highly dysfunctional for the regime. Tilman Evers claims, in this regard, that:

> Creating spaces for more comradely relationships, for conscious-
> ness less directed by the market, for less alienated cultural mani-

festations, or for different basic values and beliefs, these movements represent a constant dose of an extraneous element within
the social body of peripheral capitalism. Naturally, any result we
might expect from this micro-level "counterculture" will only appear in the long term. But during this long process it will have
demonstrated something much more indisputable and irreversible
than the multiple abrupt transformations at the pinnacle of power,
precisely because it will have put down roots in daily practice and
in the corresponding essential orientations upon which all social
structures are founded.[1]

Rock nacional represented during the dictatorship an oppositional
cultural expression of a specific social actor, youth. Its basic characteristics
were that it created its own values, which clashed with those of the regime;
it functioned as an ideology of everyday life; it generated forms of participation which were alternative in character; it was jealous of its autonomy
with respect to other actors and projects, above all of all political parties;
and it shaped its own identity in opposition to the authoritarian and
anti-democratic powers which defined it as one of their enemies. For all
these reasons, it indisputably comes into the category of counterculture.

But to say that it is a counterculture is to say, in terms of modern theories
of action, that it is a *new social movement*. In fact, following Alberto Melucci,
we can say that new social movements are characterized by making the sphere
of culture their privileged space of action (whereas traditional social movements gave battle in the field of relations of production):

> The most remarkable aspect of contemporary conflicts is that they
> overcome the distinction between public and private. Conflict and
> social struggles invade terrains hitherto considered as private, such
> as sexual relations, inter-personal relations, profound necessities
> are the basis upon which new collective identities are
> founded…This centering upon an identity which is not principally
> productive or political but founded upon more profound proper-
> ties which feel threatened, tends to accentuate the characteristics
> of fragmentation and marginality of the new movements. Revolt
> takes on existential contents the only ones which appear to the
> actors to be irreducible and not manipulable by the system.[2]

The search for a new type of inter-personal relations; the defense of
being "different" from the adults; the creation of autonomous spaces of
interaction; the proposals for the liberation of the body; the assumption by
protest of existential contents; the ambiguous and conflictive relationship
with politics; and the assumption of directly cultural character were all
characteristics present in the *rock nacional* movement during the dictatorship. Thus, the movement could be considered a particular type of new
social movement. We say that it was a particular type of social movement

because the "political function" that characterized the "old" social movements was not absent in the case of *rock nacional,* because it also played an important role in the emergence of democracy.

It should be pointed out here that references to *rock nacional* as a new social movement should be taken with the caution that all such approaches to this particular type of social actor require, especially as regards the consistency and scope of its project. Thus, if in the nucleus of the movement (musicians, journalists on alternative magazines, members of communities, young people who take on rock as their culture, etc.), such countercultural contents are found clearly delineated, the same thing does not always occur on the adolescent periphery which goes to concerts, where the same contents appear more blurred, bearing witness to the load of ambiguity which results from their being subject to other social influences (parents, school, the mass media, etc.).

Repression and Defense of Youth Identity (1976-77)

Don't lose heart
Don't let yourself be killed
There are so many tomorrows to go.
("Don't Lose Heart," Charly García, 1976)

They've offended me greatly
And no-one has explained me.
Ah, if I could kill them
I'd do it with no fear.
("The Canterville Ghost," Charly García, 1975)

With the military coup of 1976, fear appeared in Argentinian society as a social attribute: out of fear, civil society turned back in on itself in the context of a situation devoid of points of reference. In a far-reaching attempt to redefine traditional political identities, the military regime proceeded to disperse all collectivities. Political parties, trade unions, corporations, and social movements retreated (on their own initiative or under compulsion) from the public sphere. Society as a whole was privatized.

The youth movement was not unaffected by this development. On the contrary, the culture of fear made the youth movement its privileged protagonist, to the extent that it was upon the young that the bulk of the repression was exercised (67 percent of those people "disappeared" by the military were young people between the ages of 18 and 30). Basing itself on the image of "suspect youth," the repression was directed specifically to this age group: one was guilty unless one could prove the contrary. While the student movement and the political youth movements slowly disappeared as frameworks of reference and support for collective identities, the *rock nacional* movement established itself as the sphere within which a "we" was constructed. Thus, going to concerts and listening to records among groups of friends became privileged activities, as through them broad sectors of the young sought to preserve their identity, in a context in which the young felt threatened by the military by virtue of their youth:

> To go to a concert was like a need. We didn't miss a single one. There was a tremendous need to be together. You felt sure that being together nothing was going to happen to you, but if you went out onto the street something would happen to you for sure. There was a great need to participate in something, and to be safe at the same time. I think it was a state of collective energy, do you see? Which is what we were lacking.[3]

Thus the period 1976-77 was marked by a tremendous boom in *rock nacional* concerts. It was common in this period for Luna Park (the biggest covered stadium in the country, in Buenos Aires, with a capacity of 15,000) to be filled once or even twice a month, along with innumerable theater and café concerts. Nevertheless, it was not a period in which there was a noticeable increase in the sale of records of this genre, as what was taking place was a social necessity rather than an aesthetic matter. If we agree with Norbert Lechner that "considering this constitution of the 'we' as what is specific to the political, a folk performance, a strike, or a mass can also be transformed into a political act. Independent of its content, any type of ritual supposes the consciousness of a collective power."[4] The mass *rock nacional* concerts of 1976-77 provide a clear example of politicization in a period of the closure of the traditional spaces for political activity. In such concerts the movement celebrated itself and confirmed the presence of the collective actor whose identity had been questioned:

> It was as if Luna Park meant a place to meet, rather than a desire for going to see one group or another. "We are us, we are here," the twelve or fourteen thousand people who filled the place with their presence seemed to be saying.[5]

The appellation "we" necessarily signals also a "they." Who has to notice that "we shall not go un-noticed any more" (León Gieco's sentence in the concert named above)? They do, that is the "they" of Charly García's "they want to dishearten us, they want to kill us" or "they have offended us so often." From "them" comes the famous speech by Admiral Massera (a member of the military *junta*), delivered in November 1977 at the Universidad del Salvador, where he brackets rock with subversion, and which hung, framed, in the editorial office of *Expreso Imaginario* for many years:

> The young become indifferent to our world and begin to build a private universe...while they make a strong caste of themselves, they convert themselves into a secret society before everyone's eyes, celebrate their rituals: clothes, music. With complete indiffer-

ence. And they always seek horizontal identifications, spurning every vertical relationship. Later some of them will exchange their neutrality, their spineless pacifism, for the thrill of a terrorist faith, a predictable destination of an assault on the senses with no prior itinerary, which begins with so arbitrarily sacrilegious a conception of love, which for them thus ceases to be a private ceremony, leads on to promiscuity, carries on to addiction to hallucinogenic drugs and...results in the end in death, of others or of themselves, it matters little, as the destruction will be justified by the social redemption which some manipulators have generally made available to them, so that they can equate with an ideology what was a maddening race towards the most extreme exaltation of the senses.

Once again, there appears the "suspect youth" who, once initiated into rock music (that secret society which celebrates its rituals: clothes, music, drugs, free love, etc.), ends up inevitably, according to the military, in the guerrilla forces. And in 1977, when there was already talk of "the defeat of subversion," repressive action began against that cultural manifestation which appeared, in the eyes of the military, as one of its sources: rock culture.

But the "they," the enemy of the movement, the enemy of the youth, was also generalized to cover broad sectors of society, to the extent that the "anti-youth" discourse of the military obtained consensus:

> I believe that inside the concert you loved people, and outside you didn't. I don't know if it was because of the music or because you were predisposed...but it was as if you had the need to love the people, and they loved you. It's that you didn't love the people in the street...and you went to the concert wishing that everyone outside could be like those at the concert. It's that you looked at the people at the concerts and it seemed that everyone was beautiful! Because you were seeing people who looked at you like...like a human being looks, you know? With something in their eyes, and outside they all looked empty, do you see?[6]

On one side "us," the "inside," peace, freedom, and participation; and on the other "them," the "outside," violence. In this way the *rock nacional* movement was constructing the spaces which preserved the identity of the whole community of young people who felt themselves to be represented by it. The concerts thus appear as rituals on the basis of which a collectivity was constituted, and also privileged spheres of communication between the young "...to which were displaced, beyond the unattractive and scarcely credible official stage, the communicative practices in which we Argentines sought to defend the meaning of life and of our history."[7]

But it was also *rock nacional* which created, in the harshest years of the dictatorship, a very important means of communication, *Expreso Imaginario,* with a respectable print run of 15,000 copies, which proposed from its first editorial of August 1976, "…to reach those spaces of the mind which are not hardened, which still maintain, through music, poetry, and love, sufficient freshness to contain feelings of life."

So significant was the communicative phenomenon which was generated around the *Expreso* that its Letters Page became its most important section. As a sphere for the consolidation of the "we," this section laid bare the preoccupations of the young at that time, as Carlos wrote in November 1976: "You help me to lose my fear." Or, as another reader wrote:

> I am eighteen, and like most young people, the things that worry me most are violence and lack of understanding, but what upsets me most is that people reply in the same vein.[8]

As a visible expression emerging from a youth movement which had not acquired an organic character, although it was undergoing a process of consolidation, it slowly became a leader:

> you…are the ones who are doing it right…You are almost a little vanguard in these times.[9]

> The *Expreso* comes to represent the trunk, with innumerable branches, which in turn shelter all those of us who believe we love real feelings.[10]

As a refuge for sociability and a continent of solidarity, dialogue between readers is a constant feature:

> it's beautiful to find someone who thinks the same way you do. And it's beautiful that through this magazine we can communicate with each other.[11]

> good for Sandra!…you can't stand all the crap that surrounds you, and suddenly, you open a magazine and you find something as beautiful as Sandra's letter. Then…you discover, you remember, you know that there are people who are looking for something else, another life, more authentic, more natural, without lies, without poses.[12]

In this manner *Expreso Imaginario* broke, just as the concerts did on another level, with the monopoly of discourse which the regime attempted to establish, and inaugurated a current of communication which strengthened a collective actor in a period characterized by repeated attempts to secure its disintegration:

> The *Expreso* was like a drug, we rushed to buy it in the kiosks. And if it didn't come out (because the bloody thing was always late) we suffered, we cried, we went round to the offices to ask what was happening, what the hell was happening!, since it was something like two weeks since the *Expreso* came out![13]

Its function became more important still in the following period, when the military regime managed to break the concert circuit, and the *Expreso* became the last redoubt for the survival of the movement.

Regime Consolidation and the Crisis of Rock (1978-79)

> It's very sad, to let pass by
> on one side, this history.
> ("This History" León Gieco, 1976)

If, according to the logic of the dictatorship, the rock movement and subversion were linked, it was necessary to disrupt the circuit of concerts, given that this was the privileged sphere of the constitution of the "we" of the movement. Furthermore, the concerts were used by the musicians to play songs banned by the authorities.

Action against the circuit of concerts took different forms, and was carried out in a number of stages. Agents started by throwing tear-gas or stink-bomb canisters into small theaters to disrupt gatherings. Later, police repression was stepped up in the big meetings at Luna Park. Hundreds of people were literally "rounded up" and detained for police checks before and after each event. And in the end the owners of concert halls were "advised" not to rent them for rock concerts.

The offensive reached such an extent that toward the end of 1977, faced with the impossibility of putting on concerts, a great number of the groups broke up and the leading musicians were forced to go abroad in order to continue working. The winning of a certain degree of consent by the military government (the Soccer World Cup, the height of the import boom, etc.) further contributed to the inability of the national rock movement to resist this onslaught, and as a result its members "went private," as the great majority of actors against whom the military machine had gone into action had already done.

Rock nacional also had to compete against another phenomenon which was challenging it on its privileged ground. The end of 1977 saw the outbreak of *Saturday Night Fever,* as disco music performed by the Bee Gees and Donna Summer took over the musical scene. The discotheque replaced the concert. The dance replaced the song. English replaced Spanish. Lack of communication replaced communication. Participants in the movement were seized by the feeling that *rock nacional* was dying:

> What is happening to our music? Has the power of 1976 been paralyzed?…I believe in this movement. And if once we were so many that we were delighted, we must be more or less the same to help to get it out of this…chaos.[14]

In the search for explanations for what was happening, some contributions to the Letters Page refer to a change in public behavior. It would appear that the climate which engulfed the majority of the population as a consequence of the Soccer World Cup also affected the rock fans. High spirits (of an aggressive nature), chauvinism (previously unknown in the sphere of youth music), and in some cases outright violence began to make themselves felt at rock concerts, and replaced the climate of solidarity and togetherness which had always characterized them in the past. Individualism replaced solidarity, private consumption replaced sociability. Around the period 1978-79 the model of society proposed by the military (people who converge as individuals in the market, stripped of their historical connotations linked to collective actors) seemed to be imposing itself upon that other model which had guided the rock utopias, and which, to some extent, had been "rehearsed" in the concerts (people relating to each other in solidarity on the basis of giving love, and feeling they were participants in a single movement).

Nevertheless, if this was happening in the public sphere, *rock nacional* was still managing to preserve at this stage two entities which kept it going as a movement. One was *Expreso Imaginario*, the other was the small group of friends:

> For more than a year I have been receiving a share of LIFE, when *Expreso* reaches my station.[15]

> I think we all form a little under-world where we all lived separately until you arrived, *Expreso,* and began to bring us all together. If I'm not alone (or just one of a few) I can fight to turn my dream into reality.[16]

> the magazine stores up the monthly expectations of many people who aspire to change the established order of things, without yet knowing it.[17]

These comments (and numerous others along the same lines) lie thickly upon the Letters Page of the *Expreso* in those years. In a period marked by the loss of manifestations of the movement in the public sphere, the magazine functioned as the preserver of its content, through its notes and commentaries, and above all through the function of exchange and communication (that knowledge that "there is someone else") which its Letters Page fulfilled.

The other sphere in which identity was preserved was the group of friends: meetings of friends not only sustained an identity which found few external referents to aid its re-creation, but also played the crucial role of socializing new generations into the contents of the movement. Only when one realizes the importance of this exchange of lived experiences between different generations is it possible to understand the phenomenon that occurred when *rock nacional* returned to the public stage: 14- and 15-year-olds chorusing songs made popular a decade before, many of them banned and withdrawn from the record shops.

On the basis, therefore, of the contents preserved by the Expreso, the profound communication represented by its Letters Page, and the small groups of friends, the rock nacional movement "hibernated" awaiting a new spring. This was to come at the hands of the very musicians responsible for the birth of rock in Argentina. It was as if a return to origins was necessary to enable the march to begin again, to re-create the "magic" of the gathering, which the years of the military regime's greatest success seemed to have obliterated.

The Loss of Military Legitimacy and the Renaissance of Rock (1980-81)

> We are in no man's land,
> But it is mine.
> The innocent are the guilty,
> Says his highness,
> the King of Spades.
> ("Alicia's Song in the Country," Charly García, 1980)

The panorama began to show signs of change in mid-1979, and the rediscovery of the spirit of former days was celebrated with jubilation:

> What happened on May 29-30 cannot be reduced to a simple musical concert. It went beyond those bounds to turn itself into a party in which music was the element which bound us together…a climate of shared happiness, a communication which happened between all of us marked the beginning of a new move forward in the sphere of rock. A space for us, for all. For all of us who kept singing: O-OOO-O! the Woodstock song.[18]

A return to the source in order to emerge from the period of darkness: this was the slogan put forward by the most representative exponents of the movement; the recuperation of the essence, the historic banners which had "wavered a little" in the period in which the military regime seemed to have succeeded in its project of redefining the social actors; a demonstration that rock had not disappeared; and a continuation along the road which would lead to its being the point of reference for a broad sector of youth:

> to those who still live by their own instincts we say: We need a region of poetry and music which disrupts, which confuses, which illuminates. To carry on being here, and sing for a lost generation. AL-MENDRA was born and disseminated its art in terrain as muddy as that of today. That of now. A terrain drawn by the socio-economic-emotional reality of the Argentine…The present state is depressing. But to go under is not to disappear…We should today, more than ten years

on from those events, go over all that has happened; salvage the essence and continue the voyage: that of our identity.[19]

This statement belongs to the proclamation made by the mythic group Almendra on the occasion of its return. The idea appears once again of a free space, a space of one's own: that "region of poetry and music." To that sphere would belong the task of "disrupting" the route that the system (in this case the military regime) wished to impose upon the young, while at the same time "illuminating" its own. Because the generation to which it has to sing has been a "lost" generation, Almendra can perform this task because it "was born in terrain as muddy as that of today," in which authoritarian soldiers also governed, and in which the "socio-economic-emotional" reality was also depressing.

Almendra's concerts were a great success, attracting

> more than thirty thousand people and many more who could not get in. We did not go to see a foreign artist. We went to see ourselves; marginalized by the media, confused by other generations. Thus it was that the applause too was directed inwards, toward ourselves. Alongside Almendra we could say: here we are. That we have our culture, our space...everyone wanting to know that we were together, present, feeling ourselves part of something.[20]

It was happiness at the meeting itself. It was the possibility of continuing "the voyage: that of our identity," as Almendra had sensed so acutely. Almendra was only the excuse to say: "here we are...[we are] part of something," for in the liturgies of the collectivity one celebrates oneself, and "although they appear as the exaltation of a leader, this only symbolizes the confidence of the collectivity in itself to know how to establish itself in the world."[21]

From the time of the performances of December 1979 (35,000 people), there was a flood of young people to the concerts, reaching its peak in December 1980, when the group Serú Girán (led by Charly García) brought 60,000 people to Palermo.

What was the response of the military regime? Repression. The first performances of the new cycle of concerts were repressed, because toward the end of 1979 military leaders were still convinced of the viability of their socio-economic project, and acted accordingly. As the luster they had enjoyed at the time of the Soccer World Cup had faded, they now appealed directly to repression.

Part of the rock public was indisputably the same, but it had changed its attitude regarding the dusk years of 1978-79: it felt itself once again forming part of something which it considered its own. Another sector was made up of new adolescent adherents to the movement. And for the first time, university students came to *rock nacional* in massive numbers, and the "historic rock fans" raised their eyebrows at these uninvited guests at the party.

There is evidence for the emergence of a sphere of dissidence which was valued as such by the most lucid elements in the movement. This was reflected in the mass nature of the phenomenon; in the clearly questioning content of some of the most popular songs, such as "Alicia's Song in the Country" (*"Canción de Alicia en el País"*), "Collective Unconscious" (*"Inconsciente Colectivo"*: "Yesterday I dreamed of the hungry, the mad/ Those who went, those who are in prison/ Today I awoke singing this song/ Which was already written some time ago/ It is necessary to sing again, once more"), or "José Mercado"; and above all in the appearance of chants against the government (beginning with the football chant, "If you're not jumping you're a soldier" (*"El que no salta es un militar,"* which provoked the curious spectacle of the whole stadium jumping in unison upon their seats). This sphere of dissidence was also detected by the military regime, who stepped up the level of repression in response to the growing size of this oppositional challenge.

From 1981 onward, however, police action was not the only point of contact between the state and *rock nacional,* as the new military administration, in accordance with its general policy, adopted a strategy of dialogue with the movement. The political orientation of the new President, General Viola, implied a shift in the center of gravity of political power from within the military corporation onto the terrain of linkages with different actors in civil society. A future Ministry for Youth formed part of the project espoused by Viola, and he had identified the rock movement as a valid interlocutor, able to participate in the political opening in its own area: that of the young.

But unlike the political parties—who "contributed to maintaining the relative stability of the Viola government through a policy of moderation and containment of anti-military hostility...[to avoid] the production of offensive criticisms, denunciations, and frontal attacks on the military government"[22]—the human rights movement, the neighborhood movement, and also *rock nacional,* not only kept up their assault on the dictatorship, they redoubled their efforts. Thus, on the one hand the marches protesting the "disappeared" swelled in size, while on the other, the oppositional content among concert audiences became more marked: the chant *"El que no salta es un militar"* was slowly replaced in the preferences of the young by *"Se va a acabar, se va a acabar, la dictadura militar"* ("It's going to end, it's going to end, the military dictatorship").

This was the panorama presented by *rock nacional* on the eve of the Malvinas War: concerts of a size never seen before, songs with an increasingly marked oppositional content (demanded by the public themselves), and a strongly anti-military climate among the audience. The most representative actors in the movement were perfectly well aware of the ground they were treading and the role they had to play:

> García: The people are expecting a kind of message, they need strength, vitality, and in the lyrics we denounce things, and do all we can so that people go home turned upside down, and we don't need a message which says: "you must do this!"
>
> *Expreso:* So there isn't a clear message?
>
> García: No, what is happening is the message.[23]

What was happening truly was the message. Because,

> some activities acquired [during the dictatorship] a political and cultural value not so much for what they were saying, but, fundamentally, as a consequence of the very act of their taking place, which came to be part of the language. The case of what was called "national rock" is typical in this sense: it does not refer to a homogenous style of music or to a common artistic level, but to the unity of the phenomenon of youth culture which it embraces.[24]

The mass gatherings of the social movement also represented ends in themselves, and at times the music was only an excuse. A concert in which the songs were applauded more as soon as their first notes were recognized than when they finished shows clearly that the music was fulfilling something other than an aesthetic function.

Before the Malvinas War, *rock nacional* was already playing to the full its part as leader and coordinator of an oppositional movement embracing broad sectors of the young.

The War of the South Atlantic and the Access of Rock to the Media (1982-83)

> Friends on the block may disappear
> Singers on the radio may disappear
> People in the papers may disappear
> The ones you love may disappear
> ("The Dinosaurs," Charly García, 1982)

The period between December 1981 and the Malvinas War saw the return of the military "hard-liners." President Galtieri's government presented itself as a return to "the sources of the military process," through a return to military authoritarianism on the one hand (we can remember here the President's famous phrase: "the ballot boxes are under close guard") and a re-launching of the monetarist economic line associated with Martinez de Hoz on the other.

Civil society did not accept, in general, the closure of the political space which Viola had opened up, and both political parties and unions increased their opposition activity, leading up to the rally organized for March 30, 1982 by the CGT-Brasil (the most important conglomerate of trade unions of the country). In this context, the Malvinas War appears as an attempt by Galtieri, by means of a military action which struck a chord deep in the hearts of all Argentineans, to resolve "domestic political conflicts and re-establish the basis for the legitimation of an authoritarian political project."[25]

In response to an invitation from the military authorities to put on a rock music concert on account of the war, the movement mounted a Festival of Latin American Solidarity on May 16. It was guided by a double purpose: to reflect a desire for peace, and to make some kind of contribution to the needs of the young men holed up in the south, friends, brothers, comrades of the 60,000 young men and women who came to the Obras Sanitarias stadium to contribute handkerchiefs, cigarettes, sweaters, and other warm clothing:

> I went to the Malvinas concert…but I only went to take a sweater for the kids who were cold.[26]

> It's as if God had said: "Here, kids, you've got to tell him that the war's no good." And I remember that although we had to disguise the fact, all of us who were there went for peace.[27]

From the epic reconstruction of "the only ones opposed to the war" to the simple "I went to take a sweater," by way of the possible utilization on the part of the military of the intentions of the young people present, the whole range of responses picked up with regard to the Festival of Solidarity stress the commitment of those present to peace:

> I hope it will be a homage to peace and not to war, as it might appear from some points of view. We, as free musicians in our country, are totally convinced that the war offensive must end.[28]

And the way in which the festival developed finally reinforced the message of peace. After a somewhat confusing start, it was León Gieco's performance which tuned in with the feelings of the majority of the 60,000-person crowd. From that point on there was no more confusion. Everyone knew why the person at their side had come, because, as Gieco sang:

> I only ask God
> not to make me indifferent to war
> It is a great monster that tramples
> On the poor innocence of the people

Everyone remembered, too, that the peace movement in Argentina was interwoven with the rock movement, and Porchetto's "A Little Peace" (*"Algo de Paz"*) became the other big success of the night.

For *rock nacional* the seizure of the Malvinas and the consequent decision of the authorities not to transmit any more music in English meant the chance to secure massive coverage in the audio-visual media which until then had denied it space. This coverage made it possible for the music's proposals to be heard by a greater number of people, and led to an acceleration in the already marked mass nature of the phenomenon. In this context, *rock nacional,* not having supported the government in its military adventure (as the political parties had done) and representing the real losers in the war—the hundreds of young men killed or mutilated—assumed a position of outright criticism of the government. The content of lyrics became increasingly oppositional and the chants from the audience became more pointed, with some concerts echoing to the chant: "Firing squads, firing squads, for all the soldiers who betrayed the nation" (*"Paredón, paredón, a todos los milicos que vendieron la nación"*).

Thus, for example, Fito Páez described in "Difficult Times" (*"Tiempos Difíciles"*) all the horror of the figure of the "disappeared":

> The gravediggers have done their job badly
> The desecrators forgot that buried flesh
> Does not produce, but there are living branches
> And worse, they are alert.
> Mothers who cry over grey earthy
> Sons who train so as not to die…

And after having described this horror, Páez promises in his song to drink and to sing for these mothers and sons that are not going to allow for a massacre to occur anymore.

This song, along with the re-issued "Illegal Oppression" (*"Apremios Ilegales"*) by Pedro y Pablo (composed in fact for the earlier dictatorship of 1966-73),

> Illegal oppression
> Criminal abuses
> Your human condition
> Violated at their pleasure
> Shock treatment and the witnesses
> Shrieking as they die
> However loud you scream
> Your voice will not be heard

and Charly García's *"Los Dinosaurios"* and Spinetta's *"Maribel,"* dedicated to the Mothers of the Plaza de Mayo, marked the high point of the production of lyrics denouncing the situation through which the young lived in the years of the dictatorship. The privileged sphere for meeting and communication within the movement continued to be the mass concerts:

> The concerts were freedom…a meeting in freedom: a liberated zone. You wanted to get in at any price because you knew that inside something different was happening…it was a place where

people lived freedom in the music, I dont know…it was in the air, yes? We asked for freedom there.[29]

A sphere for the construction of liberty, a utopia made real, even though only between those four walls: yes, but when five, ten, twenty, and as many as 60,000 people express and feel the same thing, it makes a movement of opinion of genuine scale. The rock movement not only asked for but also, to a certain extent, anticipated the freedom that was to come.

Oppositions and the Field of Conflict Values

Rock nacional called into question the way in which adults conceive the world:

all those [adults] who surround you have their eyes closed to life, and the worst thing is that they want to get you to be the same way, and at this age you see things as they should be, not as they are.[30]

For the young, who tend to orient themselves in accordance with fundamental behaviors rooted in values, the "realism" of adults, their pragmatic behavior, is synonymous with hypocrisy. This is so because a substantial part of the values upheld by the young come from the socialization which they receive from their elders, so that their denunciations are directed against the inconsistency between the values affirmed by adult society and its social practice.

The rock movement coined a term to denote this hypocrisy: *careta* (mask). To be *careta* is to appear to be something one is not:

Argentina is *careta,* like all the countries which are coerced and under repression. It was the country of the magazine *Gente,* of marriages between artists, of the jet-set, the country where everything is beautiful, the appearance put on for outside. But inside there were people who were dying of hunger, and there isn't a single bit of political news in the papers…it's all football.[31]

In addition to those values which they absorb during the socialization process, whether adults respect them in practice or not, the young people of each generation create and uphold new values. In the context of complex modern societies, the young fulfill the function of putting forward new experimental values, which society cannot yet adopt. In this sense, certain practices of the young anticipate behavior patterns which will later be generalized through the whole of the social body, but which are temporarily repellent to it. It is there that conflict emerges over the breaking of bounds which the system is not disposed for the moment to cross, as it was expressed by teenagers such as Carlos: "Rock is against the society imposed by older people"; or Augusto: "We're against the establishment."[32]

To be against the society imposed upon them and against the establishment is to insist that other values exist to be imposed and established—one's own. For the young participants of the *rock nacional* movement, the existence of two projects in opposition to each other (those of the adult and youth worlds) was expressed in a series of opposed pairs: violence-peace (or more violence, in the case of the "heavy rock" branch of *rock nacional);* materialism-spirituality; individualism-community; greed-disinterest; routine-innovation; interest-love; alienation-creation; realism-fantasy; the constructed-the natural; the superficial-the profound; authoritarianism-liberty, etc. In this way the oppositional attitude of rock was established in the face of a social system characterized as hypocritical, repressive, violent, materialistic, individualistic, routine, alienated, superficial, and authoritarian.

Authoritarianism: The Crisis within the Crisis

If this was the characterization the rock movement made of the adult world in general, the existence of a dictatorial regime further exacerbated some of its perceived characteristics. Oppostion to the governing juntas came to monopolize the discourse of the young and the movement, to the detriment (if only temporary) of the rest. Thus violence, repression, and authoritarianism (or their opposites, peace and freedom) came to be the fundamental watchwords put forward by rock during the period of military rule. Notwithstanding this—and given the characteristic noted before, that frequently the confrontation with adults seems to be total—it was not accidental that the young linked the dictatorship to adults in general, at the same time as they signaled their clear opposition to it:

> The country has ended up penniless. Capital has been expatriated to the extent that this nation has been turned into the most dependent and indebted on the planet. What did you do about it, dad?…every son should turn himself into an inquisitor of his father. Because if the government in fact hands over to the politicians a devastated country, then also our grandfathers and fathers are handing over to us a very dubious piece of history in which they are all accomplices for what they have done or failed to do…In the eyes of their children, every father will take his share of responsibility in the face of all this mess, and we young people will be able to demand a "mea culpa" from this shrivelled and ancient society, now that its authoritarian leaders are getting older, and finding it a little harder to keep their gaze fixed upon us.[33]

It was precisely this absolute conviction of the adolescents who grew up during the military period, and of the movement they represented—the conviction of being in no way responsible for the disaster—which gave solid arguments on the one hand, and courage on the other, to confront repression. It was for that reason that the first mass setting in which slogans were chanted against the government, and the military regime was called a "dictatorship," was a national rock concert.

The Enemy within the Movement

Since its origins, the rock movement in Argentina recognized a fundamental fear, one which perhaps has its source in the fate of other youth movements at an international level, of being coopted, exploited, or "turned over" by the system. This possibility was lived as a constant threat, and these young people were highly sensitive to it. Two terms coined within the movement are of key importance to understanding the radical and non-negotiable attitude with regard to certain values: *transar* and *zafar*.

To *transar* is to enter into transactions with the system—for example, making commercial music, abandoning original values, and so on. To *zafar* is the opposite. It is to "escape" from the system, to escape from it by any means possible. When the young detected attitudes they suspected of being *transa*, comments arose such as "they're making commercial music now," "they've sold out," "they're taking the easy way," etc. Incorruptibility was demanded of all members of the movement, but of its leaders in particular.

This fear was related to the way the system might penetrate rock, producing a separation between the public and the artist. In general, it was the money the artist was (allegedly or really) earning which was accused of provoking the split. And the money comes, for the most part, from the hand of a producer. Cause and agent were thus identified. In this way the artist's representative was identified as the fifth columnist of the establishment within the world of rock. It was he or she who made money out of the music, the ideals and the poetry of the music. For a long time the utopia of the members would seem to have been to achieve the abolition of intermediations between the music and the public, with the idea that the music and the public made up the movement. All the other things were considered invasions, and the invasions were the system.

Beyond the existence of certain data which made it possible to glimpse "commercial" behavior on the part of some musicians, one would have to ask whether some of the accusations of *transa* were not linked to issues which had more to do with the young people who made them than with the musicians against whom they were directed. It might be suggested that some of those recriminations had their origins in the mythic reconstruction which each member and subgroup of the world of rock made of what was her or his moment of entry and initiation into the movement.

Curiously, practically all our interviewees, as well as the majority of readers of rock magazines writing to the Letters Page, identified the moment of the greatest authenticity of the movement (leaving aside its "untouchable origins") as the time at which they themselves were socialized into the rock culture. There was a "before" and an "after," a "paradise lost" in which, apparently, all past time was better. This intersection between the cycle of one's personal life and the history of the movement seems to mark a key point, becoming a landmark which is symbolically converted into a divisor between a mythical "before" and "after."

Perhaps the perception of how long the movement retained its "idealism" is linked to the moment at which they themselves, because of the time they had reached in their own lives, came to an equally idealistic conception of the world, governed by absolute values, purity of principles, etc., and it is possible that in part they projected their subsequent disillusionment back onto the movement as a whole. The theme is pertinent, given that the rock musicians have given eloquent signs of wishing to "escape" from the system and avoid being drawn into the bourgeoisie:

> Now that I'm part of the system…well, it's not very nice. You have to watch out all the time that the system doesn't devour you, and it wears you down…if I should happen to see that I can't keep my head together, I'll retreat and play in smaller places, without sponsors.[34]

It was a constant feature of *rock nacional* that groups broke up at the moment of their greatest success, the cases of those who broke up once they had started to decline being exceptional. The leading musicians have always attached greater importance to their creative development than to the dictates of economic success. Paradoxically, actions of this kind lead them to form new groups which themselves become successful (sooner or later), as in general the change in their style of composition corresponds to the detection of new needs which are emerging among their public. This phenomenon had led to a constant to and fro between the public and the music, which has made for their growth together.

Youth Culture and "Us"

Rock nacional for a long time defined itself as a movement. Its members were bounded together by a shared culture, an ideology of life, which had the particular characteristic of bringing into play the personality as a whole, in its rational, social, and affective aspects. It was an oppositional culture which not only embraced the political, economic, and social orders, but also called into question a form of conceiving of the world:

> Rock is our culture. The culture of a generation which rejects the inheritance of previous generations, an inheritance of crisis, blood, one of the worst in the world. It is art for today and implies a whole ideological and philosophical posture.[35]

It's a movement that goes beyond music. It's a philosophy, a way of life. For me, in personal matters, it was also a religion. Rock is your home and you feel it…it is giving you identity, speaking to you.[36]

Rock is what you were feeling and what you were living every day: your problems, your wishes, your desires. You don't carry it in long hair or faded jeans, you carry it in your heart.[37]

Rock as a form of life, as a daily concern, as ideology, as the sphere of the self, as a valid interlocutor, as a practice of freedom: these and other similar descriptions were conspicuous in the discourse of the members of the movement, revealing the resocializing function which it played in contemporary Argentina, characterized as it is by the imposition of a culture of silence and self-censorship in the family sphere. Young people were looking elsewhere for the truthful information that was being kept from them, as neither the manipulated information which they received from the mass media, nor that which they received from their teachers and lecturers, nor the dialogue they conducted with their parents (who generally appealed to self-censorship to avoid repression falling on the family) made any reference to the real country the young experience every day. To say that "rock spoke to you," or that rock was "what you felt and lived every day," is to say that the communicative practices with which many young people maintained their relationship with reality were structured around the *rock nacional* movement, not around the *careta* discourse of their parents:

It was rock which made me see the things that were all right, that you think are all right. I believe that many things you didn't have clear, or that appeared to be the case, or that you felt in a vague kind of way, became firmer or clearer through the themes of the rock songs or the musicians' statements. I think that in many cases the musicians functioned as leaders of opinion.[38]

The Concert as the Principal Channel of Participation

Although the culture of rock had multiple manifestations (a language of its own, particular types of clothes, etc.), it was centered primarily upon music, with the artists becoming the leaders of the movement. These leaders were seen as co-founders of the cultural phenomenon that had been generated, as they interpreted the feelings of the young and re-created them, not only in specific musical forms, but also in multiple common codes. The relationship between the artist and the public was practically symbiotic: one did not exist without the other. This went much further than the simple economic problem of a public supporting an artist by attending concerts or buying records, because artistic production itself depended upon the quality of this relationship. The reason for this was that it was demanded of the musicians that while their own idiosyncrasies were respected, they should continue to express the everyday experiences, the desires and the values of the young people who made them their leaders. In this way the resulting phenomenon was a shared one, given that it did not belong exclusively to the musicians, as they only transmitted back, in an artistic product, what their people first gave to them:

> the people are the main protagonist in what we are doing. The public has to provoke the phenomenon of Luis Alberto Spinetta, and Luis Alberto Spinetta has to provoke the phenomenon of his public…it's a question of making them feel that they are getting something impressive, and that they are the ones who invented it.[39]

> I believe that in the concerts there are two artists: the public and the artist. Fifty percent each.[40]

The close relationship between artist and public was the nodal point of all the phenomena known as *rock nacional,* and the concert was the physical sphere in which it was molded. In addition, this characteristic of the movement brought with it the idea of equality, absence of division: musicians were the representative of the lived experiences of their followers, and in order to continue in that position they must share these experiences with them. The logic of the equality/success held by the rock fans was a simple one: if the musician becomes a "superstar" he would not be able to share experiences with his followers, he would cease to represent his people, and then he would lose popularity. The dangers of "stardom" were perceived by the most lucid elements, and pointed out by the young fans in the majority of participant accounts:

> the musician sold me the idea that he was the same as me, and now I see that it isn't so and I have every right to tell him that he's a cretin, and to give me back what is mine.[41]

Therefore, keeping the circuit which feeds rock well oiled was not simply a matter of preserving the concert as a meeting place, but primarily of keeping open communication between the musician and the public— that recycling of messages and lived experiences which made the musician both an equal and an idol and, at the same time, transformed a leader into the most "equal" of the equal. The concert, as the principal participatory form, thus took shape as the sphere of reunion of the young with their own lived experiences. In it, ideology was renewed, the proposals of the leaders were ratified or rejected, and outsiders were given a display of the numerical size of the movement. It was lived as a ritual of re-creation, regeneration and reaffirmation of "us," of the collective identity. The slogans, the "O-OOO-O!" of Woodstock, the requests for the most significant songs, the outburst of joy at the recognition of favorite songs when the musicians play the opening chords were, more than the applause at the end, the signs of the approval and affection of the public. Applause at the end is the result of an aesthetic appreciation of the consumed artistic product, and for the movement the aesthetic was only one more component, not the principal reason for the meeting. In sum, *rock nacional* during the dictatorship was a movement which created leaders rather than idols, which demanded the reaffirmation of the commitment of musicians to the reality of their public at every meeting, in a daily plebiscite, as it were, which was the nodal point of its survival as an oppositional youth movement.

Conclusions

The *rock nacional* movement has played an extremely important part in the socialization and resocialization of broad sectors of Argentinean youth during the military period, restoring truthful communication regarding the real country, salvaging the meaning of life in a context of lies and terror, consolidating a collective actor as a means of counteracting an individualistic model of life, counterpoising a supportive community of actions and interests to the primacy of the market. The highly oppositional content of the songs, the frankly critical attitude of the audiences, and the gathering together in public places to express opposition to the military regime were some of the characteristics of this youth movement, which, in the context of the crisis of legitimacy provoked in Argentina by the emergence of successive dictatorial governments, has made itself one of the alternatives to the crisis, creating popular and communal channels of participation each time that traditional channels have been closed down.

It was a movement which had leaders but no idols, which celebrated itself in massive concerts, and which transformed some songs into genuine hymns: "Girl with Paper Eyes" (*"Muchacha Ojos de Papel"*), "Cold Tomato Juice" (*"Jugo de Tomate Frío"*), "The Raft" (*"La Balsa"*), "The Bear" (*"El Oso"*), "The March of Rage" (*"La Marcha de la Bronca"*), "Song for My Death" (*"Canción para Mi Muerte"*), "I Only Ask God (*"Sólo le Pido a Dios"*), "Alicia's Song in the Country" (*"Canción de Alicia en el País"*), or "The Canterville Ghost" (*"El Fantasma de Canterville"*). During the dictatorship, in 1983, the latter was played in the funeral cortege which followed the remains of the conscript Palacios, assassinated in the military regiment of Campo de Mayo after having been tortured for a minor infraction.

It was a movement which won the backing of adolescents who wrote on their rucksacks, as did Roberto (15 years old): "My arm is peace, my party is rock, and my eternal end is love."

Without any doubt it has been, for broad sectors of youth, a refuge, a sphere of resistance, and a channel for participation in the context of a closed and authoritarian society in crisis.

James Brown

Popular Music and the Civil Rights Movement

Reebee Garofalo

When political activists think about the music of the Civil Rights Movement, they are likely to focus on union songs and spirituals like "Which Side Are You On," "This Little Light of Mine," "Keep Your Eyes on the Prize," "This Land is Your Land," "Down by the Riverside," and, of course, "We Shall Overcome." With their roots in the labor movement and the culture of the black church, the springboards for most civil rights organizing, these songs were critical to activists in the movement. They raised our consciousness, energized our day-to-day political work, and provided us with moments of celebration in the struggle. These were, in the words of Bernice Reagon, the "songs that moved the movement."[1] To the nation-at-large, however, these songs often served as little more than the musical background for terrifying newscasts of racial violence. Interestingly, as the Civil Rights Movement exploded on the national scene, its impact on the national consciousness was more clearly reflected in popular music. As always, this was the music that moved the mass audience.

As any social phenomenon attains national recognition, popular music can be used as an important socio-political indicator of that struggle. In the case of Civil Rights, the trajectory of the entire movement can be traced through an analysis of trends in popular music from 1954 through 1973. Such analyses are often limited to a consideration of changes in lyric content. While there is no question that these changes are, at times, powerful, it is also important to note that changes in musical form, tone, instrumentation, production style, and personnel can be more telling. One pattern related to the Civil Rights Movement is that innovation in these latter areas generally preceded changes in lyric content.

Civil rights activity heated up in the 1950s when a new, activist black clergy, with the Rev. Martin Luther King, Jr., at its forefront, began to form political alliances with secular organizations like the NAACP, CORE, and, later, SNCC. "While this spiritual-secular coalition was forming in the political sector," states music journalist Nelson George, "the music world was witnessing the breaking of a longstanding taboo, as gospel began to fuse with rhythm & blues."[2] Prior to this time, gospel singers simply did not perform "the devil's music," and vice versa. But as the faithful began to take their struggle to the streets, the musical influences of gospel—the prominant use of organ, soaring vocals, background choruses, and the call-and-response style—were quickly appropriated by the secular world of rhythm and blues and brought to the attention of a mass public.

Prefigured in the 1953 releases of "Shake a Hand" by Faye Adams and "Crying in the Chapel" by Sonny Til and the Orioles (covered by June Valli for RCA), the fruits of this trend could be seen in the vocal stylings of Clyde McPhatter and Jackie Wilson, both of whom began their careers as lead vocalists for the gospel-tinged Dominoes, and in the spectacular pop career of Sam Cooke, who was already at the top of the gospel heap as the lead singer for the Soul Stirrers. But nowhere was the marriage of gospel and R&B more apparent than in the early recordings of Ray Charles ("Hallelujah, I Love Her So," "What'd I Say"). By 1954, all the elements of the fusion were already present in one of his most influential, if not most successful, releases. The impact of "I Got a Woman" is remembered by music historians as nothing short of apocalyptic. "The very strategem of adapting a traditional gospel song, putting secular lyrics to it, and then delivering it with all the attendant fanfare of a pentacostal service was, simply, staggering," writes Peter Guaralnick. "It was like a blinding flash of light in which the millenium, all of a sudden and unannounced, had arrived."[3] In popular music as in the struggle for civil rights, the black church was becoming a force to be reckoned with in the material world.

Integrating the Pop Market

The eruption of civil rights as a national issue was anticipated by a number of regional struggles which also had parallels in popular music. When Rosa Parks moved up to the front of the bus in 1955, black artists like Fats Domino ("Ain't That a Shame," "I'm in Love Again," "Blueberry Hill"), Little Richard ("Tutti Frutti," "Long Tall Sally," Good Golly, Miss Molly"), and Chuck Berry ("Rock & Roll Music," "Sweet Little Sixteen," "Johnny B. Goode") were just beginning to crossover into the pop market as heroes of rock 'n' roll. Increasingly, regional civil rights struggles, based mainly in the deep South, came to national attention, just as much of early rock 'n' roll was based on regional R&B styles from the deep South which found a national audience. The rebellious tone of this music mirrored the growing demand for political change in the black community. And just as community-based black activism would change the political face of the nation, so too would the popularization of grassroots rhythm and blues and its pop conversion to rock 'n' roll alter the popular music landscape. As early as 1956, the winds of such cultural change were already apparent. "It was not only the slicker, more pop-oriented singers like Clyde McPhatter and Otis Williams who hit in the pop market," reported *Billboard,* "but also those working in the traditional style like Shirley and Lee, Little Richard, and Fats Domino. Their impact, in fact, has virtually changed the conception of what a pop record is."[4]

With the advent of rock 'n' roll, the form and style of popular music changed dramatically and irrevocably. But these changes were not yet accompanied by analogous changes in lyric content. Brown may have rocked the Board of Education in the historic school desegregation case in 1954, but Chuck Berry's depiction of "School Days" in 1957 did not describe the educational experience in Little Rock, Arkansas that same year. Berry conjured up the image of teachers teaching "the golden rule" even as Eisenhower had to send federal troops to Little Rock to enforce the Supreme Court's school integration edict. Berry was a true storyteller in the folkloric sense of the term, but he was also a man for his time. As he recently told his audience, "I said: 'Why can't I do as Pat Boone does and play good music for the white people and sell as well there as I could in the neighborhood?' And that's what I shot for writing 'School Days.'"[5]

The strategy of the early Civil Rights Movement was integrationist, and it was in this historical context that Berry pursued his career. While he never disowned his blackness, his goal was full acceptance in the white mainstream. In keeping his eyes on that prize, Berry's intent was not significantly different than that of the other black rock 'n' rollers who crossed over. He just did it better. Interestingly, a more compelling vignette of the black educational experience was captured—albeit somewhat tongue-in-cheek—in the Coaster's "Charlie Brown" (1959), written and produced by the white songwriting team of Jerry Leiber and Mike Stoller.

Neither popular music nor the Civil Rights Movement were without their contradictions. In its integrationist phase, the movement tended to play down real differences in favor of the slogan "Black and White Together." Issues like white skin privilege on the one hand and black self-determination on the other were not yet prominant on the political agenda. If the movement itself avoided confronting pressing issues at the time, it should come as no surprise that civil rights themes were nowhere to be found in the lyric content of popular music. In this period, the movement exerted its influence on music in other ways.

Following a period of repression of both civil rights activity and rock 'n' roll in the late fifties, bland, white vocalists like Fabian, Frankie Avalon, and Bobby Rydell gradually took over the pop market. However, as civil rights activity gathered momentum once again in the early sixties with sit-ins, freedom rides, the March on Washington, and the Mississippi Summer Project, a new phenomenon appeared in popular music—the "girl groups." Black female vocal groups such as the Shirelles ("Will You Love Me Tomorrow"), the Crystals ("He's a Rebel"), the Chiffons ("He's So Fine"), and the Ronnettes ("Be My Baby") provided a polar opposite to the white males in the pop market. Corresponding to the increase in civil rights activism, there were more black women—indeed, with the continued success of artists like Sam Cooke and Ray Charles, more black artists of both genders—on the pop charts in the early sixties than at any point in history. In 1962, 42 percent of the best-selling singles of the year were by black artists. Their music was a refreshing change of pace (and race) in the pop market.

It was also during this period that Berry Gordy founded the most significant black-owned record label ever—Motown, until recently the centerpiece of the largest black-owned corporation in the United States. There can be no doubt that the growing Civil Rights Movement provided a climate which encouraged the development of such an enterprise. Gordy was brilliant as a producer in that he was able to incorporate white audience tastes without abandoning a black sound. In the process he created a formula that was the perfect metaphor for the early Civil Rights Movement—upbeat black pop that was acceptable to a white audience, irresistably danceable, and not threatening to anyone in tone or content. Dozens of early Motown releases such as the the the Marvellettes' "Please, Mr. Postman" (1961), "Dancing in the Streets" by Martha and the Vandellas (1963), the Supremes' "Where Did Our Love Go" (1964), or "My Girl" by the Temptations (1965) could serve as examples.

While the influence of the early Civil Rights Movement clearly extended to the music business, the major pop styles still showed virtually no change in lyric content. During this period, civil rights texts were performed mainly in the folk idiom and, to a lesser extent, in jazz. At the time, however, even these musics experienced some brief successes in the pop market.

In folk music, whether one looked at old-timers like Pete Seeger or new-comers like Joan Baez, the best-known performers who addressed civil rights themes in their music were white. This phenomenon probably had more to do with the process of becoming famous in the United States than who was performing civil rights-related material. In the context of the integrationist phase of the Civil Rights Movement, it was not identified as a major contradiction. The new-comer who became the most famous of all the folkies was, of course, the enigmatic Bob Dylan. With selections like "Oxford Town" (1962) and "The Lonesome Death of Hattie Carroll" (1963), Dylan was early on proclaimed a "leader" of the Civil Rights Movement. He performed his "Only a Pawn in Their Game," a song about the murder of civil rights leader Medgar Evers, at the 1963 March on Washington. That same year, the more commercial Peter, Paul, and Mary scored a Top Ten pop hit with Dylan's "Blowin' in the Wind."

Soon a number of black folk artists like the classically-trained Odetta, the unorthodox Richie Havens, and the gospel-influenced Staple Singers also gained prominence as voices of the Civil Rights Movement. As more black performers achieved recognition, the style of civil rights-related music moved closer to pop production. The Staple Singers, for example, performed "We Shall Overcome" with electric guitar and drums. Of critical importance in linking "folk consciousness" with pop appeal was the often under-appreciated Curtis Mayfield. Like fellow Chicagoan Sam Cooke before him, Mayfield left the gospel choir for the secular world of popular music, there to become, in the words of Nelson George, "black music's most unflagging civil rights champion."[6] With his pop/gospel trio, the Impressions, Mayfield utilized full studio production to achieve major pop successes with a series of "sermon" songs like "Keep on Pushing" and "Amen" in 1964, and "People Get Ready" in 1965. In 1964, Sam Cooke, inspired by Dylan's "Blowin' in the Wind," tentatively attempted a similar fusion with "A Change is Gonna Come." By the time the record was released as a single, though, Cooke had already been shot to death under unsavory circumstances. When his friend Malcolm X was assassinated on February 21, 1965, just two months later, "A Change is Gonna Come" was a pop hit. It stands as Cooke's monument to civil rights.

From Integration to Black Power

For the Civil Rights Movement, 1965 was a pivotal year. Activists marched in Alabama from Selma to Montgomery. The Voting Rights Act was passed. Rioting broke out in Watts, ushering in an era of urban unrest. And Stokely Carmichael coined the term "Black Power." In the jazz arena, Nina Simone captured the tenor of the times, in content and in tone, as her 1965 recording of "Mississippi Goddam" anticipated the militance that was about to erupt (just as her "Backlash Blues" would anticipate the reaction). This transformation was also reflected in black popular music but, again, changes in form, tone, and production style preceded changes in lyric content.

As the liberal Civil Rights Movement gave way to the more radical demand for black power, Motown's hegemony over black pop was successfully challenged by a resurgence of closer-to-the-roots, hard-driving rhythm and blues from the Memphis-Muscle Shoals region of the deep South. Chiefly responsible for the popularization of Southern soul, as this music was called, was a short-lived but highly successful collaboration between Atlantic Records and a number of Southern studios, most notably Stax in Memphis and Fame in Muscle Shoals, Alabama. From 1965 on, artists like Otis Redding ("I've Been Loving You Too Long"), Wilson Pickett ("Land of 1,000 Dances"), Sam and Dave ("Soul Man"), Arthur Conley ("Sweet Soul Music"), and Percy Sledge ("When a Man Loves a Woman") were prominant among the new chart toppers. Echoing the spirit of the emerging new militance, their recordings were raw, basic, and almost angry in tone, as compared to the cleaner, brighter Motown sound.

Striking differences between Motown and Southern soul can be seen in a comparison of Motown and its chief competitor, Stax. Both founded around 1960, Motown was as secretive and tightly controlled as Stax was open and disorganized. Stax was originally a white-owned company; its creative functions were as likely to be handled by whites as by blacks, and the "Memphis sound" which they spawned was almost invariably the product of cross-racial teamwork. Initially, the credits on all Stax recordings read simply: "produced by the Stax staff." Motown was not only black-owned, but virtually all of its creative personnel—artists, writers, producers, and session musicians—were black as well. It was clearly a haven for black talent. Paradoxically, Motown is remembered as being "totally committed to reaching white audiences," while Stax recordings, by contrast, were "consistently aimed at r&b fans first, the pop market second."[7]

In context of black pride, Motown's lavish use of multi-track studio production to achieve a more "pop" sound seemed somehow out of synch with the search for African roots. "Motown does a lot of overdubbing," commented Stax artist Otis Redding just before his death in 1967. "At Stax...[w]e cut together, horns, rhythms, and vocal...Until last year, we didn't even have a four track tape recorder. You can't overdub on a one track machine."[8] In many ways, it was the very simplicity and straight-forwardness of Southern soul production which gave the music its claim on authenticity. When this music crossed over into the pop market, it wasn't because the music had changed, it was because black pride had briefly created a climate wherein unrefined rhythm and blues could find mainstream acceptance on its own terms.

With Southern soul in its ascendency, unencumbered production was soon joined by social consciousness in black popular music. In January 1967, Aretha Franklin was signed to Atlantic Records, and after one legendary session in Muscle Shoals, she found her sound. Later that spring, she cut a version of what had been Otis Redding's signature tune. "Respect" was instantly "transformed from a demand for conjugal rights into a soaring cry of freedom."[9] Shortly thereafter, Aretha was crowned "Lady Soul." The vocal and emotional range of her early Atlantic releases ("Baby, I Love You," "Natural Woman," "Chain of Fools," and "Think," to name a few) uniquely expressed all the passion and forcefulness of the era. Fittingly, the summer of 1967 was dubbed by *Ebony* as "the summer of 'Retha, Rap [Brown], and Revolt."[10]

The insistence of black power was echoed perhaps even more force-fully in the music of James Brown. When James Brown had his first Top Ten pop hit with "Papa's Got a Brand New Bag" in 1965, he billed himself, with some justification, as "the hardest working man in show business." By 1968, he was "Soul Brother #1." His string of uncompromising Top Ten hits ("I Got You," "Cold Sweat," "I Got the Feelin' ") made fewer consessions to main-stream sensibilities than any other music in the pop market. During this period, according to critic Robert Palmer, "Brown and his musicians and arrangers began to treat every instrument and voice in the group as if each were a drum."[11] The connection to African roots and black pride was made explicit in 1968, as his hit single, "Say it Loud—I'm Black and I'm Proud," became an anthem in the struggle for black liberation.

By 1967, socially conscious texts were becoming common in popular music, as artists of all styles and personal backgrounds got on board the civil rights train. Janis Ian's "Society's Child" (1967) lamented the en-trenched separation of the races on a personal level. Releases such as Dion's "Abraham, Martin, and John" (1968), the Rascals' "People Got to be Free" (1968), and "Everyday People" by Sly and the Family Stone (1969) were reminiscent of the more moderate themes of the early Civil Rights Move-ment. Curtis Mayfield continued his run of socially conscious "sermon songs" with "We're a Winner" in 1968, and "Choice of Colors" in 1969. Even Elvis Presley's "In the Ghetto" (1969), a rather unlikely entry, went to Number Three on the pop charts.

The assassination of Martin Luther King, Jr., on April 4, 1968 left a void in civil rights leadership; the movement became increasingly fragmented. "The civil-rights struggle was not dead, but its energy was increasingly scattered," writes Nelson George. "The Black Panthers embraced commu-nism. Ron Karenga's U.S. [United Slaves] organization advocated an Afrocentric cultural nationalism... Black Power came to mean whatever its user needed it to...the assimilationists pressed on..."[12] By the early seventies, fragmentation had begun to give way to disintegration.

The career of Sly and the Family Stone echoed this phase of the Civil Rights Movement. In 1968, the group's first hit single, "Dance to the Music" transcended the confines of musical style, much as the band crossed the boundaries of race and gender. Comprised of black and white men and women, they were a model of racial and sexual harmony. Following King's death, their 1969 LP, *Stand!*, included not only the all-inclusive Number One single, "Everyday People," but also the bolder title song and the more provocative "Don't Call Me Nigger, Whitey." Turning up the heat further, their 1971 LP, *There's a Riot Goin' On*, was considered even more con-troviersial, but by this time Sly's growing militance was more than offset by his drug-induced unreliability. Following a number of personnel changes, the group, not unlike the movement itself, slowly disintegrated over the next few years. "Family Affair," released as a single in 1971, was Sly and the Family Stone's last Top Ten pop single.

The year 1971 was, in fact, a watershed year for the Civil Rights Movement as reflected in popular music. Recalling the heyday of the Black Panthers, John Lennon's exhortation, "Power to the People," tried to offer an upbeat anthem. But, Bob Dylan's tribute to the memory of slain black leader "George Jackson" reminded us that the more radical elements in the struggle for black liberation had already been neutralized. The confusion and disillusionment of the period were evident in Marvin Gaye's "What's Goin' On" and "Inner City Blues," both of 1971. On a more positive note, Aretha Franklin's recording of Nina Simone's "Young, Gifted, and Black" that same year captured the spirit of a community which had weathered a storm of urban violence. Her stirring celebration of black pride provided the musical capstone for a decade of civil rights struggle.

The Return to "Normalcy"

As radicalism in the black community was systematically repressed, either by the cooptation of key leaders or the more sinister effectiveness of the FBI's COINTELPRO agenda, there was a corresponding decline in the popularity of the more militant sounding rhythm and blues from the deep South. By the early 1970s, Stax had begun its descent into bankruptcy, the other pioneers of the Memphis-Muscle Shoals axis were no longer producing rhythm and blues, and even Atlantic had changed direction to focus on its British rock acts. Atlantic's Jerry Wexler explained that radio stations didn't want to "burden" their listeners "with the sound of breaking glass in Watts or the sirens coming from Detroit, which is what r&b music meant at the time…so they took most of it off the radio."[13]

Reflecting the "quieter" mood of the early 1970s, the black popular music which came to the fore was the "soft soul" sound pioneered by the Philadelphia-based writer-producer team of Kenny Gamble and Leon Huff, and producer-arranger Thom Bell. Joining forces with Sigma Sound Studios in Philadelphia, they developed the style in the late 1960s, working with artists like Jerry Butler and the Intruders, and Delfonics, whose classic 1968 hit, "La La Means I Love You," was a harbinger of sounds to come. But the Philadelphia enterprise didn't hit its stride until 1971, with the formation of Philadelphia International Records (PIR) and a distribution deal with CBS Records. Employing lush orchestral arrangements over a polite rhythmic pulse, groups like the Stylistics ("You Make Me Feel Brand New"), produced by Thom Bell for the Avco label, and Harold Melvin and the Blue Notes ("If You Don't Know Me By Now") and the O'Jays ("Back Stabbers," "Love Train"), produced by Gamble and Huff on PIR, set the standard in black pop for the next few years.

Personally, Gamble was a nationalist with inclinations toward Islam. He saw PIR as a platform for pushing a message. "Along the way, Gamble and Huff comtemplated slavery (the O'Jays' miniepic "Ship A'Hoy"), ecology ("The Air I Breathe"), spiritual enlightment ("Wake Up Everybody"), corruption ("Bad Luck"), and the male-dominated nuclear family ("Family Reunion")."[14] In the context of the increasingly conservative Nixon-Ford era, however, certain aspects of nationalism—like the economic self-sufficiency provided by the CBS distribution deal—were as likely to resonate with Nixon's call for "black capitalism" as with the development of a strong opposition movement. (In 1972, even James Brown endorsed Nixon for the presidency.) The bottom line was that Gamble and Huff infused the market with romantic ballads and stylish dance music more than they rejuvenated the movement with a message of black liberation. Other artists like the Chicago-based Chi-Lites ("Oh Girl"), the ever-changing Isley Brothers ("That Lady"), and the Spinners ("Could it be I'm Falling in Love") from Detroit quickly tuned into the new soft sound. Even Southern soul yielded the velvety smooth Al Green ("Let's Stay Together," "I'm Still in Love With You").

With the movement in disarray, civil rights themes were on the decline in popular music. Among the soft soul groups, the Chi-Lites had a pop hit with "(For God's Sake) Give More Power to the People" in 1971. War scored with "The World is a Ghetto" in 1972. By 1973, only Stevie Wonder's "Living for the City" was noticeable in the pop singles market. More to the point, the softer production style of the ascending Philadelphia sound clearly signaled the end of an era of turmoil, ferment, and rebellion, as it provided one of the formative influences for the style that would dominate the latter half of the decade—disco. Interestingly, in 1972, an all-time high of 44 percent of the best-selling singles of the year were by artists of color.

By the early seventies, the Civil Rights Movement appeared to have run its course. Activists knew that the issues it raised would surface again in different contexts and new organizational forms, but for the time being the movement had been forceably rendered dormant, its 20-year history of peaks and valleys, successes and failures, contradictions and divergent tendencies chronicled in popular music. Struck most by the recollection of progressive change, Curtis Mayfield offered the following summation of the previous decade:

> You know, to talk about the '60s almost brings tears to my eyes. What we did. What we all did. We changed the world—me, us, Smokey Robinson, Jerry Butler, the Temptations, Aretha, Otis, Gladys Knight, James Brown. We really did. Barriers broke down for us. And for all black musicians afterwards. I mean, to have lived through that, and to have been a part of that, is more than anyone can ask.[15]

The battles of the 1960s were hard fought; in popular music as elsewhere, they were not without their victories.

Postscript

It wasn't until 1983 that anyone recorded a song about one of the most important leaders of the entire Civil Rights era—Malcolm X. In this instance, it was Malcolm himself, from beyond the grave, who provided the content. "No Sell Out," the brainchild of a white, apolitical percussionist named Keith LeBlanc, is a rap treatment of snippets of Malcolm's actual speeches mixed over a computer drum track. It is fitting that Malcolm X should be issued on a rap record; his influence on the current generation of rappers with an Afrocentric bent has been of paramount importance.

Aretha Franklin

Women's Music

No Longer a Small Private Party

Cynthia M. Lont

We never wanted to be perceived as women's music. We don't want to be found only in the specialty bin at the record stores. We want to be in your face.
—Gretchen Phillips of 2 Nice Girls[1]

This chapter has two intentions, neither primary. First, I want to document the history of women's music. While some musicologists and cultural critics have listened to women's music, and/or know something about it, few have a firm understanding of its cultural basis. Unlike other subcultural music forms, women's music has received little attention in either mainstream or music industry media. Such "symbolic annihilation"[2] of women's music is not surprising. That is the norm concerning women and their inclusion in the media. With rare exceptions (Cris Williamson on the front cover of *Ms.* or Holly Near on the "Today Show"), women's music performers have been blatantly absent from mainstream and other subcultures' press. If the media pay no attention to you (whether it be good or bad press) you don't exist. In the case of women's music, the media's silence is mostly due to the music's foundation in the lesbian community.

My second intention is to detail the relationship between the 1970s and 1980s phenomena of women's music and the new wave of women performers who've become popular in the late '80s and '90s: Tracy Chapman, Michelle Shocked, k.d. lang, and others. Do these performers represent the cooptation of women's music by major labels that now realize the buying power of feminist and lesbian audiences (for example, Michelle Shocked's *Campfire Tapes,* an album originally recorded on a Walkman, sold 30,000 copies to the women's community in England)? Are the more "androgynous" artists (we don't say "lesbian" on major labels) now acceptable to fans who have tired of the stereotyped male fantasies of female pop singers, or is this another quickly passing trend in the music business?

I don't view optimistically the acceptance of women in the mainstream, since economics plays an enormous role; nor do I believe that there is such a large number of new female artists that feminists should be unconcerned with the 99.9 percent of female performers who continue to portray their lives as less than complete without males. Yet an incredible energy does derive from women's music that has cut a narrow path through the sexism at the heart of popular music. The question remains whether the message of women's music has been heard by enough people to result in more changes than just the acceptance of a few women performers in mainstream music.

Women's Music

Women's music was originally defined as music by women, for women, about women, and financially controlled by women.[3] By this definition, a song written by women, about women, and for women would not be considered a part of women's music if it were recorded on a major label. This alternative music industry was originally called lesbian music because many felt the music was started by lesbians for lesbians. Others believed the music was started by heterosexual feminists and taken over by lesbian-feminists when they broke away from the women's liberation movement in the early 1970s.

The term women's music stuck because it was less threatening, both to the dominant social order and to women's music performers and audiences. Women were less likely to be harassed for listening to or performing "women's music" than "lesbian music." Prior to the late '60s, the supportive gay movement and resulting gay pride were nonexistent. Thus the term women's music shielded lesbians not only from the harsh criticism of the dominant social order but from their own internal criticism.

Knowledge of women's music became a key into the lesbian community. If a woman mentioned certain performers in women's music such as Cris Williamson or Meg Christian, it identified her as a lesbian, while talking about one's interest in the music of Joan Baez or Joni Mitchell was not a clear indication that one was a lesbian or lesbian-identified.

The term women's music refers to more than music. The individuals and groups that produced the music were a tangible example of the power of women organized apart from the dominant culture. Lesbian-feminists could take enormous pride knowing that women (read "lesbians") were responsible for the record (performers, musicians, engineers, cover artists); for distribution to the local feminist (read lesbian) bookstore; and for the promotional tours to rural areas, university towns, and small cities. The lesbian-feminist movement was made visible in concert halls and coffeehouses.

The Political and (Sub)Cultural Foundation of Women's Music

Women's music didn't burst into being via one critical political and cultural moment. Instead, the explosion of disturbances from within the political left and a blatant disregard for women throughout the social order created the "space" for diverse women to form the women's music industry.

Women who began women's music labels, and later, distributors of women's music primarily came from the ranks of politically left (counterculture, student, and Civil Rights) groups which ignored women's skills and talents, and invalidated women's experiences. Lesbian organizers entered women's music from the women's liberation movement, many from the National Organization for Women, (which denied the existence of lesbians within its ranks until 1971) or from the Gay Liberation Front (which focused on gay men and their needs).

The existence of women's music (the lyrics, the music, and its support structure) directly opposed the patriarchal culture in which mainstream popular music existed. Mainstream music was based on the experiences of males, subsuming women's experiences within men's experiences or ignoring women's experiences completely. The "symbolic annihilation" of women and women's autonomous experiences within popular music was the impetus for women's music.

The absence of positive women's images within popular music paralleled a lack of opportunities for female performers.[4] In the late 1960s and early 1970s, mainstream labels signed only a few women's bands, including Fanny, Bertha, Deadly Nightshade, and Goldie and the Gingerbreads. Fanny, one of the first all-women's bands on a major record label, "served notice to the rock world that women could do more than simply sing—that women could also write and play rock passionately."[5] While these bands showed that women could play, their lyrics were no more women-centered than those of other rock music.

The women's liberation movement nurtured feminist audiences who wanted their lives portrayed as more than sexual objects for males. For the feminist music listener of the early 1970s, finding selections which didn't rock one's sensibilities was not an easy task. Even the seemingly "independent" women (Tina Turner and Linda Ronstadt) were pouring out their guts for male approval. A feminist record collection was quite limited; a lesbian collection was non-existent.

The intersection of women performers seeking a place to play women-centered music, political organizers seeking a cooperative work environment, and feminists and lesbians seeking music to reaffirm their lifestyles and experiences created the energy and space for women's music to thrive.

Early History of Women's Music

Perhaps at no other time in history could women's music have developed. Following the example of Black Liberation, women increasingly organized apart from men in the late '60s and early '70s. Lesbians faced with discrimination within feminist groups argued vehemently over whether to completely withdraw from male and straight society. "Separatism" was a tactic which focused women's energy and would give an enormous boost to the growth and development of women's music.

The first record performed and recorded by an "out" lesbian artist was Maxine Feldman's "Angry Athis," a 45-rpm single with explicitly lesbian lyrics by an "out" performer, produced by lesbians.

> I hate not being able
> To hold my lover's hand
> 'Cept under some dimly lit table
> Afraid of being who I am
> I hate to tell lies
> Live in the shadow of fear
> We've run half our lives
> From that damn word queer[6]

Like Feldman, lesbian and straight feminists were singing their politics across the country and they began to record.

In 1973, Alix Dobkin, a lesbian separatist, formed a musical group, Lavender Jane, with flutist Kay Gardner and bass player Patches Attom. Financial and emotional support from the lesbian community encouraged Lavender Jane to record an album. Dobkin located a lesbian sound engineer and, soon thereafter, *Lavender Jane Loves Women* was available. Dobkin stated on the album cover:

> For a dozen years I tried to "make it" in the music business—as a solo artist, demo artist, in groups, as a songwriter, a commercial writer and even in coffeehouse management. So many times I came so close, and felt great frustration and disappointment. Always there was this rough element of mine—an abrasive edge—an imperfection. Record and publishing executives, independent producers, managers, agents, P.R. men and assorted hustlers could never quite polish me into a neat commercial package. Lucky for me.[7]

Lavender Jane cost $3,300 for the first 1,000 copies, all of which sold in three months with no formal distribution system other than mail order and a few lesbian-feminist bookstores.

At the same time, an independent label, Rounder Records, produced *Mountain Movin' Day* by an all-straight women band, The Chicago Women's Liberation Rock Band. This band sang rock songs and pantomimed the way men perform rock, demonstrating the underlying sexist nature of the actions.

Although these recordings were important, there was little organization to the production, distribution, and promotion of women's music. In 1973, a group of politically active women (some from the disbanded Furies collective) were searching for a way to implement their lesbian-feminist politics. After meeting two performers, Meg Christian and Cris Williamson, and seeing the need for and interest in music by lesbian-feminists, they formed Olivia Records. With the exception of the short-lived Women's Music Network in New York City (1973-1976), this was the first collective attempt at an organization committed to the production, distribution, and promotion of women's music.

Olivia Records' first 45 rpm (Meg Christian's rendition of "Lady" by Carole King/Gerry Goffin and Cris Williamson's "If It Weren't For the Music") sold 5,000 copies through mail order. This enabled Olivia to produce their first album, Meg Christian's *I Know You Know*. The first year, 10,000 to 12,000 copies were sold. *I Know You Know* was followed by Cris Williamson's *The Changer and the Changed,* "one of the all-time best selling albums on any independent label—in or out of women's music."[8] Over ten years later, "Sweet Woman," one of the songs on *Changer,* continues as one of top five all-time favorite women's music songs (1987-88) in *Hot Wire's* Readers' Choice Awards.

In a few short years, the women's music industry expanded drastically and changed steadily. In 1975, Kay Gardner included classical music on her first album, *Mooncircles,* recorded on her own label, Wide Woman/Urana. Margie Adam, with Barbara Price, created her own label, Pleiades, and Holly Near and friends restructured Redwood Records. The first women of color to record on a women's music label, Sweet Honey in the Rock, had a strong feminist following in 1978 when they recorded the album *B'lieve I'll Run On...See What the End's Gonna Be* on Redwood Records. Their contemporary and traditional songs of black experience made new connections between black audiences and the predominantly white women's music audiences.

Women's music "resistance" against the dominant culture followed the example of the hippies' political strategy: cultural revolution. Rather than directly confronting patriarchy, women's music for the most part ignored it, and by its very existence, created an alternative culture. Women's music dared to emphasize the experiences of women in a culture that ignored, devalued, or subsumed women's experiences within males' experiences. Males and the dominant culture weren't portrayed negatively in women's music, they just weren't included. Instead, women's music created a space and form in which women's autonomy and, in particular, lesbian lifestyles were encouraged. Women's music portrayed women's cultures, separate and safe from patriarchal domination. Women's music portrayed women's interactions with one another, something completely counter to the dominant culture's understanding of important relationships.

By 1978, women's music labels covered over a dozen albums. Although the most well-known performers—Adam, Christian, Near, and Williamson—continued in light folk/rock style, women's music labels included other genres: new age, country, jazz, blues, etc. As the number of records grew, so did the need for a distribution network. Olivia early on recognized this need and sought volunteers to distribute their records. Women's music grew so rapidly that these volunteers formed a network called WILD (Women's Independent Labels Distributors), which distributed other women's music labels' albums. There was little competition among distributors as parts of the country were evenly assigned to WILD members, distributing women's music to individuals, feminist bookstores, and audiences at concerts and festivals. Also in 1978, Roadwork Inc., a national booking company, formed to help women's music performers book tours.

Women's music festivals showcased new women's music talent. Women's music fans from small towns came to hear their favorite artists, buy albums they couldn't obtain at home, and, in many cases, spend time in women-only space. The Michigan Womyn's Music Festival, the largest and one of the most well-known festivals, started in 1976, and continues to attract 8,000 women annually. For four days, women "live in a woman-only, idyllic world of sunny days warming bare breasts and starry nights with the full moon shining through the trees and over the stage."[9]

Profit versus Politics

The integration of politics and profit continually plagued women's music. Many felt there was no place for a discussion of profit within the confines of a politically charged organization. Alix Dobkin called the combining of good business with feminist ideals, "living with contradictions."[10] What one woman felt was a good business decision, another saw as a bad political move.

Based on a political model of social change, rather than a capitalist model of profit, women's music never intended to compete with or become part of mainstream music. Those involved in women's music wanted political change, not profit-sharing. Ginny Berson of the Olivia collective said they had two goals—to create an alternative economic institution which would employ women in a non-oppressive situation and to "be in a position to affect large numbers of women."[11]

As with most movements, money was a problem. Money for a record was donated or collected from the women's community and, after production and manufacturing, little was left for the artists or the company. While major labels spent $75,000 in 1977 to produce an album, Olivia spent $7,500.

Record-making continued, but women's music labels were always on the brink of bankruptcy. Holly Near's lesbian-identified album, *Imagine My Surprise* (Redwood Records) sold 100,000 copies, a success by women's music standards. Yet Redwood was $75,000 in debt.

The pressure on women's music performers was immense. At first, there were few performers and many stops on a tour. Everyone knew the importance of touring the small rural communities as well as the urban centers. In general, performers stayed at people's homes, were paid very little, and traveled as cheaply as they could. Producers worried about economic solvency. Women's music concerts, at first held in church basements or in university spaces, had poor or absent sound systems and a mostly volunteer production staff. Over the years, performers expected more than expenses, production crews expected to be paid, and the audience demanded better space and sound. Producers felt that performers and workers deserved the best sound, location, and payment, which meant an increase in concert ticket prices. In other words, most everyone concerned with the production of women's music needed more money.

The Move to Cross-Over or Mainstream

By the 1980s, the women's music market was saturated. While released albums increased, the audience to purchase them did not. The record industry, in general, saw a decrease in records sales. In order to survive, every level of women's music (musicians, labels, distributors, engineers, and producers) played with two options—a move toward mainstream audiences or crossing over to other political audiences.

Initially, Redwood Records sought a more mainstream audience. The resulting album, entitled *Fire in the Rain* (1981), included a commercial, slick look and sound. June Millington, one of the original members of Fanny, played electric guitar and provided direction for the album. Holly Near's voice, though kept intact, was backed up by a group of musicians more accustomed to playing mainstream music. Redwood pushed for radio airplay with one single and hired an industry professional to "work" the record. The result was sales of 30,000 copies in the first month and television appearances of Near on the "Today Show" and "Sesame Street."

Olivia Records also moved toward mainstream audiences, creating Second Wave, a subsidiary label which over the years "released less feminist-identified music and broke with its [Olivia's] commitment to use only female musicians."[12] Margie Adam summed up the early 1980s: "While reading in the feminist press that women's music was dying, I was reading in the mainstream press that several other artists were trying to distance themselves from the label 'women's music.'"[13]

As women's music peaked, problems arose. Women's music audiences expected more from women's music performers than they did from their mainstream counterparts. Performers burned out from too many tours and too many demands on their time. Meg Christian left Olivia Records and women's music in 1984. Meg Christian had given 15 years to women's music. She was among the most popular, if not *the* most popular, artist in women's music. Of the four "big cheeseburgers" (Adam, Christian, Near, and Williamson), Meg most gave of herself, and was in many ways the "ideal" lesbian performer. She was an "out" lesbian, her songs blatantly lesbian, and her rapport with an audience unprecedented—and then she was gone.

Margie Adam also left women's music. In retrospect, she expressed a political concern that as women artists began to move away from women's music "as an artistic and political principle...the possibility for radical change with our music was proportionately lessened. The power of this women-loving organizing tool began to dissipate."[14]

Olivia continued recording Cris Williamson, but her music differed greatly not only in style but in its representation of lesbianism—it was subtle, and much more accepted by mainstream audiences. According to Judy Dlugacz, co-founder and president of Olivia:

> Church groups connect and want to play Cris Williamson's music, and nuns want to take their vows to "Song of the Soul," one of Cris' classics. Girl Scout troops sing our music at the camps, and we are really looking into that homegrown type of thing because I think that is where our purpose lies.[15]

While Olivia moved toward mainstream, Redwood significantly changed its direction and built coalitions with other political and social change audiences. *Speed of Light* (1982) became the clearest declaration of Near's and Redwood's future direction. Afrikan Dreamland and Near close with the following reggae-tinged plea for political unity:

> One man fights the KKK
> But he hates the queers
> One woman fights for ecology
> It's equal rights she fears
> Some folks know that war is hell
> But then they put down the blind
> I think there must be a common ground
> But it's mighty hard to find
> Hang on, don't give up the ship
> Hang on, don't let the anchor slip
> We are all sailors and we're in mutiny
> The safety of this journey depends on Unity.[16]

Coalition-building or crossing over continues through both Near's and Redwood's albums. Near's records include collaborations with activists Ronnie Gilbert of the Weavers, Trapezoid and John McCutcheon, Inti-Illimani, Arlo Guthrie, and Pete Seeger. Near records songs by well-known political artists Phil Ochs, Malvina Reynolds, and Bernice Johnson Reagon, while Redwood Records produces or distributes artists known for their international politics: Ronnie Gilbert, Inti-Illimani, Judy Small, Guardabarranco, Salvador Bustos, and Victor Jara. Continued support for women's music includes albums by Linda Tillery, Ferron, Hunter Davis, Nancy Vogl, and Betsy Rose.

Labels were not the only component of women's music feeling the need to look elsewhere for larger audiences. Some distributors left women's music for larger salaries and better benefits. WILD included other independent labels' recordings, distributing records to political bookstores as well as feminist bookstores. As early as 1985, Sue Brown of Ladyslipper, a major distributor of women's music in the east, saw money as the big challenge. "There are few, if any feminist businesses for which cash flow and lack of capital are not constant concerns."[17] Many distributors opened up their catalogs to non-women's music. Ladyslipper broadened its catalog to include women artists who would not normally fall within women's music (Bonnie Raitt, Judy Mowatt, and the Roches). Gay and anti-sexist music by men was also included.

Boston recording engineer Karen Kane exemplifies the impact of a move from women's music. "Although in the mid-70s, women's music kept me going," she stated, "I wouldn't want to do just women's music projects in 1986—there are simply not enough people like that with the money to make the albums."[18]

The Cooptation of Women's Music?

Though mainstream female performers from Tina Turner to Laurie Anderson chipped away at the stale stereotyped male image of the female performer, the mainstream success of Suzanne Vega's song "Luka" (*Billboard's* number three hit), created avenues for a new breed of pop women. The economic success of Vega turned major labels' attention to other "serious women" performers. "In the record business new trends are not motivated by good taste or guilty consciences," stated *Musician Magazine's* editor Bill Flanagan, "Someone thinks that serious women can sell records…"[19]

Yet Vega and other mainstream artists before her did not open up these frontiers for other women performers without a lot of help. Women's music performers sang about "real women" and their needs for 20 years. In fact, many of the new performers, such as Tracy Chapman, Phranc, Ferron,

Melissa Etheridge, and Michele Shocked, got their first boost from women's music audiences. Other performers, like k.d. lang, resemble the lesbian images women's music has always portrayed. That women's music performers were not widely known was in part due to the lack of a feminist movement preceding them. Women's labels also couldn't compete with mainstream labels' marketing, which can put a half million dollars in print and media promotions and another half in radio promotion for an artist. Holly Near believes that "if we [Redwood] had been able to put a million dollars behind Ferron, she'd be a major star."[20]

So, why do performers stay with women's music labels even when mainstream labels are interested? In truth, many don't, and therein lies the conflict between the '70s and '80s generation. Older artists argue that newer performers gained access to the pop charts through the groundwork laid by women's music.[21] What, if any, repayment do the new performers owe? The women's music community varies in its response. Holly Near acknowledges that access to mainstream success is not blocked for women the way it was 15 years ago, but also points out that women pop performers "couldn't have done it without us."[22] Near and others are pleased when women performers move to major labels because one of women's music goals is to get political messages out to as many people as possible. Near describes their relationship as a parent to a child: "We feel pride that we laid the groundwork that allowed them to go on."[23]

Others' reactions are less supportive. Women's music supporters resent the mainstream press portrayals of the new women performers as if they appeared out of thin air. In fact, this music has been available through women's music labels for well over 20 years, but now no credit is given to those who worked in women's music singing about the same issues for which Tracy Chapman is being heralded. Cris Williamson explains,

> There I am, hacking with my machete, making my way through the jungle and I look behind me and Tracy's striding down the path. Part of me is a bit jealous of that success. And in my rational mind I say, Cris, this is why you did it.[24]

Another issue is the new performers' lack of gender specificity regarding their sexuality. Although Chapman, and others, have made their way into mainstream, their lesbian connections (i.e. the women's music festivals and audiences which supported them) are intentionally ignored in their promotional material and in conversations, unless they are talking to the gay and lesbian press. While gender-neutral songs are acceptable, songs with lesbians lyrics are not. Jo-Lynne Worley of Redwood Records noted that while the majors' interest was strong in Teresa Trull's album, *A Step Away,* the album "was not pursued further...because of her specific lesbian lyrics."[25] Through subtle self-presentation, new performers present themselves as objects of female as well as male desire. The argument continues: Should those in the mainstream come out and possibly lose other audiences or be more subtle in their lesbian identity to seek a broader audience? Veterans of women's music believe their lesbianism is an important part of their politics and should be presented. Other women seem less convinced.

What Young Lesbians Want is 2 Nice Girls

In the 1990s, young lesbians, both performers and fans, reject much of the politics of women's music. Lesbian musician Phranc found herself spending more time arguing politics than getting the message out in the big world, and changing attitudes and raising consciousness in the process. "It just seemed very isolated."[26] Likewise 2 Nice Girls didn't want to be in the ghetto of the women's music bin: "we want to be in your face."[27] Many young lesbians want their lifestyles to be included in the mainstream. Performers like Tracy Chapman and k.d. lang may not state that they are lesbians but they present an unmistakable image, while 2 Nice Girls and Phranc leave no doubt about their sexuality. Kathy Korniloff of 2 Nice Girls explains that although they love the early albums of Christian's and Near's, the entire women's scene is a "pre-punk experience...we've grown up in the post-punk world and our music is a reflection of that."[28]

Some would argue that Phranc and 2 Nice Girls are the future of lesbian music. "Indeed, because the band [2 Nice Girls] is willing, both personally and in their music, to state that they are queer, they have fast become role models in a community continually starved for them."[29] Phranc's record, *I Enjoy Being a Girl,* includes a description of Phranc as a "little daughter of bilitis," and her record company, Island Records, promotes her as a "basic all-American Jewish Lesbian folksinger."[30] While acknowledging Phranc's lesbian audience, the label seeks out cross-over groups—college and independent music audiences—to gain more mainstream acceptance.

Another argument for artist cross-over efforts is that acceptance of a few out-lesbians (Phranc and 2 Nice Girls) can be a way in which to inoculate the mainstream audience against reacting negatively to the potent political messages imbedded in lesbian music. Expose the audience (especially that which is less politically reactionary) to a little of the music; get them to form a non-threatened reaction to it; then when exposed to more radical music, the reaction will be mild.

What's Left for Women's Music?

> We've made the world safe for androgyny in the charts, but a few
> women musicians in the forefront is not what we wanted.[31]
>
> —Deidre McCalla

Have women's music goals been attained through the success of such
performers as Tracy Chapman? Not really. Consider the reasons women's
music began. In part, it was the desire to get their message to women, but
another goal was to get women into the production side of the business:
engineering, recording, as musicians, distributors, etc. Few such in-roads
exist. As one reads about the new breed, one also reads about their
managers, men; the musicians with whom they work, men; the distributors
of their albums, men. From this perspective, little has changed. In addition,
we shouldn't overemphasize the women who have now made it. First, you
can count on your fingers the number who are successful in the mainstream.
Compared to male performers and male-identified women, it is a small
percentage. It is also too soon to determine that the inclusion of feminist
and lesbian musicians into mainstream is a lasting trend. Popularity in pop
is notoriously short-lived for most artists. Economics determines whether
the concept of "intelligent women's music" continues with new performers
signed or present contracts extended. We should remember that a few
women in the 1970s also sang some songs of social significance. In the
1980s, they were quickly replaced.

When new women performers attain success in mainstream music,
why do others stay in women's music? For some, like Holly Near, it relates
to control. She controls her music, her schedule, her political agenda. Of
course, performers who sign with mainstream labels seek more control as
they gain more commercial success, but they rarely get it. Phranc gets her
way most of the time, but during a 1989 tour to England and Scotland, she
was unable to, along with her regular shows, do women-only or gay and
lesbian shows. "I really didn't have a choice this time. I had to play ball with
the boys."[32]

There is also a lot of pressure and a different definition of success with
a mainstream label. "If an artist at Redwood sells 100,000 records, they get
a party,…whereas a 100,000 record sales won't get the attention of the Big
Guys, certainly you can get dropped from a major label if that's all you
sell."[33] Many women prefer the lesser pressure.

Performers also get more personal attention with the women's music
labels. There isn't a huge machine to work within. And performers can have
a life-long career with a company such as Olivia or Redwood but on a major
label might be "a star for only a moment."[34]

Does all this mean that women's music will continue to keep a very narrow role within the lesbian-feminist movement? It's already obvious that women's music has changed as economics and politics have changed. The movement toward mainstream or other politically left groups seems to broaden women's music. The days of complete separateness from other subcultural groups is over. While women-only music festivals continue to attract increasing numbers of women with each succeeding year, and there are artists who continue to perform for women-only audiences, the majority of the women's music performers are forced to change or leave. The second wave of women's music (including Chapman, lang, Phranc, and all the newer performers) brings to the forefront some mainstream acceptance and some of its own radical lesbians. Anyone who thinks women's music is dead hasn't seen what it has become. Holly Near says it doesn't look like it did in the 1970s.

> It looks like Faith Nolan going into prisons and youth institutions and singing about class and drugs and health and homophobia, it look like Ronnie Gilbert going down and listening to women sing in picket lines. It's Tracy Chapman and it's K.T. Oslin singing to working class straight women about feminist issues in songs like "Ladies of the Eighties."[35]

Tracy Chapman, Abidjan, Ivory Coast. (Photo: © Neal Preston)

Afrika Bambaataa

Reconstructions of Nationalist Thought in Black Music and Culture[1]

Kristal Brent Zook

A Black Nationalist attitude is protection against a system that keeps us back.
—Chuck D (Public Enemy)

In March 1990, *Newsweek* published several articles on rap which it described as a "crude," "offensive," and "loud" music produced by "angry young males." While the introduction in the table of contents recognized that other interpretations have viewed rap as a "bold call for 'Afrocentric' political consciousness," this latter reading was apparently not to be presented in any kind of equal proportion to the former. In fact, rap's liberatory potential is completely undermined, discredited, and silenced in these articles. For example, rap group NWA is simplistically equated with rockers, Guns 'n' Roses, for having an all around "bad attitude." This attitude is so belligerent, *Newsweek* scolds, that the rappers "even got into trouble with the FBI." Similarly, 2 Live Crew is narrowly presented as the controversial Miami rap group being prosecuted for "alleged violations of obscenity laws"; Ice-T is lambasted for his sexist and violent depictions of women and intimacy; and, of course, Public Enemy's Professor Griff is slammed for attempting "to make hatred 'hip.' " Then, the article sarcastically informs us that the "bad attitude" exhibited by rappers is "a response to the diminishing expectations of the millions of American youths who forgot to go to business school in the 1980's." Futhermore, it is characterized as a "repulsive," "visceral" attitude which "resists any...attempt at intellectualizing." Unconvincingly, *Newsweek* concludes that rap "is mostly empty of political content" and, as we learned from the rock and roll of the 1960's, "has little power...to change the world."[2]

I want to make one point unequivocally clear here: I'm not about to argue that sexism, obscenity, homophobia, and even hatred haven't been present in both the musical arena of rap and in the dominant (until now) male lifestyle of its performers. They have. Rap is an expressive form which is inherently belligerent and confrontational as a result of the specific historical, socio-political, and economic context from which it comes. It is also much more than this. To say that rap is no more than a sad by-product of oppression is to take an explanatory, *defensive* stance when, in actuality, rap is a fundamental component of what may be the strongest political and cultural *offensive* gesture among African Americans today.

While I do not see myself as a missionary of rap, attempting to convert disbelievers who remain untouched by its power, I am concerned with the ways in which propaganda like the *Newsweek* article are formulated from specific social locations in order to uphold specific (usually unspoken) ideological and political agendas. My suspicion is that the need to repudiate rap's liberatory potential is in reaction to a deeply rooted fear of African-American empowerment. Because it is situated within a comprehensive, historical frame of reference (nationalism) which evokes radical traditions of racial solidarity and resistance, rap is quite capable of sensitizing people and of fostering a sense of political consciousness. This consciousness may then be used to subvert, and even, to dislodge hegemonic powers that be.

My main argument, then, is two-fold. First, I believe that there are persistent elements of Black Nationalist ideology which underlie and inform both rap music and a larger "hip hop" culture. These elements include a desire for cultural pride, economic self-sufficiency, racial solidarity, and collective survival. They are manifested in certain aesthetic moods and attitudes and are present in contemporary fashion, language, dance, and overall lifestyles. I argue that nationalism has continued to manifest itself through cultural expressive forms, as well as through various political arenas, precisely because of the fact that complete racial equality has not yet been achieved in this country. Within this context, nationalism represents a necessary vision of safety, protection, and what I refer to as an empowering "home."

The second part of my argument is simply that nationalist elements are presented, not only within the creative content of rap and other expressive forms (in film, literature, and television), but they are also manifested through the modes of production and consumption which surround these forms. In other words, nationalism is not just a metaphoric or aesthetic vision which appears in the creative product, but it is also that which informs the actual material mechanisms of cultural production itself (i.e., the marketing, promotion, and distribution of this product).

There are various reasons why I name this tradition "nationalist" as opposed to using what I consider to be milder terms such as "Afrocentric." It is interesting that while there has been quite an explosion of cultural commentary surrounding rap in recent years, few people, other than a handful of African Americans, have been seriously willing to engage the terms of nationalism as they are presented in the music itself. This is due, in part, to a deeply rooted understanding that the terms of Black Nationalism are actually quite radical in all of their ambiguous, and even frightening implications. In fact, its history as a "scary" word is tied to powerful visions of physically robust African-American men dressed in black leather jackets, displaying a firm military posture, espousing "revolution" (another scary word) by any means necessary, and defiantly naming themselves the "Black Panthers." This image was apparently so frightening to the status quo that a massive government-sponsored FBI campaign called "COINTELPRO" was instituted in order to destroy the collective.[3] In short, if nationalism is a complex, contradictory, dynamic, historically loaded, "scary" word, then I embrace it precisely for this reason. By engaging a term which immediately calls to mind a certain confusion, I am insisting on more complex, richer interpretations. Another term which could be used to describe current trends in hip hop culture is "Afrocentricity." And while I agree that the promotion of an "Afrocentric" world view is undoubtedly an aspect of nationalism, it does not provoke the same fullness of connotations that nationalism does; it does not describe the intricacies of nationalist desire which extend far beyond cultural affirmation.

A Brief History of Rap

Emerging in the mid- to late-1970s among black and Puerto Rican male youths of the South Bronx, rap music was clearly an extension of African expressive forms such as "signifying," "playing the dozens," and creating praisesongs in the tradition of the *griot,* or the African storyteller. Along with these earlier traditions, rap also traces its antecedents to the bebop singers, the funk of James Brown, and the rhythmic jazz of The Last Poets, to name but a few influences.[4] What was immediately clear about this cultural movement (which came to be called "hip hop" and included other activities such as graffiti-art and breakdancing) was that it expressed certain sentiments that genuinely reflected the lives of working-class Black and Puerto Rican male youths in a way that the more romanticized disco scene, popularized by middle-class whites, did not.

Part of rap's streetwise edge came, undoubtedly, from the fact that most of its participants were from the "'hood," that is, the neighborhoods of New York which required this edge for day-to-day survival, such as the South Bronx. For example, Grandmaster Flash and the Furious Five's 1982 hit, "The Message," bitterly refers to living conditions of the ghetto.

> Don't push me cuz, I'm close to the edge,
> I'm trying not to lose my head.
> It's liked a jungle sometimes, it makes me wonder

how I keep from going under...
broken glass everywhere,
people pissing on the stair,
you know they just don't care.
I can't take the smell, I can't take the noise.
Got no money to move out,
I guess I got no choice.[5]

While cuts such as "The Message" are part of a long tradition of politically conscious black music (Curtis Mayfield is another precursor to this kind of rap), such "conscious" raps are only a fragment of that which sells and gains widespread recognition among consumers. It is important to recognize that a great deal of commercially popular rap is little more than self-aggrandized boasting. Highly politicized rap is often overlooked by the average consumer since it doesn't receive the same radio airplay, and other such advantages. For instance, Brother D's (Daryl Asmaa Nubyah), "How We Gonna Make the Black Nation Rise?" (1980) was, in spite of its limited recognition, one of the first "message" raps to be recorded. And although the desire for some kind of safe home or "nation" is one which was rarely articulated explicitly in the early days of rap, the existence of this, and other, similar cuts indicates that many of the underlying assumptions behind rap were, in fact, profoundly nationalistic.

The experience of Afrika Bambaataa—ex-gang member and founder of the Zulu Nation, a hip hop community numbering in the hundreds—is another especially vivid example of the connection between cultural expressive forms such as rap and political consciousness. Bambaataa had hung around the Black Panther Information Center since the age of twelve and when he became a member of the Black Spades, the largest black gang in New York, he found some of the same "unity" and sense of "family" that was at the center. Later, when he joined the Nation of Islam in the 1960s, Bambaataa felt a continued sense of belonging and eventually moved away from the street gang. In the 1970s, it seems that the hip hop lifestyle popular among his peers was able to fulfill some of the same needs he had been searching for in the Nation and in The Black Spades. Bambaataa himself notes this shift from street gangs to hip hop and comments that, at that time, "the 70's was coming more into music and dancing and going to clubs...The lifestyle was changing."[6]

Significantly, Bambaataa was one of the first in a long line of "gang bangers" to leave that lifestyle for one involved in rap. West Coast L.A. rappers Ice-T, Tone Loc, Ice Cube, and Eazy E all follow in this tradition. It is not a coincidence that the New York police department reported a decline in gang violence in the early- to mid-1970s, when rap was clearly becoming an influential force. Nor is it a coincidence that many rappers are also members of the Nation of Islam and even the 5 percent Nation. While

I would not say that this latter point is necessarily an encouraging sign of an evolving, progressive nationalism, it is, nevertheless, important to note the ways in which such traditions reinforce one another in useful ways as the persistent search for home continues.

A Brief History of Nationalism

Until very recently, nationalism (particularly of the black variety) was regarded as a dirty word to be whispered only in hush-hush tones among politically "progressive" groups. There are numerous reasons for its alleged, post-1960s "fall from grace." For one, it was, and still is, embraced by "boy-men" around the globe who have been less interested in truly liberatory strategies for change than in revitalizing their own depressed state of masculinity.[7] These male-centered myth-makers have often employed nationalist tenets to construct narcissistic mirror images of the dominant patriarchal and heterosexist culture—the only difference between theirs and the original illusion being its colored tint.

In this way, proponents of nationalist thought have seriously undermined its emancipatory capacity through their own refusal to engage in dialogue with women as well as through their reactionary stance against homosexuality. I'm thinking, specifically, of the way in which key members of the 1960s Black Aesthetic Movement (a cultural arm of the Black Power/Black Nationalist Movement) were later lambasted for their homophobic viewpoints. Haki Madhubuti (Don L. Lee), for example, continues to see black male homosexuality as a direct result of white oppression or as a product of internalized oppression which, although its cause is "understandable," is, nevertheless, a sign of our "abnormality" and continued "backwardness."[8]

Furthermore, critiques from the "outside," particularly from Eurocentric and/or white Marxists, have further contributed to the marginalization of nationalist thought by insisting that it is nothing more than a mere phase, a temporary aberration which will eventually pass, leaving a clear road to internationalism.[9] Perhaps this latter group's most devastating oversight was its inability to see culture as a legitimate tool of resistance, a catalyst for change. By not recognizing popular expressive forms as "transmitted historical consciousness"[10] with revolutionary potential, intellectuals in the Marxist tradition have been unable to see the ways in which various strands of nationalist thought have been, and continue to be, empowering reference points for black people.

It follows, then, that while many have rightfully pointed to the problematic and contradictory aspects of nationalist thought, not all have had the desire (or the power) to "officially" ban it from "legitimate" intellectual and political discourse. Instead, it has simply been diffused and debilitated by traditional historical discourses—discourses which offer dry categorizations of nationalist thought, giving it a precise chronological past, and neatly packaging its tenets within some forgotten historical moment. Although both the dominant mass media and academic power structures have historicized the 1960s as a fixed period of political protest, which began and ended at concrete moments in time, many, including myself, have resisted this particular version of (his)story. Instead, we have resurrected nationalist narratives, memories, and myths which may have resurged in the 1960s but which originate in traditions begun long before then. In challenging the historicization of the 1960s, it becomes possible to identify elements of ideological continuity, such as Black Nationalism, which have resurfaced in any number of cultural contexts. Such nationalist narratives are empowering precisely because of the fact that they are neither stable, homogenous, nor chronologically linear. Instead, they lend themselves to dynamic reformulation and reinterpretation as the need arises.

Continued Expressions of Nationalism

In fact, the need has arisen at the present moment. I write this essay now because it has become painfully obvious that my generation maintains a desire for some kind of nationalistically rooted "home." Black articulations of the "nation" which were voiced in the political realm of the 1960s have not died in the popular memories of the people. Instead, they have been transferred to a cultural arena and reformulated in popular expressive forms such as film, television, rap music, clothing, literature, and language. I argue that there is evidence of a collective desire to identify a usable past among a large number of African-Americans of my generation (16 to 25 years old). This usable past is one which will aid in the regeneration of a nationalistically centered present. Most important, it is a past which must be imaginatively remembered and constantly re-visioned in order to remain valuable.

Cultural critic Greg Tate has identified this desire for a nation/home convincingly. With references to such foundational cultural nationalists as Amiri Baraka and Ron Karenga, Tate ties their work to contemporary artistic expression:

> While the founding fathers have long taken deserved lumps for the jiver parts of their program (like the sexist, anti-semitic black supremacist, pseudo-African mumbo-jumbo paramilitary adventurist parts), to their credit they took black liberation seriously enough to be theoretically ambitious about it...the cult-nats [cultural nationalists]...did produce a postliberated black aesthetic, responsible for the degree to which contemporary black artists and intellectuals feel themselves heirs to a culture every bit as def as

classical Western civilization...This cultural confidence has freed up more black artists to do work as wonderfully absurdist as black life itself.[11]

I find it significant that Tate's elaborate critique of the cult-nats is, by necessity, parenthetical. This stylistic choice is a reflection of his need both to valorize healthy strands of nationalist thought (such as racial solidarity) and to simultaneously (and strategically) question and reformulate these doctrines where they may be destructive. Such a tension between these two tasks is what lead Tate to help form the Black Rock Coalition, on the one hand,[12] and to publicly slam Professor Griff (who returned the insult by calling Tate a "white booty nigger") for his highly polemic comments regarding Jewish people, on the other. Tate is positioned, therefore, as a cultural worker involved in both the productive remembering and the reformulation of usable Black Nationalist thought.

Trey Ellis, black novelist and critic, echoes Tate's sentiment that the cultural nationalists have paved the way for much of what is expressed by today's younger generations. In his somewhat problematic, and yet highly compelling essay, "The New Black Aesthetic," Ellis refers to a large collective which includes George Clinton, Ishmael Reed, and Toni Morrison in order to highlight one of their most important contributions. That is,

[an ability to] strip themselves of both white envy and self-hate [and to produce] supersophisticated black art that either expanded or exploded the old definitions of blackness, showing us as the intricate, uncategorizeable folks we had always known ourselves to be.[13]

Writer Lisa Jones continues this work as well. Through her repeated challenges to those who would argue for any one model of "authentic" black music (or blackness), she is refusing traditional notions of the restrictive, homogenous black "nation." Yet, her work with both Spike Lee and the Black Rock Coalition testifies to her commitment to revise useful nationalist assumptions, such as, economic autonomy, cultural pride, and collective political awareness.

These examples are evidence of a need (among cultural critics, anyway) to situate and contextualize current manifestations in popular culture as extensions and reworkings of the nationalist legacy of the 1960s. Rap music, as one of these manifestations, forms part of a larger conduit of culturally specific, "in-house" intercommunication among blacks. It is also "cross-medial" in the sense that the various media such as television, music, film, and video speak to and through one another and are intimately connected by a growing number of black men (for the most part) who insist on capturing full productive control over their artistic works.

As an aside, it is important to note that the terrain of black cultural expression is primarily, but not exclusively, black. It is not the sole terrain of black subjects since any number of non-black participants can be affiliated with such productions through the ever-increasing accessibility of technological communication. These spectators, who would traditionally lie somewhere "outside" of such expression, are now able to create spaces of entry for themselves through affinities of age, geography, class, gender, sexual lifestyle, and most important, through technology.

The example of white rapper, Vanilla Ice, who lied about having a black step-father and half-brother in order to appear more "authentic," demonstrates that an increasing sense of African-American solidarity seems to inspire an increasingly blatant demand for inclusion among (some) white people who now sense themselves uncomfortably shifting from center to margin.

In terms of theoretical productions, Dick Hebdige's book *Cut 'n' Mix* is another example of this kind of arrogant self-insertion into a space of black aesthetic expression and political discourse. By emphasizing the notion that hip hop is nothing more than a "fusion" of elements from hard rock to electro funk, salsa, soul, new wave, etc., he is able to conclude that

> We shouldn't be so concerned about where a sound comes from...Nobody can own [it]. It's there for everyone to use. Nobody can pin it down or put a copyright on it. It's better not to try.[14]

Most revealing are the last three pages of his book in which Hebdige discusses the impossibility of locating his own, personal, ethnic roots. He states that he is a "white Englishman" with no detailed knowledge of his ancestry. This revelation is juxtaposed with Hebdige's insistence that music is a shared commodity to be freely "cut" and "mixed" under any circumstances. Finally, Hebdige concludes with the words of a white reggae fan who, by his own definition, is half Scottish and half Irish. These words offer fascinating insight as to why black cultural production is in such high demand among some white consumers.

> Who am I?...Tell me who do I belong to? They criticize me, the good old England. Alright, where do I belong? You know I was brought up with Blacks, Pakistanis, Africans, Asians, everything, you name it...who do I belong to?... I'm just a broad person. The earth is mine...[15]

In fact, that it is no longer "your" earth is precisely why "you" are now so concerned with the idea of "ownership" in the first place. I include this aside as a reminder that through such disruptive insertions, the mass appropriation of rap is promoted. Consequently, its political strength, which is dependent on a sense of collective, in-house dialogue, is necessarily diffused.

On the whole, however, internal spaces of contestation are being constructed across the boundaries of various media and, yet, are remaining within a relatively closed circle of black cultural production. Such circles, networks, or (borrowing from Benedict Anderson) "imagined communities" serve as evidence of a desire for some kind of nationalistic shelter or "home."[16] Both the form and content of rap express black autonomy, self-determination, and cultural pride. But what is perhaps most fascinating is not only the way that rap confirms a sense of imagined, metaphorical community, but rather, the fact that this fantasy of "home" is simultaneously constructed materially through the very modes of production, marketing, and the critical discourses which surround it. In other words, just as Anderson argues that literary forms such as the newspaper and the novel made European nationalisms possible, I would say that the forms of television, music videos, film, literary works, and the networks involved in producing these forms are also nurturing a heightened sense of racial collectivity, group solidarity, and even political responsibility—all of which are important elements of nationalist thought.

A clear example of such material nationalism is Nelson George and Ann Carlin's organization of the "Stop the Violence movement," a collective of noted rappers who participated, as a group, in the making of the recording and video, *Self-Destruction*. This album contained powerful messages about gang violence, education, racism, and resistance. Because of its production, over $200,000 was sent to the National Urban League in an effort to combat illiteracy and black-on-black crime.[17] Interestingly, Nelson George was also an early investor in Spike Lee's first film and consequently, Lee, with his "Forty Acres and an Empire," was in a position to help finance production of *Self-Destruction,* which he has done.[18] The recent production of *We're All in the Same Gang* is another good example of a black coalition of rappers working toward the collective "uplift of the race." With lyrics which repeatedly emphasize the idea that black genocide is being committed by black people themselves, "Same Gang" is, in fact, a powerful statement against self-destruction.

Another case in point: when rapper Ice Cube left the group N.W.A. (Niggas With Attitude) as a result of pay inequities between he and his white manager (who made $23,000 and $130,000 in 1989, respectively), Public Enemy's Chuck D and Hank Shocklee agreed that they would produce his solo album. This is clearly an example of what some have traditionally referred to as "economic nationalism," or self-sufficiency. Placing rap music within a historical context rife with white appropriation and the theft of Black creativity, it becomes essential to look at the ways in which this theft is being resisted and subverted. The early productions of Spike Lee's "Forty Acres" enterprise as well as his recent decision to found "Forty Acres and a Mule Music Works," his own record label, are further examples of a move away from exploitative commodification toward black productive control over black creativity. This developing trend is one which has undoubtedly created an atmosphere conducive to partnerships such as that between Ice Cube and Chuck D. It is a mood which has fostered and nourished a sense of racial solidarity and empowering economic autonomy.

Similarly, the recently released film, *Listen Up: the Lives of Quincy Jones* emphasizes common ties between musical legends such as Miles Davis, Sara Vaughn, and contemporary rappers. This connection is further reinforced in *The Fresh Prince of Bel Air,* rap's initiation into prime-time commercial television. Being a Quincy Jones Production, this phenomenally successful experiment is in keeping with what seems to be Jones's political agenda: the bridging of gaps between generations, economic classes, and most importantly, between African-American individuals who seem to have acculturated themselves into mainstream U.S. culture and those who have not.

In a recent episode of *The Fresh Prince,* contemporary male heroes such as Kadeem Hardison, Malcolm Jamal-Warner, Bo Jackson, Al B. Sure, Heavy D, and Quincy Jones himself appeared on the show as "close personal friends" of Will Smith's character, each of them either requesting or offering assistance to one another in a time of need. Again, what makes this example so profound is the fact that the imagined community/nation is being constructed both in the minds of an internal (black) audience and externally, with the financial resources as well as the actual, material bodies of black subjects.

The list of examples could go on: On television sitcoms *A Different World,* and *The Cosby Show,* Heavy D shows up to make a pitch for the artistic value of rap; characters often wear T-shirts with statements such as "Support Black Colleges" or "Malcolm-Martin-Mandela-Me: Inheritors of a Tradition" across them (unproblematically evoking an all-male tradition, of course); and they have also been known to scold one another for not knowing that "Simply Red got their lyrics from Black writers." As Reebee Garofalo reminds me, "even Cosby went to the barricades with the network over the 'Abolish Apartheid' bumper sticker which appeared on Theo's [his son in the series] bedroom door."

Similarly, Keenen Ivory Wayans, part of a closely knit crew of young independent black film-makers, comedians, actors, and actresses is the only African American to produce, direct, and star in his own television series *(In Living Color).* This show, which has had guest appearances of rappers, Monie Love, Queen Latifah, and Flavor Flav, is grounded in a definitive hip hop aesthetic manifested in dress styles, graphic art, music, and language.[19]

Interestingly, Robert Townsend, who co-wrote the film, *I'm Gonna Git You Sucka* with Wayans, has released another film called *The Five Heartbeats.* Although it began as "pure comedy," it took a different turn after Townsend "travelled on the road for a few months with an actual group from the '60s, (the Dells), and heard their stories of being ripped off and taken advantage of by people in the business." Also in the works for Townsend is a filmmaking workshop for inner-city children, since an important part of his agenda is "giving back to the community" some of what he has received.[20]

Finally, rappers Big Daddy Kane, Chuck D, Flavor Flav, and Ice Cube joined together (with Spike Lee, whose name is invoked but who does not appear in the actual video) in a recently released music video called *Burn Hollywood Burn,* a commentary on the racist control of representation and production in Hollywood's film industry. Not coincidentally, this video is strongly reminiscent of *Hollywood Shuffle,* one of Townsend's earlier films. While it is an example of what is positive and hopeful in the current resurgence of nationalist thought, its narrow demand for the "black man's" rights must, nevertheless, be recognized as a dangerous and disheartening mimicry of patriarchal Black Nationalism.

This somewhat random sample of nationalistic practices calls to mind "the net," described by Erik Davis in his account of the 1989 New Music Seminar. In his overview of the "Afrocentricity" panel, Davis quoted Public Enemy's Chuck D as saying, "The enemy is not a person but a structure." This structure, Davis continued, must be slowly seized through coalitions of multimedia black artists so that new networks can be established. "Michael Jordan forcing Nike to hire Spike Lee to shoot his ad may just shuffle cash between big boys, but as a trend it has profound structural implications."[21]

I suspect that there are many more examples of quiet, behind-the-scenes-back-scratching which may not even be explicitly articulated as nationalistic moves but which are, nevertheless, implicated in these conversations. Whereas we do not yet have electoral power, there is more and more potential for economic leverage as the percentage of black-owned businesses continues to climb at a faster rate than the national average.[22]

Furthermore, while concrete political goals, strategies, and agendas may not be made explicit in black cultural expressive forms, some emergent practices serve as evidence of future possibilities. For example, Spike Lee and Tawana Brawley appear together in Public Enemy's *Fight the Power* video, and graffiti which reads "Tawana Told the Truth" appears in Lee's film, *Do the Right Thing,* as well. What would happen if these kinds of affiliations were to inspire in-depth, en masse conversations about the ways in which black women and men are prey to very distinct (but related) kinds of persecution in a society such as this one—a society with such an insidious system of linked racial and sexual oppressions? Then, what would happen to those conversations if they expanded to include the dialogue already taking place between Yo-Yo, rapper and founder of the Intelligent Black

Women's Coalition, and Ice Cube, a male rapper who has been noted for his sexist lyrics while simultaneously promoting Yo-Yo's career. Or if Joie Lee were to write a screenplay for her brother, Spike, as she has indicated that she would like to do. What kinds of black male and female representations would materialize from this perspective? As rapper and writer Dominique DiPrima notes, female rappers are clearly expressing a woman-centered Black Nationalism, particularly as more and more of them are no longer dependent on male writers and producers.[23] Interestingly, both DiPrima and Lisa Jones are daughters of Amiri Baraka, each continuing to expand upon the nationalist tradition their father helped to articulate.

If my suspicions have foundation, then these cultural manifestations may, in fact, be the impetus for increasing awareness and insight in a way that is not clearly measurable at this historical moment. Just as Malcolm X eventually moved beyond bourgeois, economic nationalism and into the realm of a more fundamentally revolutionary socialist thought, my hope is that we, as a people, have both the desire and the imagination to move beyond the nationalistic trend that bell hooks calls "a gesture of powerlessness." At the same time, I firmly believe that the nationalist vision of home is a necessary one which we need to offer us strength and relative safety in this endeavor.

Queen Latifah

Chicano Rock

Cruising Around the Historical Bloc

George Lipsitz

During his first visit to Los Angeles, Octavio Paz searched in vain for visible evidence of Mexican influence on that city's life and culture. The great Mexican writer found streets with Spanish names and subdivisions filled with Spanish Revival architecture, but to his surprise and dismay he perceived only a superficial Hispanic gloss on an essentially Anglo-American metropolis. Mexican culture seemed to have evaporated into little more than local color, even in a city that had belonged to Spain and Mexico long before it became part of the United States, a city where one-third of the population traced its lineage to Olmec, Mayan, Toltec, Aztec, Spanish, and Mexican ancestors, and a city which had more Mexican residents than all but two of Mexico's own cities. Paz detected a "vague atmosphere" of Mexicanism in Los Angeles, manifesting itself through "delight in decorations, carelessness and pomp, negligence, passion and reserve." But he felt that this "ragged but beautiful" ghost of Mexican identity only rarely interacted with "the North American world based on precision and efficiency." Instead, this Mexicanism floated above the city, "never quite existing, never quite vanishing."[1]

As both the oldest and the newest immigrants to Los Angeles, Mexican-Americans have faced unique problems about cultural identity and assimilation. But the anguish of invisibility that Paz identified among them is all too familiar to minority ethnic communities around the globe. Everywhere, cultural domination by metropolitan elites eviscerates and obliterates traditional cultures rooted in centuries of shared experience. For ethnic minorities, failure to assimilate into dominant cultures can bring exclusion from vital economic and political resources, but successful assimilation can annihilate prized traditions and customs essential to individual and collective identity. Cultural institutions and the mass media alike depict dominant cultures as "natural" and "normal," while never representing the world from the vantage point of ethnic communities. Active discrimination and economic exploitation reinforce a sense of marginality among aggrieved peoples, but mass media images rarely grant legitimacy to marginal perspectives. Traditional forms of cultural expression within ethnic communities lose their power to order and interpret experience, yet they persist as important icons of alienated identity. Surrounded by images that exclude them, included in images that seem to have no real social power, ethnic communities come to feel that they never quite exist and never quite vanish.

But the transformation of real historical traditions and cultures into superficial icons and images touches more than ethnic communities. A sharp division between life and culture provides an essential characteristic of life in all modern industrialized societies, affecting dominant as well as subordinated groups. As Walter Benjamin points out, the production and distribution of art under conditions of mechanical reproduction and commodity form lead to an alienated world in which cultural objects are received outside of the communities and traditions that initially gave them shape and meaning.[2] Created artifacts from diverse cultures blend together into a seeming contextless homogenized mass, encountered independently from the communities that gave birth to them. Mass communications and culture rely on an ever-expanding supply of free-floating symbols only loosely connected to social life. Experience and traditions seem to have no binding claims on the present. Ours is a world in which "all that is solid melts into air" as Marshall Berman asserts in a phrase appropriated from the *Communist Manifesto*.[3]

Members of dominant social groups might not feel quite the same anguish of invisibility that oppresses cultural minorities, but cultural identity for them has become no less an exercise in alienation. The seeming collapse of tradition and the tensions between cultural commodities and social life make mass cultural discourse a locus of confusion and conflict. A proliferation of composite cultural creations and marginal subcultures claim the same "authority" wielded by traditions rooted in centuries of common experience. The revered "master narratives" of the past—religion, liberal humanism, Marxism, psychoanalysis—survive in truncated form, influencing but not dominating social discourse. Instead, a multivocal and contradictory culture that delights in difference and disunity seems to be at the core of contemporary cultural consciousness. This "postmodern" culture allows the residues of many historical cultures to float above us, "ragged but beautiful," "never quite existing and never quite vanishing."[4]

Postmodern culture places ethnic minorities in an important role. Their exclusion from political power and cultural recognition has allowed aggrieved populations to cultivate sophisticated capacities for ambiguity, juxtaposition, and irony—all key qualities in the postmodern aesthetic. The imperatives of adapting to dominant cultures while not being allowed full entry into them leads to complex and creative cultural negotiations that foreground marginal and alienated states of consciousness. Unable to experience either simple assimilation or complete separation from dominant groups, ethnic cultures accustom themselves to a bifocality reflective of both the ways that they view themselves and the ways that they are viewed by others. In a world that constantly undermines the importance and influence of traditions, ethnic cultures remain tied to their pasts in order to explain and arbitrate the problems of the present. Because their marginality involves the pains of exclusion and exploitation, racial and ethnic cultures speak eloquently about the fissures and frictions of society. Because their experience demands bifocality, minority group culture reflects the decentered and fragmented nature of contemporary human experience. Because their history identifies the sources of marginality, racial and ethnic cultures have an ongoing legitimate connection to the past that distinguishes them from more assimilated groups. Masters of irony in an ironic world, they often understand that their marginalized status makes them more appropriate spokespersons for society than mainstream groups unable to fathom or address the causes of their alienations.

Discussions about postmodern sensibilities in contemporary culture often revolve around trends and tendencies in painting, architecture, and literature, but they have even greater relevance to analyses of commercialized leisure. It is on the level of commodified mass culture that the most popular, and often the most profound, acts of cultural *bricolage* take place.[5] The destruction of established canons and the juxtaposition of seemingly inappropriate items characteristic of the self-conscious postmodernism in "high culture" have long been staples of commodified popular culture. With their facility for cultural fusion and their resistance to univocal master narratives, expressions of popular culture contain important lessons about the problems and promises of culture in a world in which "all that is solid melts into air."

The Mexican-American community of Los Angeles that so disappointed Octavio Paz provides an instructive example of how ethnic minority groups can fashion forms of cultural expression appropriate to postmodern realities. Paz's static and one-dimensional view of Mexican identity prevented him from seeing the rich culture of opposition embedded within the Los Angeles Chicano community. What seemed to him like an ephemeral cloud "hovering and floating" above the city, in actuality represented a complicated cultural strategy designed to preserve the resources of the past by adapting them to the needs of the present. In many areas of cultural production, especially in popular music, organic intellectuals within Mexican-American Los Angeles pursued a strategy of self-presentation that brought their unique and distinctive cultural traditions into the mainstream of mass popular culture. Neither assimilationist nor separatist, they drew upon "families of resemblance"—similarities to the experiences and cultures of other groups—to fashion a "unity of disunity."[6] In that way, they sought to make alliances with other groups by cultivating the ways in which their particular experiences spoke with special authority about the ideas and alienations felt by others. They used the techniques and sensibilities of postmodernism to build a "historical bloc" of oppositional groups united in ideas and intentions, if not experience.[7]

Popular Music in Mexican-American Los Angeles

During the 1940s, defense spending and war mobilization changed the face of Los Angeles, stimulating a massive inmigration of whites, blacks, and Chicanos. Traditional residential segregation confined African-Americans to the south-central area while limiting Chicanos largely to housing in downtown East Side neighborhoods.[8] Private bankers and government planners encouraged housing segregation by class and race, viewing ethnic heterogeneity in Los Angeles (as in other cities) as a defect of urban life rather than as one of its advantages. In this way vicious prejudice became written into federal loan policies and private commercial practices. For example, the Home Owners Loan Corporation City Survey File on Los Angeles for 1939 contained a confidential memorandum that argued against the feasibility of loans to Mexican-Americans because

> While many of the Mexican race are of high caliber and descended from the Spanish grandees who formerly owned all of the territory in Southern California, the large majority of Mexican peoples are a definite problem locally and their importation in the years gone by to work the agricultural crops has now been recognized as a mistake.[9]

Translated into public policy, that perception of Mexican-Americans meant that Chicano neighborhoods would not be eligible for housing loans, thereby assuring residential segregation in the region. Federal appraisers rated the eligibility of each Los Angeles neighborhood for home loans, giving the highest rating to areas reserved for the exclusive use of white Christians, while assigning the lowest ratings to black, Chicano, and mixed neighborhoods. The Federal Housing Authority gave its lowest possible rating to Boyle Heights in East Los Angeles because its mixture of Chicano, Jewish, and Eastern European residents convinced the appraisers that

> This is a "melting pot" area and is literally honeycombed with diverse and subversive racial elements. It is seriously doubted whether there is a single block in the area which does not contain detrimental racial elements and there are very few districts which are not hopelessly heterogeneous...[10]

Yet the opening of new shipyards and aircraft assembly plants combined with Los Angeles' severe housing shortage to produce unprecedented inter-ethnic mixing in Los Angeles. Official segregation gave way, bit by bit, as Chicanos and European ethnics lived and worked together in Boyle Heights and Lincoln Park, while blacks and Chicanos lived in close proximity to each other in Watts and in the San Fernando Valley suburb of Pacoima.[11] On the factory floor, on public transportation, and on the streets of thriving commercial districts, diverse groups mixed with each other as never before. Wherever one traveled in the city's *barrios,* ghettos, and mixed neighborhoods, one could easily find the potential for inter-group conflicts and rivalries; sometimes they took the form of actual racial and ethnic violence. But there also existed a vibrant street life built upon communication and cooperation in community organizations and in neighborhood life.

In 1948, a record by Los Angeles' Don Tosti Band titled "Pachuco Boogie" went on to sell more than two million copies, an extraordinary total for any Spanish language record in the United States, but especially for one that glorified one of the *barrio's* more reviled subcultures—the Pachucos.[12]

In many ways, Pachucos embodied the defiance of conventional authority that came to symbolize the appeal of rock and roll. Pachucos were teenaged gang members sporting zoot suits, ducktail haircuts, and distinctive tattoos; they had attracted public attention during the war years when newspaper stories blamed them for much of the youth crime in Los Angeles. Tensions peaked in June 1943 when hundreds of sailors invaded the East Los Angeles community to beat up Mexican-American youths who wore zoot suits. The police, prosecutors, and city council joined forces to praise this criminal attack, lauding the sailors for the efforts to "clean up" the city. But the racism manifest in the attacks caused many Mexican-Americans to start looking at the Pachucos as defenders of the community against outside encroachments, and as symbols of Chicano victimization and marginality.[13]

The Don Tosti Band's "Pachuco Boogie" captured the spirit of that new-found admiration for street rebels. The song's lyrics employed *calo,* the street slang associated with Pachucos but considered vulgar by "respectable" Mexican-Americans. "Pachuco Boogie" blended Mexican speech and rhythms with African-American scat-singing and blues harmonies to form a provocative musical synthesis. Some Spanish language radio stations refused to play the song, but Anglo disc jockeys, programming black rhythm and blues shows aimed at white teenagers, put it on their playlists, to the delight of their listeners. Band member Raul Diaz remembers what it was like before that record became a hit, how Mexican-American musicians like himself often had to wear sombreros and tropical outfits to get work playing music during intermissions at motion picture theaters. "We wanted to play Chicano music, not come on like some clowns," Diaz recalls, "but at the time the scene was dominated by people like Desi Arnaz and Xavier Cugat and the music was really bland."[14] The Don Tosti Band changed that situation when "Pachuco Boogie" sold more than two million copies. Itself a blend of Chicano, Anglo, and African-American musical forms, "Pachuco Boogie" garnered commercial success by uniting a diverse audience into a new synthesis—a "unity of disunity."[15]

The ability of musicians to learn from other cultures played a key role in their success as rock and roll artists. For example, in 1952, black saxophonist Chuck Higgins had a hit recording with "Pachuko Hop"—a song he wrote as a tribute to the dancing, style, and slang of the Mexican-American youths he encountered while playing dances at East Los Angeles union halls.[16] White songwriter Jerry Leiber's widowed mother operated a grocery store near a black neighborhood in Baltimore in the early 1940s where he first became exposed to black music. The family moved to Los Angeles in 1945, and as a teenager he resumed his infatuation with the blues while working in a record store with a largely black clientele. A high school classmate introduced Leiber to another middle-class white fan of black music, Mike Stoller, who had grown up on Long Island but had taken piano lessons in Harlem as an 11-year-old student of the great jazz and blues pianist James P. Johnson. As a teenager, Stoller joined a Harlem "social club" before moving to Los Angeles with his family in 1949. "I learned the pachuco dances and joined a pachuco social club," Stoller later explained when asked how he got his start as a musician.[17] He played piano with the Blas Vasquez band which exposed him to Chicano appropriations of African-American and Euro-American forms and styles as well as to indigenous Mexican music. Within a year after joining the Vasquez band, Stoller began writing rhythm and blues songs for black vocal groups along with his writing partner Jerry Leiber. "We found ourselves writing for black artists," recalls Leiber, "because those were the voices and rhythms that we loved. By the Fall of 1950, when both Mike and I were in City College, we had black girlfriends and were into a black lifestyle."[18] Leiber and Stoller went on to write the original "Hound Dog" for Big Mama Thornton, and they fashioned dozens of best-selling songs for black artists that celebrated the speech, folklore, and subcultures of African-American city life.

The pinnacle of this brown-white-black mixing in rock and roll music in Los Angeles came with the enormous popularity of Ritchie Valens, East Los Angeles' best-selling and most significant rock and roll artist. Independent record producer Bob Keane discovered Valens when he noticed that the car club *cholos* of East Los Angeles and of the San Fernando Valley responded to a band called the Silhouettes and their lead singer, Richard Valenzuela. Shortening (and Anglicizing) the youth's last name to Valens, Keane signed him to a contract and recorded the singer with the same back-up musicians that Keane used on sessions by the black gospel and rock singer Sam Cooke. These session musicians brought a wealth of musical experience to Valens' recordings—bass player Red Callendar had played with jazz great Art Tatum, and drummer Earl Palmer had recorded with rhythm and blues artists in New Orleans, including Roy Brown, Fats Domino, and Little Richard.[19] But Ritchie Valens did not have to learn his cultural pluralism in a studio; life in postwar Los Angeles prepared him well for the mixing of forms and styles that would come to characterize his recorded music.

More than any other artist, Valens brought the folk traditions of Mexican music to a mass audience via rock and roll, but his music also reflected an extraordinary blending of traditions and styles from other cultures. Valens' father Steve and his mother Concepción met while both were employed at a munitions factory in Saugus, California, north of the city of San Fernando. He was born in 1941, in the San Fernando Valley suburb of Pacoima, where he learned music by listening to his relatives sing Mexican songs as they gathered at each others' homes in the evenings. At the age of five, Valens made a toy guitar out of a cigar box and learned to fret it with the help of an uncle who taught him how to play his first song—the traditional Mexican *huapango* "La Bamba." In Pacoima, Valens met William Jones, a black musician who lived across the street from the youth's Aunt Ernestine. Jones taught Valens how to tune a guitar and play chords. After building a green and white electric guitar for himself in his junior high school wood shop class, Valens began to experiment with the African-American rhythm and blues songs that he heard on the radio. But he liked country music as well, idolizing Roy Rogers and Gene Autry, and delighting his classmates in school with a parody of the theme song to the Walt Disney television program "Davy Crockett."[20] The very plurality of the industrial city excited Valens, and he drew his friends from diverse communities. As classmate Manny Sandoval recalls, "They used to put Ritchie down, especially the Mexican kids. They used to call him *falso* and call me that, too, because we liked to be with everybody—Blacks, Mexicans, whites, whatever. So they [Chicanos] wouldn't come around that much to group into the music thing with us. It would be the Blacks, some of the whites, and a few Chicanos."[21] In 1957, he joined the Silhouettes, a mostly Chicano but multiracial band put together by vibraphonist Gil Rocha that included Valens on guitar, William Jones' African-American sons Conrad and Bill on drums and woodwinds, Italian-Americans Dave Torreta and Sal Barragan on trumpet and alto saxophone, and Japanese-American Walter Takaki on tenor saxophone. Although primarily a rock and roll band, the Silhouttes' Chicano members were well schooled in traditional musics; when the occasion called for it they could break into Mexican *corridos* as easily as they played "Shake, Rattle, and Roll."[22] Valens became the featured vocalist with the band, and his tributes to the black rhythm and blues singer Little Richard motivated his admirers to start calling him "Little Ritchie."[23]

In the brief period between Valens' emergence on the best-selling record charts and his death in a plane crash early in 1959, he brought an extraordinary range of musics before pop audiences. He borrowed from white rockabilly, black blues, and Mexican folk musicians because they all made up parts of his cultural environment in postwar Los Angeles. "La Bamba" and "Come On, Let's Go" featured variations on melodies and harmonies common to Mexican fiesta music, while "Ooh My Head" employed the boogie-woogie form and vocal mannerisms common to African-American music. One of Valens' unfinished records included an attempt to lay the rhythm popularized by blues guitarist Bo Diddley underneath the melody of "Malaguena" (a song originally written by Cuban bandleader Ernesto Lecuona, but blended by Valens with the Mexican march "Espani Cani"). Radio programs and phonograph records made Eddie Cochran's rockabilly and Bo Diddley's rhythm and blues songs an organic part of Valens' life, while the limited but nonetheless real cultural mixing in working-class neighborhoods enabled young people to explore the culture of their neighbors. Valens wrote his big hit song "Donna" about a failed romance with an Anglo classmate whose father ordered her to stop going out with "that Mexican," and he recorded a version of his favorite rhythm and blues song "Framed," which had originally been recorded by a Los Angeles rhythm and blues group, The Robins, but which had been written by Mike Stoller and Jerry Leiber.[24]

Valens' tragic death at age 17 deprived the Los Angeles Chicano community of its biggest star, and it cut short the career of one of rock and roll's most eclectic synthesizers. But despite the variety of influences on his music, his status as a Chicano had an enormous impact on his community. "Back then," explains Gil Rocha of the Silhouettes, "he gave us the conviction that a Mexican could make it in a white man's world."[25] But other artists carried on his propensity for blending the folk musics of the *barrio* with the styles and forms circulated within popular music. In the late 1950s and early 1960s, groups including the Salas Brothers, Carlos Brothers, Rene and Ray, and the Romancers had regional and national hit songs that reflected the *barrio's* dialogue with mainstream rock and roll music. Just as Ritchie Valens established himself as a commercial performer by playing rhythm-and-blues-styled versions of Anglo and Mexican songs for a mixed audience, later Chicano musicians played a combination of musics for a combination of audiences. In concerts at East Los Angeles College and at El Monte Legion Stadium, at dances held in youth centers and union halls, and in popular nightclubs like the Rhythm Room and Rainbow Gardens, Chicano rock and rollers learned to blend Mexican and rock musics into a synthesis that won them admirers both inside and outside the *barrio*.[26]

In 1965, Frankie "Cannibal" García and his group, the *Headhunters*, brought Los Angeles Chicano rock music to new audiences when their

"Land of a Thousand Dances" entered the national best-seller charts. García got his start as a rock singer when the lead vocalist for the Royal Jesters (another East Los Angeles rock group) got sick, and the band recruited García to take his place "because I sang in school with a mariachi band, doing traditional Mexican music."[27] García later joined with some friends of friends from the Ramona Gardens Housing Project to form Cannibal and the Headhunters, taking their name from García's "street" (gang) name of "Cannibal," gained when he bit an opponent in a fight. One of their most effective songs in live performances had been Chris Kenner's "Land of a Thousand Dances," but at one show García forgot the words at the beginning of the song and ad-libbed "na-na-na-nana" to the delight of the crowd. In the studio they retained Cannibal's accidental improvisation to give the record a captivating introduction. They also borrowed the double drum sound prominent in Stevie Wonder records to forge a synthesis that attracted the attention of audiences all over the country.

Yet however much they might influence popular culture, Chicano rock musicians could not be completely assimilated. Frankie "Cannibal" García feels that his group's Chicano identity prevented them from attaining greater success after they reached *Billboard's* Top Forty with "Land of a Thousand Dances" in 1965. García remembers "They didn't know how to market us, for one. There were basically only black or white groups in the early 1960s, not even many mixed groups. The people didn't even know what we were half of the time; a lot of people thought we were Hawaiian or something. And with the name Cannibal and the Headhunters, most people just assumed we'd be black."[28]

Whether the audience knew what they were or not, Cannibal and the Headhunters found that they could not forget who they were. Remembering a tour through the southern states with the Rolling Stones, García relates, "It was a shock to us to go somewhere and see restrooms that would say 'white only' or 'black only.' I'd say 'Where do we go? We would get kicked out of restaurants, no Latins allowed. There was a big billboard in Jacksonville, Florida that said 'No niggers, no spics, no Mexicans allowed.' I wrote home and said 'You know what Mom? There's this big marquee that says they don't like us here.'"[29]

Other Chicano musicians in the 1960s combined a fusion of popular and Mexican musics with lyrics that evoked the complex pluralities of the city streets. The Midnighters scored a national hit in 1965 with "Whittier Boulevard," a song honoring the main traffic artery of the East Los Angeles *barrio*. Drawing inspiration from the energy and imagination of the car customizers and cruisers who claimed the boulevard as their own territory on weekend nights, the Midnighters presented the activities of the car club *cholos* to the outside world, while at the same time elevating the self-image of the cruisers by inserting their subculture into the discourse of mainstream popular culture. As the Midnighters' lead singer Little Willie G (for García) once explained, "A lot of people say you guys made Whittier Boulevard famous, but we just took the action off the boulevard and made it into a song."[30]

The car culture's quest for fun and good times expressed a desire for the good life of material success, but it also provided a means for satirizing and subverting ruling icons of consumer society. Just as Chicano car customizers "improved" upon the mass-produced vehicles from Detroit, Chicano rock songs like "Whittier Boulevard" celebrated Mexican-American appropriations of automobiles as part of a community ritual. By the late 1960s, that dialogue between the images of mass culture and the realities of *barrio* life increasingly took on an expressly political cast. At that time, changes in urban economics and politics threatened to destroy the social basis for the cultural pluralism of Los Angeles rock and roll by undermining the social and economic infrastructure of the central city. The cumulative effects of postwar highway and housing policies had subsidized suburban growth at the expense of the inner city, had exacerbated racial and class polarizations, and had encouraged residential segregation. For Chicanos, increased migration from Mexico, inadequate access to decent housing, and discrimination within a segmented labor market all combined to help create a new consciousness.[31]

The failures of 1960s social programs including the War on Poverty, the effects of the Vietnam War on poor and working-class youths, and the repressive policies of the Los Angeles Police Department all contributed to a growing political activism and cultural nationalism. On August 29, 1970, the Chicano community mobilized for a massive anti-war demonstration that expressed anger over many pent-up grievances and complaints. Taking their opposition to the war and their growing nationalism to the streets, demonstrators relied on their cultural traditions to give form to their protest activity. As one participant chronicled the start of that day's events,

> The boulevard was filled with gente, doing Latino chants and playing musica right in the streets. It started taking on the atmosphere of a carnival. Some even danced.[32]

This demonstration involved an attempt to reclaim city streets as a terrain for culture, politics, and celebration. But its aggressive festivity provoked a violent reaction from the authorities. Los Angeles police officers used force against the demonstrators; one officer shot and killed *Los Angeles Times* columnist Ruben Salazar. The Salazar killing outraged many people within the Mexican-American community and helped mobilize subsequent activism and demonstrations.[33]

The political ferment surrounding the 1970 demonstration found its way into Mexican-American rock and roll music in significant ways. The

Midnighters (who had recorded "Whittier Boulevard") recorded a song titled "Chicano Power" in 1970, and the group the V.I.P.'s changed their name that same year to El Chicano. In the early 1970s, East Los Angeles musicians began to feature Latin musical forms and Spanish language lyrics more prominently in their songs, and they attached themselves to a variety of community icons and subcultures. A series of outdoor music festivals, known popularly as "Chicano Woodstocks," showcased the community's musicians and provided an arena for displaying and celebrating diverse images of Chicano identity. The band Tierra emerged as a favorite of the "low rider" car customizers in the early 1970s, while Los Lobos got their start with an album recorded under the aegis of Cesar Chavez's United Farm Workers union. Mixing images from the past of *pachucos* and *cholos* with contemporary ones like low riders, these bands and their audiences placed current struggles in historical perspective, preserving a measure of continuity in a period of extraordinary change.[34]

Yet the music of East Los Angeles still had significant influence on artists and audiences outside the *barrio*. In 1975, for example, a mostly African-American jazz/funk ensemble from Long Beach calling themselves War recorded "Low Rider," a tribute to Chicano car customizers, cruisers, and musicians.[35] One of the year's best-selling records, "Low Rider" expressed War's own experiences playing dances and concerts for Mexican-American audiences throughout southern California, but the song also reflected demographic trends in Los Angeles that encouraged black-Chicano cultural interaction. In 1970, more than 50,000 Hispanics lived in the traditionally black south-central area of Los Angeles; by 1980 that figure had doubled, with Chicanos making up 21 percent of the total population of the south-central area.[36] The clear Latin influence on the subject and style of "Low Rider" testifies to the importance of Chicano music to American popular music, even when Chicano artists themselves might not enjoy access to a mass audience.

The commercial popularity of Los Lobos in the 1980s provides another example of the capacity for Los Angeles Chicano rock and roll musicians to form a historical bloc with other groups based on families of resemblance. Los Lobos proudly affirm their cultural heritage, but they reject separatism. They insist on acceptance as "legitimate contributors to contemporary music" without having to hide their ethnic identity. Aware of the ways in which they might be perceived as a novelty by a mass audience, they attempt to use their marginality to find families of resemblance connecting themselves to other groups. Drummer Louis Perez explains the group's philosophy by talking about the title song from their 1984 album *How Will the Wolf Survive?* Perez recalls that he read a *National Geographic* article about wolves as an endangered species and that he compared their plight to those of people that he knew. As he describes writing the song,

It started out being about the wolf and the next verse turned into a message of hope for the middle class. And the last verse is about how bands all over the country are trying to preserve something close to the heart of America. So yeah, it's about whether or not Los Lobos will survive. Not only us...[37]

Perez's lyrics talk about a wolf "running scared now forced to hide, in a land where he once stood with pride"—a clear reference to the Chicano people and to Los Lobos ("the wolves" in Spanish) themselves. The narrator predicts that the hunted creature will somehow find its way, and concludes with a tribute to the "young hearts and minds" in bands whose "songs of passion" keep alive the wolf's hope for survival. For Perez, the world of rock and roll music does not obliterate local cultures by rendering them invisible; rather it is an arena where diverse groups find common ground while still acknowledging important differences. The prefigurative counter-hegemony fashioned by Los Lobos has succeeded in winning the allegiance of musicians from other marginalized cultures. Their songs have been recorded by polka artist Frankie Yankovic as well as by country and western star Waylon Jennings. The southern "swamp rocker" Tony Joe White introduced Jennings to "How Will the Wolf Survive?" At first, Jennings could not make out all the lyrics in the song, but he loved the record's sound, so he decided to record it himself. He recalls,

The funny thing is, we couldn't understand all the words on the record, and that often means the lyrics are bad and they are trying to cover them up. Still, I loved the feel of the record and we decided to record it—even without knowing what it said completely. When we got the words from the publisher, I was knocked out. The words were great. I think everyone can relate to that song.[38]

The Cajun accordion player and singer Jo-El Sonnier views Los Lobos as artists whose cultural struggles parallel his own. As he explains:

I've sold myself as French, as R&B, as country, and as rock. But I want to do it all if I can; I think we could open doors for this music. Look at what Los Lobos has done for ethnic music, and they got signed without really changing. It can't just be that all people want is Madonna and punk music! All I've ever wanted to do is bring my music and my culture to the people. I have a message about the preservation of it. I feel like if I let my culture die, I die with it.[39]

Sonnier's strategy of using the plasticity of popular music as a means of preserving his ethnic culture echoes the efforts to build a historical bloc by Chicano musicians like Los Lobos; his acknowledgement of their importance as a model reveals a self-conscious understanding of the families of resemblance that they nurture and cultivate. Almost 40 years after Octavio Paz's visit to Los Angeles, Mexican-Americans in that city still suffer from the anguish of invisibility. Their numbers have increased, but discrimination and exploitation still leave them under-represented and under-rewarded. The expanded reach and scope of the mass media over the past four decades has exacerbated the cultural crisis facing Mexican-Americans; rarely do they see their world presented sympathetically or even accurately in the communications media that reinforce and legitimate Anglo cultural hegemony. But the "vague atmosphere" of Mexicanism perceived by Paz persists in the present as well. In community subcultures and styles, in the prefigurative counter-hegemony of organic intellectuals, it continues to inform the struggles of the present with the perceptions and values of the past. Conscious of the fragmentation of the modern world, this constantly changing "Mexicanism" cultivates its own marginality even as it reaches out to other groups. It is not a buried master narrative, but rather a conscious cultural politics that survives by "floating and hovering," never quite existing and never quite vanishing. Invisibility has its psychic and political costs, but for Chicano musicians in Los Angeles, it provides the ultimate camouflage for the difficult but necessary work of building a historical bloc.

Rubén Blades

Amnesty International concert, Costa Rica. (Photo: © Neal Preston)

Footnotes

Introduction

1 See, for example, Jorge Duany, "Popular Music in Puerto Rico: Toward an Anthropology of Salsa." *Latin American Music Review,* Volume 5, No. 2, 1984; and Felix M. Padilla, "Salsa Music as Cultural Expression of Latino Consciousness and Unity." *Hispanic Journal of Behavioral Sciences,* Volume 11, No. 1. February 1989.

2 Steven Feld, "Notes on World Beat." *Public Culture Bulletin,* Volume 1, No. 1. Fall 1988. p. 32.

3 Dave Laing, "The Music Industry and the 'Cultural Imperialism' Thesis." *Media, Culture and Society.* London: Sage, Volume 8, 1986. p. 331.

4 Roger Wallis and Krister Malm, *Big Sounds from Small Peoples: The Music Industry in Small Countries.* London: Constable, 1984. pp. 298-299.

5 *Rolling Stone.* October 23, 1986. Cited in Feld, 1988. p. 33.

6 For a fuller discussion of this process, see Reebee Garofalo, "The Internationalization of the U.S. Music Industry and its Impact on Canada." *Cultural Studies,* Volume 5, No. 3. October 1991.

7 See *Billboard.* April 6, 1991. p. 80; and Michèle Hung and Estaban Garcia Morencos, Eds., *World Record Sales 1969-1990,* London: International Federation of the Phonographic Industry, 1990.

8 See Nicholas Garnham, "Public Service Versus the Market." *Screen,* Volume 24, No. 1. 1983. p. 16. Also Wallis and Malm, 1984. p. 74.

9 For a detailed discussion of these various influences see George Lipsitz, " 'Ain't Nobody Here but us Chickens': The Class Origins of Rock and Roll," in George Lipsitz, Ed., *Class and Culture in Cold War America.* South Hadley, MA: Bergin and Garvey, 1982; Portia K. Maultsby, "Africanisms in African-American Popular Music," in Joseph E. Holloway, Ed., *Africanisms in American Culture.* Bloomington, IN: Indiana University Press, 1990; Reebee Garofalo, "Crossing Over, 1939-1989," in Jannette L. Dates and William Barlow, Eds., *Split Image: African-Americans in the Mass Media.* Washington, DC: Howard University Press, 1990.

10 Andrew Goodwin and Joe Gore, "World Beat and the Cultural Imperialism Debate." *Socialist Review,* Volume 20, No. 3. July-September, 1990. p. 71.

11 Wallis and Malm, 1984. pp. 300-301

12 Goodwin and Gore, 1990. p. 73.

13 Wallis and Malm, 1984. p. 302.

Chapter 1

1 Michael Goldberg, "Bill Graham: The Rolling Stone Interview." *Rolling Stone*. December 19, 1985. p. 138.

2 For a more developed discussion of this process as it relates to the civil rights movement, see Reebee Garofalo, "The Impact of the Civil Rights Movement on Popular Music," *Radical America,* Volume 21, No. 6. November-December 1987. pp. 15-22.

3 Particularly as this analysis relates to popular music, see Theodor W. Adorno, "On Popular Music." *Studies in Philosophy and Social Science.* No. 9. 1941, and "Culture Industry Reconsidered." *New German Critique.* Fall, 1975.

4 See the chapter on "Cultural Theory" in Raymond Williams, *Marxism and Literature.* Oxford: Oxford University Press, 1977; and Stuart Hall, "Rethinking the 'Base-and-Superstructure' Metaphor," in John Bloomfield, Ed., *The Communist University of London: Papers on Class, Hegemony and Party.* London: Lawrence and Wishart, 1977.

5 Laurence Kenneth Shore, *The Crossroads of Business and Music: A Study of the Music Industry in the United States and Internationally.* Unpublished Doctoral Dissertation. Stanford University. 1983. p. 248.

6 Michèle Hung and Estaban Garcia Morencos, Eds., *World Record Sales, 1969-1990.* London: International Federation of the Phonographic Industry, 1990. p. 83.

7 Personal interview with Little Steven. July 18, 1989.

8 Shore, 1983. pp. 283-284.

9 Roger Wallis and Krister Malm, *Big Sounds from Small Peoples: The Music Industry in Small Countries.* London: Constable, 1984. p. 302.

10 Ibid. p. 301.

11 Niles Rogers, quoted in Ted Fox, *In the Groove.* New York: St. Martins, 1986. p. 334-336.

12 Simon Frith, Ed., *Facing the Music.* New York: Pantheon Books, 1988. p. 129.

13 Tony Hollingsworth, Panel on "Mass Concerts/Mass Consciousness: The Politics of Mega-Events." New Music Seminar. New York. July 17, 1989.

14 Will Straw, "Rock for Ethiopia." Panel presentation at the Third International Conference on Popular Music Studies. Montreal, Canada. July 1985. p. 28.

15 Michael Goldberg, 1985. p. 169.

16 Simon Frith, "Crappy Birthday to Punk." *In These Times.* April 23-29, 1986. p. 20.

17 *Rock 'n' Roll Confidential.* September 1985. p. 1.

18 Michael Goldberg, "Live Aid Take May Hit $60 Million." *Rolling Stone.* August 29, 1985. p. 19.

19 Correspondence from Jennifer Davis, Executive Secretary of the Africa Fund, to Artists United Against Apartheid. September 10, 1985.

20 David Breskin, "Bob Geldof: The Rolling Stone Interview." *Rolling Stone*. December 5, 1985. p. 67.

21 Griel Marcus, "Rock for Ethiopia." Panel presentation at the Third International Conference on Popular Music Studies. Montreal, Canada. July 1985. p. 17.

22 Stan Rijven, "Rock for Ethiopia." Panel presentation at the Third International Conference on Popular Music Studies. Montreal, Canada. July 1985. pp. 3-7.

23 Simon Frith and John Street, "Party Music." *Marxism Today.* June, 1986. p. 29.

24 *Rock 'n' Roll Confidential*. September 1985. p. 1.

25 John Rockwell, "Leftist Causes? Rock Seconds Those Emotions." *New York Times*. December 11, 1988. p. 23.

26 "Concert Aid: Music to the Rescue." *Billboard*. December 28, 1985. p. T-7.

27 Telephone interview with Tony Hollingsworth. September 15, 1988.

28 Jack Healy, Panel on "Mass Concerts/Mass Consciousness: The Politics of Mega-Events." New Music Seminar. New York. July 17, 1989.

29 Breskin, 1985. p. 33.

Chapter 2

1 Peace Choir, "Give Peace a Chance." Produced by Sean Ono Lennon and Lenny Kravitz, Virgin Records 4-98839, 1991. It is interesting to note that while a documentary on the making of "Give Peace a Chance" is available on home video, it was never aired.

2 Alvin Eng, "News Lines." *PULSE!,* No. 90. February 1991. p. 14.

3 Nelson George, *Stop the Violence: Overcoming Self-destruction: Rap Speaks Out.* New York: National Urban League/Pantheon, 1990.

4 Arnold Shaw, *The Rockin' '50s*. New York: Hawthorn, 1974. p. xv.

5 Mick Jagger and Keith Richards, "Satisfaction." Out of Our Heads. London Records, 1965.

6 John Berger, *Ways of Seeing*. London: Pelican, 1972. p. 131.

7 Evan Eisenberg, *The Recording Angel*. New York: Penguin, 1987. p. 24.

8 *McKinley Morganfield (AKA Muddy Waters), "Can't be satisfied."* Chess 2CH-60006, 1948.

9 See Simon Frith, *Sound Effects: Youth, Leisure and the Politics of Rock 'n' Roll.* New York: Pantheon, 1981; and Jeremy Hawthorne, *Identity and Relationship*. London: Lawrence & Wishart, 1973; as well as Steve Chapple and Reebee Garofalo, *Rock 'n' Roll is Here to Pay: The History and Politics of the Music Industry*. Chicago: Nelson Hall, 1977; and Walter Benjamin, *Understanding Brecht*. London: New Left Books/Verso, 1973. p. 93.

10 Peter Hillmore, *Live Aid*. Parsippany, NJ: Unicorn, 1985; "We Are the World." *United Support of Artists for Africa*. Columbia Records 40043, 1985.

11 Various artists. "Land of Africa," RAS Records RAS 5001, 1985.

12 Gilda Berger, *USA for Africa: Rock Aid in the Eighties*. New York: Watts, 1987. p. 55.

13 Robert Allan, "Bob's Not Your Uncle." *Capital & Class,* No. 30. Winter 1986. pp. 31-37.

14 Susan Sontag, *Styles of Radical Will*. New York: Delta, 1969. p. 111.

15 Phil Slater, *Origin and Significance of the Frankfurt School*. Boston: Routledge & Kegan Paul, 1977. p. 133.

16 Walter Benjamin, "The Work of Art in the Age of Mechanical Reproduction,"*Illuminations*. New York: Harcourt, Brace & World, 1968.

17 See Ian Chambers, "Some Critical Tracks." *Popular Music,* No. 2. 1982. pp. 19-36.

18 Larry Grossberg, "Another Boring Day in Paradise: Rock 'n' Roll and the Empowerment of Everyday Life." *Popular Music,* No. 4. 1984. p. 232.

19 Reebee Garofalo, "How Autonomous is Relative? Popular Music, the Social Formation and Cultural Struggle." *Popular Music,* Volume 6, No. 1. January 1987. p. 84.

20 UB40, "I'm not Fooled so Easily." *Geffery Morgan...Loves White Girls*. DEP/International/New Claims A&M SP5033, 1984.

21 Grossberg, 1984. p. 232.

22 Ibid.

23 Stuart Hall, "Culture, the Media and the 'Ideological Effect'," in James Curran, et al., Eds., *Mass Communication and Society*. London: E. Arnold, 1977. pp. 315-348.

24 Malcolm X and Keith Le Blanc, "No Sell Out." Tommy Boy Music TB840, 1984.

25 Todd Gitlin, *The Whole World is Watching: Mass Media in the Making and Unmaking of the New Left*. Berkeley: University of California, 1980. p. 237.

26 Dave Marsh, *Rock 'n' Roll Confidential,* No. 32. January 1986. p. 2.

27 Chris Heath, "Tribal in Mind." *Details*. January 1991. p. 91.

28 Michel Foucault, "Sexuality, Discourse, Politics." Interview by Bernard-Henri Levy, *The Oxford Literary Review,* Volume 4, No. 2. 1980. p. 13; and *Power/Knowledge*. New York: Pantheon, 1980. p. 93.

29 Bob Geldof with Paul Vallely, *Is That It?* New York: Weidenfeld & Nicolson, 1986.

30 Roland Barthes, "Myth Today," *Mythologies*. New York: Hill & Wang, 1972. pp. 109-159; Goran Therborn, "The Social Order of Ideologies," *The Ideology of Power & the Power of Ideology*. London: Verso/Schocken, 1980. pp. 77-92.

31 Walter Benjamin, "Theses on the Philosophy of History," *Illuminations*. New York: Harcourt, Brace & World, 1968. p. 265.

32 See Larry Grossberg, "Farm Aid: The Politics of Music, Media and Morality." Champaign: photocopy, 1985.

33 Artists United Against Apartheid. *Sun City*. Manhattan/Capitol Records EP - ST53019, 1985; Karl Lorimar Home Video 012-VHS; Dave Marsh, *The Making of the Record*. New York: Penguin, 1985.

34 James Henke, *Human Rights Now!* New York: Amnesty International/Salem House, 1988.

35 Ibid. p.150.

36 GreenPeace/various artists, *Rainbow Warriors*. Geffen Records M5G 24236, 1989.

37 John Street, "If You Care About Our World, You'll Buy This Album: Green Politics and Rock Music." *ONE TWO THREE FOUR: A Rock 'n' Roll Quarterly,* No. 8. Winter, 1990. p. 27.

38 André Carothers, "Can Rock 'n' Roll Save the World?" *Greenpeace,* Volume 14, No. 6. November/December 1989. p. 11.

39 Street, 1990.

40 Various Artists, *Red Hot & Blue*. King Cole Music, Chrysalis Records F4 21799, 1990; Arista/6 West Home Video SW-5718.

41 Ernest Hardy, "Did You Evah?" *Outweek,* No. 75. December 5, 1990. p. 51.

42 Pat Benatar, "Love is a Battlefield," *Live from Earth*. Chrysalis Records FV41444, 1983.

Chapter 3

1 The bill included Whitney Houston, Sting, Stevie Wonder, Dire Straits, Tracy Chapman, Peter Gabriel, The Fat Boys, Jackson Browne, Natalie Cole, Little Steven, Eurythmics, Freddie Jackson, Phil Collins, UB40, Al Green, Midge Ure, Miriam Makeba, Hugh Masekela, Simple Minds, Aswad, The Bee Gees, Youssou N'Dour, Salt-n-Pepa, and more.

2 Personal interview with Peter Jenner. July 19, 1988.

3 Telephone interview with Tony Hollingsworth. September 15, 1988.

4 Ibid.

5 *New York Times.* June 24, 1988. p. A31.

6 Anthony De Curtis, "Rock & Roll Politics: Did the Nelson Mandela Tribute Make its Point?" *Rolling Stone*. August 11, 1988. p. 34.

7 Hollingsworth interview, 1988.

8 Ibid.

9 Fox broadcast, Freedomfest. June 11, 1988.

10 Ibid.

11 Ibid.

12 Hollingsworth interview, 1988.

13 Fox broadcast, 1988.

14 Ibid.

15 Jenner interview, 1988.

16 Ibid.

17 Hollingsworth interview, 1988.

18 Ibid.

19 DeCurtis, 1988. p. 34.

20 Ibid. p. 33.

21 Hollingsworth interview, 1988.

22 Personal interview with Paolo Pratto. August 1988.

23 *The Making of Sun City*. Karl-Lorimar Home Video. 1985.

24 Telephone interview with Danny Schechter. January 22, 1992.

25 Telephone interview with Themba Vilakasi. January 22, 1992.

26 According to Danny Schechter (January 22, 1992), there was an "awkward structure" comprised of Hollingsworth's Tribute Productions, the London-based Anti-Apartheid Movement, and the ANC's International Reception Committee which formed the production team for the second Mandela concert.

27 Schechter interview, 1992.

28 Simon Applebaum, "Mandela Mistake." *Cablevision*. May 7, 1990. Last page.

29 Schechter interview, 1992.

30 Danny Schechter, "Why We Didn't See Wembley." *Africa Report*. July-August 1990. p. 65.

31 Schechter, 1990. p. 66.

32 Jenner interview, 1988.

33 DeCurtis, 1988. p. 29.

34 Schechter, 1990. p. 66.

Chapter 4

1 Neither movement has formally died, though Rock Against Racism ceased to be much more than a slogan after 1981, and it is unclear as we write whether Red Wedge will reappear in the next general election campaign.

2 Robin Denselow, *When the Music's Over*. London: Faber, 1989. p. 139.

3 Quoted in Denselow, 1989. p. 140.

4 David Widgery, *Beating Time: Riot 'n' Race 'n' Rock 'n' Roll*. London: Chatto & Windus, 1986. p. 53.

5 One other organization to emerge at roughly this time was Rock In Opposition, organized around avant-garde bands like Henry Cow. See Chris Cutler, *File Under Popular: Theoretical and Critical Writings on Music*. London: November Books, 1985.

6 Widgery, 1986. p. 54.

7 Ibid. p. 58.

8 Ibid. p. 62.

9 Ibid. 1986. p. 43. The SWP's own involvement was largely organized through the Anti-Nazi League, which was formed in 1977 as a popular front against the National Front. It built a large following through its distinctive slogans and clever images. A series of badges proliferated: Teachers Against the Nazis, Well-Meaning Socialists Against the Nazis, Drunks Against the Nazis, and so on. For most people RAR and ANL events were indistinguishable. For the SWP's reading of events, see J. Rose, "Rocking Against Racism"; A. Callinicos, "When the Music Stops"; and J. Hoyland & M. Flood Page, "You can lead a horse to water," all in *Socialist Review*. June 1978. pp. 13-17.

10 Quoted in Denselow, 1989. p. 151.

11 Red Wedge, *A State of Independence*. London, n.d. p. 1.

12 In 1987, 32 percent of first-time voters failed to vote at all, and of those that did, 45 percent voted Conservative and only 32 percent Labor. This was a small gain in votes over 1983, putting Labor in second place, instead of the third they achieved in the previous election.

13 *New Socialist*. March 1986. p. 8.

14 Widgery, 1986. p. 67.

15 Quoted in Ibid. pp. 54-55.

16 Ibid. p. 42.

17 Ibid. p. 56.

18 Dick Hebdige, *Hiding in the Light*. London: Routledge, 1988. p. 214.

19 Dave Laing, *One Chord Wonders: Power and Meaning in Punk Rock*. Milton Keynes: Open University Press, 1985. p. 111, his emphasis.

Chapter 5

1 This chapter is based on a lecture entitled "The Influence of Rock Music on Political Changes in East Germany" delivered at the Centre for Research on Culture and Society at Carleton University, Ottawa, Ontario, Canada, November 17, 1990.

2 See also Peter Wicke, "The Role of Rock Music in the Political Disintegration of East Germany," in James Lull, Ed., *Popular Music and Communication*. Beverly Hills: Sage, 1992 (Second Edition).

3 Wolf Biermann was born in 1940 in Germany. His parents were in the German Communist Party for many years before World War II. His father died in a Nazi concentration camp and his mother became a prominent member of the West German Communist Party after the war. Because of this background he decided, in 1956, to emigrate from Hamburg to East Berlin to finish high school and to study philosophy at Humboldt University. He became a singer-songwriter, working briefly with Bertolt Brecht and studying with Hans Eisler. He then embarked on a career as a political singer-songwriter, winning the National Award for the Arts, the most prestigious award for artists of any kind in the GDR. His critical songs soon led him into political trouble with the authorities, however, and caused him to be publicly criticized at the 1965 meeting of the Central Committee of the Communist Party. As a result of this, he was prohibited from performing. Attempts on the part of the state authorities to make him return to West Germany failed, and because of the prominent position occupied by his mother in the Communist Party of West Germany, it was not possible for the security services to handle his case in the usual manner (that is, to imprison him on charges of undermining the state). As a result of this, he came under heavy surveillance by the security services. Despite this, he was able to produce records in his East Berlin apartment which were then sent to West Germany for pressing and distribution. This made him very famous, and caused the state to become obsessed with him as a public figure of resistance. Finally, in 1976, he suddenly received permission (which had hitherto been denied) to accept an invitation from the West German trade union movement to give a concert in Cologne. He accepted on condition that he would be allowed to return to the GDR. Despite these assurances, however, the state authorities cancelled his GDR citizenship immediately upon his departure to West Germany, thus making it impossible for him to return to the GDR. This forced expulsion of Wolf Biermann resulted in significant political unrest among artists and intellectuals. Many of these artists and intellectuals then left the country.

4 The Committee for Entertainment Arts was formed in 1972 as a separate organization set up and funded by the state. It functioned as a cross between a trade union for artists and a governing body for their activities. The term "entertainment arts" refers to all those artistic and cultural practices which fall outside the English designation of "high culture" or "serious art" (for example, popular music, all kinds of variety acts, journalism, circus acts, and so on). Half the members of the governing council of the committee were appointed by various branches of the state or the state media, and half were elected by different sections of member artists (for example, rock musicians, jazz musicians, singer-songwriters, journalists, comedians, and so on). The president of this committee for some years was Gisela Steineckert, one of the most popular song lyric writers. The president of the rock section was for many years Toni Krahl, the lead singer of one of the top GDR rock bands, City. The committee provided a route for the funding of popular culture, and was the organization which facilitated institutionalized negotiations between popular artists on the one hand and the party and state authorities on the other.

Footnotes/289

Chapter 6

1 George Lipsitz, *Time Passages: Collective Memory and American Popular Culture.* Minneapolis: University of Minnesota Press, 1990. pp. 16-17.

2 Robert Wuthnow, *Meaning and Moral Order: Explorations in Cultural Analysis.* Berkeley and Los Angeles: University of California Press, 1987.

3 Miklós Sükösd has characterized the youth movements of the mid- and late 1980s as being comprised of various tendencies. They include cultural movements: a) literary and artistic groups; b) alternative life-style groups; religious movements: a) groups within established churches; b) groups within various "free" churches; political movements: a) single-issue movements; b) peace and environmental groups; c) political and social science clubs; d) university clubs; e) popular movements consisting of 1) conservative nationalist societies; 2) democratic societies; f) "urbanite" European-oriented movements consisting of 1) liberal socialist associations; 2) liberal democratic associations (quoted by Elemér Hankiss in *Kelet-Európai Alternatívák.* Budapest: Közgazdasági és Jogi Könyvkiadó, 1989. pp. 126-127. In English: *East-European Alternatives—Are There Any?* Oxford: University Press. 1990.

4 Wuthnow, 1987. p. 158.

5 For more on this, see Anna Szemere, "Pop Music in Hungary." *Communication Research,* Volume 12, No. 3. 1985. pp. 401-411.

6 Ian Chambers, *Urban Rhythms: Pop Music and Popular Culture.* London: Macmillan, 1985. pp. xi-xii.

7 Miklós Hadas, " 'Ugy Dalolok, Ahogy én Akarok': A Popzenei ipar Müködésének Vázlata." *Valóság,* Volume 26, No. 9. 1983. pp. 71-78.

8 Anna Szemere and András Bozóki, "Interjú Menyhárt Jenővel, Müller Péterrel és Bárdos D. Agnessel." Budapest: Institute for Musicology, 1984. Typescript.

9 Simon Frith, *Sound Effects: Youth, Leisure and the Politics of Rock 'n' Roll.* London: Pantheon, 1983.

10 See János Sebők, *Magya-Rock,* Volumes 1-2. Budapest: Zenemükiadó, 1983-84; and László Dám, *Rockszámla.* Budapest: IRI: Reflex, 1987.

11 See "Local Musician Survey." Budapest: Institute for Musicology. 1986. Prepared by Hajnóczy, Kenderesi, and Szemere for the International Communication and Youth Culture Consortium's comparative study on the impact of the transnational music industry on peripheral popular music production. Its results are included in Deanna C. Robinson, et al., *Music at the Margins.* London: Sage, 1991.

12 My use of the terms "politics" and "politicization" do not connote resistance or progressiveness. Despite a tacit semantic convention in Western leftist discourses, I do not believe that such a restriction of the meaning of politics to the activities of resisting subjects is justified in cultural analysis since it deprives us of a conceptual tool to describe the behavior of other actors in the political and other arenas of social life, most notably, as in my discussion of cultural life in state socialism, the state itself.

13 Peter Wicke, "The Influence of Rock Music on Political Changes in East Germany," First Annual Public Lecture, The Centre for Research on Culture and Society, Carleton University, Ottawa, 1990. p. 10.

14 See Dénes Csengey, "Es mi most itt vagyunk," Budapest: Magvetö, 1983; and István Csörsz, "Elhagyott a közérzetem," Budapest: Magvetö, 1986.

15 János Köbányai, "Biztosítötü és börnadrág," *Mozgó Világ,* Volume 5, No. 2. 1979. pp. 6-77.

16 Chris Bohn, "Hungarian Rhapsody and other Magyar Melodies." *New Musical Express,* Volume 17, No. 16. 1981. p. 18.

17 The so-called democratic opposition was formed in the latter years of 1970s and comprised an active group of people with diverse political orientations. The core was made up of "hard core" Liberals and Social Democrats who engaged in extensive underground political activities. (For an excellent account of liberalism as the rhetoric of progressive politics in Eastern Europe, see Tony Judt, "The Unmastered Future: What Prospects for Eastern Europe?" *Tikkun,* Volume 5, No. 2. 1990. pp. 11-18.) This included the circulation of *samizdat* [self-published] writings and later, after the acquisition of a printing machine, the publication of their own underground journals *(Beszélö, Hírmondó)* and a variety of Hungarian and foreign, classic, and contemporary books put on index by the state. They drafted petitions and manifestos to the Hungarian government as a protest against human rights violations in Hungary and other Warsaw Pact countries. The democratic opposition cooperated with organizations of similar purpose in Czechoslovakia (subscribers to Charta '77), Poland (Solidarity, KOR), the GDR (the Evangelic Church) and the Soviet Union (*samizdat* writers) as well as in the West (Amnesty International). The idea and practice of the so-called "moving universities" consisted of a series of illegal gatherings at private apartments where the lectures, usually held by social scientists, voiced illegitimate political/ideological positions. (The adjective "moving" refers to the fact that these lectures had to be held at different places in order to avoid the blatant provocation of the authorities.) In 1989, members of the democratic opposition established the Alliance of Free Democrats, which is currently the largest oppositional party in the Parliament.

18 A memorable incident of political maneuvering took place around the journal *Mozgó Világ,* dedicated to publishing the work of young avant-garde writers, poets, essayists and radical social scientists. Since the journal was sponsored by the Communist Youth League, the Communist Party and the Cultural Ministry employed a variety of measures to smooth off its oppositional edges. Eventually, when the chief editor was removed, the whole staff abandoned the journal as a gesture of protest. The Ministry appointed a new chief editor to run the journal under the same name but most of the earlier contributors and readers withdrew their loyalty from the new *Mozgó.*

19 Simon Frith and Howard Horne, *Art into Pop.* New York: Methuen, 1987. p. 124.

20 Rumor had it that originally the band had used the name Central Committee but they were pressed by some official to drop the adjective. One member of the

band, when asked in an interview, denied that the story was true. Just like Feró, he also seemed uncomfortable about the over-politicization of their joke. Certainly, in changing the name, he may have intended to protect the band from potential harassment by the officialdom. Besides, this elusive behavior may also be seen as a postmodernist play on ambiguities.

21 Dave Laing, *One Chord Wonders: Power and Meaning in Punk Rock.* Milton Keynes: Open University Press, 1985. p. 44.

22 The hard-core punks represented another populist, working-class sub-trend. They mostly drew on the British "oi" movement. Some bands were persecuted for propagating racism (anti-Gypsy) among their public. See more on this in Timothy Ryback's chapter on Hungary in his account of Eastern European rock, *Rock Around the Bloc: A History of Rock Music in Eastern-Europe and the Soviet Union.* New York: Oxford University Press, 1990. pp. 174-177.

23 Szemere and Bozóki, 1984.

24 Ibid.

25 Hankiss, 1989. pp. 117-132. The notion of second publicity has been theorized by Hankiss as an aspect of the second society in socialist Hungary. According to his structuralist model, the official or first society, which represented the embodiment of certain socialist (i.e., Marxist/Leninist/Stalinist) ideals, can be contrasted through binary opposition with the second one, a spontaneously existing, entirely unplanned social realm, along a set of criteria such as homogeneity vs. differentiation and integration; hierarchical vs. horizontal organization; the downward vs. upward flow of information; the presence vs. absence of the state; centralization; political vs. economic/social predominance; the presence vs. absence of the dominant ideology; visibility; and legitimacy. The second society is assumed to embrace a very tangible but chaotic second economy, a more-or-less organized second political publicity, a second cultural sphere (subcultures and countercultures), a second consciousness (identified by Hankiss, somewhat imprecisely, with a set of political philosophies and belief systems); and a second, mostly hidden domain of political and social interactions.

26 Roger Wallis and Krister Malm, *Big Sounds from Small Peoples: The Music Industry in Small Countries.* London: Constable, 1984.

27 From the early 1980s, small-scale private enterprise was granted further concessions and thus started to play an increasingly significant role in the Hungarian economy. In the music business the easing of tax regulations led to the mushrooming of small record boutiques selling self-imported foreign pop music. Parallel to this, new channels opened up for foreign bands to visit Hungarian venues. As a result, all pop musical tastes began to be catered to in the marketplace, even if without the abundance and ease characterizing the workings of its Western counterpart.

28 Lawrence Grossberg's writings ("Another Boring Day in Paradise: Rock and Roll and the Empowerment of Everyday Life," in Richard Middleton and David Horn, Eds., *Popular Music 4.* New York: Cambridge University Press, 1984. pp. 225-258; and "Teaching the Popular," in Cary Nelson, Ed., *Theory in the Classroom.* Urbana

and Chicago: University of Illinois Press, 1986. pp. 177-200) have dealt extensively with the ways in which rock fans use the term "rock-and-roll" to demarcate their difference both from other music fans and from straight society.

29 Frith and Horne, 1987. p. 132.

30 L. Beke and A. Szöke, Eds., *Jó Világ, Bölcsész Index.* Budapest: ELTE BTK, 1984. p. 7.

31 Grossberg, " 'I'd Rather Feel Bad than not Feel Anything at All': Rock and Roll, Pleasure and Power." *Enclitic 8.* 1984. p. 107.

32 Csengey, 1983.

33 Quoted by Laing, 1985. p. 76.

34 Csaba Hajnóczy, *Voice of Hungary 1.* Vienna-Budapest-New York: International Network Rittn Tittn, 1984.

35 On the women punks' use of the chanteuse image and of fetishistic clothes, see Laing, 1985. pp. 94-95.

36 This perceptive phrase was suggested by János Maróthy in one of our extensive discussions on the Hungarian avant-garde rock bands.

37 For a perceptive discussion of the relationship between lyrical subjects and performers in various pop styles, see Laing, 1985. pp. 63-68.

38 Much of Bockris and Malanga's account of Andy Warhol's complex use of images and of the portrayal of the Velvet Underground could describe the Trabant and Balaton live shows: "The movies were portraits of the people on stage. The people on stage were portraits of themselves. The songs the Velvets were singing were portraits of people." Quoted by Frith and Horne, 1987. p. 112.

39 Grandpierre is also a Ph.D. in astronomy, a physicist, a poet, and a self-taught anthropologist.

40 Attila Grandpierre, "Punk as a Rebirth of Shamanist Folk Music." 1984. p. 1. Typescript.

41 Beke, in Beke and Szöke, Eds., 1984. p. 136.

42 It must be noted that the researcher addressing such issues must be aware of some special methodical problems in disentangling the relations between a cultural form and politics. In an authoritarian society, such as Hungary was during the early 1980s, the question of the artists' political intentions and interpretations of particular songs simply could not be straightforwardly discussed without threatening the delicate legitimacy of the art form itself as a site of political communication. In more profane terms, the artists were reluctant to talk about the political contents of their practice unless they felt completely safe with their interviewer. But even when they felt safe, they enjoyed playing on the opacity of their texts.

43 Szemere and Bozóki, 1984. pp. 19-20.

Chapter 7

1 This collaboration is the result of research conducted independently by the authors and published in *Asian Music,* Volume 22, No. 2. Spring-Summer 1991, as Tim Brace, "Popular Music in Contemporary Beijing: Modernism and Cultural Identity," and Paul Friedlander, "China's 'Newer Value' Pop: Rock-and-Roll and Technology on the New Long March." The authors would also like to thank the Kaltenborn Foundation for funding some of the research upon which some of this analysis is based.

2 *Gangtai* is a term which refers to the cultures of Hong Kong and Taiwan. It is formed by joining the second syllable of Hong Kong, *Xianggang,* to the first of Taiwan.

3 In order to protect the identity of informants, the quotations in this chapter will be unattributed.

4 This reasoning is echoed in the official music press. See, for example, Zeng Suijin, *"Gangtai Liuxing Gequ Chongji Hou de Huigu"* (A Look Back at the Influx of *Gangtai* Popular Songs). *Renmin Yinyue (People's Music),* Volume 2, No. 44. 1988. p. 51; and Shu Zechi and Zeng Yi, *"Liuxing Yinyue yu Cidai Shichang Xianzhuang Pingxi"* (Popular Music and the Cassette Market: A Critical Appraisal of the Present Situation). *Yinyue, Wudao Yanjiu (Music and Dance Research),* Volume 5, No. 15. 1989. p. 16.

5 This reference is to the severe governmental restrictions concerning what was and what was not allowed over both live and mass-mediated musical presentations during the years of the Cultural Revolution (1966-69) and up until the Open Door Policy of the late 1970s. At their most severe, during the mid-1970s, these restrictions were the work of the so-called Gang of Four (Jiang Qing, Zhang Chunqiao, Yao Wenyuan, and Wang Hongwen).

6 For a discussion of how popular music "creates our understanding of what popularity is," see Simon Frith, "Towards an Aesthetic of Popular Music," in Richard Leppert and Susan McClary, Eds., *Music and Society: The Politics of Composition, Performance and Reception.* Cambridge: Cambridge University Press, 1987. pp. 137-138.

7 For example, see Yang Ruiqing, *"Xibeifeng Gequ Heyi Chengchao"* (Why the *Xibeifeng* Wave?). *Yinyue, Wudao Yanjiu (Music and Dance Research),* Volume 5, No. 15. 1989.

8 These forces were dominated by a combination of influences from outside the country, namely from Hong Kong and Taiwan, and internally-generated, politically-motivated developments of governmental instigation.

9 Shu Zechi and Zeng Yi, 1989. p. 16.

10 Authors' translation. The same title is translated in Chapter 8 as "I'm Left with Nothing." Original words copyright Cui Jian, China Tourist Audio-Visual Publishers, 1989.

11 For further discussions of this point, see Peter Manuel, *Popular Musics of the Non-Western World: An Introductory Survey.* Oxford: Oxford University Press,

1988. Especially pp. 6-7; and Simon Frith, "The Industrialization of Popular Music," in James Lull, Ed., *Popular Music and Communication*. Beverly Hills: Sage, 1987. pp. 53-77.

12 There is (and has been since the late 1970s) a tradition of hand-to-hand dissemination of those tapes—mostly imported—which are not allowed in public stores. In this sense, the simple copying of a cassette tape becomes a political act which, combined with thousands of others, constantly works (or struggles) to defeat the hegemonic goals of the Party.

13 Manuel, 1988. p. 6.

14 Ibid. p. 14.

15 For example, see Sun Sheng, *"Yi Shou Zhua Zhengdun, Yi Shou Zhua Fanrong"* (Reorganize With One Hand, and Prosper With the Other). *Renmin Yinyue (People's Music)*, Volume 2, No. 8. 1991. For an account of a more pointed criticism of Cui Jian's work—criticism which, it is claimed, appeared in the original Sun Sheng speech, see Xia Hanhua, *"Dalu Yuetan Xin Yi Lun de Pidou Yundong"* (A New Criticism Campaign in the Music World of Mainland China). *Jiushi Niandai Yuekan (90's Monthly)*, Volume 4, No. 102. 1991.

16 This term is an adaptation of Raymond Williams' "structure of feeling": it attempts, as does Williams' term, to refocus the traditional term "worldview" away from the distanced "view" and toward closer "feelings": the affective element in any lived process. See Raymond Williams, *Marxism and Literature*. Oxford: Oxford University Press, 1977. pp. 128-135.

17 Charles Hamm, "China's Great Leap Into the World of Rock Music." *New York Times*. April 16, 1989. p. 27.

Chapter 8

1 First verse of "You Awaken My Soul" (Music: D. Bohlen; Lyrics: Lin Zhenqiang), © BMG Pacific Ltd., taken from an album of the same title. All the Cantopop lyrics in this article are translated by Janet Mui-Fong Ng (Columbia University). Cf. Appendix 1: Selected List of Cantopop Albums for release date and record information.

2 Hans Ebert, Hong Kong correspondent to *Billboard,* coined the term "Canto-rock" in 1974, but changed it to "Cantopop" in 1978. Discussions in this article deal only with Cantopop produced and marketed primarily in Hong Kong.

3 *Contemporary,* No. 10. February 3, 1990. p. 31.

4 Hong Kong island and Kowloon peninsula were ceded to Britain in 1842 and 1860 respectively. The New Territories were leased to Britain in 1898 for 99 years. However, Hong Kong cannot be separated into three political or economic entities. When the British and Chinese negotiated the future of Hong Kong, they considered Hong Kong as an undivided unity, although legally Hong Kong island and Kowloon peninsula were supposedly "permanent" British colonies.

5 This figure is based on Hong Kong government statistics released in 1989.

6 The Sino-British Agreement for the return of Hong Kong to China was initialed on September 26, 1984 between Margaret Thatcher and Deng Xiaoping, and then officially signed as the Joint Declaration between the British and Chinese governments on December 19, 1984. Prior to 1984, Hong Kong citizens were not consulted via any public channels regarding the return to China. The Sino-British Agreement states that Hong Kong will be a "Special Administrative Region" of the People's Republic of China. Hong Kong's post-1997 "Basic Law" was finalized on April 4, 1990.

7 For example, on September 20, 1983, the Hong Kong Stock Market index plummeted by 73.86 points due to the uncertain outcome of the Sino-British talks about the colony's future. On June 4, 1989, the stock market dropped an even bigger margin of 22 percent. Smaller fluctuations of the Hong Kong Stock Market index always occur when there are political reshuffles or policy changes in China.

8 The emigration numbers (in round figures) are as follows: before 1987: less than 20,000 per year; 1987: 30,000; 1988: 45,800; 1989: 42,000; 1990: 62,000.

9 Up to 1985, the only government council that contained elected members was the Urban Council, which only dealt with Hong Kong's sanitation, hygiene, and cultural policies. The other two Legislative and Executive Councils contained only appointed members. In late 1985, the first elections for a limited number of seats at the Legislative Council took place, but only selected professional or interest groups could elect their representatives. The first direct elections will be held in late 1991.

10 The demography of Hong Kong is unique: it has been the haven for Chinese legal and illegal immigrants before and after 1949. Throughout the 1950s and early 1960s, when political turmoil occurred in China, many immigrated to Hong Kong. These immigrants helped to establish Hong Kong as an industrial city in the 1960s. The colony's growth as a financial center in the 1970s was partly due to the political and economic developments in China.

11 As British Dependent Territories citizens, Hong Kong citizens do not have the right of abode in the United Kingdom. See later discussion.

12 See, for example, "Next Door and Eight Years Away," *Time.* June 5, 1989. p. 29; and "Fear and Anger in Hong Kong," *Time.* June 19, 1989. p. 22.

13 Hu Yaobang was forced to step down because of pro-democracy demonstrations in Beijing in December 1986. His death was not officially mourned by the authorities in the People's Republic of China, nor were his achievements in the past decade acknowledged by the official press. The Beijing students wanted to mourn Hu's death; therefore, they organized rallies in university campuses and in Tiananmen Square on April 17, 1989.

14 The May 4 Movement of 1919 changed the path of modern Chinese society, culture, and politics. When the student leaders learned that Mikhail Gorbachev would be visiting Beijing at the time of the anniversary, and that the international media would all be stationed there for the state visit, they decided to stage a media coup-d'état.

15 Historically, overseas Chinese have played major roles in the political changes of the Chinese mainland. The 1911 revolution that deposed the last Qing monarch was heavily financed by overseas Chinese.

16 Official and unofficial estimates range from 1 million to 1.5 million.

17 Cf. Appendix 2: A Selected List of the Major Rallies organized by the Hong Kong Alliance in Support of Patriotic Democratic Movement in China (May 1989-December 1990).

18 There was a small output of Cantonese popular music from the 1960s, but its importance and its market were marginal.

19 It is difficult to quantify the extent to which Anglo-American pop lyrics are understood by the listeners in Hong Kong, but this question is not directly related to this article.

20 There were sympathetic riots in Hong Kong in 1967 during the Chinese Cultural Revolution. Martial law was declared in the colony by the governor of Hong Kong during that time.

21 Hong Kong Cantopop and Hong Kong television shows are marketed in all Southeast Asian countries that have a significant Chinese population: namely Singapore, Thailand, Malaysia, Indonesia, Taiwan, and the Philippines. Chinatowns throughout Europe, Canada, and the U.S. are also markets for such audio and video programs.

22 Nearly all the major international record companies have branches in Hong Kong: e.g., EMI and Polygram have been producing local popular music in Hong Kong since the 1960s (and Cantopop since the 1970s); WEA joined the Cantopop market in 1979; and BMG took over a successful local record company, Current, in 1989.

23 Some Cantopop songs from the late 1980s were straight borrowings of famous tunes, including the mellower music of Miami Sound Machine, George Michael, Madonna, and Richard Marx.

24 There are a few exceptions: George Lam, who has incorporated dixieland jazz and some hard rock, and Lowell Lo, who has a strong blues influence in his music.

25 The Hong Kong Alliance in Support of Patriotic Democratic Movement in China began as a coalition of 40 civic groups on May 21, 1989. By December 1990, there were 218 civic groups which formed the Alliance, including labor unions, political associations, district communities, and college student unions. The chairman of the Alliance, Mr. Wah Szeto, was the president of the Professional Teachers Union of Hong Kong. The Alliance was formed in a hurry, because the organizers wanted to coordinate all sorts of fundraising and supportive actions for Beijing. Its goals then were to provide material support to the Beijing students, who at that time were on hunger strikes. That goal was the only reason that joined these 40 civic groups together. The Hong Kong Alliance took on a different life immediately after its inception, due to the rapid development of events in China. Money was collected in the rallies in Hong Kong starting from May 21; but the main boost of the Alliance's financial and popular status came a week later, with the "Concert

for Democracy in China." The amount of $170,000 was channeled to the Beijing students prior to June 3, 1989. Since June 4, 1989, the Alliance has not been able to channel money into China, but has donated money to support some of the Chinese dissidents who are in exile and their political associations. The Alliance now funds many activities that constantly remind Hong Kong citizens of the long struggle to democracy in China. However, there is a clear indication of a lack of interest and of public support in this political venture, reflected by the smaller number of demonstrators in recent rallies. Cf. Appendix 2.

26 According to the figures released in the financial report of the Hong Kong Alliance in Support of Patriotic Democratic Movement in China, released on February 15, 1990.

27 More than 20,000 cassettes of "All for Freedom" were sold in 1989, and a total of more than $28,000 was raised in this venture. Cf. Appendix 1.

28 "All for Freedom" (Music: Lowell Lo. Lyrics: Susan Tang), © Hong Kong Alliance in Support of Patriotic Democratic Movement in China, 1989.

29 See later discussion of Lo's album *1989*.

30 The Hong Kong weekly pop chart is calculated according to the frequency of airplay in the four local Cantopop music channels. The frequency of airplay, however, is conditioned by the policy whereby a "suggested list of newly released Cantopop" is sent from the music directors to the disc jockeys.

31 Eamonn Fitzpatrick, "Pop Stars Unite to Sing for Freedom." *South China Morning Post*. May 24, 1989.

32 Ibid.

33 Although some Cantopop singers were unable to attend the recording of "All for Freedom" due to their concert or film engagements abroad, they phoned in from Japan, Canada, and the U.S. during the "Concert for Democracy in China," and these conversations were broadcast. Cui Jian's video of "I'm Left with Nothing" was also premiered in the "Concert for Democracy in China."

34 This was inspired by Corizon Aquino's yellow ribbon and the subsequent success of her People's Movement in the Philippines.

35 "Question" (Music: G. Moroder/P. Bellote. Lyrics: Liu Zhuohui), © BMG Pacific Ltd., 1989. Music is taken from Moroder's soundtrack to *Metropolis*.

36 "Mama, I've Done Nothing Wrong" (Music: Mahmoud Rumajan. Lyrics: Liu Zhuohui), © BMG Pacific Ltd., 1989. The first collective hunger strike started on May 13, 1989. Mahmoud Rumajan was inspired by the democracy movement in China when he wrote the music. He wanted to emulate the successful examples of songs such as "Give Peace a Chance" in support of the Beijing students' actions.

37 Cf. Appendix 1.

38 Information supplied by BMG Pacific Ltd.

39 Between June 11 and August 5, 1989. This song is still used as a rally song by the Hong Kong Alliance even in late 1990.

40 Widely reported in all the local newspapers on May 24, 1989.

41 "1989 Prelude" and "1989" (Music: Lowell Lo. Lyrics: Susan Tang), © EMI Hong Kong Ltd., 1989. Cf. Appendix 1.

42 Cf. Footnote 28.

43 Articles have appeared in China's *People's Daily,* since June 1989, which referred to Hong Kong as the home base of "counter-revolutionary activities" to topple the Chinese government.

44 Two other songs from this album, "No Regrets" and "Never to Face Darkness Again," did enter the Hong Kong pop chart briefly in November and December 1989.

45 "Blood-red Dawn" (Music: Lowell Lo. Lyrics: Liu Zhuohui), © EMI Hong Kong Ltd., 1989. Liu Zhuohui completed the lyrics within days after the massacre, prompted by the following event: On June 9, 1989, Deng Xiaoping made his first public appearance after the crush of the democracy movement. Deng was seen congratulating members of the People's Liberation Army.

46 This album is marketed by EMI Hong Kong Ltd. It was relaunched on the market on December 12, 1990 for the Christmas season. Cf. Appendix 1.

47 An article in the Hong Kong Alliance in Support of Patriotic Democratic Movement in China *Newsletter,* No. 2, December 2, 1989, specifically explains the Hong Kong Alliance's position of including musical performances in the memorial rally.

48 Cf. Appendix 2.

49 The six cities are Vancouver, Toronto, Los Angeles, San Francisco, Washington DC, New York.

50 Mr. Wah Szeto sang "Descendants of the Dragon" by Hou Dejian. Hou was among the remaining four hunger-strikers in Tiananmen Square on June 3, 1989. It was rumored that Hou sought refuge in the Australian embassy in Beijing immediately after the June 4 massacre. By July 1989, Hou was interviewed by the Chinese authorities in Beijing, and his "official" but untruthful account of June 4 was widely publicized throughout the world. Hou escaped to Taipei in 1990.

51 Apart from "All for Freedom," two other rally songs were sung: "Bloodstains" was a revolutionary song of the People's Republic of China. It was also *the* rally song that Beijing students used in Tiananmen Square. "Wounds of History" is a Taiwanese variation of "All for Freedom."

52 "Ten Firefighter Boys" (Music: Wang Yaoming. Lyrics: Pan Yuanliang), © Polygram Records Ltd., Hong Kong, 1990. "Ten Firefighter Boys" was among the Top Thirty in the pop chart from January 21 to March 31, 1990.

53 The Chinese phrase *shen jing* can be translated as "madness" or "mental illness." This double meaning suggests medical diagnoses of the Chinese rulers who crushed the democracy movement. Cf. Appendix 1.

54 "This list contains left, right, good, evil, big, and small: arranged not in order of importance" was among the Top Thirty in the pop chart from January 7-20, 1990.

The personalities whose names were used include: (in one verse) Deng Xiaoping, Anita Mui (pop singer), Alan Tam (pop singer), Jackie Chan (film star), David Wilson (governor of Hong Kong), Martin Lee (famous political figure, then vice-chairman of the Hong Kong Alliance), Chow Yun Fatt (film star), and Wuer Kaixi (charismatic Chinese student leader in the democracy movement).

55 "Questioning Heaven" (Music: Liu Yida. Lyrics: Zhou Yaohui), © PolyGram Records Ltd., Hong Kong, 1990. The author wishes to acknowledge Janet Ng for this insight into the reference to *Chuci*.

56 "We Are Both Watching" (Music: Liu Yida. Lyrics: Zhou Yaohui), © PolyGram Records Ltd., Hong Kong, 1990. This song is also taken from *Madness*. The "Hong Kong People Save Hong Kong Campaign" began on June 18, 1989. This movement is a sequel to Hong Kong's involvement in the democracy movement in China. It is also a middle-class movement. The campaign organizers asked Hong Kong citizens to redirect their energies from China to the political future of Hong Kong. Between June and October 1989, the "Hong Kong People Save Hong Kong Campaign" organized rallies and petitions in Hong Kong, and visits to London to lobby for the right of abode in the United Kingdom. The British Nationality (Hong Kong) Act of 1990 came into effect on December 1, 1990. Under this Act, the Hong Kong Governor can recommend to the British government up to 50,000 heads of households in Hong Kong to be registered as British citizens.

57 "God save the Queen" is used as a title in another song in *Madness*.

58 "Farewell to England" (Music: Chen Guangrong. Lyrics: Liu Zhuohui), © Pacific Music Publishing Ltd., 1990. It is taken from the album *Chapter Two*. Cf. Appendix 1.

59 "Farewell Song" (Music & Lyrics: Cai Guoquan) © PolyGram Records Ltd., Hong Kong, 1990. It is taken from the album *Dreams on Stage*. Cf. Appendix 1.

60 Cf. Appendix 1. The reference material about *Dreams of Hong Kong*, provided by Radio Television Hong Kong, states that "(t)he International Bank of Asia contributed close to US $100,000 to this project as part of the bank's campaign to underline its confidence and long-term commitment in Hong Kong." The entire project also included a music competition, pop concerts, youth projects, school activities, and a television series.

61 Other albums include *Love of Hong Kong* and *Wish*. Cf. Appendix 1.

62 Quoted from reference materials provided by Radio Television Hong Kong.

63 Ibid.

64 Twenty local Taiwanese and Chinese singers were involved in the recording of *Dreams of Hong Kong*. "The Lights of the City," "Growing Up," and "Our Roots" were all recorded in the "We are the World/All for Freedom" format.

65 "The Lights of the City" (Music: Chris Babida. Lyrics: Zheng Guojiang), © Radio Television Hong Kong, 1990, was on the pop chart from May 27 to September 1, 1990. An English version of this song, translated as "We Love Hong Kong," was recorded in October 1990 to publicize the *Dreams of Hong Kong* project abroad.

Chapter 9

1 Carl Lumholtz, *Among Cannibals*. Canberra: Australian National University Press, 1980. p. 173.

2 T.G.H. Strehlow, *Songs of Central Australia*. Sydney: Angus and Robertson, 1971. p. 7.

3 Cited in Trevor Jones, "The Traditional Music of the Australian Aborigines," in Elizabeth May, Ed., *Music of Many Cultures: An Introduction*. Berkeley: University of California Press, 1962. p. 162.

4 Bruce Chatwin, *The Songlines*. London: Pan Books, 1988. p. 79.

5 Cath Ellis, *Aboriginal Music: Cross-Cultural Experience from South Australia*. Brisbane: University of Queensland Press, 1985. p. 17.

6 Ibid. p. 17.

7 Karl Marx, "The Origins of Art: Historical Development of the Artistic Sense," in Karl Marx and Fredrick Engels, *On Literature and Art*. Moscow: Progress Publishers, 1976. pp. 126-128.

8 Eric Willmot, "Australia: The Last Experiment." *St. Mark's Review*. December 1978. pp. 23-27.

9 Christina Spurgeon, "Challenging Technological Determinism: Aborigines, Aussat and Remote Australia," in Helen Wilson, Ed., *Australian Communications and the Public Sphere: Essays in Memory of Bill Bonney*. Melbourne: Macmillan, 1989. p. 30.

10 Ibid. p. 31; Mark Brolly, "Church Deplores 'Genocide' of Aborigines." *The Age*. February 5, 1991. p. 3.

11 Spurgeon, in Wilson, 1989. p. 30.

12 Guy Tustall, participating author in Marcus Breen, Ed., *Our Place, Our Music, Aboriginal Music: Australian Popular Music in Perspective,* Volume 2. Canberra: Aboriginal Studies Press, 1989. p. 7.

13 Chester Schultz, participating author in Breen, 1989. p. 15. The destruction of traditional cultures by Christian missionaries as part of a process of "culturation" and modernization is a familiar story to people who know the history of colonization. It has been seen in a pernicious form in recent years with the Christianization of Central and South American Indians by the fundamentalist Protestant interdenominational organization Wycliffe Bible Translators (Summer Institute of Linguistics).

14 Marcus Breen, "Fundamentalist Music: the Popular Impulse," in Marcus Breen, Ed., *Missing in Action: Australian Popular Music in Perspective,* Volume 1. Melbourne: Verbal Graphics, 1987. p. 14.

15 Schultz, in Breen, 1989. p. 15; Eric Watson, "Country Music: The Voice of Rural Australia," in Breen, 1987. pp. 48-77.

16 Schultz, in Breen, 1989. p. 25.

17 Doug Petherick, participating author in Breen, 1989. p. 29.

18 Dave Laing, "The Grain of Punk: An Analysis of the Lyrics," in Angela McRobbie, Ed., *Zoot Suits and Second Hand Dresses: An Anthology of Fashion and Music.* London: Macmillan, 1989. pp. 74-102.

19 Steve Warne, "Beyond the Echoes: A Look at Public Radio," in Breen, 1987. p. 170.

20 Tony Bennett, "The Political Rationality of the Museum." *Continuum,* Volume 3, No. 1. 1990. pp. 35-55.

21 Marcus Breen, "Writing Songs to Inspire a Brand New Day." *Sunday Herald.* September 10, 1989.

22 CAAMA Catalogue, 1990. A mix of Aboriginal media workers and trainees, assisted by two or three specialist Europeans (media lawyers and technical personnel) has always been the trademark of CAAMA from the early days to the present. Aboriginal members through the CAAMA Board have ultimate control over the station and its affiliates.

23 Marcus Breen, "Desert Rhythms Fulfill an Aborignal Dream." *The Herald.* August 9, 1988.

24 Ibid.

25 Liora Salter, "Two Directions on a One Way Street: Old and New Approaches in Media Analysis in Two Decades." *Studies in Communication,* No. 1. 1980. pp. 85-117.

26 Sam Paltridge, "Australian Remote Television Services." Centre for International Research on Communication and Information Technologies, Policy Research Paper, No. 8. October 1990.

27 Spurgeon, in Wilson, 1989. p. 28.

28 Ibid.

29 Louise Bellamy, "Black and White TV from the Heart." *The Age.* October 22, 1987.

30 Eric Michaels, *Aboriginal Invention of Television in Central Australia 1982-1986.* Canberra: Aboriginal Studies Press, 1986.

31 Tim Rowse, "Review of Aboriginal Invention of Television in Central Australia 1982-86." *Oceania,* Volume 57, No. 4. June 1987. pp. 316-317.

32 Spurgeon, in Wilson, 1989. p. 43.

33 *Communication Update,* 21. Communication Law Centre, Sydney. 1987.

34 Department of Transport and Communication. Press Release. September 28, 1990.

35 Breen, "Writing Songs to Inspire a Brand New Day." 1989.

36 Helen Molnar, "The Broadcasting for Remote Areas Community Scheme: Small vs Big Media." *Media Information Australia,* No 58. November 1990. pp. 147-154.

37 Ibid.

38 Marcus Breen, "Black Gold." *Sunday Herald.* November 25, 1990.

Chapter 10

1 Haunai-Kay Trask, "Interview," *Honolulu Star-Bulletin.* November 7, 1982. p. C-9. Arthur Godfrey was well-known for his 1930-1940s radio shows that featured artificial, tourist-oriented "Hawaiian" music and his own ukelele playing.

2 Debbie Maxell, "Hawaiian Awakening." Caleb Music, 1976. Translated from the Hawaiian, as are several other lyrics of the "new" Hawaiian music that are quoted in this essay.

3 Ethel Damon, *Sanford Ballard Dole and His Hawaii.* Palo Alto, CA: Pacific Books, 1957. p. 317.

4 Samuel Elbert and Noelani Mahoe, *Na Mele o Hawai'i Nei.* Honolulu: University of Hawaii Press, 1970. p. 63.

5 Ibid. p. 72.

6 George Awai, "Interview," *Ha 'Ilono Mele,* Volume 3, No. 8. 1977. pp. 5-6.

7 Harry Owens, "Princess Poo-Poo-Ly," Royal Music Publishers, 1935.

8 Harry Owens, *Sweet Leilani.* Pacific Palisades, CA: Hula House, 1970.

9 De Soto Brown, *Hawaii Recalls: Selling Romance to America.* Honolulu: Editions Limited, 1982. p. 96.

10 Ibid. p. 99.

11 Interestingly, Crosby felt that "Sweet Leilani" (named for Harry Owens' little daughter) was the *only* authentic song in the film. Crosby had met Owens while on vacation in Hawaii and had learned the song from him. When he came back to Hollywood to do *Waikiki Wedding,* all the songs had been written by mainland composers and were ready for him to sing. He insisted on inserting "Sweet Leilani" and was at first turned down. Only by threatening to walk out on the production did he force the producer to include Owens' song.

12 Charles E.K. Davis, "Interview," in Robert Kamohalu and Burt Burlingame, Eds., *Da Kine Sound.* Honolulu: Press Pacifica, 1978. p. 93.

13 Don Ho, "Interview." *Honolulu,* Volume 15, No. 9. 1982. p. 50.

14 Krash Kealoha, "Krash Kealoha Tells Why He Left KCCN." *Ha 'Ilono Mele,* Volume 7, No. 4. 1981. pp. 1, 6-8.

15 Ibid. p. 7.

16 Gabby Pahinui, "Interview," in Robert Kamohalu and Burt Burlingame, 1978. p. 21.

17 Peter Moon, "Moon Bridges Gap." *Ha 'Ilono Mele,* Volume 3, No. 2. 1977. p. 7.

18 Jerry Hopkins, "Slack Key and Other Notes." *Hawaii Observer,* No. 123. 1978. p. 22.

19 Peter Moon, "Interview." *Ha 'Ilono Mele,* Volume 3, No. 3. 1977. p. 2.

20 George Helm, "Language-Pain Revolution." *Ha 'Ilono Mel,* Volume 2, No. 6. 1976. p. 3.

21 Walter Ritte, "Interview," *Honolulu,* Volume 15, 1982. p. 68.

22 Jerry Santos, "Olomana Interview," *Da Kine Sound.* Honolulu: Press Pacifica, 1978. p. 47.

23 Palani Vaughn, "Interview," *Honolulu,* Volume 12, 1979. p. 149.

24 'Ilimia Pi'ianai'a, "Liner Notes," on *Music of George Helm.* Honolulu: Gold Coin Records # G.C. 1001.

25 Hopkins, 1978. p. 21.

26 George Kanahele, "Hawaiian Renaissance Grips, Changes Island History." *Ha 'Ilono Mele,* Volume 5, No. 7. 1979. pp. 3-4.

27 George H. Lewis, "Beyond The Reef: Role Conflict and the Professional Musician in Hawaii," *Popular Music 5.* Cambridge: University Press 1985. pp. 189-198.

28 Pahinui, 1978. p. 21.

29 Peter Moon, "Interview," in Kamohalu and Burlingame, 1978. p. 22.

30 Ibid. p. 42. Moon knew what he was talking about in 1978. In 1982, he experimented with reggae rhythms on songs like "Guava Jelly," and by 1991, the Hawaiian/Reggae sound had become the "new hot thing" on the Hawaiian pop charts.

31 Peter Moon, *Chinatown.* Kanikapila Record #KC 1003, 1986.

Chapter 11

1 Antonio Gramsci, *Selections from Prison Notebooks.* London: Lawrence and Wisehart, 1971.

2 Hans Magnus Ensenburger, *The Consciousness Industry.* New York: Seabury Press, 1974.

3 C.W.E. Bigsby, Ed., *The Politics of Popular Culture.* London: Edward Arnold, 1976.

4 James Carey, "A Cultural Approach to Communication." *Communication,* 2. 1975. pp. 1-22.

5 Raymond Williams, "On High and Popular Culture." *The New Republic.* November 23, 1974. p. 15.

6 Ibid.

7 James Lull, Ed., *Popular Music and Education.* Beverly Hills: Sage Publications, 1987.

8 D. Marks, "Pop and Folk as a Going Concern for Sociological Research." *International Review of the Aesthetics and Sociology of Music,* 14. 1983. pp. 93-98.

9 Paul Rutten, "Youth and Music in the Netherlands." Paper presented at the International Association for Mass Communications Research, Prague, 1984.

10 Roger Wallis and Krister Malm, *Big Sounds from Small Peoples: The Music Industry in Small Countries*. London: Constable, 1984.

11 David Coplan, "The Urbanization of African Music: Some Theoretical Observations," in Richard Middleton and David Horn, Eds., *Popular Music 2*. Cambridge: Cambridge University Press, 1982. Also by Coplan on South Africa is *In Township Tonight*. South Africa: Ravan Press, 1985.

12 E.J. Collins, *Music Makers of West Africa*. Washington, DC: Three Continents Press, 1985.

13 T.O. Ranger, *Dance and Society in East Africa*. Heinemann Educational Books, 1975. pp. 116-117.

14 J.H.K. Nketia, "Observations on the Study of Popular Music in Africa." Paper presented at the Conference of the International Association for the Study of Popular Music (IASPM), Accra, Ghana, August 1987. p. 12.

15 A term used by Raymond Williams in *Marxism and Literature*. Oxford University Press, 1977; and also by Angelika and Charles Keil in "In Search of Polka Happiness," *Cultural Correspondence*, 14. 1977.

16 John Szwed, "Afro-American Musical Adaptation," in N. E. Whitten Jr. and J. Szwed, Eds., *American Anthropology: Contemporary Perspectives*. New York: Free Press, 1970. pp. 219-228: 226.

17 E.J. Collins, "The Man Who Made Traditional Music." *West Africa Magazine*. London, December 19-26, 1983. p. 2946.

18 Leonard Lynn. *The Growth of Entertainment of Non-African Origin in Lagos from 1860-1920*. Masters Thesis. University of Ibadan, 1967.

19 E.J. Collins and Paul Richards, "Popular Music in West Africa: Suggestions for an Interpretive Framework," in Simon Frith, Ed., *World Music, Politics and Social Change*. New York: University of Manchester Press, 1989. pp. 12-46.

20 M.J.C. Echeruo, "Concert and Theatre in Late 19th Century Lagos, Nigeria." *Magazine* (Lagos). September 1972. pp. 68-74.

21 P.D. Cole. *Modern and Traditional Elites in the Politics of Lagos* and *Modern and Traditional Elites in Late 19th Century Lagos*. Cambridge: Cambridge University Press, 1975.

22 J.S. Coleman, *Nigeria: Background to Nationalism*. Berkeley: University of California Press, 1960.

23 Coplan, 1985. p. 235.

24 Christopher Waterman, *Juju: The Historical Development, Socio-Economic Organization and Communicative Function of a West African Popular Music*. Ph.D. Thesis. University of Illinois, 1986. p. 72.

25 Phillip Donne, "Music forms in Tanzania and their Socio-Economic Base." *Jipemoyo,* No. 3, and *Transactions of the Finnish Anthropological Society,* No. 9. 1980. pp. 88-97.

26 From a UNESCO report, "Cultural Policy in the Revolutionary People's Republic Guinea," published by the Guinea Ministry of Education and Culture, 1979. pp. 80-83.

27 Graham Ewen, *Luamba Franco and Thirty Years of O.K. Jazz.* London: Off the Record Press, 1986. p. 45.

28 E.J. Collins, *E.T. Mensah, The King of Highlife.* London: Off the Record Press, 1986. p. 45.

29 Flemming, Harrev, "Goumbe and the Development of Krio Popular Music in Freetown, Sierra Leone." Paper presented at the Fourth International conference of IASPM, Accra, Ghana, August 1987.

30 A.A. Mensah, "Jazz, the Round Trip." *Jazzforschung,* Volume 3, No. 4. 1971. p. 2.

31 This is mentioned by both David Coplan (1985) and Veit Erlmann, "A Feeling of Prejudice: Orpheus McAdoo and the Virginia Jubilee Singers in South Africa 1890-1898." *Journal of Southern African Studies,* Volume 14, No. 3. April 1988. pp. 331-350.

32 E.J. Collins, "Jazz Feedback to Africa." *American Music,* Volume 5, No. 2. Summer 1987.

33 Gerhard Kubick, "Neo-Traditional Popular Music in East Africa since 1945," in Richard Middleton and David Horn, Eds., *Popular Music.* Cambridge: Cambridge University Press, 1981. p. 86.

34 Afolabi Alajo-Brown, *Juju Music: A Study of its Social History and Styles.* Pittsburgh: Pittsburgh University Press, 1985.

35 Waterman, 1986.

36 Coplan, 1982. p. 123.

37 Coplan, 1985. pp. 42, 79.

38 A.A. Mensah, "Highlife." Unpublished manuscript.

39 Waterman, 1986.

40 Coplan, 1982 and 1987.

41 The idea of cultural analogues occurs in several writings: in Alan P. Merriam's "The Use of Music in the Study of the Problem of Acculturation." *American Anthroplogist,* No. 57. 1955. pp. 28-54; in Richard A. Waterman's "African Influences in the Music of the Americas," in Sol Tax, Ed., *Acculturation in the Americas.* Chicago: University of Chicago Press, 1952; and in Waterman, 1986. p. 28.

42 Theodor Newcomer, "An Approach to the Study of the Communicative Act." *Psychological Review,* No. 60. 1953. pp. 393-404.

43 Luke Uche, "Imperialism Revisited." *The Media Education Journal*, No. 6. 1987. pp. 30-33.

44 Coplan, 1985. p. 3.

45 Melville J. Herskovitz, *The Anthropology of the American Negro*. New York: Columbia University Press, 1930.

46 Rudi Blesh, *African Retentions in Jazz*. New York: Cassell Publications, 1949.

47 Waterman, 1952.

48 LeRoi Jones (Amiri Baraka), *Blues People: Negro Music in White America*. New York: William Morrow, 1963.

49 Paul Oliver, *The Savannah Syncopators*. London: Vista Publications, 1970.

50 John Storm Roberts, *Black Music of Two Worlds*. New York: William Morrow, 1974. p. 245.

51 J.H.K. Nketia, *Folk Songs of Ghana*. Accra: Ghana University Press, 1973. p. 66.

52 K. Little, *The Mende of Sierra Leone*. London: Routledge and Kegan Paul, 1987.

53 John Blacking, "The Value of Music in Human Experience." *The Yearbook of the International Folk Music Council*, No. 1. 1969. pp. 33-71.

54 Grace Sims, "Inversion in Black Communication," in T. Kochman, Ed., *Rappin' and Stylin' Out*. University of Illinois Press, 1972. p. 152-159.

55 Keith Warner, *The Trinidad Calypso*. London: Heinemann Educational Books, 1982. p. 13.

56 Ranger, 1975. p. 166.

57 K. Little, *West African Urbanisation, a Study of Voluntary Associations in Social Change*. Cambridge: Cambridge University Press, 1970.

58 N. Sithole, *African Nationalism*. Oxford: Oxford University Press, 1970.

59 Collins, 1986. p. 6.

60 E.J. Collins, "Comic Opera in Ghana." *African Arts*, Volume 9, No. 2. January 1976. pp. 50-57.

61 Ebun Clark and Herbert Ogunde, *The Making of Nigerian Theatre*. Oxford: Oxford University Press, 1979.

62 Fred Zindi, *Roots Rocking in Zimbabwe*. Harare: Mambo Press, 1985.

63 Waterman, 1986. p. 4.

64 Roberts, 1974. p. 254.

65 Ranger, 1975. p. 3.

66 Ibid. p. 113.

67 Collins, 1986. p. 6.

68 Sjaak Van der Geest and Nimrod Asante-Darko, "The Political Meaning of Highlife Songs in Ghana." *African Studies Review,* Volume 5, No. 1. 1982.

69 Roland Barthes, *Elements of Semiology.* London: Jonathon Cape, 1967.

70 Stuart Hall, "The Rediscovery of Ideology: Return of the Repressed in Media Studies," in M. Gurevitch, et al., Eds., *Culture, Society and Media.* London: Methuen, 1982.

71 Collins, 1986. p. 6.

72 W. Banton, *West African City: A Study of Tribal Life in Freetown.* Oxford: University Press, 1957.

73 Collins, 1983. p. 2946.

74 Mosumola Omibiyi-Obidike, "Women in Popular Music in Africa." Paper presented at the Fourth International Conference of IASPM, Accra, Ghana, August 1987. p. 7.

75 Collins, 1987. p. 7.

76 Sjaak Van der Geest and Nimrod Asante-Darko, "Men and Women in Ghanaian Highlife Songs," in Christine Oppong, Ed., *Female and Male in West Africa.* London: George Allen and Unwin, 1983. pp. 242-255.

77 Collins, 1985.

Chapter 12

1 This study is based in part on information collected during a visit to Johannesburg financed by le Programme Quadriennal de Recherche sur l'Afrique Australe de la Maison des Sciences de l'Homme d'Aquitaine, in conjunction with le Groupe Afrique Australe du Centre d'Études d'Afrique Noire de l'Institut d'Études Politiques de Bordeaux.

2 Muslim name used since 1969 by pianist, composer, and bandleader Dollar Brand.

3 Interview, Johannesburg. December 14, 1990.

4 For example, the series of volumes edited by Bailey's African Photo Archives Productions; the reproduction of *Drum* articles in Michael Chapman, Ed., *The Drum Decade: Stories from the 1950s.* Pietermaritzburg: University of Natal Press, 1989; or Jurgen Schadeberg's documentary, *Have You Seen Drum Recently?* produced by Claudia Schadeberg for Bailey's African Photo Archives, 1988.

5 Stan Motjuwadi, "Lest We Forget," in Jurgen Schadeberg, Ed., *The Fifties People of South Africa, Black Life: Politics, Jazz, Sport.* Johannesburg: Bailey's African Photo Archives Production, 1987. pp. 5-6.

6 B. Modisane, cited in Deborah Hart, Gordon H. Pirie, "The Sight and Soul of Sophiatown." *The Geographical Review,* Volume 74, No. 1. January 1984. p. 42.

7 Shamil Jeppie and Crain Soudien, Eds., *The Struggle for District Six, Past and Present.* Le Cap: Buchu Books, 1990. p. 13.

8 Hugh Masekela, Miriam Makeba, Letta Mbulu, Abdullah Ibrahim, Chris McGregor, Johnny Dyani, Louis Moholo, Dudu Pukwana, Ronnie Beer, Jonas Gwangwa, Makaya Ntshoko, Mongezi Feza, Ernest Mothle, Harry Miller, and Gwigwi Mwrebi, to name but a few.

9 See Deborah James, "Musical Form and Social History: Research Perspectives in Black South African Music." *Radical History Review,* Volume 46, No. 7. 1990. pp. 309-319; and David Coplan, "The African Musician and the Development of the Johannesburg Entertainment Industry, 1900-1960." *Journal of Southern African Studies,* Volume 5, No. 2. April 1979. pp. 135-164.

10 See Muff Andersson, *Music in the Mix, The Story of South African Popular Music.* Johannesburg: Ravan Press, 1981, especially pp. 80, 85, and those following.

11 Conversation with Sipho "Hotstix" Mabuse, Johannesburg. December 14, 1990. See also "A Great Year for SA Music." *Pace.* December/January 1986, where Ray Phiri explained: "We hated ourselves and even looked down on our culture. We tried hard to be duplicates of overseas artists, and in the process, local music lovers despised us. They did not want to identify with people who hated themselves so much that it was coming through in their music." p. 32.

12 "Soleil de Soweto," interview with Rashid Vally conducted by Denis Constant. *Jazz Magazine,* (Paris) 320. July/August 1983. pp. 55, 74.

13 Dollar Brand/Abdullah Ibrahim, *Mannenberg.* The Sun (SA) SRK 786134, 1974.

14 Harari, *Rufaro, Happiness.* Fiesta (F) 360 095, 1976.

15 Johnny Clegg, *Dance and Society in Africa South of the Sahara,* unpublished Master's Thesis. University of Witwatersrand, 1977.

16 Philippe Conrath, *Johnny Clegg: La Passion Zoulou.* Paris: Seghers, 1988.

17 Interview with Victor Ntoni, Johannesburg. December 13, 1990.

18 Paul Simon, *Graceland.* Warner Bros (F) 925 447-4, 1986.

19 See Denis-Constant Martin, *Aux Sources du Reggae: Musique Société et Politique en Jamaïque.* Marseille: Parenthèses, 1986.

20 See Joe Khumalo, "The Rise and Rise of Reggae." *Pace.* December/January 1991. pp. 22-27.

21 Listen particularly and view the accompanying video to: Lucky Dube, "Prisoner," *Captured Live.* (SA) DC 6, 1990.

22 Cited in Andersson. 1981. p. 13.

23 Compare, for example, Brenda and the Big Dudes, *Week End Special.* CCP (SA) FLY (V) 4, 1983, with Brenda Fassie, *Black President.* CCP (SA) L4 BREN (V), 4064854, 1990.

24 Chicco, *Papa Stop the War.* Dephon (SA) MCRBL 175, 1990.

25 Fassie, 1990.

26 Yvonne Chaka Chaka, *Be Proud to Be an African.* Dephon (SA) MCRBL 170, 1990.

27 Pure Magic, *Bhay' Lam'*. Flame (SA) (V) 406 601, nd. (c. 1990)

28 Barney Rachabane, *Barney's Way*. Jive (SA) HIP (V) 9001, 1989; Jonas Gwangwa, *Flowers of the Nation*. The Sun (SA) AI 7864, 1990.

29 Sakhile, *Phambili*. The Sun (SA) ZAE 7861, 1989.

30 Ratau Mike Makhalamele, *Thabang*. Tusk (SA) ZTUC 5, 1990.

31 Sankomata, *The Writing is on the Wall*. L4 Flame (SA) (EV) 4064634, 1989.

32 Tananas, *Tananas,* Celluloid (F) 66862-2, nd. (c.1989).

33 *Iscathamiya, Zulu Worker Choirs in South Africa*. Heritage (UK) HT 313, 1986.

34 For example, Ohisson's Lager beer presents, in the foreground, a young "whitish" man, and in a blurred background, a "black," commenting: "I have seen the future, and it's wearing a blue label" (like that on the bottle), with the caption "The beer for a new generation." Among others, *Drum,* December 1990/January 1991. p. 23.

35 See "Quels sont les Sens des Sons? Clefs pour L'Analyse," in Didier Levallet and Denis-Constant Martin, *L'Amérique de Mingus, Musique et Politique: Les "Fables of Faubus" de Charles Mingus*. Paris: P.O.L., 1991. pp. 57-96.

36 Sipho "Hotstix" Mabuse, *Burn Out*. Gallo (SA) HUC 509, 1984.

37 Sipho "Hotstix" Mabuse, *Chant of the Marching*. Gallo (SA) HUL 40185, 1989.

38 Ray Phiri and Stimela, *The Unfinished Story*. Celluloid (F) 66850-2, 1988.

39 *Top 40,* December 1990/January 1991. p. 9.

40 *Weekly Mail*. November 9, 1990.

41 Marcalex, *Boys B Boys*. Tusk (SA) A TUC (FC) 9, 1990.

42 P. J. Powers (Thandeka), *Back Again*. FMC V1035, 1990.

43 Bright Blue, *The Rising Tide*. EMI (SA) L4 EMCJ (N) 406 3774, 1988.

44 Amply discussed by Andersson, 1981.

45 See David Coplan, *In Township Tonight!: South Africa's Black City Music and Theatre*. London: Longman, 1985.

46 See Denis-Constant Martin, "Le Triolet Multicolore, dans la Musique Sud Africaine, une Blanche N'Égale pas Nécessairement Deux Noires." *Politiques Africaine,* 25. March 1987. pp. 74-81.

Chapter 13

1 Tilman Evers, "Identidad: la Faz Oculta de los Nuevos Movimientos Sociales." *Punto de Vista,* No. 25. 1985. p. 34.

2 Alberto Melucci, "L'azione Ribelle: Formazione e Struttura dei Movimenti Sociali," *Movimenti di Rivolta*. Milan: Etas Libri, 1976. p. 57.

3 Ricardo, 31, bank employee, author's interview, 1984.

4 Norbert Lechner, "Especificando la Política." *Crítica y Utopía*. No. 8, 1982. p. 47.

5 Concert report, *Expreso Imaginario*. August 1976.

6 Carlos, 30, office worker, author's interview, 1984.

7 Oscar Landi, "Cultura y Política en la Transición a la Democracia en Argentina." *Crítica y Utopía*, Nos. 10/11. 1983. p. 81.

8 Liliana, *Expreso Imaginario*, Letters Page. November 1976.

9 Laura, *Expreso Imaginario*, Letters Page. September 1977.

10 Juan, *Expreso Imaginario*, Letters Page. August 1977.

11 Mariana, *Expreso Imaginario*, Letters Page. July 1977.

12 Jorge, *Expreso Imaginario*, Letters Page. July 1977. Jorge's letter was followed by an editor's note: "The flood of letters congratulating Sandra on her letter is staggering." A couple of months later Sandra Russo became part of the *Expreso Imaginario* staff, inaugurating a path followed by some other *Expreso Imaginario* fans: from readers to writers.

13 Carlos, 30, employee, author's interview, 1984.

14 Silvia, *Expreso Imaginario*, Letters Page. February 1978. A note from the editors followed Silvia's letter: "All the musicians (and we ourselves) are passing through a strange period of confusion."

15 Freddy, *Expreso Imaginario*, Letters Page. November 1977.

16 Guillermo, *Expreso Imaginario*, Letters Page. April 1978.

17 Ernesto, *Expreso Imaginario*, Letters Page. April 1979.

18 Ralph Rothschild, *Mordisco—Expreso Imaginario's* rock music *separata*. July 1979.

19 Almendra, *Mordisco*. September 1979.

20 Ralph Rothschild, *Mordisco*. January 1980.

21 Lechner, 1982. p. 47.

22 Andrés Fontana, *Fuerzas Armadas, Partidos Políticos y Transición a la Democracia en Argentina*. Buenos Aires: CEDES, 1984. p. 23.

23 Interview with Charly García, *Expreso Imaginario*. December 1981.

24 Landi, 1983. p. 82.

25 Fontana, 1984. pp. 30-31

26 Oscar, 24, day laborer, author's interview. 1984.

27 Roberto's interview quoted in Pitman and Gerber, Label and Piccolini, "¿Por qué los Adolescentes Invierten su Tiempo Libre en el Rock Nacional?" Buenos Aires, UNBA, *mimeo*, 1983. p.6.

28 Luis Alberto Spinetta, leader of Almendra, *Pan Caliente, Expreso Imaginario's* succesor. June 1982

29 Carlos, 19, student, author's interview. 1984.

30 Rodolfo, *Expreso Imaginario,* Letters Page. October 1977.

31 Roberto's statement in Pitman, et al., 1983. p. 4

32 Carlos, 19, student; Augusto, 17, student; author's interviews. 1984.

33 Miguel Cantilo, leader of the group Pedro y Pablo and author of the song "Illegal Opression" quoted above, *Primera Plana.* April 1983.

34 Charly García, *Clarín.* March 6, 1983.

35 Andrés Calamaro, keyboard player, *La Razón.* December 16, 1984.

36 Ruben's interview in Pitman, et al., 1983. p. 5.

37 Federico, *Humor.* 1984.

38 Jorge, 22, military cadet, author's interview. 1984.

39 Luis Alberto Spinetta, *Expreso Imaginario.* August 1980.

40 Jorge, 22, military cadet, author's interview. 1984.

41 Pablo, 22, student, quoted in Pitman, et al., 1983. p.6.

Chapter 14

1 Bernice Reagon, "Songs That Moved the Movement." *Civil Rights Quarterly.* Summer 1983.

2 Nelson George, *The Death of Rhythm & Blues.* New York: Pantheon Books, 1988. p. 69.

3 Peter Guaralnick, *Sweet Soul Music.* New York: Harper and Row, 1986. p. 50.

4 *Billboard.* December 22, 1956. p. 10.

5 Chuck Berry interviewed in the Taylor Hackford documentary, *Hail! Hail! Rock 'n' Roll.* 1987.

6 George, 1988. p. 85.

7 Ibid. p. 86.

8 *Rolling Stone.* January 20, 1968. p. 15.

9 Guaralnick, 1986. p. 332.

10 Ibid. p. 345.

11 Robert Palmer, "James Brown," in Jim Miller, Ed., *The Rolling Stone Illustrated History of Rock '& Roll.* New York: Rolling Stone Press, 1976. p. 136.

12 George, 1988. p. 98.

13 *Billboard.* November 20, 1971. p. 103.

14 George, 1988. p. 145.

15 Guaralnick, 1986. p. 20.

Chapter 15

1 Arlene Stein, "Androgyny Goes Pop: But Is It Lesbian Music?" *Out/Look*. Spring 1991. p. 31.

2 Gaye Tuchman, A.K. Daniels, J. Benet, *Hearth and Home: Images of Women in the Mass Media*. New York: Oxford University Press, 1978.

3 Toni Armstrong, Jr., "An Endangered Species: Women's Music By, For, and About Women," *Hot Wire: The Journal of Women's Music and Culture*, 5. September 1989. p. 17. See also Cynthia M. Lont, *Between Rock and a Hard Place: Subcultural Persistence and Women's Music*, Ph.D. Thesis. University of Iowa, 1984.

4 Steve Chapple and Reebee Garofalo, *Rock and Roll is Here to Pay: The History and Politics of the Music Industry*. Chicago: Nelson Hall, 1980.

5 Laura Post, "The Institute for the Musical Arts." *Hot Wire: Journal of Women's Music and Culture*, 5. September 1989. p. 47.

6 Maxine Feldman, "Angry Athis." Athis Music Publishers BMF, 1969, 1972. Used with permission.

7 Alix Dobkin, *Lavender Jane Loves Women*. Project 1, 1975. Insert.

8 Laura Post, "Olivia Record Artist Profiles." *Hot Wire: Journal of Women's Music and Culture*, 4. July 1988. p. 32.

9 Maida Tilchen, "Lesbians and Women's Music," in Trudy Darty and Sandee Potter, *Women-Identified-Women*. Palo Alto, CA: Mayfield Publishers, 1984. pp. 287-303.

10 Maida Tilchen, "Women's Music: Politics for Sale?" *Gay Community News*. June Supplement 1982. p. 2.

11 Jorjet Harper and Toni Armstrong, Jr., "Meg Departs." *Hot Wire: Journal of Women's Music and Culture*, 5. January 1989. p. 21.

12 Stein, Spring 1991. p. 29.

13 Toni Armstrong, Jr. "Welcome Back Margie Adam." *Hot Wire: Journal of Women's Music and Culture*. January 1992. p. 2.

14 Ibid.

15 Sheila Rene, "No Madonnas: Olivia Records, the Premiere Women's Music Label, Celebrates 15 years in the Trenches." *Indie Special*. 1989. p. 53.

16 Holly Near, *Speed of Light*. Redwood Records, 1982.

17 Susanna J. Sturgis, "Ladyslipper: Meeting the Challenges of Feminist Business." *Hot Wire: Journal of Women's Music and Culture*. May 1985. p. 38.

18 Susan Wilson, "Women's Music: Then and Now." *The Boston Sunday Globe*. March 9, 1986. p. 68.

19 Susan Wilson, "Talkin' 'bout Revolution For Women in Pop?" *The Boston Sunday Globe*. November 20, 1988. p. 101.

20 Sandy Carter, "Redwood Records: Slippin and Sliding." *Z Magazine*. May 1989. p. 65.

21 Noelle Hanrahan, "A New Wave of Women on Vinyl." *Coming Up!* August 1988. p. 45.

22 Scott Alarik, "Does Women's Music Have Any Place Left To Go?" *The Boston Sunday Globe*. November 12, 1989. p. B7.

23 Carter, *Z Magazine,* 1989. p. 64.

24 Wilson, 1988. p. 96.

25 Hanrahan, 1988. p. 45.

26 Confabulation, "Hi, Phranc. This is Alix Calling." *Hot Wire: The Journal of Women's Music and Culture.* January 1990. p. 17.

27 Stein, 1991. p. 31.

28 Larry Kelp, "Getting in Tune with the Times." *The Tribune Calendar.* July 9, 1989. p. 24.

29 Rachel Pepper, "The Winning Duo...er...Threesome." *Outweek.* September 19, 1990. p. 39.

30 Confabulation, 1990. p. 17.

31 Stein, 1991. p. 32.

32 Confabulation, 1990. p. 16-17.

33 Carter, *Z Magazine.* 1989. p. 64.

34 Carter, *Z Magazine.* 1989. p. 65.

35 Alarik, 1989. p. B7.

Chapter 16

1 An earlier version of this chapter was first presented at the annual conference of the International Association for the Study of Popular Music (IASPM) in May 1990. I am grateful to the members of this organization who offered me very generous feedback (especially Herman Gray, who first encouraged me to present this paper, Reebee Garofalo, Portia Maultsby, Venise Berry, and Rosalinda Fregoso) and to the Feminist Research and Action Group at UC Santa Cruz (FRA) for their financial support.

2 This special section in "The Arts" is actually composed of two essays. The first, "The Rap Attitude" begins with the following subheading in bold print: "A new musical culture, filled with self-assertion and anger, has come boiling up from the streets. Some people think it should have stayed there." The essay which follows is called "Decoding Rap Music," and it begins with a clear indicator of who

Newsweek believes its audience to be: "Feeling out of it 'cause you're not into it?...Sooner or later you're just going to have to deal with it. The guys with the names you don't understand—what is a Tone-Loc, anyway?" The collective title for both essays is "Rap's Mixed Message: Rage and Responsibility." *Newsweek*, March 19, 1990. pp. 56-63.

3 The history of the FBI's infiltration into the Black Panther Party has been heavily documented. See, for example, Ward Churchill and Jim Vander Wall, *Agents of Repression: The FBI's Secret War Against the Black Panther Party and the American Indian Movement*. Boston: South End Press, 1988; and Clayborne Carson. *In Struggle: SNCC and the Black Awakening of the 1960s*. Cambridge: Harvard University Press, 1981.

4 For a more detailed elaboration of these traditions see David Toop, *The Rap Attack: African Jive to New York Hip Hop*. London: Pluto Press, 1984.

5 "The Message." Sugarhill Records, 1982.

6 Steven Hager, *Hip Hop: The Illustrated History of Break Dancing, Rap Music and Graffitti*. New York: St. Martin's Press, 1984. p. 10.

7 The term "boy men" is used by Toni Cade Bambara in her novel, *The Salt Eaters*. New York: Random House, 1980. For a further discussion of this point, see Cynthia Enloe, *Bananas, Beaches & Bases: Making Feminist Sense of International Politics*. Berkeley: University of California Press, 1990. Chapter 3, "Nationalism and Masculinity," is particularly useful.

8 See Haki Madhubuti, *Enemies: The Clash of Races*. Chicago: Third World Press, 1990 (originally published in 1978). pp. 147-48.

9 Manning Marable has implicitly called for a dialogue between those engaged in critical Marxist theories and those who highlight systems of oppression rooted in racial hierarchies. He notes that "The majority of white American Marxists are hostile, if not downright antagonistic, toward black nationalists, movements, theorists, and organizations. On the other side of the color line, black activists who view themselves as both socialists and nationalists reciprocate the feeling of distrust." From "The Third Reconstruction: Black Nationalism and Race Relations After the Revolution." *Black Praxis I*. Dayton: Black Research Associates, 1980. p. 6. Revolutionary theorist Cornel West has also sought, quite effectively, to heal the split between those who utilize various materialist analyses of history and those who rely on theories involving the racial dynamics of oppression. See, for example, his "Marxist Theory and the Specificity of Afro-American Oppression," in Lawrence Grossberg and Cary Nelson, Eds., *Marxism and the Interpretation of Culture*. Urbana: University of Illinois Press, 1988. pp. 17-29.

10 Cedric Robinson, *Black Marxism*. London: Zed Books, 1983. p. 78.

11 Greg Tate, "Cult-Nats Meet Freaky-Dede: The Return of the Black Aesthetic." *Village Voice Literary Supplement*. December 1986. Emphasis in original.

12 The Black Rock Coalition (BRC) is an organization which formed in response to the historical theft and appropriation of black music and which attempts "to give voice and spiritual refuge to those musicians of color who feel isolated and

ostracized by club owners, record labels and radio because they want to create in other genres than the established bantustans of funk, R&B and pop jazz." Tom Terrell, "Rock Beat of a Different Colour." *Emerge Magazine.* January 1991. pp. 51-53. The B.R.C. is interesting in its simultaneous demands for both (economic) inclusion and (cultural) autonomy. It represents what sociologist John Brown Childs calls a "third possibility," which goes beyond simplistic integrationist/segregationist dichotomies; see his "National Identity and Racial/Ethnic Diversity: Toward Conflict or Cooperation," Project Concept Paper. University of California, Santa Cruz. November 1990.

13 Trey Ellis, "The New Black Aesthetic." *Callaloo,* Volume 12, No. 1. Winter 1989. pp. 233-43.

14 Dick Hebdige, *Cut 'N' Mix: Culture, Identity and Caribbean Music.* New York: Methuen, 1987. p. 158.

15 Ibid. p. 159.

16 Benedict Anderson, *Imagined Communities.* London: Verso, 1983.

17 Nelson George, Ed., *Stop the Violence: Overcoming Self-Destruction: Rap Speaks Out.* New York: National Urban League, 1990. p. 19.

18 Nelson George describes the nature of this empire and the decidedly nationalist stance of its owner in "Forty Acres and an Empire: Spike Lee Plants the New Motown in Brooklyn." *Village Voice.* August 7, 1990. p. 61.

19 It is both ironic and distressing that members of the musical group, Living Colour (also co-founders of the Black Rock Coalition, a group with inherently nationalist assumptions) have recently been engaged in litigation with Wayans about his unauthorized use of their name. See *Jet Magazine.* May 28, 1990. p. 37.

20 Allison Samuels, "This Time, It Isn't About Jokes." *Los Angeles Times,* Calendar Section. September 1990.

21 Erik Davis, "New Music Seminar: Wireheads and Cybergunk." *Village Voice.* August 8, 1989. pp. 67-73.

22 *Emerge Magazine* reported that black-owned businesses increased by 38 percent between 1982 and 1987, while the total number of U.S. businesses grew by only 14 percent. *Emerge* also reported an increase in African-American consumer support for these businesses during that same period. February 1991. p. 31.

23 Dominique DiPrima, "Beat the Rap." *Mother Jones,* Volume 15, No. 6. September/October 1990. p. 32.

Chapter 17

1 Octavio Paz, *The Labyrinthe of Solitude.* New York: Grove Press, 1961. p. 13

2 Walter Benjamin, *Illuminations.* New York: Harcourt, Brace, and World, 1968. p. 255

3 Marshall Berman, All That Is Solid Melts Into Air. New York: Simon and Schuster, 1982.

4 Paz, 1961. p. 13.

5 The term *bricolage* is from Claude Levi-Strauss, who uses it to propose a universal description of innate human characteristics, but, is used here simply as a description of cultural amalgamation processes.

6 Berman, 1982. p. 15.

7 Antonio Gramsci, *Selections From the Prison Notebooks*. New York: International Publishers, 1971.

8 Eshref Shevky and Marilyn Williams, *The Social Areas of Los Angeles*. Berkeley: University of California Press, 1949; Ricardo Romo, *East Los Angeles*. Austin: University of Texas Press, 1983. Romo also reveals some long standing ethnic interaction between blacks and Chicanos.

9 Home Owners Loan Corporation City Survey Files. Los Angeles, 1939. National Archives, Washington, DC. p. 7.

10 Ibid. Area D-53.

11 Gilbert G. Gonzales, "Factors Relating to Property Ownership of Chicanos in Lincoln Heights, Los Angeles." *Aztlan*, Volume 2. Fall 1981. pp. 111-114.

12 Lindsey Haley, "Pachuco Boogie." *Low Rider*. June 1985. p. 34. *Los Angeles Times*, Calendar Section. October 12, 1980. p. 6; Roberto Caballero-Robledo, "The Return of Pachuco Boogie." *Nuestro*. November 1979. pp 14-17.

13 Mauricio Mazon, *Zoot Suit Riots*. Austin: University of Texas Press, 1984; George Lipsitz, *Class and Culture in Cold War America: A Rainbow at Midnight*. South Hadley, MA: Bergin and Garvey, 1982. pp. 26-28.

14 *Los Angeles Times*, 1980; *Nuestro*, 1979.

15 Berman, 1982. p. 15.

16 Ray Topping, "Chuck Higgins Pachuko Hop." Liner notes, Ace Records. Ch 81. 1983.

17 Robert Palmer, *Baby That Was Rock and Roll*. New York: Harvest/HBJ, 1978. p. 19.

18 Ibid. p. 16.

19 Jim Dawson and Bob Keane, "Ritchie Valens: His Life Story." Rhino Records insert. 1981. p. 10.

20 Beverly Mendheim, *Ritchie Valens: The First Latino Rocker*. Tempe, AZ: Bilingual Press, 1987. pp. 18, 21.

21 Ibid. p. 23.

22 Ibid. p. 34.

23 Jim Dawson, "Valens, The Forgotten Story." *Los Angeles Times*. February 3, 1980. p. 100; Dawson and Keane, 1981. p. 5.

24 Dawson and Keane, 1981. pp. 3-5; Dawson, 1980. p. 100.

25 Dawson, 1980. p. 100.

26 Don Snowden, "The Sound of East L.A., 1964." *Los Angeles Times,* Calendar Section. October 28, 1984. p. 6.

27 Ethlie Ann Vare, "Cannibal and the Headhunters." *Goldmine.* November 1983. pp. 26, 53; Snowden, 1984. p. 7.

28 Vare, 1983. p. 26.

29 Ibid. p. 53.

30 Snowden, 1984. pp. 6-7.

31 For a detailed explanation of the urban crisis of the 1960s and 1970s, see John Mollenkopf, *The Contested City.* Princeton: Princeton University Press, 1983.

32 Luis Rodriguez, "La Veintineuve," *L.A. Latino Writers Workshop, 201—Latino Experience in Literature and Art.* n.d. p. 9.

33 Ruben Guevara, "The View From the Sixth Street Bridge: The History of Chicano Rock," in Dave Marsh, Ed., *Rock 'n' Roll Confidential Report.* Pantheon: New York, 1985. p. 120.

34 Guevara, in Marsh, 1985. p. 120. *Los Angeles Times,* Calendar Section. November 9, 1980. p. 69; El Larry, "Los Lobos." *Low Rider.* March-April 1984. p. 34.

35 Joel Whitburn, *The Billboard Book of Top 40 Hits.* New York: Billboard, 1984.

36 Melvin Oliver and James Johnson, Jr., "Inter-Ethnic Conflict in an Urban Ghetto." *Research in Social Movements: Conflict and Change,* Volume 6. JAI Sage. pp. 57-94.

37 Rob Tannenbaum, "Los Lobos." *Musician,* 77. March 1985. p. 19.

38 Robert Hilburn, "Willie Packs 'Em In, Down on the Farm." *Los Angeles Times,* Calendar Section. July 13, 1986. p. 63.

39 Judy Raphael, "Ragin' Cajun: Jo-El Sonnier's Last Stand." *L.A. Weekly.* August 8-15, 1985. p. 57.

Bibliography

Adorno, Theodor W., "On Popular Music." *Studies in Philosophy and Social Science,* No. 9, 1941.

Adorno, Theodor W., "Culture Industry Reconsidered." *New German Critique.* Fall 1975.

Alajo-Brown, Afolabi, *Juju Music: A Study of its Social History and Styles.* Pittsburgh: Pittsburgh University Press, 1985.

Alarik, Scott, "Does Women's Music Have Any Place Left to Go?" *The Boston Sunday Globe,* November 12, 1989.

Allan, Robert, "Bob's Not Your Uncle." *Capital & Class,* No. 30, Winter 1986.

Anderson, Benedict, *Imagined Communities.* London: Verso, 1983.

Andersson, Muff, *Music in the Mix, The Story of South African Popular Music.* Johannesburg: Ravan Press, 1981.

Armstrong Jr., Tony, "An Endangered Species: Women's Music By, For, and About Women." *Hot Wire: The Journal of Women's Music and Culture,* September 1989.

Armstrong, Jr., Tony, "Welcome Back Margie Adam." *Hot Wire: The Journal of Women's Music and Culture,* January 1992.

Banton, W., *West African City: A Study of Tribal Life in Freetown.* Oxford: Oxford University Press, 1957.

Barthes, Roland, *Elements of Semiology.* London: Jonathan Cape, 1967.

Barthes, Roland, *Mythologies.* New York: Hill & Wang, 1972.

Benjamin, Walter, *Illuminations.* New York: Harcourt, Brace & World, 1968.

Benjamin, Walter, *Understanding Brecht.* London: New Left Books/Verso, 1973.

Berger, Gilda, *USA for Africa: Rock Aid in the Eighties.* New York: Watts, 1987.

Berger, John, *Ways of Seeing.* London: Pelican, 1972.

Berman, Marshall, *All That Is Solid Melts Into Air*. New York: Simon and Schuster, 1982.

Bigsby, C.W.E., Ed., *The Politics of Popular Culture*. London: Edward Arnold, 1976.

Blesh, Rudi, *African Retentions in Jazz*. New York: Cassell Publications, 1949.

Bohn, Chris, "Hungarian Rhapsody and other Magyar Melodies." *New Musical Express*, Volume 17, No. 16, 1981.

Breen, Marcus, Ed., *Missing in Action: Australian Popular Music in Perspective*, Volume 1. Melbourne: Verbal Graphics, 1987.

Breen, Marcus, Ed., *Our Place, Our Music, Aboriginal Music: Australian Popular Music in Perspective*, Volume 2. Canberra: Aboriginal Studies Press, 1989.

Breskin, David, "Bob Geldof: The Rolling Stone, Interview." *Rolling Stone*. December 5, 1985.

Brown, De Soto, *Hawaii Recalls: Selling Romance to America*. Honolulu: Editions Limited, 1982.

Caballero-Robledo, Roberto, "The Return of Pachuco Boogie." *Nuestro*, November 1979.

Carey, James, "A Cultural Approach to Communication." *Communication*, 2, 1975.

Carothers, André, "Can Rock 'n' Roll Save the World?" *Greenpeace*, Volume 14, No. 6, November/December 1989, p. 11.

Carter, Sandy, "Redwood Records: Slippin' and Sliding." *Zeta Magazine*, May 1989, pp. 63-68.

Chambers, Ian, "Some Critical Tracks." *Popular Music*. No. 2, 1982.

Chambers, Ian, *Urban Rhythms: Pop Music and Popular Culture*. London: Macmillan, 1985.

Chapman, Michael, director, *The Drum Decade: Stories from the 1950s*. Pietermaritzburg: University of Natal Press, 1989.

Chapple, Steve, and Reebee Garofalo, *Rock 'n' Roll is Here to Pay: The History and Politics of the Music Industry*. Chicago: Nelson Hall, 1977.

Chatwin, Bruce, *The Songlines*. London: Pan Books, 1988.

Christina Spurgeon, "Challenging Technological Determinism: Aborigines, Aussat and Remote Australia," in Helen Wilson, Ed., *Australian Communications and the Public Sphere: Essays in Memory of Bill Bonney*. Melbourne: Macmillan, 1989.

Churchill, Ward, and Jim Vander Wall, *Agents of Repression: The FBI's Secret War Against the Black Panther Party and the American Indian Movement.* Boston: South End Press, 1988.

Clark, Ebun, and Herbert Ogunde, *The Making of Nigerian Theatre.* Oxford: Oxford University Press, 1979.

Clayborne Carson. *In Struggle: SNCC and the Black Awakening of the 1960's.* Cambridge, MA: Harvard University Press, 1981.

Clegg, Johnny, "Dance and Society in Africa South of the Sahara." Unpublished master's thesis, University of Witwatersrand, 1977.

Cole, P.D., *Modern and Traditional Elites in the Politics of Lagos.* Cambridge: Cambridge Unviersity Press, 1975.

Coleman, J.S., *Nigeria: Background to Nationalism.* Berkeley: California Press, 1960.

Collins, E.J., *Music Makers of West Africa.* Washington, D.C.: Three Continents Press, 1985.

Collins, E.J., *E.T. Mensah, The King of Highlife.* London: Off the Record Press, 1986.

Collins, E.J., "Jazz Feedback to Africa." *American Music,* Volume 5, No. 2, Summer 1987.

Confabulation, "Hi, Phranc. This is Alix Calling." *Hot Wire: The Journal of Women's Music and Culture,* January 1990,

Conrath, Philippe, *Johnny Clegg: La Passion Zoulou.* Paris: Seghers, 1988.

Constant, Denis, *Aux Sources du Reggae: Musique Société et Politique en Jamaïque.* Marseille: Parenthèses, 1986.

Coplan, David, "The African Musician and the Development of the Johannesburg Entertainment Industry, 1900-1960," *Journal of Southern African Studies,* Volume 5, No. 2, April, 1979.

Coplan, David, "The Urbanization of African Music: Some Theoretical Observations," in Richard Middleton and David Horn, Eds., *Popular Music 2.* Cambridge: Cambridge University Press, 1982.

Coplan, David, *In Township Tonight!: South Africa's Black City Music and Theatre.* London: Longman, 1985.

Cornel West, "Marxist Theory and the Specificity of Afro-American Oppression," in Lawrence Grossberg and Cary Nelson, Eds., *Marxism and the Interpretation of Culture.* Urbana: University of Illinois Press, 1988.

Cutler, Chris, *File Under Popular: Theoretical and Critical Writings on Music.* London: November Books, 1985.

Dám, László, *Rockszámla*. Budapest: IRI: Reflex, 1987.

Damon, Ethel, *Sanford Ballard Dole and His Hawaii*. Palo Alto, CA: Pacific Books, 1957.

Dawson, Jim, "Valens, The Forgotten Story." *Los Angeles Times*. February 3, 1980.

De Curtis, Anthony, "Rock & Roll Politics: Did the Nelson Mandela Tribute Make its Point?" *Rolling Stone,* August 11, 1988.

Denselow, Robin, *When the Music's Over: The Story of Political Pop*. London: Faber, 1989.

DiPrima, Dominique, "Beat the Rap." *Mother Jones,* Volume 15, No. 6, September/ October 1990.

Duany, Jorge, "Popular Music in Puerto Rico: Toward an Anthropology of Salsa." *Latin American Music Review,* Volume 5, No. 2, 1984.

Eisenberg, Evan, *The Recording Angel*. New York: Penguin, 1987.

Elbert, Samuel, and Noelani Mahoe, *Na Mele o Hawai'i Nei*. Honolulu: University of Hawaii Press, 1970.

Ellis, Catherine, *Aboriginal Music: Cross Cultural Experience from South Australia*. Brisbane: University of Queensland Press, 1985.

Ellis, Trey, "The New Black Aesthetic." *Callaloo,* Volume 12, No. 1, Winter 1989.

Enloe, Cynthia, *Bananas, Beaches & Bases: Making Feminist Sense of International Politics*. Berkeley: University of California Press, 1990.

Ensenburger, Hans Magnus, *The Consciousness Industry*. New York: Seabury Press, 1974.

Erlmann, Veit, "A Feeling of Prejudice: Orpheus McAdoo and the Virginia Jubilee Singers in South Africa 1890-1898." *Journal of Southern African Studies,* Volume 14, No. 3, April 1988.

Evers, Tilman, "Identidad: la Faz Oculta de los Nuevos Movimientos Sociales." *Punto de Vista,* No. 25, 1985.

Ewen, Graham, *Luamba Franco and Thirty Years of O.K. Jazz*. London: Off the Record Press, 1986.

Feld, Steven, "Notes on World Beat." *Public Culture Bulletin,* Volume 1, No. 1, Fall 1988.

Fitzpatrick, Eamonn, "Pop Stars Unite to Sing for Freedom." *South China Morning Post,* May 24, 1989.

Foucault, Michel, *Power/Knowledge*. New York: Pantheon, 1980.

Frith, Simon, *Sound Effects: Youth, Leisure and the Politics of Rock 'n' Roll.* New York: Pantheon, 1981.

Frith, Simon, "Towards an Aesthetic of Popular Music," in Richard Leppert and Susan McClary, Eds., *Music and Society: The Politics of Composition, Performance and Reception.* Cambridge: Cambridge University Press, 1987.

Frith, Simon, Ed., *Facing the Music.* New York: Pantheon Books, 1988.

Frith, Simon, Ed., *World Music, Politics and Social Change.* New York: University of Manchester Press, 1989.

Frith, Simon, and John Street, "Party Music." *Marxism Today,* June 1986.

Frith, Simon, and Howard Horne, *Art into Pop.* New York: Methuen, 1987.

Garnham, Nicholas, "Public Service Versus the Market." *Screen,* Volume 24, No. 1, 1983.

Garofalo, Reebee, "How Autonomous is Relative? Popular Music, the Social Formation and Cultural Struggle." *Popular Music,* Volume 6, No. 1, January 1987.

Garofalo, Reebee, "The Impact of the Civil Rights Movement on Popular Music." *Radical America,* Volume 21, No. 6, November-December 1987.

Garofalo, Reebee, "Crossing Over, 1939-1989," in Jannette L. Dates and William Barlow, Eds., *Split Image: African-Americans in the Mass Media.* Washington, DC: Howard University Press, 1990.

Garofalo, Reebee, "The Internationalization of the U.S. Music Industry and its Impact on Canada." *Cultural Studies,* Volume 5, No. 3, October 1991.

Geldof, Bob, with Paul Vallely, *Is That It?* New York: Weidenfeld & Nicolson, 1986.

George, Nelson, *The Death of Rhythm & Blues.* New York: Pantheon Books, 1988.

George, Nelson, Ed., *Stop the Violence: Overcoming Self-Destruction: Rap Speaks Out.* New York: National Urban League, 1990.

George, Nelson, "Forty Acres and an Empire: Spike Lee Plants the New Motown in Brooklyn." *Village Voice,* August 7, 1990.

Gitlin, Todd, *The Whole World is Watching: Mass Media in the Making and Unmaking of the New Left.* Berkeley: University of California Press, 1980.

Goldberg, Michael, "Live Aid Take May Hit $60 million." *Rolling Stone,* August 29, 1985.

Goldberg, Michael, "Bill Graham: The Rolling Stone Interview." *Rolling Stone,* December 19, 1985.

Gonzales, Gilbert G., "Factors Relating to Property Ownership of Chicanos in Lincoln Heights, Los Angeles." *Aztlan,* Volume 2, Fall 1981.

Goodwin Andrew, and Joe Gore, "World Beat and the Cultural Imperialism Debate." *Socialist Review,* Volume 20, No. 3, July-Sept., 1990.

Gramsci, Antonio, *Selections from Prison Notebooks.* London: Lawrence and Wisehart, 1971.

Grossberg, Lawrence, " 'I'd Rather Feel Bad than not Feel Anything at All': Rock and Roll, Pleasure and Power." *Enclitic 8.* 1984.

Grossberg, Lawrence, "Another Boring Day in Paradise: Rock and Roll and the Empowerment of Everyday Life," in Richard Middleton and David Horn, Eds., *Popular Music 4,* New York: Cambridge University Press, 1984.

Grossberg, Lawrence, "Teaching the Popular," in Cary Nelson, Ed., *Theory in the Classroom.* Urbana and Chicago: University of Illinois Press, 1986.

Guaralnick, Peter, *Sweet Soul Music.* New York: Harper and Row, 1986.

Guevara, Ruben, "The View From the Sixth Street Bridge: The History of Chicano Rock," in Dave Marsh, Ed., *Rock 'n' Roll Confidential Report.* New York: Pantheon, 1985.

Hager, Steven, *Hip Hop: The Illustrated History of Break Dancing, Rap Music and Graffitti.* New York: St. Martin's Press, 1984.

Hajnóczy, Csaba, *Voice of Hungary 1.* Vienna-Budapest-New York: International Network Rittn Tittn, 1984.

Haley, Lindsey, "Pachuco Boogie." *Low Rider,* June 1985.

Hall, Stuart, "Culture, the Media and the 'Ideological Effect,' " in James Curran, et al., Eds., *Mass Communication and Society.* London: E. Arnold, 1977.

Hall, Stuart, "Rethinking the 'Base-and-Superstructure' Metaphor," in John Bloomfielf, Ed., *The Communist University of London: Papers on Class, Hegemony and Party.* London: Lawrence and Wishart, 1977.

Hall, Stuart, "The Rediscovery of Ideology: Return of the Repressed in Media Studies," in M. Gurevitch, et al., Eds., *Culture, Society and Media.* London: Methuen, 1982.

Hamm, Charles, "China's Great Leap Into the World of Rock Music." *New York Times.* April 16, 1989. p. 27.

Hanhua, Xia, "Dalu Yuetan Xin Yi Lun de Pidou Yundong" (A New Criticism Campaign in the Music World of Mainland China). *Jiushi Niandai Yuekan (90's Monthly),* Volume 4, No. 102, 1991.

Hankiss, Elemér, *Kelet-Európai Alternatívák*, Budapest: Közgazdasági és Jogi Könyvkiadó, 1989. (In English: *East-European Alternatives: Are There Any?* Oxford: University Press, 1990.)

Hanrahan, Noelle, "A New Wave of Women on Vinyl." *Coming Up!*, August 1988.

Harper, Jorjet and Toni Armstrong Jr., "Meg Departs." *Hot Wire: The Journal of Women's Music and Culture*, January 1989.

Hart, Deborah and Gordon H. Pirie, "The Sight and Soul of Sophiatown," *The Geographical Review*, Volume 74, No. 1, January, 1984.

Hawthorne, Jeremy, *Identity and Relationship*. London: Lawrence & Wishart, 1973.

Heath, Chris, "Tribal in Mind." *Details*, January, 1991.

Hebdige, Dick, *Cut 'N' Mix: Culture, Identity and Caribbean Music*. New York: Methuen, 1987.

Hebdige, Dick, *Hiding in the Light*. London: Routledge, 1988.

Henke, James, *Human Rights Now!* New York: Amnesty International/Salem House, 1988.

Hillmore, Peter, *Live Aid*. Parsippany, NJ: Unicorn, 1985

Hung, Michèle and Esteban Garcia Morencos, Eds., *World Record Sales, 1969-1990*. London: International Federation of the Phonographic Industry, 1990.

James, Deborah, "Musical Form and Social History: Research Perspectives in Black South African Music." *Radical History Review*, Volume 46, No. 7, 1990.

Jeppie, Shamil and Crain Soudien, Eds., *The Struggle for District Six, Past and Present*. Le Cap: Buchu Books, 1990.

Jones, LeRoi (Amari Baraka), *Blues People: Negro Music in White America*. New York: William Morrow, 1963.

Judt, Tony, "The Unmastered Future: What Prospects for Eastern Europe?" *Tikkun*. Volume 5, No. 2, 1990.

Kamohalu, Robert, and Burt Burlingame, Eds., *Da Kine Sound*. Honolulu: Press Pacifica, 1978.

Keil, Angelika and Charles, "In Search of Polka Happiness." *Cultural Correspondence*, No. 14, 1977.

Kelp, Larry, "Getting in Tune with the Times." *The Tribune Calendar*, July 9, 1989.

Köbányai, János, "Biztosítótü és Börnadrág." Mozgó Világ, Volume 5, No. 2, 1979.

Kubick, Gerhard, "Neo-Traditional Popular Music in East Africa since 1945," in Richard Middleton and David Horn, Eds., *Popular Music*. Cambridge: Cambridge University Press, 1981.

Laing, Dave, *One Chord Wonders: Power and Meaning in Punk Rock*. Milton Keynes: Open University Press, 1985.

Laing, Dave, "The Music Industry and the 'Cultural Imperialism' Thesis." *Media, Culture and Society*. London: Sage, Volume 8, 1986.

Landi, Oscar, "Cultura y Política en la Transición a la Democracia en Argentina." *Crítica y Utopía,* Nos. 10/11, 1983.

Lechner, Norbert, "Especificando la Política." *Crítica y Utopía*. No. 8, 1982.

Levallet, Didier, and Denis-Constant Martin, *L'Amérique de Mingus. Musique et Politique: Les "Fables of Faubus" de Charles Mingus,* Paris: P.O.L., 1991.

Lewis, George H., "Beyond The Reef: Role Conflict and the Professional Musician in Hawaii." *Popular Music 5*. Cambridge: Cambridge University Press, 1985.

Lipsitz, George, *Class and Culture in Cold War America: A Rainbow at Midnight*. South Hadley, Massachusetts: Bergin and Garvey, 1982.

Lipsitz, George, *Time Passages: Collective Memory and American Popular Culture*. Minneapolis: University of Minnesota Press, 1990.

Little, K., *West African Urbanisation, A Study of Voluntary Associations in Social Change*. Cambridge: Cambridge University Press, 1970.

Lont, Cynthia M., "Between Rock and a Hard Place: A Model of Subcultural Persistence and Women's Music." Ph.D. Thesis, University of Iowa, 1984.

Lull, James, Ed., *Popular Music and Communication*. Beverly Hills: Sage Publications, 1987.

Lumholtz, Carl, *Among Cannibals*. Canberra: Australian National University Press, 1980.

Manuel, Peter, *Popular Musics of the Non-Western World: An Introductory Survey*. Oxford: Oxford University Press, 1988.

Martin, Denis-Constant, "Le Triolet Multicolore, dans la Musique Sud Africaine, une Blanche N'Égale pas Nécessairement Deux Noires." *Politiques Africaine 25,* March 1987.

Marx Karl, and Fredrick Engels, *On Literature and Art*. Moscow: Progress Publishers, 1976.

Maultsby, Portia K., "Africanisms in African-American Popular Music," in Joseph E. Holloway, Ed., *Africanisms in American Culture*. Bloomington, IN: Indiana University Press, 1990.

May, Elizabeth, Ed., *Music of Many Cultures: An Introduction*. Berkeley: University of California Press, 1962.

Mazon, Mauricio, *Zoot Suit Riots*. Austin: University of Texas Press, 1984.

McRobbie, Angela, Ed., *Zoot Suits and Second Hand Dresses: An Anthology of Fashion and Music*. London: Macmillan, 1989.

Melucci, Alberto, "L'azzione Ribelle: Formazione e Struttura dei Movimenti Sociali," *Movimenti di Rivolta*. Milan: Etas Libri, 1976.

Mendheim, Beverly, *Ritchie Valens: The First Latino Rocker*. Tempe, AZ: Bilingual Press, 1987.

Merriam, Alan P., "The Use of Music in the Study of the Problem of Acculturation." *American Anthroplogist*, No. 57, 1955.

Michaels, Eric, *Aboriginal Invention of Television in Central Australia 1982-1986*. Canberra: Aboriginal Studies Press, 1986.

Mollenkopf, John, *The Contested City*. Princeton: University Press, 1983.

Molnar, Helen, "The Broadcasting for Remote Areas Community Scheme: Small vs Big Media." *Media Information Australia*, No. 58, November 1990.

Motjuwadi, Stan "Lest We Forget." In Jurgen Schadeberg, Ed., *The Fifties People of South Africa, Black Life: Politics, Jazz, Sport*. Johannesburg: Bailey's African Photo Archives Production, 1987.

Nketia, J.H.K., *Folk Songs of Ghana*. Accra: Ghana University Press, 1973.

Nketia, J.H.K., "Observations on the Study of Popular Music in Africa." Paper presented at the Conference of the International Association for the Study of Popular Music (IASPM), Accra, Ghana, August 1987.

Oliver, Paul, *The Savannah Syncopators*. London: Vista Publications, 1970.

Omibiyi-Obidike, Mosumola, "Women in Popular Music in Africa." Paper presented at the Fourth International Conference of IASPM, Accra, Ghana, August 1987.

Owens, Harry, *Sweet Leilani*. Pacific Palisades, CA: Hula House, 1970.

Padilla, Felix M., "Salsa Music as Cultural Expression of Latino Consciousness and Unity." *Hispanic Journal of Behavioral Sciences*, Volume 11, No. 1, February 1989.

Palmer, Robert, *Baby That Was Rock and Roll*. New York: Harvest/HBJ, 1978.

Paz, Octavio, *The Labyrinthe of Solitude*. New York: Grove Press, 1961.

Pepper, Rachel, "The Winning Duo...er...Threesome," *Outweek,* September 19, 1990.

Post, Laura, "The Institute for the Musical Arts." *Hot Wire: The Journal of Women's Music and Culture,* September 1989.

Post, Laura, "Olivia Record Artist Profiles." *Hot Wire: The Journal of Women's Music and Culture,* July 1988.

Ranger, T.O., *Dance and Society in East Africa.* Heinemann Educational Books, 1975.

Reagon, Bernice, "Songs That Moved the Movement." *Civil Rights Quarterly,* Summer, 1983.

Rene, Sheila, "No Madonnas: Olivia Records, the Premiere Women's Music Label, Celebrates 15 years in the Trenches." *Pulse Indie Special,* 1989.

Roberts, John Storm, *Black Music of Two Worlds.* New York: William Morrow, 1974.

Robinson, Cedric, *Black Marxism.* London: Zed Books, 1983.

Robinson, Deanna C., et al., *Music at the Margins.* London: Sage, 1991.

Rockwell, John, "Leftist Causes? Rock Seconds Those Emotions." *New York Times,* December 11, 1988.

Romo, Ricardo, *East Los Angeles.* Austin: University of Texas Press, 1983.

Ruiqing, Yang, "Xibeifeng Gequ Heyi Chengchao" (Why the Xibeifeng Wave?), *Yinyue, Wudao Yanjiu (Music and Dance Research),* Volume 5, No. 15, 1989.

Ryback, Timothy, *Rock Around the Bloc. A History of Rock Music in Eastern-Europe and the Soviet Union.* New York: Oxford University Press, 1990.

Schechter, Danny, "Why We Didn't See Wembley." *Africa Report,* July-August 1990.

Sebök, János, *Magya-Rock Volumes 1-2.* Budapest: Zenemükiadó, 1983-84.

Shaw, Arnold, *The Rockin' '50s.* New York: Hawthorn, 1974.

Sheng, Sun, "Yi Shou Zhua Zhengdun, Yi Shou Zhua Fanrong" (Reorganize With One Hand, and Prosper With the Other), *Renmin Yinyue (People's Music),* Volume 2, No. 8, 1991.

Shevky, Eshref, and Marilyn Williams, *The Social Areas of Los Angeles.* Berkeley: University of California Press, 1949.

Shore, Laurence Kenneth, *The Crossroads of Business and Music: A Study of the Music Industry in the United States and Internationally.* Unpublished Doctoral Dissertation, Stanford University, 1983.

Sims, Grace, "Inversion in Black Communication." In T. Kochman, Ed., Rappin' and Stylin' Out: Communication in Urban Black America, Urbana: University of Illinois Press, 1972.

Sithole, N., *African Nationalism*. Oxford: Oxford University Press, 1970.

Slater, Phil, *Origin and Significance of the Frankfurt School*. Boston: Routledge & Kegan Paul, 1977.

Snowden, Don, "The Sound of East L.A., 1964." *Los Angeles Times,* October 28, 1984.

Sontag, Susan, *Styles of Radical Will*. New York: Delta, 1969.

Stein, Arlene, "Androgyny Goes Pop: But Is It Lesbian Music?" *Out/Look,* Spring 1991.

Street, John, "If You Care About Our World, You'll Buy This Album: Green Politics and Rock Music." *ONE TWO THREE FOUR: A Rock 'n' Roll Quarterly,* No. 8, Winter 1990.

Strehlow, T.G.H., *Songs of Central Australia*. Sydney: Angus and Robertson, 1971.

Sturgis, Susanna J., "Ladyslipper: Meeting the Challenges of Feminist Business." *Hot Wire: The Journal of Women's Music and Culture,* May 1985.

Suijin, Zeng, "Gangtai Liuxing Gequ Chongji Hou de Huigu" (A Look Back at the Influx of Gangtai Popular Songs), *Renmin Yinyue (People's Music),* Volume 2, No. 44, 1988.

Szemere, Anna, "Pop Music in Hungary," *Communication Research,* Volume 12, No. 3, 1985.

Szwed, John, "Afro-American Musical Adaptation," in N.E. Whitten Jr. and J. Szwed, Eds., *American Anthropology: Contemporary Perspectives*. New York: Free Press, 1970.

Tannenbaum, Rob, "Los Lobos." *Musician 77,* March, 1985.

Tate, Greg, "Cult-Nats Meet Freaky-Dede: The Return of the Black Aesthetic." *Village Voice Literary Supplement,* December 1986.

Therborn, Goran, "The Social Order of Ideologies," *The Ideology of Power & the Power of Ideology*. London: Verso/Schocken, 1980.

Tilchen, Maida, "Women's Music: Politics for Sale?" *Gay Community News,* June Supplement 1982.

Tilchen, Maida, "Lesbians and Women's Music," in T. Darty and S. Potter, *Women-Identified-Women,* Palo Alto, CA: Mayfield Publishing, 1984.

Toop, David, *Rap Attack: African Jive to New York Hip Hop*. London: Pluto Press, 1984.

Uche, Luke, "Imperialism Revisited." *The Media Education Journal,* No. 6, 1987.

Van der Geest, Sjaak, and Nimrod Asante-Darko, "Men and Women in Ghanaian Highlife Songs," in Christine Oppong, Ed., *Female and Male in West Africa.* London: George Allen and Unwin, 1983.

Van der Geest, Sjaak, and Nimrod Asante-Darko, "The Political Meaning of Highlife Songs in Ghana." *African Studies Review,* Volume 5, No. 1, 1982.

Vare, Ethlie Ann, "Cannibal and the Headhunters." *Goldmine,* November 1983.

Wallis, Roger and Krister Malm, *Big Sounds from Small Peoples: The Music Industry in Small Countries.* London: Constable, 1984.

Warner, Keith, *The Trinidad Calypso.* London: Heinemann Educational Books, 1982.

Waterman, Christopher, *Juju: The Historical Development, Socio-Economic Organization and Communicative Function of a West African Popular Music.* Ph.D. Thesis, University of Illinois, 1986.

Waterman, Richard A., "African Influences in the Music of the Americas," in Sol Tax, Ed., *Acculturation in the Americas.* Chicago: University of Chicago Press, 1952.

Widgery, David, *Beating Time: Riot 'n' Race 'n' Rock 'n' Roll.* London: Chatto & Windus, 1986.

Williams, Raymond, "On High and Popular Culture." *The New Republic,* November 23, 1974.

Williams, Raymond, *Marxism and Literature.* Oxford: Oxford University Press, 1977.

Willmot, Eric, "Australia: The Last Experiment." St. Mark's Review, December 1978.

Wilson, Susan, "Talkin' 'bout Revolution For Women in Pop?" *The Boston Sunday Globe,* November 20, 1988.

Wilson, Susan, "Women's Music: Then and Now." *The Boston Sunday Globe,* March 9, 1986.

Wuthnow, Robert, *Meaning and Moral Order: Explorations in Cultural Analysis.* Berkeley and Los Angeles: University of California Press, 1987.

Zechi, Shu, and Zeng Yi, "Liuxing Yinyue yu Cidai Shichang Xianzhuang Pingxi" (Popular Music and the Cassette Market: A Critical Appraisal of the Present Situation), *Yinyue, Wudao Yanjiu (Music and Dance Research),* Volume 5, No. 15, 1989.

Zindi, Fred, *Roots Rocking in Zimbabwe.* Harare: Mambo Press, 1985.

Tim Brace has taught courses on Western art music history, theory and performance, and on popular music in America. His special interests include musical aesthetics, hermeneutics, and the relationship of musical practice to political economy. He recently finished his doctoral dissertation on the modernization of music in the People's Republic of China at the University of Texas at Austin.

Marcus Breen is a freelance writer living in Melbourne, Australia, where he is the Australian correspondent for *Music Business International.* He is the editor of *Missing in Action: Australian Popular Music in Perspective* (Vol. 1), and *Our Place, Our Music, Aboriginal Music: Australian Popular Music in Perspective* (Vol. 2). He is currently working on a major study of the Australian music industry.

John Collins is a graduate of the University of Ghana, and the author of *African Pop Roots,* among many other publications. He is a frequent contributor to such publications as *West Africa Magazine, Afrique, Africa Journal,* and *Music Express.* He has been active in the West African music scene for over 20 years as a musician and a producer as well. He operates his own recording studio, Bokoor House, near Accra and works closely with the Ghana Arts Council.

Paul Friedlander is the Assistant to the Dean and Professor of Music Management at the Conservatory of Music, University of the Pacific in Stockton, California. He is Chair of the U.S. Chapter of the International Association for the Study of Popular Music, author of *That Rock and Roll Music,* to be published by Schirmer Books, and a tenor in the rockapella quartet "The Tones."

Simon Frith is Professor of English at Strathclyde University, Glasgow, Scotland, and co-director of the John Logie Baird Centre. He is the "Britbeat" columnist for the *Village Voice* and currently chairs the International Association for the Study of Popular Music.

Reebee Garofalo is an activist and Professor at the University of Massachusetts at Boston. Co-author of *Rock 'n' Roll is Here to Pay: The History and Politics of the Music Industry,* he has written numerous articles and has lectured internationally on music and politics. He is a past chairman of the U.S. Chapter of the International Association for the Study of Popular Music and a co-founder of Massachusetts Rock Against Racism. He is currently writing a social history of popular music in the United States. For relaxation, he enjoys drumming and singing with the Blue Suede Boppers, a fifties rock 'n' roll band.

Joanna Ching-Yun Lee was born and educated in Hong Kong. She studied at the Royal College of Music in London, before pursuing her graduate work in historical musicology at Columbia University. She has delivered papers on Cantopop at the Society for Ethnomusicology, the Society for Asian Music, and the International Association for the Study of Popular Music. She is currently finishing her doctoral dissertation on the composition, performance, and reception history of György Ligeti's *Aventures* and *Nouvelles Aventures*.

George H. Lewis is Professor of Sociology/Anthropology at the University of the Pacific, Stockton, California. Long interested in the sociology of popular music and culture, he is the author of numerous articles appearing in journals ranging from *American Music* and *Tracking* to *Theory and Society* and the *British Journal of Sociology*. He is the author of *Side-Saddle on the Golden Calf: Popular Culture and Social Structure in America* and is presently at work on a book on modern country music, *All That Glitters*, to be published by Bowling Green Popular Press. He has been a visiting professor at the University of Hawaii, and has lectured on popular Hawaiian music in places as far removed as Kennebunkport, Maine and Paris, France.

George Lipsitz is Professor of Ethnic Studies at the University of California, San Diego. Active in struggles concerning labor, education, and popular culture, he is also the author of *Class and Culture in Cold War America* (Bergin and Gervey, 1982), *A Life in the Struggle: Ivory Perry and the Culture of Opposition* (Temple University Press, 1988), and *Time Passages: Collective Memory and American Popular Culture* (University of Minnesota Press, 1990).

Cynthia M. Lont is an Associate Professor at George Mason University, where she teaches video production, women in media, and communication theory. Her interests also include feminist media, critical studies, and subcultural theory. She has been an avid listener of women's music for well over 15 years.

Denis-Constant Martin holds a doctorate from the Sorbonne, and is Director of Research at the Fondation Nationale des Sciences Politiques in Paris, where he also teaches at several institutions of higher learning. He has done field research in Eastern Africa and in the English-speaking

Caribbean. He has authored numerous articles in academic journals and has been a regular contributor to the French *Jazz Magazine* for more than 20 years. His books include: *Aux Sources du Reggae: Musique, Société et Politique en Jamaïque, Tanzanie, l'Invention d'une Culture Politique, L'Amérique de Mingus: Musique et Politique, les "Fables of Faubus" de Charles Mingus* (with Didier Levallet), and *Les Afriques Politiques* (with Christian Coulon).

John Street is a Lecturer in Politics at the University of East Anglia, Norwich, England. He is the author of *Rebel Rock: The Politics of Popular Music,* and occasionally he writes rock reviews for the *London Times.*

Anna Szemere is a Research Associate at the Institute for Musicology, Hungarian Academy of Sciences. She has published numerous articles and chapters with a focus on popular music, politics, and youth. She is an Advisory Editor to the journal *Popular Music.* She currently lives and works in San Diego, California.

Neal Ullestad works at Pima Community College in Tucson, Arizona, where he lives with his wife Kathy. His articles and reviews have appeared in *Popular Music* (Cambridge, England), Los Angeles' *International Reggae Beat,* Chicago's *In These Times,* and New York City's *Guardian,* as well as various local publications. In addition to being active with KXCI community radio, he has worked with the publications committee of the International Association for the Study of Popular Music (IASPM-USA) for nearly ten years.

Pablo Vila is a researcher for CEDES (Centro de Estudios de Estado y Societad) in Buenos Aires, where he is involved in projects concerned with *rock nacional* and with the politics of everyday life, in the light of re-emerging democracy. He also teaches sociology at the Universidad de Buenos Aires.

Peter Wicke is the Director of the Center for Popular Music Research at Humboldt University in Berlin. Active in the East German popular music scene for many years as an author and a critic, he is the author of *Rock Music: Culture, Aesthetics and Sociology.* He currently serves as the General Secretary of the International Association for the Study of Popular Music.

Kristal Brent Zook is a Ph.D. Candidate in the History of Consciousness Program at the University of California/Santa Cruz and is writing about nationalist thought in contemporary black culture. She has also written about black film and television for such publications as *The Village Voice* and *The L.A. Weekly.*